THE AMATEUR MAGICIAN'S HANDBOOK

THE AMATEUR MAGICIAN'S HANDBOOK

FOURTH EDITION

NEWLY REVISED AND EXPANDED

by Henry Hay

PHOTOGRAPHS BY AUDREY ALLEY

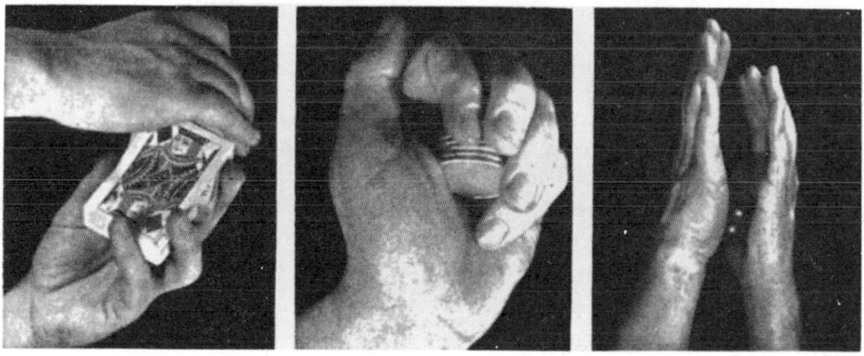

CASTLE BOOKS

a division of Book Sales, Inc.

PO Box 7100

Edison, NJ 08818-7100

This edition is published by CASTLE BOOKS
a division of Book Sales, Inc.
PO Box 7100
Edison, NJ 08818-7100
by arrangement with HarperCollins Publishers, Inc.

ISBN 0-7858-0204-5

Library of Congress Cataloging in Publication Data

The amateur magician's handbook.

Bibliography: p.
Includes index.
1. Conjuring. 2. Tricks. I. Title.
GV1547.M845 1982 793.8 80-7878
AACR2

In Memoriam THOMAS NELSON DOWNS

"The Great Man" of my boyhood

and, alas, JOHN MULHOLLAND

What shall we do without him?

Contents

PART III · APPARATUS MAGIC

PART IV · MENTAL MAGIC

PART V · INTIMATE MAGIC

PART VI · CHILDREN'S SHOWS

PART VII · PLATFORM MAGIC

APPENDIX

Introduction

by Milbourne Christopher

INTEREST IN THE ART of legitimate deception rocketed to a new high soon after the third edition of *The Amateur Magician's Handbook* was published in 1972. A new generation of mystifiers captivated audiences. Doug Henning, an exuberant Canadian, achieved stardom in "The Magic Show," a Broadway musical. David Copperfield, a personable American, won acclaim in Chicago in "The Magic Man." Harry Blackstone, Jr. enlarged his repertoire, toured from coast to coast, then brought his conjuring spectacle to Broadway in 1980.

When in March 1976 I played the role of Houdini and re-created his "Magic vs. the Occult" at Alice Tully Hall, Lincoln Center in New York City, tickets sold out weeks in advance. Responding to public demand, Siegfried and Roy, long a major Las Vegas attraction, added extensively to their fantastic feats with jungle beasts. Richiardi, Jr., a dynamic Peruvian deceptionist, delighted spectators in the United States with artistically staged mystifications. Paul Daniels, a witty British wizard, progressed from night clubs to the stage, then began a long run in a London theater.

Television magic specials became more prevalent, featuring, in addition to the performers previously cited, such adept deceptionists as Mark Wilson, Haruo Shimada, James Randi, Marvyn Roy, and Ricky Jay. The renaissance of magic as an important phase of show business swelled the ranks of amateurs and increased the membership of magic societies to an all-time high.

Keeping pace with the times, Henry Hay has revised and expanded this fourth edition of his popular handbook. His advice to those who wish to entertain at children's parties is especially noteworthy. An informative new chapter by James Randi explains how videotape machines can be used as a rehearsal tool and to analyze the presentations of other performers.

Few books cover as wide a scope; fewer list so many sources for further study. Study is essential for one to understand why spectators are mystified and how to practice, prepare for, and present a magic show. Precise instructions for sleight-of-hand moves and the handling of equipment are given. Biographical notes vividly convey data on the development and lore of legerdemain.

Once the basic techniques are mastered, the next step—one of the greatest pleasures in magic—is to create novel presentations, and then to stage them in a personal, not imitative, style.

If magic is your hobby it will help you to acquire digital dexterity, enable you to gain poise and confidence, and give you insight into the way people think. A knowledge of the psychology of deception will also make you a less likely victim of business, political, and psychic frauds.

If your aim is to perform professionally, the future in this field is brighter than it has been for many decades—if you can adapt your shows to conform with contemporary trends. Vaudeville and night-club magicians could and did present the same acts for years. Television is more demanding. The more versatile and inventive you are, the greater your chance for achieving and continuing success. Ingenious trade show magicians design routines to illustrate the selling points of products and devise illusionary devices to introduce new campaigns. I have produced an automobile, changed the colors of fabrics, and caused gallons of orange juice to flow from an empty metal cylinder.

Magic shows can be staged under almost every conceivable condition—aboard ships and planes, on football fields and in arenas, for a single spectator or an audience of thousands. If you enjoy performing, audiences will reflect your mood and have a good time. That in essence is the purpose of magic—to delight and astonish with seemingly impossible mysteries.

A Few Words Before Curtain Time

THIS BOOK first appeared in 1950. Fifteen years later I was flattered by a letter from a magician I did not know, beginning, "Let me say that even though books by Hugard, Blackstone, Hoffmann, *et al.* have been lauded as classics in magic literature, there is, in my opinion, no better book than *The Amateur Magician's Handbook* for presenting the subject of magic. Indeed, I feel that your book must be the melting pot of all the best points, plus many other new effects as well, of the 'classics.' "

FOUR KINGS: Nate Leipzig, Harry Blackstone, John Mulholland, Thomas Nelson Downs. (Courtesy of Pauline Mulholland)

This awakened me to the discovery that what I too remembered as the classics of conjuring, the cornerstone works of Professor Hoffmann, Lang Neil, Hilliard, Hugard, and the rest, were out of print. The authors were better men than I, but they were gone. So a new, expanded edition of this volume seemed a good idea.

I wound up the foreword to it by saying, "The surprising thing, really, is that in the electronic age conjuring should have changed so little. The decline of the waistcoat has affected magic more than the invention of communications satellites."

On the whole I still think so, and the London *Daily Telegraph* quoted the remark when a British edition of the book appeared in 1971. But see page 305 for an instance where I must eat my words.

When the expanded edition in its turn went out of print, I asked Lewis Ganson (who has become a grand old man of British conjuring since we met in the 1950s; then he was merely the leading English magical writer) what material we might usefully add to the next edition.

I asked the same question of two valued pen pals, the late Colonel Richardson Greene of Pelham, Massachusetts (then in his mid-seventies; we have been corresponding at intervals since about 1948), and Rodney M. Heft of Canada, a magic student and historian who was six years old when *Amateur Magician's Handbook* first appeared.

All three counselors gave substantially the same advice, which is reflected in the new Part Five, Intimate Magic. They, together with John Braun, also brought the bibliography up to date.

More startling to me, Rodney Heft sent a clipping from a leading American conjuring journal, *The Linking Ring,* reprinting the letters of Thomas Nelson Downs (the father of modern coin manipulation and one of the two or three greatest all-round sleight-of-hand experts who ever lived) to a friend in Rhode Island. Downs was fifty-four, and thoroughly enjoying a prosperous retirement in his native Marshalltown, Iowa, when he began to correspond with Edward G. McGuire in 1922.

On April 12, 1924, he wrote, "The Kid arrived Sat. nite & left Monday. Smart kid—very enthusiastic, very fond of the coin work. Did not believe it possible to palm & produce 35 to 40 half dollars so I had to show him. . . . He landed in full Turk costume. We had a BIG visit."

John Braun of the *Linking Ring* editorialized in the April 1971 issue, "Wonder who 'the KID' was who arrived in full Turk costume?" In August he headlined, "A mystery solved": Two collector-historians, H. Adrian Smith and C. R. Tracy, had both shown him clippings to prove I must be the one.

I could have told them that, but I had to wait forty-eight years for the *Linking Ring* to tell me Downs had thought the visit worth recording—quite enough to swell my chest retrospectively for any remaining fragment of my magical career.

In another book I remarked many years ago, "When I was thirteen years old, and had only been doing magic for three years, I had the Arabian

THE YOUNG TURK: The author in magical costume at age thirteen.

Nights dream experience of spending two days with the late Nelson Downs. . . . I felt very sheepish because I dropped the coins every time I tried to do what he showed me. 'Son,' he said, 'I've been doing magic for forty years, and I still drop the coins, so what can you expect?' "

At one point I complained that my hands were small. He held out one of his, palm to palm with mine: same size as near as no matter.

As I observe on a later page about his friends Cardini and Nate Leipzig, the work of people like Downs can be more astounding if you know how they do it than if you don't. For instance, when he made sixty coins disappear from his closed fist, it was merely a diverting illogicality; but if you knew that they disappeared because he had noiselessly palmed the whole stack in the innocent hand so carelessly spread against his knee, that approached the incredible.

Equally stunning to a diffident learner was the Great Man's absolute nerve. He showed me how to fan a pack of cards behind your back and still make a spectator take the one card you wanted: "Just back into 'em." He used to say anybody could force a card that way if his feet were big enough.

And then his beautiful deliberation. During my visit, the man from downstairs with his son, aged seven or eight, looked in, and Downs made me do a trick, after which of course I insisted on his doing one. The man said to me, "You're pretty good, but you're not as fast as Tommy yet."

Under the hypnotic influence of those leisurely hands I felt moved to say, "You know, the real reason he's so great is because he's slow, not fast."

After they left, Downs said, "You don't ever want to tell 'em that about being slow; let 'em think you're fast"—advice I pass on for your consideration and possible appropriate action.

As for my "Turk costume," which you see here, it was what I decided to wear on a trip organized by my mother (a lifelong devotee of everything theatrical), during which friends of the family arranged for full-scale performances in eight or nine cities between Boston and Iowa. Marshalltown was the high point and turning point, really the main reason for the enterprise in my eyes.

What first caught Downs's fancy in our preliminary correspondence was an invitation (found among my grandmother's papers) to a London garden party given by Queen Victoria, at which T. Nelson Downs was the star attraction. Perhaps even he had not very many third-generation fans. (I had supposed a command performance would be all in the day's work for him, but he seemed to have a lively recollection of this one.)

The name I have added, with a heavy heart, to the memorial dedication is John Mulholland's. This immensely tall, ungainly, chinless man with the panoramic ears (he would have been the first to accept the description) spent sixty-five of his seventy years studying and doing magic. He knew people who had seen Robert-Houdin, Signor Blitz, Robert Heller, Alexander Herrmann; he was friends with every contemporary magician of the slightest consequence from England to India; his collection of books and memorabilia (now housed in a special suite at the Players' Club in New York) may well have been the world's largest, and it certainly had no superior in its share of rarities.

"John Mulholland is the most knowledgeable magician in the world today," said an authority, William W. Larsen Jr., in 1965.

Houdini, striving for culture, hired the young Mulholland to take the raw edges off his circus-barker delivery—to make a lecturer of the jailbreaker. The result was a tempestuous but lifelong friendship. "The final Houdini, the one most of us remember, the crusading, fabulous earthshaker, was shaped to some extent by John," an admirer wrote.

Five years after my visit to Tommy Downs, John gave me the run of his New York apartment (he spent his entire life, globetrotting apart, within a mile or two of the spot). That was my senior year at college; naturally the hours with him taught me more than anything alma mater had to offer.

A little later he helped me over a rough patch by making me temporary managing editor of his magazine, *The Sphinx*, and letting me work on one of his books.

Those were just two visible specimens of his kindness to one person among the scores who loved him and the hundreds who had reason to.

You mustn't suppose from this that he was a darling of the gods with all magic falling into his lap. Universally known as a wit and raconteur, he taught himself that art as he did history-writing and editing and collecting and the manual skill of his profession—by unremitting application. Nothing that ever happened to him went unused.

The Great Man of my boyhood, Nelson Downs, was obviously born to magical greatness; John Mulholland, the great model of my youth, was self-made.

As the *Handbook*'s thirtieth anniversary in print rolled around I began discussing with my editor, Hugh Rawson, what was urgent to catch up on for the next generation. He said children's shows were becoming more and more the way to one's first paying jobs; I thought videotape for self-criticism was the most noteworthy innovation. So we compromised by doing both, and Mr. Rawson persuaded The Amazing Randi to give us the benefit of his broad videotape expertise, for which we cannot thank him enough.

Another pen pal, Dan Barstow (Merlyn's Apprentice) of Hartford, Conn., responded nobly with a virtual essay on kid shows, much of which you will find embodied in the new Part VI. Old reliable Lewis Ganson and Rodney Heft again offered wise suggestions.

I have, of course, seized the opportunity to go over the book line by line for small corrections and updating.

Finally, last-minute glad tidings. My friend Hayward Cirker of Dover Publications, who had already pleased me by reviving my *Learn Magic* and *Cyclopedia of* Magic in his impressive list of conjuring reprints, is now bringing back Professor Hoffmann; he even gave me the privilege of writing an introduction for *More Magic*. (In the process I learned that Professor Hoffmann himself died exactly the proverbial fairy-tale year and a day before *Modern Magic* under my Christmas tree launched me into conjuring; and that Howard Thurston, whose show in Washington had prompted the gift, was another pupil of the Professor.)

H.H.

I pause in fond memory of Lewis Ganson, who died in December 1980.

1. *The Magic State of Mind*

THE PURPOSE of this volume is to help you become a good magician: one who can entertain others as well as himself with the wonders he works.

Now everyone knows that being a magician at all—just knowing how to do tricks—is endless fun and a ready source of eminence among your friends, not to mention your automatic membership in the world's most delightful secret fraternity. This stage accounted for my first five years or so in magic.

The next twenty-five went into learning how to please other people as much as I pleased myself with what I could do. I came to appreciate both sides of Susanne Langer's remark: "Every play has its intended audience, and in that audience there is one pre-eminent member: the author."

At that point I wrote the original edition of this book. The hardest part of magic to teach, I said then, and the part most shamefully neglected, is the art of making puzzling tricks pleasing. I shall return to this in the next chapter, and in every chapter that follows.

First, however, come the tricks—simply because without tricks you can be a juggler, a comedian, a dancer, a violinist, an actor, but not, by definition, a conjurer. And besides, the tricks were probably what attracted you to magic in the first place. It won't do to talk them down.

After I had learned *how* most magical effects are produced, and could show a fair number without disappointing a paying audience, I began to wonder *why* conjuring works. Still later I had some thoughts, to be discussed in a moment, about the emotional basis of different sorts of effect.

Now these are philosophical questions—thin stuff, one might think, to the twelve-year-old tackling the two-handed pass. But if we can get hold of them, we (the twelve-year-old included) shall have a much easier time both learning and selling to the audience any trick we undertake.

To begin, we must consider magic itself: what are we talking about?

1. "White," or "natural," magic or conjuring is the art—let's say the game—of entertaining by tempting a particular audience to accept, temporarily, minor infractions of natural law.

If you ask them to accept permanently—to *believe*—you are a charlatan, a messiah, perhaps both; not a prestidigitator.

"Black," so-called "primitive" magic tries to soften the impartiality of natural law—to give a pet enemy a pain in the neck, to make it rain today instead of next week. The object is not entertainment but results.

2. And how do we go about tempting our audience?

The central secret of conjuring (and of art and literature and politics and economics) is a *manipulation of interest.* (Not just of *attention,* as we shall see in a moment.)

What, in turn, is interest? *Interest is a sense of being involved in some process, actual or potential.*

(Potential processes—will it or won't it?—create curiosity; they are the mainspring of conjuring and of drama in general.)

Processes too big, too small, too fast, too confused, or too slow for you to take in can't give any sense of involvement; they aren't interesting. That much is obvious.

Not obvious but equally important is something else—a point that nothing I've ever read about magic, drama, advertising, or even psychology has made in so many words:

Interest is not the same as attention. Attention is a simple response to a stimulus—either to a loud bang or (much more powerful) to a feeling of interest.

Interest is selective, an expenditure of energy by the interested party. You, the performer, can never command it, only invite it.

Attention you may compel briefly with a wham or a bright light; it can be sustained only by interest. Enforced attention without interest is a fine definition of boredom; try memorizing strings of random figures. You can't even keep at it for long unless you add interest by discovering some progression in the numbers.

You, as a magician, may encourage interest by offering the spectator a process to involve himself in. That is, you can demand his attention, and if you don't forcibly disappoint him, he may well follow up with interest.

Not only that, you can take heart: merely because interest is an effort on his part, don't think he automatically shuns it. He'll gladly volunteer the work so long as you let him, instead of trying to drive him. Nobody is lazy about anything he's truly interested in. More than that, unless he keeps letting off his energy somehow, he'll go crazy. Shut a man up in a blank cell and he'll hunt for designs in the cracked plaster. Some psychologists call boredom "structure hunger."

For the magician, this means a trick must hang together; that it must not be scrambled by irrelevant objects, motions, or even surprises. As Henning Nelms says in his magnificent *Magic and Showmanship*, of which more later, to find a chosen card by mind-reading and then turn the back a different color is to undo your whole psychic illusion.

To sum up, every normal person projects interest in something every waking moment, and many sleeping moments (you can dream, can't you?). With luck and good management you can usually win him for what you're interested in, your performance. Just remember it's always his choice.

Another piece of practical philosophy follows from this:

3. *Memory is an internally edited record of interest (not of attention, much less of "events")*. Memory creates surprise at magic, because the event seems to contradict what the spectator remembers has gone before (though, of course, not what the performer remembers has gone before).

Incidentally, Cagliostro and other medicine men have set us an example here: a really convincing wizard at least half believes his own story. As William Cowper put it in 1785,

> ". . . Katterfelto, with his hair on end
> At his own wonders, wond'ring for his bread."

Our friend Henning Nelms offers a magic tool for doing this—what he calls the "silent script." "Every performer," he says, "needs lines to *think* whenever he is silent. . . . The technique consists of writing out on paper enough lines to fill all the gaps in your speech. Then recite these lines mentally while you perform. Do not attempt to memorize them exactly, just get the basic ideas in mind. . . . Note that although both the spoken and silent scripts fit your assumed character, the silent lines do not fit your real situation at all. . . . On points like these . . . you must forget the facts as they are and think as you would if the facts were what you pretend them to be. . . . The silent script . . . provides an easy way to believe in your own miracles."

Now memory comes in again to help the conjurer: selecting only what's interesting, it magnifies its choices. People sketching from memory make the colors brighter and the design bolder than the original. In describing a magic trick, they make it good.

Suppose you vanish four or five small oranges, and then catch them from empty air—a modest little trick that you can do before you are halfway through the section on hand magic. If you are any showman at all, ten to one that people will quite honestly remember that you caught half a bushel of grapefruit, and piled them up on the stage.

We've seen that interest is projected by the interested person, not by the "interesting" object. Next step for the performer to grasp:

4. *Perception, too, originates with the perceiver, not with the object.* No two people see or hear a given event or even a given body exactly the same. (Think of "the moment that seems a year.")

You couldn't do magic at all if this weren't so: people would take in everything, would attach the appropriate physical meaning to it, and nothing would seem surprising—or even very interesting, since there would be little uncertainty, few potential processes.

Take note that I don't mean mere "optical illusions." A baby perceives his mother as a huge body; his father perceives her as a rather small one. Light and sound waves have independent existence; but "sight" and "sound" are names for perception, not for what evokes perception when someone happens to be paying attention (i.e., projecting interest).

In other words, *the magic show takes place ultimately in the spectator's head.* Any single performance (or TV program or painting) has as many versions as it has viewers.

Nevertheless, the wizard may exert a certain degree of control: he determines what the audience shall not pay attention to (a process known in conjuring as misdirection), and he restricts so far as he can the ways in which each onlooker shapes his own private performance. What you must realize is that your game is angling, not shooting. You don't propel, you lure. The "fly" is in the trout's appetite, not on the hook.

You let the audience perform their own magic, with coaching from you.

This brings up another consideration: what you might call the basic distinction between "Want to bet?" and "What if?" in magic.

With due allowance for the fact that all explanations are partial, all motives mixed, I hazard the opinion that every beginning conjurer wants first of all to distinguish himself in some unusual way—by being unique, not just by outrunning the field. He wants to set himself apart.

This may well involve conspiracy; it certainly brings involvement with audiences. That involvement necessarily starts as a contest: the performer must prove himself cleverer than the spectators. A young magician's first business is to fool his contemporaries.

What we overlook—or at least I did until well past middle age—is that not all magic falls in this class. To rise above ordinary clowning, magic must fool to a certain minimum extent, of course, but its essence may rather be to charm or to amuse. An adult performing for children lives (as we shall see in Chapter 20) by joining in a game of make-believe where tricks are just part of the scenery. And you must have met people who earnestly say, "I don't want to know how he does it."

Please don't think I'm urging moral categories, friendly over hostile.

I just say it's a useful classification in programming and presentation.

For instance, playing cards on their very faces typify opposition, "taking tricks." From the back, in flourishes, they serve for a form of dance. (Jumbling the two categories is probably a mistake; show one, follow with the other. Decide for yourself which should come first. And consider Cardini as against Nate Leipzig: the cards connoted different personalities.)

Houdini was the ultimate adversary: people came hoping to see him fail. This is, in fact, the essence of all escape tricks, and also of what the profession calls "sucker gags"—pretended blunders or exposures with a sting in the tail, leaving the audience more puzzled than ever.

Pretty effects—silks, billiard balls, productions—live more by the eye than by rational analysis. Productions, puzzling as they may be, essentially summon one and all to join in the fun.

In short, whenever you consider a trick, you may learn a good deal just by asking yourself, "Am I running with 'em or against 'em?"

So much for philosophy. Now for some basic practical applications—techniques of "coaching" the spectators.

The "trick" part of magic (misdirection, the "psychology of deception") is essentially a guiding of interest. Once a person starts to perceive a process, he will probably carry it through to his own conclusion; and when he misidentifies the process for reasons I'm about to explain, the result is a successful deception. Not necessarily an entertaining one, as you will be reminded in the next chapter; but at least an undetected trick.

Perhaps the most important element in the process you want perceived is *association*—the great labor-saving device of the brain, the short cut that saves all the time we live on.

After two images have been perceived together once or twice, you automatically associate them: the wooden handle goes with the ice pick attached to it. The feel of a hard disk provokes the image of money.

Here "magic" comes into play. Bore an ice pick into the elbow of a volunteer from the audience. Where you drive a pick, there must be a hole. But this pick sinks back into a hollow handle: the hole is in the handle beforehand, not in the elbow afterward.

The hard disk that someone holds through a handkerchief instantly says "half dollar" to him, particularly since but a moment before he actually saw the money. Instead, however, you have handed him a glass disk, which will become invisible when he drops it into a tumbler of water.

If you simply gave someone the disk under a handkerchief and asked him what it was, he probably wouldn't call it money; the glass does not really feel like a coin. So you let *him* do the trick by association.

Not only apparatus magic but hand magic rests on association. (Hand magic is what the profession knows as sleight of hand—the operation of pure manual skill, rather than of mechanical devices or guile.)

Of all the wonderful sleight-of-hand experts in the world, probably not a dozen can stand up against a slow-motion camera. Take away the misdirection and the timing, and anyone can see the coin revolving to the back of the hand, the billiard ball being gobbled by the left fist instead of carried away by the right.

Slow-motion-camera perfection is the last stage that even a great expert attains, and on balance it may not be very much more effective than the showman's "good enough." It is certainly not sufficient in itself. Keep on practicing your sleights, but remember that the onlookers, guided by association, are the ones who do the real work. Neat manipulation won't necessarily compel them to cooperate; clumsiness will prevent them.

You take a silver dollar in your hand. Your hand goes gently down, then sharply up. "Toss!" says association, steering eyes to the ceiling. The spectator with an agile, well-trained mind will actually see the silver gleam as it flies upward.

His three-year-old son, having a tenth of his father's practice at associating cause and effect, is not so smart: he sees no dollar at all after your hand starts down. Instead, he may even see your fingers pressing the coin into your palm, where it sticks while the adults are gaping at the ceiling.

(This, incidentally, is why you had better give really young audiences a wide berth until you have grown practiced in wizardry. The lovable kiddies have too few associations—and no inhibitions. When you get ready to take the plunge, read chapter 20.)

We have been considering misdirection as the fabricated association of cause and effect, of an object and its properties. Another way of manipulating cause and effect is time.

You have a silver dollar in each hand. You say "Go!" Suddenly there is a clink, and both coins are in one hand. Of course people really know better, but still they can't help *feeling* that the dollar went when you told it to. Actually it had moved some time before, while the audience was involved in a different stage of the apparent process.

Sometimes you can make a secret move *after* people's attention has passed on. A dollar is palmed in your left hand. You boldly grab at the air with your right, which is plainly empty, and seem to catch something. Your look of satisfaction makes people think you have succeeded. You casually "put" the "thing" into your left hand; only then does anyone actually see the dollar.

These are a few ways of demanding attention (to be sustained, as we saw, by continuing interest).

Within a process the loudest noise, the fastest motion, the brightest color will ordinarily capture attention. People watch the hand that moves. They ignore the hand that stays still.

Say you are making a thimble disappear. Apparently you pass it from your right hand to your left; actually, your right forefinger sticks the thimble into the fork of your right thumb, then straightens out to touch your left hand, which closes. The actual motions are not half so hard as you may have thought when you bought this book. But no matter how perfectly they are done, you will still be caught out unless you end by stopping your right hand still and moving your left hand away.

The motion carries people's eyes with it. (If you were to forget and withdraw your right hand, they would sense something wrong.)

In performance you also have another, even better tool for launching the process you want people to share in: *imitation*, or let's say *suggestibility*—a force that reaches down the biological scale at least to swarms of gnats. Every practical joker knows that he can collect a gaping crowd by just standing and staring. (Man to member of a street-corner gathering: "What's going on here?" Answer: "I don't know, I've been waiting for an hour to find out.")

Wherever you look fixedly, the audience will look also. Even a set of magicians can hardly refrain. So the very first hurdle you must clear in learning sleight of hand is making your eyes behave. You tend to forget that the ball is supposed to be in your left fist; though you'll scarcely glance at your right palm, you may look at the audience to see how they're taking it—with the result that they don't take your motions seriously. But one or two such small flops will cure you, and your eyes will blandly follow the mythical ball to the wrong spot.

In the case of the thimble, when you move your left hand, point with your right (suggestibility again), and follow through with your eyes, people will be fooled even though your small finger motions are not altogether invisible: the audience gets caught up in the larger process.

The crucial movement need not even be invisible at all: it just has to seem insignificant. Here is an easy trick you can try right now, though (for reasons that will appear in the next chapter) you may not succeed with it very well. At any rate it will give you an example of misdirection that relies on rendering the vital detail uninteresting—on turning away attention, association, and memory.

Take a quarter at the finger tips of your right hand. Hold your left hand out, palm up. Lay a quarter on your left palm, and close your left hand. Toss the quarter back from your left hand to your right.

Repeat the act of putting the coin in your left hand, only this time close the left hand before anyone can see the coin very plainly.

Toss the coin back to your right hand, but fumble it so that it falls on the floor roughly in front of your right foot.

Don't pause, and don't hurry—the process must go evenly on. Stoop, put the tip of your right second finger on the quarter, and snap your hand shut. The motion shoots the quarter under your right foot.

This is the crucial point, the place for your "silent script," which reads, "How could I have been so clumsy? I'll really hang on to it this time." Thus you instantly forget the quarter under your foot, and concentrate on the imaginary quarter in your closed right hand.

Keep your eyes on the right hand as you straighten up. Make the same motion of putting the "coin" into your left hand, and closing the left hand, as you did before. Follow through with your eyes from the right hand to the left, which is now closed, while the right hand hangs slack.

If you have not allowed your mishap of dropping the coin to interrupt the process, association leads people to expect that you will toss the quarter back to your right hand.

Instead, toss upward, following the "quarter" with your eyes.

The coin has vanished. Both hands are empty. (For heaven's sake don't say so. Just hold out your palms, look at them, and put on a surprised or pleased expression.)

Since I am merely giving you a small sample of misdirection, I shall leave you with the coin under your foot. When we come to consider routines, you will see various ways to get out of this fix.

That will do for a start on why magic works.

Soon—perhaps within hours—your very success will face you with new problems. The first is that people will ask you how you did it.

This may be a compliment, or perhaps (as Nelms says) simply the "I give up" that follows a riddle, when the rules of social intercourse seem to demand that you reciprocate.

Anyhow, you must find means to resist graciously. If a trick is so ingenious that it can't be seen through, you should cherish it as a priceless possession. If, as is usually the case, the method is simple, people will be annoyed with themselves when it's explained—and therefore with you.

When the pressure to expose grows strong, you have two ready recourses. One is a good-natured little remark that says you won't tell, but hope to be forgiven as part of the game. "Well, I do it mostly with wires and mirrors. I sometimes surprise myself."

John Mulholland, the eminent wizard and magical scholar who taught me at least half of anything I've ever known about our art, suggested, "I'm sorry, but I promised not to tell"—nothing said about whom you promised. Perhaps Mulholland's shade, yourself, or me. (As a matter of fact, such a promise is part of joining any magical society.)

The best way when you can, though, is to do another trick that professes to be an explanation of the one you have just shown. It may in fact be altogether different, or it may be a sucker gag.

Here let me give you a related piece of advice, which time has elevated to the dignity of a rule: Don't tell just what you are going to do until you are in the clear; don't warn people what to expect until after the secret maneuvers are accomplished. Otherwise they will have three times the chance to detect your feat.

By the same token, you should never do a trick over, because that is the same as telling exactly what comes next.

You may perfectly well *seem* to do it over; in fact we've just seen that you often should. But the "repetition" should be a sucker gag, or else you must have a different means of producing the same effect.

When you get just a little further into magic, you will have to make a decision based on your personal style. Either you must learn your effects so perfectly that they never go wrong; or you must learn a variety of methods to cover repetitions and predicaments. You must decide, that is, between technical perfection and improvisation.

Actually this is no choice because sooner or later something always will go wrong. All you can do is take every precaution, and have some means of covering up the slip. Many teachers of conjuring say they judge a performer most of all by how he surmounts a mishap.

So you are virtually driven to learn a variety of ruses and recoveries; a solid background of these is what makes you a conjurer rather than just the life of the party. But a good many hard-working performers carry their passion for moves, variations, and refinements too far; they have never been told that the audience re-creates their tricks—that the magician's mechanical perfection doesn't assure a perfect show in the spectator's head.

Still, no amount of skill and learning will hurt you if you can also do justice to the next chapter. I have provided a good deal of the added information you may want in later pages.

2. *Hard Easy Tricks and Easy Hard Tricks*

PROBABLY you are wondering whether you haven't tackled something pretty formidable in deciding to study magic. The hours of practice that go with being a wizard are almost as traditional as the rabbit from the hat. Some of the most substantial textbooks on conjuring start off by remarking that of course the neophyte must practice indefatigably before he can hope for success.

When the craze for "ten easy lessons" hit the world, writers on magic began claiming that they could make a magician out of you with no work at all.

Strangely enough, both parties are telling the truth—if they find the right pupil. A patient, persistent student can make himself into a smooth manipulator by dogged practice. A born comedian can show tricks entertainingly with hardly more effort than reading the directions on the box.

But in this book, which takes nothing for granted except that you want to be a magician, I must start by explaining the paradox of practice, of hard and easy tricks.

The chapters that follow will probably strike you as being arranged backward: first come the tricks of manual skill, then the ones so misleadingly known as "self-working."

The reason is this. I have loved magic since the 1920s, and I want every one of my readers to love it also.

If you start off with a few self-working tricks that you can plod through undetected, you may puzzle people, but you won't entertain them. Worse, you won't have entertained yourself. Easy come, easy go. Familiarity breeds contempt.

A parlor accomplishment as simple as that scarcely seems worth having. At this perfunctory stage, indeed, it isn't.

Understand, some self-working tricks are intrinsically among the most beautiful things in magic. If you think my reasoning is wrong, you can turn straight to the section on head magic. The natural-born comedian I mentioned above can well afford to do just that.

But if you are starting in magic as a normal person of ordinary dramatic gifts, you haven't yet acquired the timing, the splash, the showmanship to convert an ingenious puzzle into a pleasing surprise.

Some notion, at least, of magical acting can be taught in a book; but it takes time to sink in. The time required to memorize a self-working trick is not long enough.

The time required to learn a fairly simple sleight (a manual artifice) probably will be long enough for you to absorb the acting that goes with it.

In short, you can learn to do a moderately difficult trick *well* more easily than you can a perfectly easy trick. On a sleight-of-hand trick you can't skimp; on an easy trick the temptation is almost irresistible. You won't dare to show a feat of skill that is only half practiced—and this is one of the basic axioms in all conjuring.

Don't be frightened by the word "difficult"; it is altogether relative.

Learning to write the letter W by hand strikes the five-year-old as a formidable task. He can do it much more easily by finding the right key on a typewriter and punching it.

But if he does that, he will learn neither to write nor to typewrite.

Learning your first sleight is of about the same order of difficulty as learning to write a W. Learning the equivalent of the alphabet will render you a competent sleight-of-hand magician.

It does take practice—but practice that is almost pure pleasure. The celebrated card manipulator Jack Merlin wrote, "Practice is something I cannot resist. I practice because I enjoy it. When I force myself to it, I accomplish nothing."

With cards, coins, and other small staples of conjuring you can practice where you like, when you like, and what you like. When you get tired or bored, you stop.

The result is that you hardly ever grow bored; and, though you tire, you don't realize it.

Indeed you should remind yourself to call a halt now and then. Psychologists have shown that we learn faster and better with frequent short rests than with dogged, unremitting effort.

An English professional, Robertson-Keene, put it this way: "There is such a thing as learning a thing too well. I have frequently back-palmed cards so continually that my grip and control of them were visibly lessened, and I have found that moderation is necessary in this, as in all things."

Another pitfall is that of starting to practice too eagerly. You should read the whole way through a trick two or three times before you tackle it at all. Understand what you are trying to do, and how you are to do it; *memorize* the complete process. Then you are ready to start practicing.

I have spoken about showmanship, dramatic ability, proper presentation—call it what you like—but so far I have not come to grips with it.

Showmanship is not to be confused with volubility. Half-informed people often think that a conjurer, like an auctioneer, succeeds just by fast, bewildering patter. This is hardly ever true. Auctioneers and conjurers both rely on timing and judgment of public temper; the patter (which is the technical name for *all* magical talk) merely sets a certain tempo. The auctioneer's tempo has to be fast to hold his buyers' attention. The magician's tempo should harmonize with his own personality. He has a set of cunningly contrived plots and properties to hold interest; he can afford a leisurely, conversational pace if he is a leisurely, conversational person.

The naturally quick performer can go his own gait—as long as he does not outrun his audience. If they can't keep up with events, he must slow down willy-nilly. Otherwise his whole act is just shadowboxing before onlookers too bewildered to be mystified. This is fully as bad as the act so slow that people go to sleep between tricks.

The naturally slow performer can go his own gait too—as long as he offers enough interest, in talk or action, to keep people entertained. When you see them strolling off to the group around the piano, speed up.

Nothing is so profoundly a performer's own as his patter. You can change the color of your eyes more easily than the color of the patter that suits you. I say this with full realization that the writing of canned patter (some of it, God help us, in rhyme!) is a busy industry. There are books upon books of patter; well-informed magical critics laud new volumes for their wealth of intelligent patter; dealers sell tricks whose sole novelty is an intricate "patter story" to account for the outlandish properties used. (This has its place, though, in children's shows.)

You have about one chance in ten—a poor chance, but still a chance—that any particular prefabricated patter can be twisted to suit you. My urgent advice is, don't fool around with it. The chance isn't good enough.

You can grow your own patter more easily and far more successfully. Study the new trick a little. Grasp the plot—ball keeps coming back; red silk turns green; chosen cards rise. See if the plot would be clear with no patter at all.

Then see if misdirection requires bits of patter nevertheless. If not, try the trick without patter. Some of the greatest magicians have done "silent acts." These acts put a severe strain on your skill and your pantomime; they are excellent training.

Your study soon shows you what must be said, and when. That is all you need to give you the patter. You have the outlines of your story; let it come out according to plan, but in your own natural words.

Book patter abounds in words like "endeavor" and "observe." Don't be taken in: go right ahead saying "try" and "see." But maybe you're the "endeavor" sort of fellow. Very well, "endeavor" it is—for you. You are in a small gathering of friends; talk that way. Don't talk like Professor Hoffmann; don't talk like me; talk like you.

Good patter is quite as much knowing what to say, and when to say nothing, as it is smooth palaver. In this it brings us back to showmanship.

The highest art of showmanship cannot be taught, and can be learned only to a degree. If you and I struggled as long and as hard as Houdini did to teach ourselves showmanship, we should still be far below Houdini's level; but we might be equally far above the level of some very skillful performers with greater natural gifts than ours.

Good, workable showmanship, on the other hand, is just a matter of common sense and reasonable planning. The difficulty about it is that most learners of magic become fascinated with the tricks—the means of producing effects—and so forget the effects themselves, the whole reason for their efforts.

The commonest faults in showmanship are ones that nobody would commit knowingly.

Turning your back on the audience in the struggle to hide a difficult manipulation is an elementary mistake. If you find a sleight so hard that you have to hide it in this way, you shouldn't be showing it yet.

Nothing is so crippling to smooth presentation as trying to show a trick that you cannot yet do with perfect ease.

Another fault is not letting people know what you claim to be doing. A trick may be so familiar to you that you quite forget it is all new to the audience.

Say you are going to change a red billiard ball into a white one. Of course the rule says you must not announce this in advance; yet on the other hand you must let everyone, no matter how thick headed, see—and more important, realize—that you have a ball in your hand. A red ball. One red ball, and nothing else.

The more complicated your trick, the more difficult is this first part of your task. There are a number of tricks (not in this book, I hasten to add) that are just plain too complicated. They are no good, and should never be shown: they demand too much concentration from an audience that rightfully expects you to do most of the work.

One way you can judge an effect for simplicity, as I have already suggested, is to see how far you can get with it in dumbshow. One red billiard ball in an empty pair of hands speaks for itself: a pause, a look, and the gesture of holding up the ball are all anyone could need. To say, as some magicians still do, "I have here an unprepared billiard ball, and I want you to notice that my hands are absolutely empty," is to give the audience a rude nudge in the ribs. If you admit thinking them as stupid as that, you will never be a showman.

But actually some of them are as stupid as that—or will be so if you forget to give them a chance. The pause, the look, the emphatic gesture, all are essential. Omit just one, and you spoil your trick.

Not all good tricks can be started in pantomime. However, if a trick demands much explaining, you should ask yourself whether it is good enough to keep, and then whether it can't be simplified somehow.

The fact is that nearly all complications in presenting a trick are there for your technical convenience. If you were a true wizard, you wouldn't need any complications.

Say you are going to do the Book Test—a standard trick in which you write down beforehand the word someone will pick out of a book. As a real magician you probably wouldn't use a book at all; you would walk up to a stranger, hand him a sealed envelope, and ask him to mention a word. The word would be written inside the envelope.

Since you are only a make-believe magician, you have to use a book, and for your convenience you elaborate the method of choosing a word. First a page is chosen, then a number that indicates the position of the word on the page.

Inherently this is such a serious flaw in the Book Test that I have never liked the trick. Nevertheless it is possible to show the effect entertainingly. By misdirection you make the elaboration appear a safeguard. You suggest that any one person who merely opened the book and picked a word might be in league with you. Therefore you have one man choose the page, another the number, a third count to the word. The complication becomes build-up, a stroke of showmanship.

Furthermore, you can create the impression of simplicity by stating very simply what you want done. "Here is a dictionary, with twenty thousand entries. I would like you to choose one of those twenty thousand words in such a way that nobody can possibly know what the word is going to be."

At this point you hand around a dictionary. You hand it around. You *don't* say, "Please examine this ordinary, unprepared dictionary."

Very likely it is nothing of the sort, but unless you bring up the subject, the natural association of "dictionary" and "commonplace" will protect you.

When you say your hands are empty, you merely affront people's intelligence. When you say the dictionary is unprepared, you arouse their intelligence, which is far worse.

There are tricks (such as stage escapes) in which rigid scrutiny of the properties is the very foundation of the effect. These feats, however, are far rarer than most conjurers suppose. Generally you want people to forget that you have used any boxes, covers, or contraptions at all.

To put the lesson of the Book Test in plainer form, showmanship demands that you have an apparent reason for anything you do. You need not explain your reason: the more self-evident, the better. In showing the Miser's Dream, the coin-catching trick, you take a hat in your left hand for the most obvious of reasons—to hold the money. This is another effect where explanation might get you into serious trouble.

The Book Test you do need to explain because of the aforementioned complications. You explain that you introduce them merely to make things hard for yourself.

You must have a reason all along the line. You must have a reason not only for the way you do a trick, but for the trick itself.

The Miser's Dream offers the best example in all magic of a convincing reason for doing the trick. What else would a real wizard ever do besides catch money?

More usually the reason is a desire to prove your magic powers—say by sawing a woman in two and restoring her. But in that case you must have especially good reasons for the way you do it. A real magician could just chop her in half with a meat cleaver on the stage, and stick her right together again. Accordingly the box she lies in is to protect squeamish members of the audience.

For a quick, startling effect, sometimes the total absence of any reason is a reason in itself. But then the reasons for how you do it must be perfect.

You show a fan of cards. Clap your hands—gone!

The next moment, you slide the cards ribbonwise out of your mouth.

There is no reason to make them disappear, except that you are a magician. But the way you do it is simple, natural, magical. There is no reason for the cards to reappear in your mouth except that they have to reappear somewhere; but then they come back smoothly and surprisingly.

If you did this trick with a nickel-plated box to vanish the cards, and a garrulous explanation, it would be intolerable. You would then have no reason for using the nickel-plated box except to make the disappearance easy for yourself—obviously nothing like real magic.

If you want to use the nickel-plated box (which you can get at a magic shop by asking for a "card box") legitimately, you must do as you did in the Book Test: claim to be putting a particular card where no one can get at it, even the spectator who holds it.

Here is another reason that hand magic is the easy way. It generally takes less explaining and looks more like a truly magical process.

I don't want to claim too much for my own admitted preference. Some sleights are laborious and utterly unmagical; some apparatus is unobtrusive and convincing. Yet in general I think you will agree that it is more like real wizardry to toss a silver dollar into the air, bingo, than to drop it in a gaudy tin cup, which you can show empty after an appropriate pause.

So far, so good. You have allowed the audience to realize what you are working with. The trick is not too hard for you, and you are facing forward, where they can see you do it. You have done nothing without a reason. You have not verbally insisted on anything obvious (obvious, though of course it may be quite untrue).

In short, you have refrained from all the usual thoughtless mistakes.

The big moment of your trick is at hand. The red ball is about to turn white; the fan of cards is going to disappear as you clap your hands.

Remember the timid man and the barking dog? "Barking dogs never bite. You know it; I know it; but does the dog know it?"

You are trying your magic on the dog. You know the climax is coming; does the dog know it? Again you must steer between announcing the trick too soon and losing the whole point of your effect.

Often the secret part of the trick will be done already, so that you may baldly state your intentions. At all events you must put up a conspicuous warning sign: Caution! This is it! Wizard at work!

Almost any kind of accent may serve to alert the audience—a pause, a fixed gaze, the gesture of pointing, the mere word "Look!"

Really you are calling into play your old friend suggestibility. If you obviously think this moment of a feat the most important, the audience thinks likewise. If you were lackadaisical, they would settle back for a cat nap, during which you could safely march the vanishing elephant right off the stage.

But you have already done that part. Now you must do just one thing: pull them to the edge of their chairs. Convince them that this they've got to see.

I have emphasized this point because it is the biggest single thing in presentation. It is a positive knack that you must acquire. The "don'ts" are just elementary reminders. This "do" is basic.

The knack is easy enough to learn; I shall remind you of it, off and on, throughout the chapters on hand magic, by the end of which it should be automatic. But I want you to realize now what you will be doing, and why, instead of just following my directions mechanically.

The last step in a successful trick is to take a bow. This is an important step, and young magicians surprisingly often forget it.

I don't mean that you must literally bob your head or bend from the waist. I do mean that you must pause definitely until everyone knows the trick is done. Then pause just a little longer. Give them time to decide whether they will applaud.

Nine chances out of ten they *will* applaud because they have been watching you for their own pleasure, and only a serious interference will spoil it. But one serious interference is hurrying on to the next trick before the last is well over.

Here, as always, your own attitude is very important. Above all, you must not be tentative; don't let the audience wonder whether you really *are* done. Depending on your personality and your trick, you may be pleased, relieved, surprised, triumphant, smug. Whichever it is, be definite about it. And give them time to get it.

To sum up, the four important steps in presenting a trick are these: show them what's what; get them on the edge of their chairs; spring your surprise; and notify them to sit back and applaud.

There are as many different ways of doing this as there are conjurers who do it. I can't tell you how to do it; I can tell you how I do it, and how men far better than I do it; I can tell you that in your own way you must do it too.

After you have learned some of the tricks in this volume, and thus struck up a working practical acquaintance with conjuring, you will certainly not regret the few dollars you spend to buy a copy of *Our Magic*, by Nevil Maskelyne and David Devant. A good many beginners have been disappointed in this masterpiece because it was not a book of tricks they cared to do. The wonderful lessons in presentation that the authors have to teach cannot, in fact, be appreciated without some background of magical knowledge.

The same is true of an even more expensive but highly rewarding volume, Dariel Fitzkee's *Showmanship for Magicians.*

If you want just one book to unlock the secrets of conjuring stagecraft, though, let it be the one I have already quoted, of which my sole complaint is that it appeared forty years late for my own career: *Magic and Showmanship, a Handbook for Conjurers,* by Henning Nelms. He wrote to me recently, "I am not a magician—just a showman with a lifelong interest in magic. Although I never perform myself, I have been saddened by the fact that a tremendous amount of valuable material which is commonplace to people in the theater seems completely unknown to magicians." The book is a paperback, and any performer who remains ignorant now has only himself to blame.

Enjoyment of Laughter, by Max Eastman, is another work that will amply repay your study. It gives a clear analysis of how to shape a joke, how to tell it, and why people laugh at it. The inquiring wizard can easily apply many of Eastman's observations to the planning and presentation of tricks.

Take a look at chapter 22, later in this book.

For now, however, let's interrupt our theorizing to learn some tricks. If you will reread these first two chapters *after* you have gone part way through the book, you'll find they tell you twice as much as they did before.

The same is true of some other general instructions I might give you, so I shall put them in at intervals as you need them. And if you feel you've missed anything, or want more information, you can probably find it in the back of the book.

PART ONE · HAND MAGIC

3. *Hand Magic with Cards*

HAND magic, as I have mentioned, is known to conjurers as sleight of hand. The lay public is just as likely to apply the latter term to almost any magic, large or small.

We of the trade distinguish illusions (stage tricks involving people or large animals); escapes; mind reading (or "mentalism"); apparatus conjuring; and sleight of hand. Under the general heading of sleight of hand comes a subheading, "manipulation." This is the technical term for a routine or act done with one particular kind of small object.

Thomas Nelson Downs was the greatest coin manipulator who ever lived; he improved the century-old Miser's Dream and made of it a complete vaudeville act. Howard Thurston began as the outstanding card manipulator of his day; later he bought the big show created by the great Harry Kellar and became an illusionist. As part of the show, however, he still did a brief routine of card manipulation.

Thus you can be a magician without being an illusionist or a sleight-of-hand man, and a sleight-of-hand man without being a manipulator. Whether you will become any or all of these is for you to decide from the samples I give you.

The only guidance I can offer is this. Illusions are at present in a decline among professionals and are not suitable for most amateurs because of their bulk, cost, and the necessary elaborate cooperative rehearsal. Escapes are subject to about the same drawbacks and in addition are physically strenuous. They are almost a separate art in themselves and are barely touched on in this book.

Mental effects enjoy an ever growing popularity. Only remember that they give the audience nothing to look at and so demand the utmost in presentation to keep them from dragging.

Apparatus conjuring is beloved of many well-to-do amateurs. Besides money, it requires careful, intelligent rehearsal and well-rounded showmanship. It has rather a bad name among magicians simply because too many amateurs stop short with the money, and skimp on the rehearsal.

Sleight of hand frightens many beginners by its supposed difficulty, while those who have become proficient look down loftily on all the rest of the magic world. Actually, as you will see in the next section, it is not remarkably difficult, and its acquisition is so pleasant that sleight-of-hand men should feel grateful instead of superior.

HAND MAGIC

Sleight of hand, I freely admit, is my own absorbing passion. I have nothing to say against other branches of the art; but in which one can you come so close to the qualities of genuine magic? Nothing to buy, nothing to cart around, nothing to get ready tediously in secret. If anyone says, "Do some magic," you do it on the spot; you are completely self-contained and self-reliant.

Incidentally, when the methods of a Cardini or a Nate Leipzig are explained, they seem more like magic than the tricks themselves. The sleight-of-hand man is the only performer who can never be made ridiculous, and may even grow in stature, by exposure.

The satisfactions of hand magic I have already touched on, and I hope you will soon experience them for yourself.

They also bring with them their own pitfalls. Sleight of hand is the most introverted magic. A man too easily becomes so absorbed in sleights that he forgets his audience. What should be a means becomes an end. For a time, the young student's absorption serves him instead of showmanship, carrying indulgent spectators along. But out in the cold world where magicians play for money, he falls behind in competition with genial, extroverted entertainers who can raise a laugh without necessarily knowing a side steal from a Charlier pass.

He tends to think the world is neglecting his hard-won merits—which, in a sense, it is. But in a wider sense magic is the art of compelling the world to admire and enjoy your merits. The sleight-of-hand man who cannot do that still has his hardest lessons ahead of him.

Now, how to become one of these fortunate beings.

Hand magic though it is, the hands can be dismissed at once. Any hand big enough to cover the cards or other objects you use has all the natural requirements. Such special suppleness as you need will come when you need it.

Long fingers are quite irrelevant, though bony hands may leave cracks between fingers and complicate your card-palming.

Hard, dry palms are a nuisance that can be largely offset by using a lanolin hand lotion.

Finger exercises, as divorced from specific sleights, are nonsense.

The best gift you can have is placid nerves and a gentle touch; and if you lack that gift, you can acquire it.

HAND MAGIC WITH CARDS

Card manipulation is incomparably the widest field for sleight of hand. Card tricks sometimes threaten to run away with the whole art, trailing all other magic in their wake. There are certainly far more books on card tricks than on any other one type of effect.

Of these books you will certainly require the card manipulator's bible, *The Expert at the Card Table,* by S. W. Erdnase; probably also T. Nelson Downs's *The Art of Magic* and its sequel, *Greater Magic,* by John Northern Hilliard; and perhaps *Expert Card Technique,* by Jean Hugard and Fred Braue. In addition there are specialized books within the specialty, some of which you will find listed at the back of this volume.

Along with the sleights, the card trickster has a whole army of mechanical and mathematical aids, which will be treated in subsequent sections. Once again, I warn you not to let the ingrown fascinations of card sleights blind you to sometimes subtler ways of entertaining with card tricks.

The cards themselves are important, though you must learn to perform the general run of tricks with whatever cards people hand you.

The first choice to be made is between bridge and poker sizes. I find bridge size slightly easier to handle, so I always use poker size, on the principle of a ball player warming up by swinging two bats.

There are three common finishes: ivory, air cushion, and linen. In addition there are soft, unglazed cards called Steamboats.

For card *tricks* (as distinct from flourishes) I like the ivory finish; some far-greater card manipulators than I use the air cushion; I do not happen to know of anyone who prefers the linen finish.

For fancy palming, and particularly back palming, the uncalendered

Steamboats are preferable. For fanning flourishes the ivory finish works best.

For all purposes the cards should be thin, flexible, and elastic.

Never use cards with gilt or silver edges if you can help it; they are stiff, thicker at the edges, and will give trouble in such sleights as the dovetail false shuffle.

Back patterns come in bewildering variety. Often they are quite immaterial to sleight of hand. Sometimes the scotty dogs, fruits, and flowers of cheap bridge cards are better avoided. A number of sleights, such as the second deal and the fan force, are more deceptive when the cards have an all-over pattern with no white border.

Having told you what kind of cards you want, I must reiterate that three-quarters of any card conjurer's reputation depends on his readiness to use borrowed cards. You must work at the basic sleights until you can do them with any pack short of laundry board.

The fancy flourishes will work only with proper cards, but that is quite legitimate and another matter altogether.

Now for the sleights. They are arranged roughly in order of importance. They are definitely not in order of difficulty. If you get discouraged with one, try another for a while.

And remember the basic rule in hand magic: gently does it.

For every single time that you drop the cards because your grip is too loose, you will scatter them five times with a tight grip that skids. Relax, relax, relax.

1. BREAKS

Breaks are divisions or openings created in the edge of the deck for the purpose of locating a particular card. They may be held as required by the tip of any finger, the thumb, or the flesh at the base of the thumb.

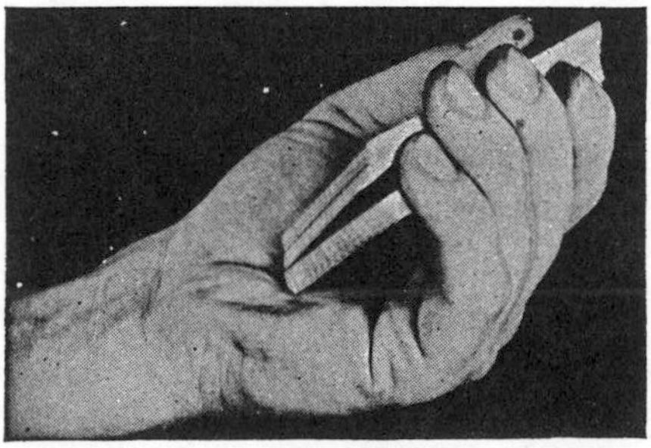

Fig. 1

1a. The little-finger break (Fig. 1). Except for the overhand shuffle (5*a*), this is by far the most useful break for all purposes. It is the easiest and best method of getting set for the side steal (2*b*).

As depicted in the illustration, it is being used to locate a card that a spectator has peeked at.

For this purpose proceed as follows:

Hold the cards in your left hand, in the normal position for dealing. The deck should be beveled somewhat toward the right, and the tip of your little finger should lie comfortably against the beveled right edge. Once you get the correct position, the rest of the sleight is almost automatic.

Hold the pack out to a spectator. Tell him that you wish him, instead of drawing a card, just to lift up the corner of the pack enough to peek at one card. Naturally, you offer him (from your point of view) the outer right-hand corner, which has the indices.

As far as possible don't make a point of it, but you must prevent the victim from riffling the deck and seeing more than one card. I always say quite simply, "Just lift up a corner and get a look at one card."

His natural tendency will be to pry up the corner nearest to himself. As he starts to do this, relax your whole left hand, particularly the thumb. This lets the lower part of the deck sag half an inch all along the right edge, for the spectator is supporting the upper part.

Bend your little finger a trifle, and slightly straighten the other three fingers.

By this time the spectator will have noted his card and released the corner he was bending back.

Press down with your left thumb.

The front end of the pack, toward the audience, is now flush, with no separation visible. But your little finger is holding open a break at the end toward you. You have "taken a little-finger break."

Usually the matter can rest there. In suspicious company, however, bring your right hand over to take the deck with the second (middle) finger at the center of the outer end, and the thumb at the center of the near end. You can square up the bevel and any slight step that remains at the outer end without losing the break at the inner end. Then keep the pack in your right hand, and make some explanatory or emphatic gesture with your left. The right thumb, meanwhile, holds the break open perfectly comfortably, ready to be picked up again at need by the left little finger.

To see through this dodge takes a very knowing spectator indeed.

The simple break is just a stage in various sleights, of which perhaps the simplest, and among the most useful, is the next item.

1b.. The glimpse. This is the name given to any method of surreptitiously sighting a chosen card. Different occasions may require different methods, but the following is the smoothest, subtlest, and simplest.

Proceed to take a little-finger break below the chosen card, exactly as in *1a.* This leaves the deck beveled to the right.

Move your thumb out so that it lies along the left edge of the pack, and squeeze to the left with your fingers, beveling the whole pack to the left (Fig. 2).

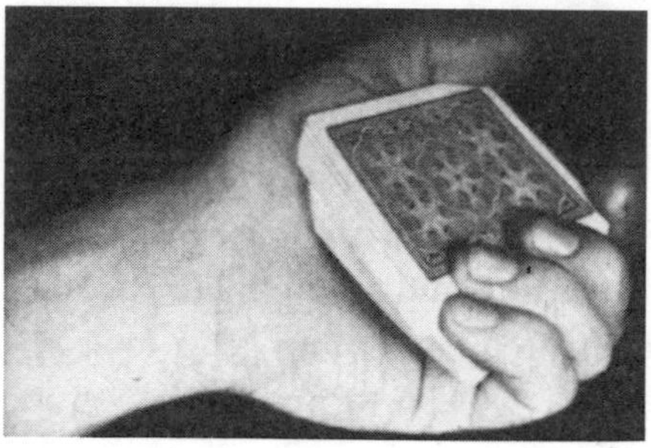

FIG. 2

This converts the break into a step: the upper half of the pack juts out to the left over the lower half.

Now you make two motions together: turn your left hand over, bringing its back upward; and start your right hand, thumb uppermost, toward the pack.

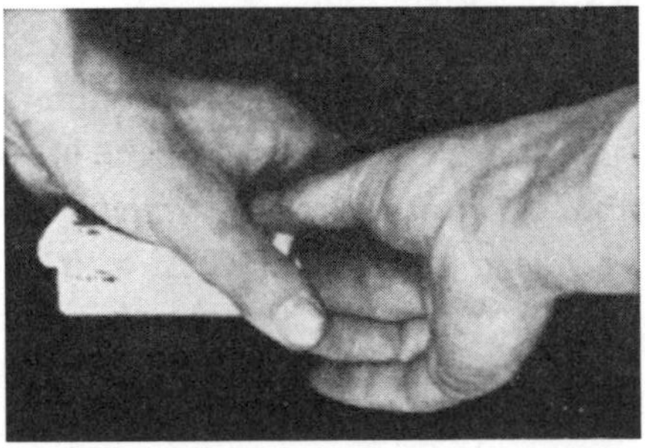

FIG. 3

As you see in Fig. 3, this brings the lower index corner of the chosen card into view below the heel of your left hand. It takes you but an instant to discover that the spectator has peeped at (in this case) the four of clubs.

Grab the pack between your right thumb and middle finger, and draw it forward out of your left hand, squaring up the step by this motion.

Probably you will now hand the deck to your victim for shuffling, safe in the knowledge that you can find his card when you want it.

The question of when to have a spectator shuffle is one that demands judgment. The safe rule is, don't unless you have to.

You may have to because your trick is pointless unless everyone knows that the chosen card has been hopelessly lost, or that the deck could not possibly be stacked. In those tricks, having someone shuffle is part of your regular routine, and I shall call your attention to it.

You may have to let a spectator shuffle because he insists, trying to stump you. This is much better than requesting him to shuffle: he will be more impressed when you succeed with your trick on his terms, whereas if you offer to let him shuffle, he will rightly conclude that it makes no difference. Here is a point of showmanship that builds up your effect without cost to you. To have people forever shuffling as a routine matter, on the other hand, does not impress them, but does make your show drag intolerably.

Example of a trick using the glimpse: As Easy as Spelling Your Name. This is a feat where you must have the audience shuffling, for several reasons.

To give the trick its fullest effect, you should work it on a stranger whose name you can manage to find out quietly. Be sure you have the correct spelling—an extra *e* on Brown, or a Chumley who spells it Cholmondely, will trip you up.

Failing this, it is still a good trick when done for a friend.

The effect is that someone peeks at a card, shuffles, and then deals one card off the top of the deck for each letter of his own name. On the last letter he turns up his card.

The special merit of the trick is that the spectator does most of it himself, yet has no involved directions to follow. It is really as simple as spelling his name.

Having picked your victim and ascertained his name, offer him the deck for a peek. Take a glimpse as you have just learned to do in 1*b*, and hand him the pack to shuffle as long as he likes.

When he says he is satisfied, take it back from him.

Tell him that you find people often imagine that you would not let them shuffle unless you had managed to sneak their card out of the pack.

You don't want him to think this, so you will run through and let him see that his card is still there.

Turn the deck face upward, and take it in dealing position in your left hand.

(In studying directions for card tricks, remember that the top of the pack and the back are synonymous. Although the faces of the cards may be turned upward, as here, the face side is still the bottom of the deck—that is, the bottom is on top.)

Run the cards casually into your right hand, one behind another, so as not to disturb their order.

Tell your victim to give no sign when he spots his card; and point out that you won't watch his face. (You are too busy to, but you don't tell him that.)

When you see his card, which you learned by means of the glimpse, start mentally spelling his name. Count his card as the first letter, the next card—the one to your *left* of it—as the second letter, and so on to the end.

Pass the card representing the last letter into your right hand.

Separate your hands, breaking the pack at this point, and gesture with your right hand toward the man. "Is it still there?"

He is pretty sure to say yes; whereupon you simply slap all the cards in your left hand in front of those in your right hand.

Square up the pack, and hand it to your victim.

Sometimes, instead of admitting that his card is there, he will tell you to keep going. If he does, bring your hands together, putting the left-hand cards behind the right-hand cards as they were before, but don't be too neat about it. Work the last right-hand card (the one standing for the last letter of the name) out of line. (See jogs, *5a*.) Run all the way through the pack, and then simply cut it above the jogged or projecting card.

Mechanically, in either case the trick is now done. You have observed the rule of not telling too soon what was going to happen, and now you must start your build-up, warn the customers that the big moment is here.

Point out to your victim that he himself has shuffled his card into the pack, and has lost it. Is there any way of finding it?

None at all.

Oh, on the contrary, it's as easy as spelling his name. He has shuffled the deck; he has it now; you won't touch it; he has done everything else so far (an untruth that he will probably remember in preference to the actual facts); now he will find the card by spelling his name out loud, and dealing one card for each letter.

He does: R-O-B-E-R-T-C-R-O-W-E-L-L, and on the last *L* his card turns up.

It is good showmanship to have your victim name his card just before he turns it over. This marks unmistakably both the climax and the conclusion. Remember, also, that so far only one person has seen the chosen card, and nobody can really enjoy this sort of trick until he personally knows the card. The word of your volunteer afterward that "That was it" is not nearly so effective.

1c. Permanent breaks: the crimp, or bridge. On many occasions you want a break to stay put while you let the pack out of your hands. This is very simply accomplished by the several forms of crimp—the gambler's word for putting a bend in part of the deck, leaving the remainder flat.

The oldest method is still usually known by its British name of the "bridge." Hold the pack in dealing position in your left hand, but with about half of it projecting beyond your first finger. Cover the pack with your right hand, thumb at the near end, fingers at the far end. Bend the whole pack sharply against your left forefinger; then pull up the upper half alone with your right fingers, against the fulcrum formed by your left thumb.

This gives the two halves of the deck opposing bends. Usually you will now transpose them by the shift (*2a*); and then cutting the pack will merely restore the original position.

The best method in general, however, is that shown in Fig. 4.

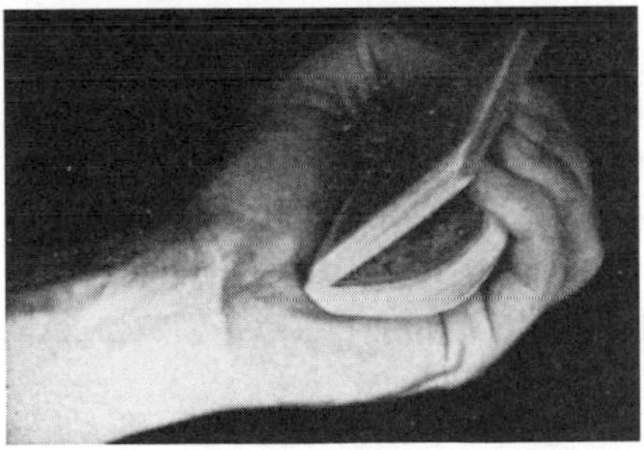

Fig. 4

Let us assume, for instance, that you are holding a little-finger break below a particular card, but want for some purpose to drop the pack on the table.

Bring your right hand over the pack as you would do if you were about to pick up the little-finger break with your right thumb (1*a*). This is simply to hide the action of your left fingers, which squeeze smartly inward, bending or crimping the lower half of the deck lengthwise.

You can now find the break under almost any conditions—on the table, behind your back, in your pocket.

A refinement of this crimp is to bend only the rear or inner end of the lower half, leaving the spectators' end unmarred.

Some occasions require the crimp to be made in the opposite direction, upward. You can insure this by curling your left forefinger under the pack and pushing up while the other three fingers squeeze in as usual.

Example of a trick using the crimp: Paul Rosini's Location. This trick is too simple to have been first used by Paul Rosini, but as I once saw that brilliant card manipulator fool a large roomful of magicians with it, it deserves to pass under his name.

Lay the pack face down on your flat left hand. Ask a spectator, not to peek at a card, but simply to lift off a bunch and keep his cut.

Then have him look at the bottom card of the cut, and show it to several other people. (This, naturally, is a way of getting more of the audience into the game.)

While he is doing this, all eyes are bound to be on him and his half of the deck. Drop your left hand to your side and crimp the lower half of the pack lengthwise upward (instead of downward as shown in Fig. 4).

If possible, you want a fairly new pack for this trick. The older and flabbier the cards, the sharper must be your crimp.

Hold out the lower half in your left hand toward the volunteer, asking him to replace his cut on the pack.

When he does so, square the cards up carefully with your right hand in the now familiar position, thumb at the near end, fingers at the front end. Make considerable fuss about it.

Finally take the pack in your right hand, holding it by the ends between thumb and second finger. Press down on the top with your forefinger. This gives the pack a slight crosswise bend and temporarily removes the crimp.

Holding the pack thus in your right hand, lay the right long edge against a table or wall, and pound the outer edge with your left fist.

The entire point of this trick is to make it absolutely plain that all four edges of the pack are smooth and unbroken.

Some magicians commit the gross blunder of mentioning an artifice in order to prove that they are not using it. This comes under the head of exposing magic, and is sheer suicide. In the present trick you will certainly not say, "No jogs, no breaks, no crimps." Nine out of ten spectators do not know such things exist; the tenth shouldn't be reminded.

But on the other hand you certainly will make it plain that there is no possible mark of any kind whatsoever on the pack.

Point out that you don't know what the card is, or where it is; that it is wholly buried in the pack. "If you tell me what it is, though, I'll see how fast I can find it."

As you say this, take the pack in your left hand, in position to start the Charlier pass (2*f*). This means that the pack is held very nearly on edge, with the tip of the thumb on the upper long edge; the second and third finger tips opposite, on the lower long edge; the forefinger curled under the pack; and the little finger acting as a stop across the near end.

If you push upward with the forefinger, the upper half of the pack, down to the crimp, will spring away from the tip of your thumb. This creates a wide opening along the upper edge of the pack.

Straighten your forefinger, allowing the lower half (the crimped half) to drop into the crotch of your thumb; at the same time, slide the tip of your thumb down the face of the upper half. This face card is the chosen one.

Move your thumb upward. After a few trials (moistening the thumb is a big help), you can make the thumb tip carry the bottom card up with it.

When your thumb clears the upper edge of the pack, the top half will drop back on the lower half, flipping the one loose card over sidewise as it does so.

Thus you end the trick with the chosen card (once so hopelessly lost) face up under your thumb on top of the deck.

From the description you may feel you are already entering the higher realms of manipulation. Actually, all these moves are about as simple as they come. Try them out with the cards, and you will agree.

2. SHIFTS, OR PASSES

The pass with cards, which gamblers always, and magicians often, call the shift, is a sleight for transposing the halves of the pack.

You may need a moment to appreciate the full value of such a move. In addition to restoring the cut, you can put any given card at any place you like in the pack. The commonest use of the shift is to bring a chosen card from the middle to the top. For the conventional fan force (3*a*) you bring the "force" card from the bottom to the middle.

There is almost no predicament in card conjuring that the shift won't help you out of.

In consequence, the magicians of four centuries have striven to perfect new and better shifts, with the odd result that there are at least twenty variants, one-handed and two-handed—and the oldest of all is still the best.

2a. The conventional two-handed shift. This shift is about as hard a lesson as any the young card conjurer will have to master. It probably accounts in good part for the old theory that assiduous practice alone makes a magician.

In his monumental *Greater Magic,* the late John Northern Hilliard wrote, "If I had one word of advice to give the beginning magician, it would be this—practice the pass daily, if only as a finger exercise, as a musician practices his scales. Half an hour a day devoted to this exercise will not only give you, in time, a perfect execution of this difficult maneuver, but it will also keep your fingers in training for all sleight-of-hand work. It is the basic exercise of magic."

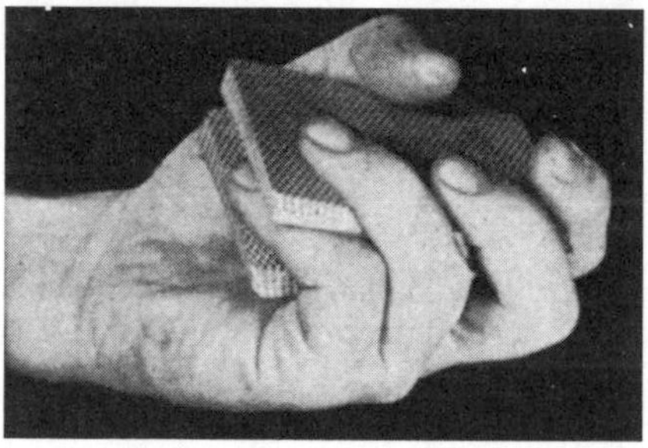

Fig. 5

The first step is to learn the position shown in Fig. 5 so thoroughly that it becomes a muscular habit. The little finger will usually rest on top of the chosen card, which itself is on top of the lower half.

This position is called a little-finger separation, as distinct from a little-finger break. Simply to hold a location, the break is far superior to the separation, which it has superseded. To start the shift, however, you must have a separation.

The next step is to cover the pack with the right hand and assume the position of Fig. 6, which is seen from your own point of view. Notice that the right forefinger and thumb seize the *lower* (or face) half of the pack by the ends, not too near the left-hand corners. You still find some teachers instructing you to use the thumb and *second* finger; but, unless your hands are minute, the forefinger lets you cover the pack better.

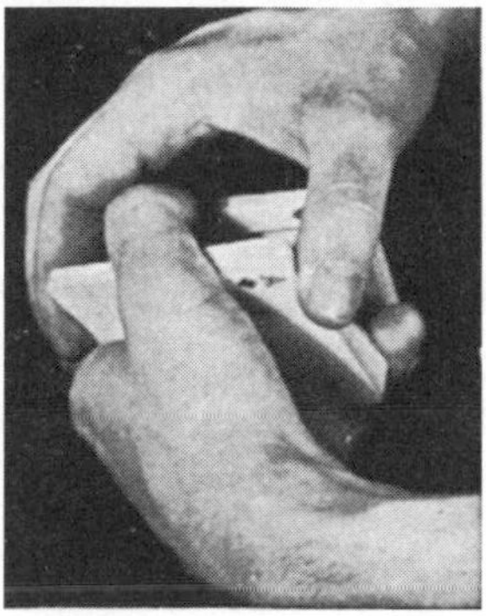

FIG. 6

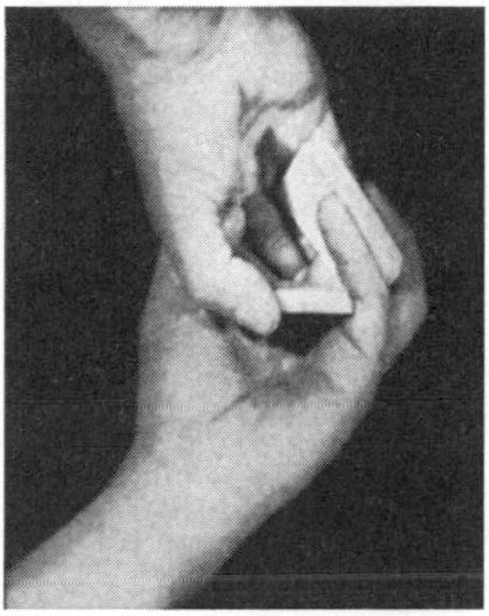

FIG. 7

You now find yourself holding the lower half of the pack from above with your right hand, and the upper half from below with your left fingers.

The next step, and the first actual motion, is depicted in Fig. 7: you straighten your left fingers (but *not* your thumb), tilting the upper half on edge.

This puts you in position for the next stage (Fig. 8), which is accomplished by simply drawing down your left hand.

Let me warn you that the right hand should never stir during a properly executed shift: it is a cover and a pivot only.

When the left hand moves down, the hooked thumb tilts the lower half toward the left; the upper half, already tilted by the left fingers, clears the lower half with almost no sidewise motion.

This is the crucial point in the two-handed shift. The edges of the

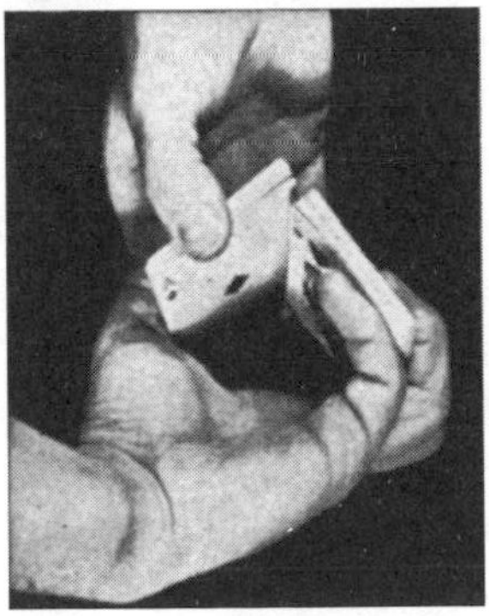

FIG. 8

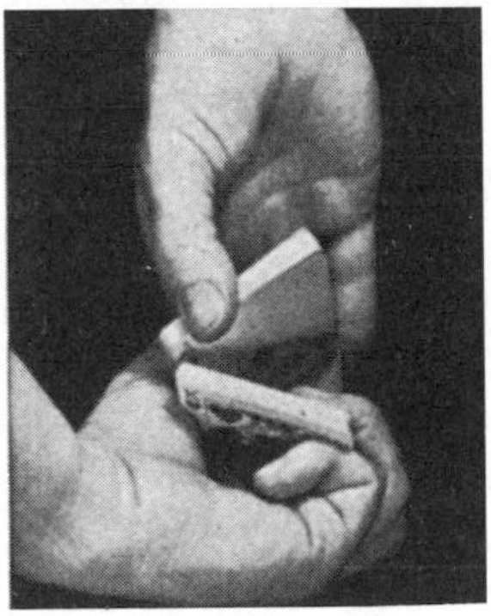

FIG. 9

two halves must not brush in passing, or they will "talk." They must not clear each other by much, or the motion will be visible. Remember what I said at the start of this section: relax. Gently does it.

The final stage (Fig. 9) is accomplished by simply closing the left hand again.

There are several bad habits much better avoided than broken.

First, don't let your left forefinger stick out; keep it curled across the far end of the deck, lest it wigwag a warning to everyone in the room.

Second, I say again, don't lift up with your right hand; pull down with your left.

Third, don't use your right middle finger to help tilt the lower half; the bend of your left thumb does the whole job.

Fourth, *don't blink*. This is a very easy and a very bad habit to acquire.

Fifth, don't sway your hands about in a misguided effort to cover a small motion with a big one. The only good shift is an invisible one; if you can't make it invisible (which naturally you cannot at first), you need misdirection, distraction, not a "cover" that draws all eyes to your hands.

The best cover that I know for the shift is so simple that I do not remember having seen any other writer suggest it. Just *wait until they look away from your hands.*

Any short, quick remark draws people's eyes to your face, a fact on which you can rely in emergencies. But in my experience you have only to keep your hands still for a few seconds, and people get tired of looking at them. *Then* make your pass.

It is better to make the shift slowly and quietly than quickly and noisily. Never tolerate noise, and speed will come with practice.

Example of a trick using the shift: The Stabbed Pack. This effect was a favorite for years on the vaudeville stage, and it is just as good now as it ever was. You need a paper knife, a rubber band, and about half a page of newspaper.

Two people choose cards, which are shuffled back into the pack. The pack is wrapped in the newspaper and secured with the rubber band. You jab the paper knife into the edge of the wrapped deck, which is torn open, revealing one of the two chosen cards on each side of the knife.

The preliminaries can be done in many ways, so the following sequence is just a suggestion.

Have someone peep at a card, and hold a little-finger break below it. Make the shift, bringing his card to the bottom.

Let someone else draw a card from the pack as you fan it before him, running the cards from your left hand into your right by pushing with your left thumb. Get him to show his card to several other people.

While he is doing this, make the shift again, bringing the first chosen card back to the middle. Stretch out your left hand, containing all the cards *below* the first chosen one, for the second victim to replace his card.

Drop the upper half on the lower, but get your left little finger between the two halves—and so between the two chosen cards.

Make the shift again. The first chosen card is at the bottom; the second is at the top.

A casual false shuffle (section 5) makes the trick more convincing.

Make a bridge (1*c*) by the first method, concluding with one last shift.

There is now an elliptical opening in the sides of the pack, dividing the two chosen cards.

Wrap the deck in the piece of newspaper. If you can't make a neat package, get some shopkeeper or shipping-clerk friend to teach you. I can only warn you that too little paper is far better than too much.

Put the elastic lengthwise around the package.

As you are doing this, press your left thumb firmly against a long edge of the package, near the center. This should press the paper into the gap of the bridge. You enlarge the mark by poking with your thumbnail.

Show the package from all sides, keeping your thumb over the tear in the paper.

Now your build-up begins. "I wonder where those cards could have got to. They're certainly well wrapped up; I can't find them by looking. I suppose I'll have to do it by magic. I hope this paper knife is sharp enough. Ouch! It is. Well, here goes!"

So saying, jab the paper knife into the crack you have opened with your thumbnail. Hold the stabbed pack up in one hand. You want to give the impression of a deft, clear-cut action, not of rooting in a mass of old newspapers.

Cut the package open with the knife far enough so that you can tear the paper the rest of the way. All this you can do, and should, under the very noses of the audience. Don't give anyone a chance to suppose that you smuggled the cards into the package as you were tearing it open.

There, on each side of the knife, is a chosen card.

Caution: At some stage in the proceedings when you are not being too closely watched, bend the deck to and fro to remove the bridge.

2b. The side steal, or side slip. This invaluable sleight comes among the shifts because it brings a chosen card to the top of the deck; but it does not transpose the halves. It was invented by Nelson Downs, the coin manipulator, and has since become virtually the trademark of expert card-handlers.

The corner peep as a means of having a card chosen was first introduced in connection with the side steal.

Have a card peeped at, and hold a little-finger break below it (1*a*).

Here, as in the standard shift, you may very well wait until people are thinking of something else.

Then bring up your right hand, and grasp the upper half of the deck with your forefinger at the far right corner, your thumb at the near right corner. This leaves the whole top of the pack exposed.

Tilt the lower half down and to the left until you have room to curl your left second finger in against the face of the chosen card, on the bottom of the upper half.

Straighten your left second finger, sliding the chosen card to the right.

The chosen card will travel out fairly straight until its far right corner bumps into the tip of your right little finger. Then the card pivots, the near end swinging to the right (Fig. 10).

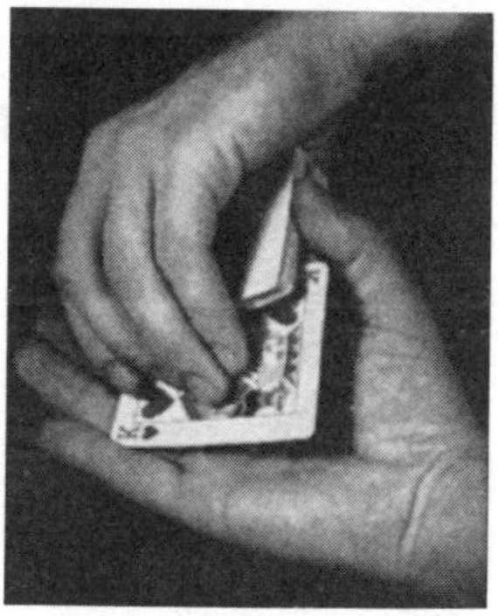

FIG. 10

Bend the last joint of your right little finger just enough to catch the card by diagonally opposite corners between the finger tip and the fleshy base of your right thumb. This amounts to the same thing as palming it (section 4).

Don't waggle your right thumb in getting this grip, and don't stick the thumb out at right angles to your hand.

You now have two courses open: one, to put the chosen card right back on the deck; the other, to palm the card while the deck is being shuffled or otherwise worked on.

In the first case, simply run your right forefinger and thumb back and forth along the ends of the deck two or three times, as if squaring up, and drop the palmed card on top of it.

In the second case, move your *left* hand away with the pack, and don't be in a hurry to drop your right hand to your side. Remember, people watch what moves. You don't want them watching your right hand.

The side steal, more than any other card sleight, demands perfect gentleness of handling. The only real difficulty you must meet is the tendency of the chosen card to scrape or "talk" as the last corner clears the pack, just when you thought you were safe. Complete relaxation of both hands is the cure for that, slightly dropping the right.

You will probably find it a help to moisten the tip of your left second finger before you start.

Move smoothly, gently, and deliberately, and you will have a perfect side steal.

Example of a trick using the side steal: You Must Be Wrong. You can scarcely call this an effect to stand by itself. It does make a good member of a series, and has the special advantage of apparently turning out just like a dodge that you will often have to use when you get into trouble, which is treated in chapter 5, (1*c*).

Someone peeps at a card; you promptly hand him the pack, asking him to shuffle. Then you tell him he has done too good a job of mixing things up, and you will have to start over. Ask him to find his card and remove it.

He runs all the way through the pack, but can't find his card.

You ask what it was. He tells you.

"Oh, you must be wrong. Any card but that. I put that in my pocket before we started." And you pull the missing card from your right trouser pocket.

You will scarcely need my explanation of how this trick works. You hold a little-finger break below the chosen card, which you side-steal and palm. Hand the deck over for shuffling with your left hand.

Warning: Don't hurry the card into your pocket. Wait until the spectator has begun to shuffle. Then, with an I'm-ready-when-you-are air, put *both* hands into your trouser pockets simultaneously.

Always in magic when you need to put one hand into a pocket unnoticed, make the same motion with both hands. This is a complete disguise.

You remember in chapter 2 I talked about having a reason for things. Now you need a reason for asking the victim to find his card. If you have no reason, he is quite justified in telling you snappishly to find it yourself.

Your reason is that he has shuffled the pack beyond your power to finish the trick. Your surprise and dismay must therefore seem utterly real. Try to convince yourself, as well as him, that he has spoiled your trick.

By this time it is safe to take your hands out of your pockets, leaving the palmed card behind.

The rest of the trick is entirely a matter of your portraying repeated surprise. The whole effect rests on unexpectedness. Simply to produce a chosen card, in cold blood, from your pocket is a very small trick indeed, and quite an easy one to detect. At each step you must leave the audience surprised and expecting something different from what actually follows.

First they expect you to find the card, and you can't. Then they expect the volunteer to find it, and it's gone. They must not expect it to be in your pocket until the actual moment that it emerges from there.

In finally reaching to bring out the card, give everyone a good look at your empty hand first. Don't say it. Just look; then dip.

2c. The Herrmann pass. Alexander Herrmann, still rightfully remembered by some as Herrmann the Great, made a specialty of this pass. When done with the proper attention to angles of sight, it is absolutely invisible. It is not, however, so universally helpful as the conventional shift, nor so smooth as the side steal.

Angles of sight are such an endless problem to magicians that we call them simply "angles." Any sleight that is "angle proof" is much to be prized. Angles forever remind us that we conjurers live in a half world, divided into out front (which is magical) and backstage (where the wires are). Some magic can be done when you are surrounded, and it falls in the highest category of the art.

The Herrmann pass is not angle proof, and you should try it in front of a mirror before you risk it with a live audience. The angles you get

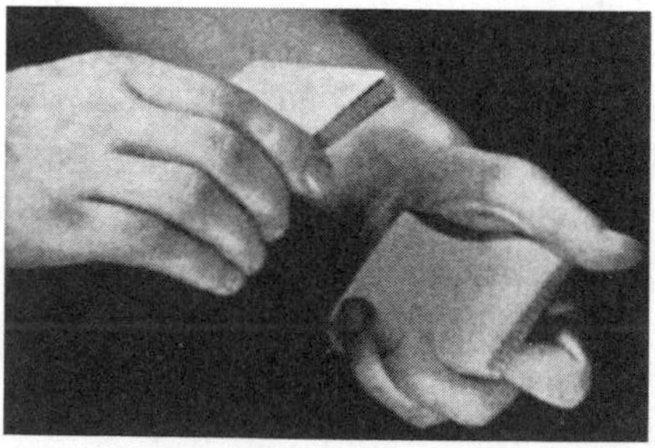

FIG. 11

from a mirror are not exactly the same as the angles with an audience, but at least you can check the more glaring faults.

To do the Herrmann pass, divide the deck. Hold the lower half in your left hand with first and fourth fingers drawn underneath; hold the upper half between forefinger and thumb of your right hand, exposing the whole top of the pack (Fig. 11).

The standard procedure is to have the spectator put the card he has drawn on top of the lower half. Then you seem to drop the upper half on top of that.

Actually, however, as your right hand comes down upon the lower half, it furnishes a wide screen. Under this cover, you straighten your left fingers, tilting the lower half up on edge. It passes just to the right of the upper half (Fig. 12), which now takes the place in the palm of the left hand occupied but a moment before by the lower half.

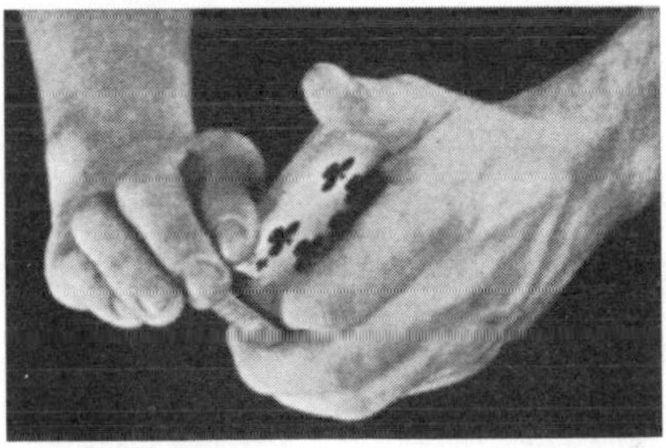

FIG. 12

Now roll your left wrist, turning the back of the hand uppermost and so bringing the two halves together in reverse order, with the chosen card on top.

It is not necessary to start the Herrmann pass with the two halves separated. Instead, you may hold a third-finger break, get the correct grip with the left hand, and make the shift in the act of apparently turning the deck face up.

Most tricks that you can do with the standard shift will also work with the Herrmann pass.

2d. One-handed shifts: "new method" (Robert-Houdin). It once occurred to me that the two-handed shift should be possible to do with the left hand alone. I tried it, and decided I was wrong.

Then Luis Zingone showed me that it could be done. I supposed the method was the product of his own marvelously skillful fingers, until I came upon it where I should have looked in the first place, in the classic

Secrets of Conjuring and Magic, by the revered "father of modern conjuring," Jean Eugene Robert-Houdin.

No one-handed shift can be called a necessary accomplishment. The most you can say is that there are means of rendering a one-handed shift almost as good as a two-handed shift. Every magical writer since the late 1800s has pointed this out, and still the one-handed shifts survive. I suspect they are simply fun to do, and magicians enjoy the feeling of mastery when they have learned them.

This particular shift should really give you quite a sense of accomplishment: it is undeniably hard.

Hold the pack just as if you were starting a regular two-handed shift (Fig. 5).

The motions of the shift are the same, too, but the rhythm is different. Open the fingers, standing the upper half of the pack on its right edge.

Press down with your thumb on the extreme upper left corner of the lower half, tilting this up on its left edge (Fig. 13).

The right front corner of the lower half is all too likely to root up the bottom card of the upper half. This is cured partly by sheer practice, partly by straightening the forefinger so as to prop up the lower half and hold back the upper half. The forefinger is a sort of rock on which the pack splits.

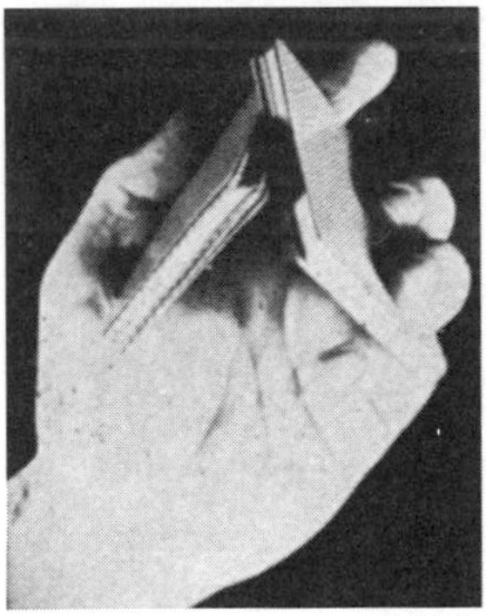

FIG. 13

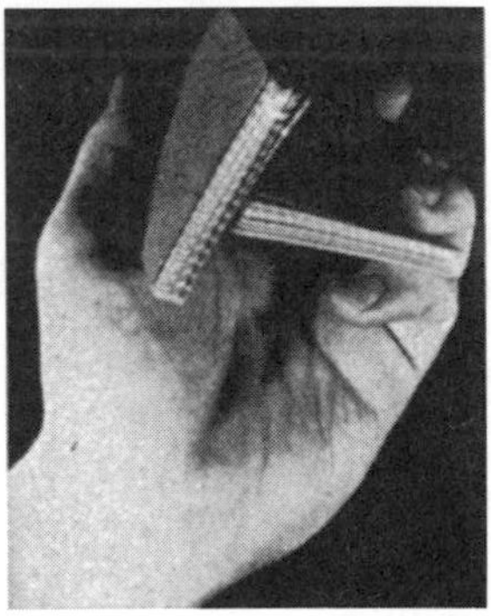

FIG. 14

Once the right edge of the lower half has traveled up the face of the upper half, and cleared its edge, you close the fingers, pushing down the upper half, and move your thumb to the right (Fig. 14), pushing down the original lower half on top of the upper.

That is all. The necessary rhythm is a sort of flip or sudden burst, a sequence of loose-tight-loose. You start with a loose grip, flip up the lower half with a sudden tightening, and instantly relax again as the halves fall into the new position.

2e. One-handed shifts: old method. If the last was the regular two-handed shift done with one hand, this is the Herrmann shift with one hand.

Start with a third-finger break. Then change to the grip shown in Fig. 15. You will notice that the third finger now holds a separation, while the tip of the second finger presses the edge of the upper half.

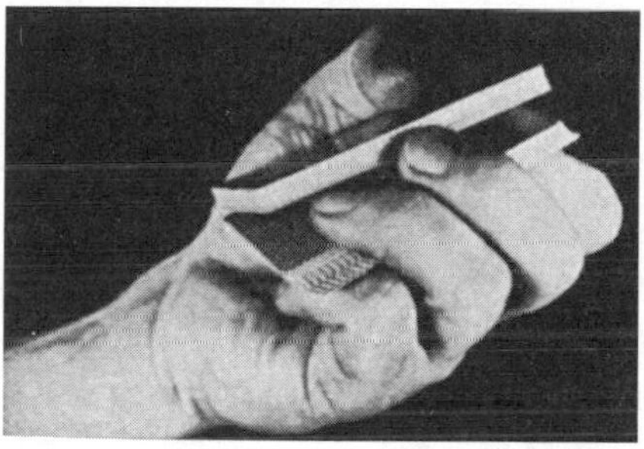

FIG. 15

This is because the whole difficulty of the sleight comes at the start. You straighten your fingers, carrying the lower half to the right and tilting it up on its right edge (Fig. 16), while your thumb holds back the upper

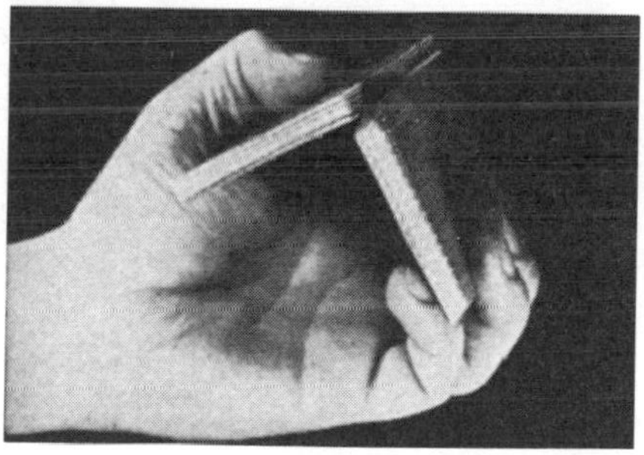

FIG. 16

half. Unless you give the upper half a push with your second finger, it is likely either to escape from the thumb and spill, or to rub against the left edge of the lower half so hard that its own bottom card is dragged out of place.

Once the halves have cleared each other, the fingers close and square them up in their new position.

Gentleness leads to success in this sleight, as in most others.

2f. One-handed shifts: The Charlier pass. This is really more of a flourish than a shift, and is so easy that a complete novice can learn it in ten minutes. Nevertheless some eminent performers have put it to use.

The position is different from that for any other pass. The deck is held by the *tips* of the left second and third fingers on the right long edge as you pick up the deck and the tip of the thumb on the left long edge. The end of the little finger lies across the middle of the near end. The forefinger is curled underneath the pack.

In order to keep a particular location, you must either crimp the lower half upward, as described for the trick in 1*c*, or you must hold a thumb break.

In either case, bend your thumb enough to let the lower half drop into your palm. The two halves should be like a book, open along the left side, closed along the right.

With your forefinger, push up the right edge of the lower half until it touches your thumb (Fig. 17).

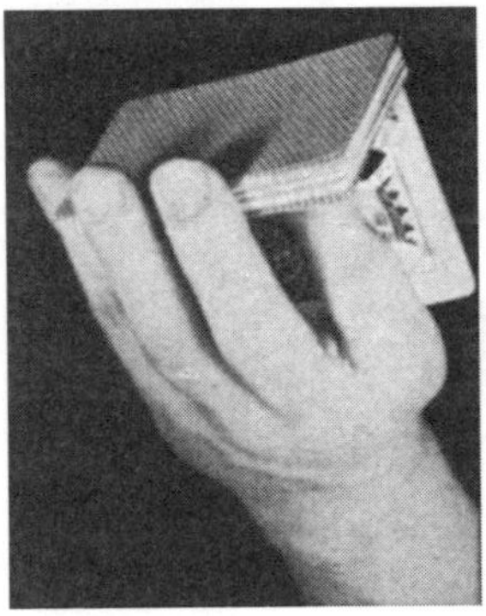

Fig. 17

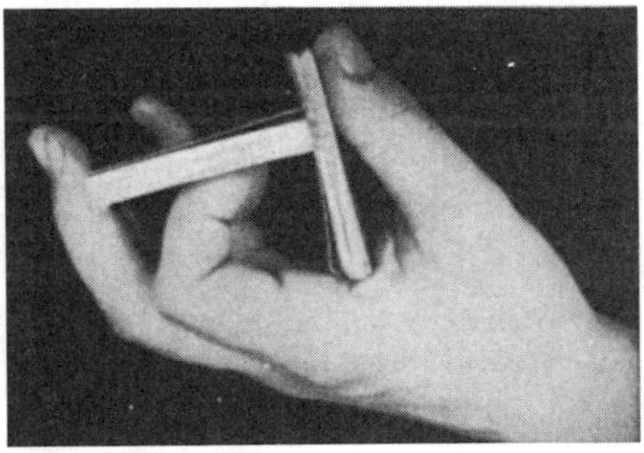

Fig. 18

Straighten your fingers enough to carry the upper half a little to the right. It thus clears the lower half, and slides beneath it (Fig. 18). Relax your hand completely, dropping the lower half on top, and the pass is finished.

Since this is not only the easiest but also the quietest one-handed shift, most of the thought expended on means of covering such shifts has been applied to it.

It can be hidden by stretching out your right arm to the left, bringing your left hand up inside the right elbow to draw back the sleeve, and executing the pass before you pull. You must immediately follow this, of course, by pulling up your left sleeve with a tug at the elbow from your right hand.

If you are working with a volunteer who has chosen a card, you may ask him to move a little, putting your left hand behind his back as if to steer him.

Robert-Houdin's "new method" (*2d*), if you are very good at it, can be used just as your right hand advances to take the pack—a sort of anticipated standard shift.

All the one-handed shifts may be covered by holding the pack behind your back for a card to be replaced. As you turn around and bring your hand to the front, the shift will be hidden.

The two-handed shift is still better, though.

3. FORCING

"Forcing" in magic is not a way to grow fruit out of season, but a way to make a spectator choose some one particular object, number, word, or the like, out of an assortment, when he thinks he has had a perfectly free selection. Forcing is done more often in card tricks than in any other class of effects, but it is used constantly in all magic. Theo Annemann's little book, *202 Methods of Forcing*, is a very valuable asset to any magician. I have borrowed from it here, and so no doubt will you.

Forcing of other objects besides cards usually falls under head magic or apparatus magic, and many card methods also depend on ingenuity. The ones that follow, however, are pure manipulation.

3a. The fan force. This is the classical force and still without an equal when perfectly done. It is not illustrated because there is hardly any movement to depict and no difficult mechanics to rehearse over and over. This force has the one great difficulty that it must be practiced on a living victim; a mirror is no help at all.

The principle of fan forcing is utterly simple: you fan the cards face down, invite the spectator to draw one from the fan, and when he starts to do so, you make sure that your particular "force" card comes between his fingers.

Elementary as the move is, I cannot even tell you how to do it because you will have to find the method that works for you on the victims you have to deal with.

One step is always necessary; by the shift or by casually cutting, bring the force card from its original hideout at top or bottom to about the middle of the deck. Then hold a little-finger break there.

Harry Blackstone, the great illusionist whose hobby was card manipulation, put on a bustling air, running the cards rapidly from his left hand into his right, deliberately trying to hurry and fluster the chooser, and almost poking the card at him.

Other performers work altogether by timing, running the cards over slowly until the spectator puts forward his hand, then contriving to work the force card just to that point as his fingers close.

John Mulholland contributed almost the only novelty in three centuries of fan forcing. Instead of moving the cards in his hands, he moved his entire body, swaying on the ball of the left foot. In this way he brought the force card into place with no suggestion of fidgeting; and the moment the spectator touched it, Mulholland swayed back, taking the rest of the pack out of reach.

It seems fairly generally agreed that an atmosphere of total indifference is best calculated to bring success to the fan force. If the spectator thinks you don't care, he won't bother being choosy.

A certain amount of experience is very necessary in deciding whom you will work a force on. For one thing, people who are very anxious to choose a card should be avoided in forcing. Some performers find they can force more easily on women, some on men. If you do many tricks involving the fan force, you will get an instinct for proper victims.

The fan force can also be done with one hand. Spread the deck into a neat, even fan, exposing the force card perhaps a quarter of an inch more than the others, and take the pack in your right hand. Start it moving slowly to the right with a motion of your wrist. Good timing of this movement, together with the extra surface that catches the eye, will enable you to force your card just as surely as any other method—if you can get the knack.

If the force fails, you mustn't bat an eye. Do a different trick with the card actually chosen. In a set show where the force is essential, have the refractory chooser use his card as the indicator for the slip or Collins force (3*c* and 3*d*).

3b. Thought forces. These are even more difficult, and, when successful, more rewarding, than the classical force. Strictly speaking, most of them are half way between forces and locations, since it is rarely possible to decide in advance, "I will force this man to think of the two of diamonds," and be sure of doing it. Still, you may be one of the fortunate few who can attain even that level.

All thought forces depend on having a spectator remember (rather than actually think at random of) one card among several shown to him. Either the force card must stand out among the many, or it must be in actual fact the only one the spectator can see.

The former method is less certain and correspondingly less obvious. You may arrange an ace among a number of miscellaneous spot cards; hold a little-finger break there, and start running the cards over with their faces to the spectator. Run almost to the force card before you tell him what he is to do. As you say, ". . . remember one card," you pause the merest tenth of a second longer at the ace, and then run on quickly, closing up the pack well before you come to the end.

This force is precarious when used for one card, but in an effect like the mental-selection spelling trick (see chapter 5, section 4), where the force can be any of six cards, it is practically infallible.

The other type of thought force, where the victim can see only the force card, will not work on a suspicious customer; he will probably demand a fair choice. In this case, at least, you know when you are about to fail and can take measures accordingly.

The basic method of this type is the "step" riffle. Hold the pack in your left hand in dealing position, but rather far forward, exposing nearly half of the face.

Keep a little- or third-finger break below the force card.

Cover the deck with your right hand, fingers in front, thumb at the back. If you draw your right fingers up, the front ends of the cards snap away singly in rapid succession, constituting a "riffle."

You present the cards to a spectator in this fashion, asking him to remember one of those he sees. The normal riffle, however, is so fast that he can hardly see any except the bottom card. So before you start to riffle, you push the upper half of the deck (above the break) forward perhaps a sixteenth of an inch, forming a step.

Now when you riffle, the stepped card is visible just an instant longer than any of the others—long enough to be distinguished, whereas the others cannot.

The same principle operates in springing the cards from hand to hand (9*b*) face up. The first time you go too fast for any card to be seen. The next time the spectator is on his mettle to see one, and takes the only one he can, exposed when you stop the cascade for an instant. You see it also, and get a little-finger separation. This, of course, is a location rather than a manageable force.

3*c*. *Sure-fire force: the slip.* Instead of having a card peeped at, or fanning the deck for selection, you may have the spectator stick a pencil, knife, or indifferent card into the front end of the pack as you riffle it or merely hold it in dealing position. This is the procedure for the sure-fire methods, both sleight-of-hand and mechanical.

The slip is a very old sleight, but was practically neglected until it was revived as a force.

Start with the force card on top of the deck.

Your left hand holds the card very nearly in dealing position, except that your fingers should stretch almost to the middle of the top card.

Riffle the front end with your right fingers, asking the victim to poke his knife or pencil in wherever he pleases.

When he does so, stop riffling. Move your left thumb out of the way, and tilt the upper half up open like a book along the left side.

In theory the volunteer will look at the card below the knife. To help him do so, you thrust out your left hand toward him, carrying the lower half of the pack out from under the upper half (and also from under the knife).

As you do this, your left finger tips press down and carry off the top card of the upper half (Fig. 19), which you remember is the force card.

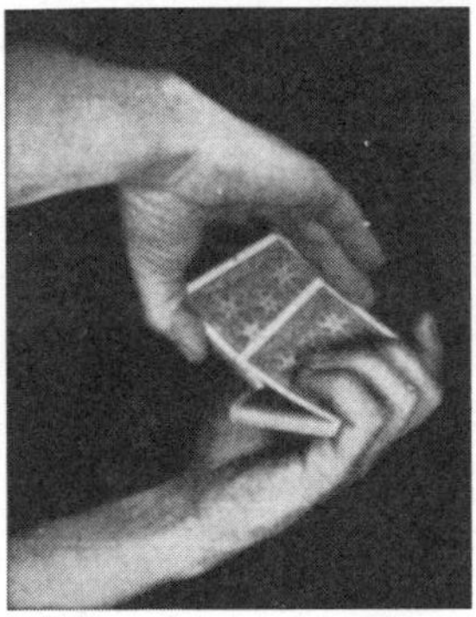

Fig. 19

There are two points to be careful about. Be gentle as always, or the force card will talk. And don't draw back your right hand; just shoot forward your left.

Obviously if you want to force several cards in succession you can simply arrange them on top of the pack.

3d. Sure-fire force: Stanley Collins' method. Here the card to be chosen comes above the knife. The method is practically indetectable.

Get the force card about one-third of the way down in the deck, and hold a little-finger break below it.

By experimentation you could very likely use the step riffle (3*b*) to make the spectator insert his knife exactly at the force card. In the present case, however, you have only to be sure that he sticks it in somewhere *below* your little-finger break.

Grab the upper half of the pack and the knife simultaneously in your right hand (fingers at the far end, thumb at the near), clipping the knife between your first and second finger tips to hold it in its place.

Slide the right hand forward, dividing the pack at your break, and offering both upper half and knife to the victim.

The result is to withdraw the knife from where the spectator stuck it, and bring it up against the force card, which is at the face of the upper half (as divided by you, not by the victim).

It is possible to modify this sleight so that the force card appears below the knife, but I think the result is less convincing.

The Collins force and the slip are probably both better when worked in combination.

Example of a trick using the force: Everybody's Card. The Collins force is the most natural for this effect.

For uniformity of association you will have to use a pencil or knife throughout the trick. Have someone choose a card in this way. To do the trick at its simplest, eliminating all intermediate steps, you can make the spectator put in his knife about a third of the way from the top, the right place for the force card to be in the Collins force.

Hold a little-finger break there after he has looked at the card and replaced it.

Now you must make a sort of tacit intermission, dropping your left hand with the pack to your side, telling the first victim not to forget his card, and in general diverting all attention from the deck.

Go to another spectator, and force on him the same card that the first man chose. Pick up your break again, and sparkle with some more patter.

Force the same card on a third man. Take your break again; more patter.

Force the same card on a fourth man. Take up your break again, and this time bring everybody's card to the bottom by the shift.

Lay the pack on the table, and start building up to a climax (*a*, not really *the*, climax). Dust off your hands, pull at your sleeves, or do whatever you have found brings the customers to the edges of their chairs.

Pick up the pack in your left hand in dealing position, but with the top of the pack against your palm, and keep the back of your left hand uppermost, so that no one can see the bottom card.

Go over impressively to the first man who chose a card. Tell him you and he are going to have a secret together: just for him, you will find his card by striking the pack.

Turn the face of the cards toward yourself, and slap it with your right palm. Then show him the front card, but don't let anyone else see it.

Ask him if that was his card, and tell him the trick isn't over yet, so he must still remember it.

Apparently you now draw his card off the bottom of the pack, and lay it face down on the table.

Actually, you turn your left hand knuckles up again, reach forward with your right hand, palm up, and move to pull the bottom card out from the far end of the pack by the pressure of your right second finger. At that moment your left third finger moves half an inch to the left, drawing the bottom card back with it (whence this move is technically known as the "glide" or "draw back"). Your right second finger, accordingly, gets hold of the next above the bottom card, and draws it out; it is laid face down on the table.

Ask your first man to put his forefinger on the card, pinning it down.

You go through the whole procedure again with the second, third, and fourth spectators.

Thus everyone believes that the four people have chosen four different cards, and are holding them; whereas actually they have all chosen the same card, which remains on the bottom of the deck.

Palm this bottom card by the side steal or the bottom palm (4*b* and 4*c*), and lay the pack on the table. Load the card into your trouser pocket as you learned to do so smoothly in 2*b*.

"Now for a concentration test," you announce. "I want to see if you have all been concentrating on your various cards so intently that you can call them out together when I give the signal. Can you? Ready, *now!*"

"Four of diamonds!" they bellow with one voice.

"Everybody with the four of diamonds? Nonsense! It can't be. You're each holding down your own card. You must have forgotten. Let's look."

The four cards are all different, and none is the four of diamonds.

"Not more than one of you could possibly have had the four of diamonds. In fact, I doubt even that. Why don't you take it out of the pack, and we can start over?"

The only result of the search, of course, is at last to coax the four of diamonds from your trouser pocket.

3e. Sure-fire force: the shift. Get the force card to about the center, and hold a break above it.

Ask a victim to call a number. When he does, deal cards off the top, counting slowly and distinctly as you do so. When you are one short of the number, pause, and bring your hands together.

"You said eight, did you?"

This question brings all eyes to your face just long enough for you to make the shift (or do the side steal, in which case your break will have been *below* the force card).

The next card, at the number the victim has called, is thus forced with dead certainty.

4. PALMING

To most laymen, "palming" is just another name for sleight of hand. Anything that isn't done by wires and mirrors or up your sleeve is accounted for by palming.

In card tricks, palming occupies no such important place; nor is it so difficult as you will find palming in most other types of tricks to be.

You have already mastered the rudiments of palming if you have learned the side steal (2*b*).

Fig. 20 shows a card correctly palmed as seen by yourself. The point to notice is that the card is held entirely by gentle pressure against the two index corners, exerted by bending the tip of the little finger.

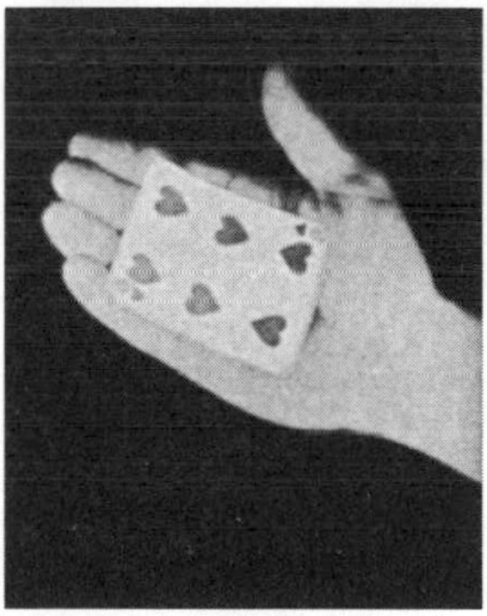

FIG. 20

Some performers have the habit of holding the card by bending in the second and third fingers, leaving the first and fourth fingers straight. This is no doubt very graceful, but the only time anyone really holds his hand like that is when he is palming a card. Don't do it.

You may find it natural to close all four fingers halfway into a fist, bending the card into a full semicircle. This is all right when the bend in the card can be straightened or won't be noticed. The vital point is to keep your hand looking natural. Everything else is secondary.

Holding a card palmed is hardly more difficult than wearing a hat. Getting the card there, like putting on the hat at a becoming angle, is the trick.

4a. The top palm. The primary, almost the standard, use of palming is to steal the top card off the pack. There are many different top palms, and every performer has his own private twists. The following method is the simplest good one.

The pack is held in the left hand, not in dealing position, but pressed by the fingers against the heel of the hand, while the thumb lies along the left side.

The right hand approaches, and the right little-finger tip pushes the top card forward about half an inch (Fig. 21).

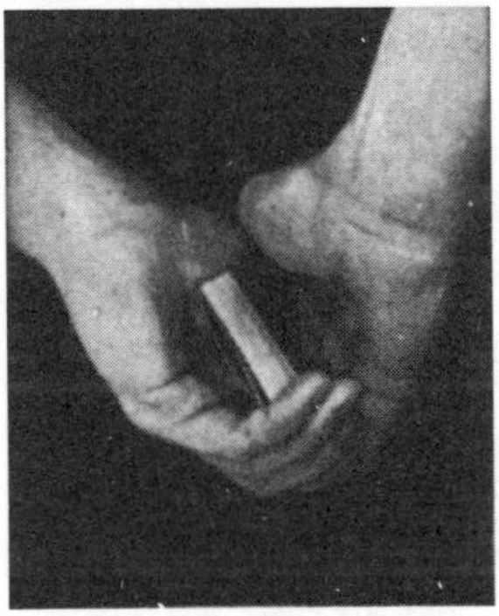

FIG. 21

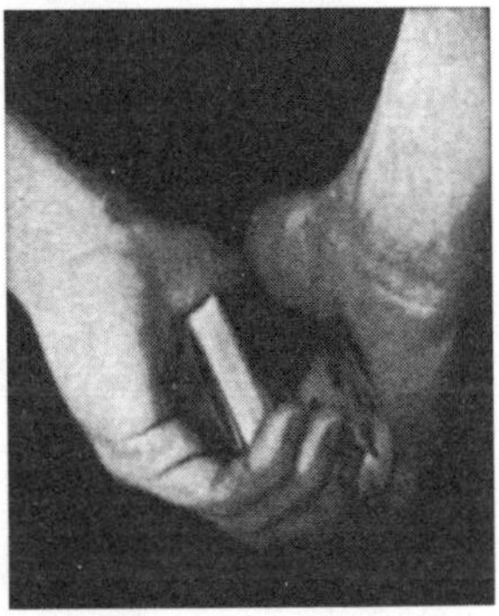

FIG. 22

With the same motion, the right finger tips go out and down, tilting the overhanging top card into perfect palming position (Fig. 22). The far end of the pack serves as a fulcrum.

Still with the same motion, the right hand grasps the deck by opposite ends between thumb and forefinger, and slides from side to side as if squaring up.

Then the left hand carries the pack away, while the right hand stays behind.

In order to palm more than one card from the top, keep a little-finger break below the cards you want to palm. Instead of tilting these by sliding them forward, just boost them into your palm by a push of the left little finger.

Another deceptive method is to riffle off with your left thumb, at the left side of the pack, as many cards as you want to palm. When your right hand covers the deck, simply shove your left thumb under the left edge of the cards riffled off; the thumb pokes them straight into your palm.

Example of a trick using the top palm: Charles Bertram's Four-Ace Trick. This splendid version of a classic effect is admirably described in C. Lang Neil's *The Modern Conjurer*, a book that every magician should own. I give Lang Neil's instructions with minor changes.

You ask for a volunteer to help you. The four aces are taken out of the pack and put on top. The volunteer deals the four aces separately onto the table, and on each ace deals three other cards. He then chooses three of the heaps, which are put back in the pack, leaving one ace and three other cards on the table. He puts his hand flat on these, while you take the pack, make a riffling noise, and produce the three indifferent cards from under his arm. You make two more riffles, and the volunteer finds he now has all four aces under his hand. You tell him to feel in his breast pocket, and there he finds the three indifferent cards that you took away from him.

Receive your volunteer on your left, and while doing so, pick up your pack and palm the top four cards. Put the deck on the table, and ask the volunteer to pick out the four aces and give them to you. He is also to make sure there are only four.

As he reaches to pick up the pack, check his arm with your left hand, and plunge your right hand (containing the four palmed cards) into his breast pocket. Leave three of the palmed cards, and bring out one, which you put on the pack, remonstrating, "Please, we may need all the cards before we're through."

Now have him lay the four aces on the table, and tell you whether there are any more than four.

As he says no, put the rest of the pack on the table, and ask him to put the four aces on top of the deck.

Pick up the pack, riffle it officiously, and deal the four aces face downward on the table.

Try to sound as positive yet dishonest as possible when you say, "The four aces are on the table now, aren't they?"

Aroused by the riffle and your con-man demeanor, the volunteer will probably say he doesn't think they are.

Tell him caution is a wonderful thing, but can be carried too far; and turn the aces up one by one on the table.

Palm off three cards, and put the pack on the table, asking the volunteer to put the four aces on top. Then pick up the pack with your right hand, leaving the three palmed cards on top.

Run four cards off the pack into your right hand, counting one, two, three, four, and turn them up as one, so that only the ace shows.

"That's right, they're still here." Put the four cards back on top. "There seems to be some doubt about the way I handle the cards, so suppose you do this yourself."

Hand him the pack in his left hand and tell him to deal the four aces in a row face downward on the table. As he moves his right hand to the pack, you put your left hand gently and persuasively on his forearm, and guide each card down to the table, saying, "One here, and one here, and one here, and the fourth one here."

As the fourth card (which is an ace) goes down, you briefly show it, then say, "Deal three cards on this ace." He does so; you guide his hand again, since the three cards are the other three aces, and must not be seen. As soon as the three aces are safely on the fourth ace, you stop guiding his hand.

"And three on the next ace, and three on the next. You can take them from anywhere in the pack you like. And now three on the last ace. You see I'm not even touching them. Now will you please put the pack on the table, and tell everyone what you have just done? You have put one, two, three, four aces on the table, and you have put three other cards on each ace. Is that right?"

Ask him to touch two of the heaps.

If he touches two that include the pile of aces, remove the other two piles, and stick them into the pack. If he touches two that don't include the aces, remove the ones he touches.

Ask him to touch one more, and on the same principles leave the pile of aces behind, and put the third pile back in the pack. (You will use this elementary method of forcing time and again; it is known as an equivoque, or conjurer's choice.)

You now pick up the pack, and say, "You had a free choice of one heap, and you have left me one ace and three small cards. Now will you put your hand firmly on this last ace and the three other cards?"

The volunteer does so.

"Now, no matter how hard you lean on the cards, I'm going to make you lift your hand while I take away the three odd cards and give you the other three aces from the pack."

As you speak, palm three cards. Run your hand up his arm, and bring the three cards out in a fan from under his elbow. Put them on the pack. "There are the three odd cards. Now for the three aces."

Run the pack down his arm, riffling loudly. "There they go."

Give a sharp upward movement with the pack, riffling again in the direction of his breast pocket, where you loaded the three palmed cards at the start of the trick. Spread the pack face upward on the table with a sweep of your arm. "And I'll just put the three odd cards in your pocket. Please see if you have the aces, and if so, show them to the audience.

"Now may I have the three cards from your pocket? Try that one." Point to a side pocket.

They aren't there.

"How about this one?" Point to the other side pocket.

Not there.

"How about that one?" Point to the breast pocket. The volunteer reaches in and brings out the missing three cards.

"Thanks very much for helping me. And one other favor, please don't tell anyone how it's done."

4b. The bottom palm (right hand). Sometimes you need to steal the bottom card of the pack in your right hand—palming it, that is, face toward you.

Hold the pack by the tips of your left fingers and thumb, with the forefinger resting at the far end of the bottom card.

Bring up your right hand as if to do the top palm. As your right hand moves forward, the left forefinger shoves the bottom card out (Fig. 23),

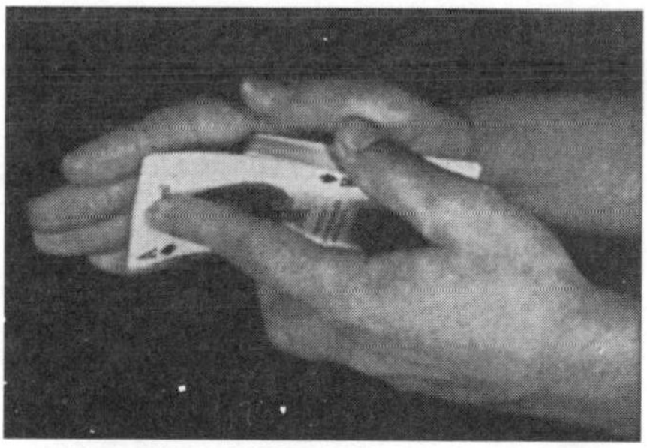

FIG. 23

pressing it against the middle fingers of the right hand until it clears the pack, and can be palmed.

This requires a rather unnatural motion, which can perhaps be covered best by immediately taking the pack at the far end with the right thumb on top and the right second finger underneath.

4c. The bottom palm (left hand), Erdnase method. If you want the bottom card back outward in your left hand, this move is a thing of beauty.

The important point to get is the exact starting position, which Fig. 24 shows better than a page of directions. Your left forefinger, close to the near end, holds a break above the cards to be palmed.

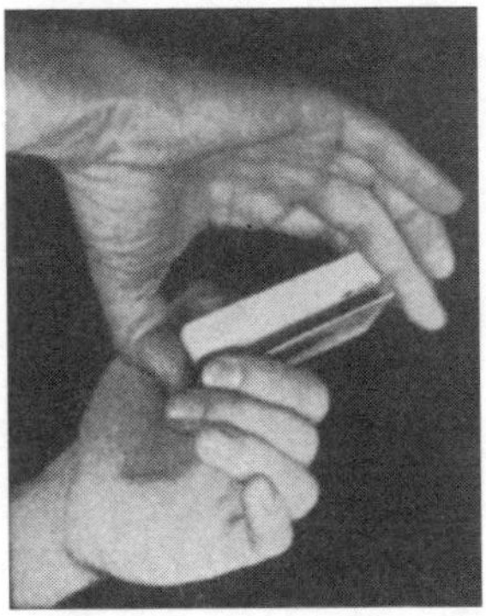

FIG. 24

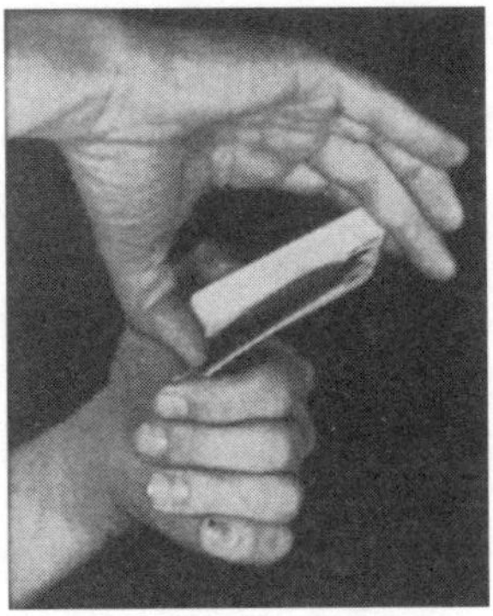

FIG. 25

Swing the tip of your left forefinger toward you and to the left, revolving the cards to be palmed against the crotch of your left thumb as a pivot (Fig. 25).

Then put the tip of your *right little* finger against the end of the pivoting cards, and carry them around until they reach palming position for the left hand (Fig. 26).

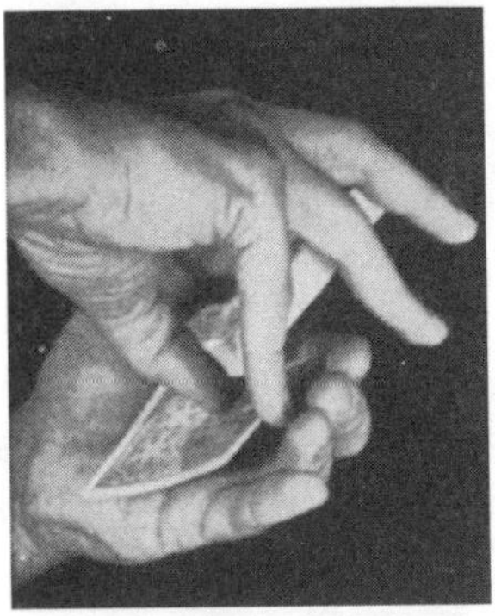

FIG. 26

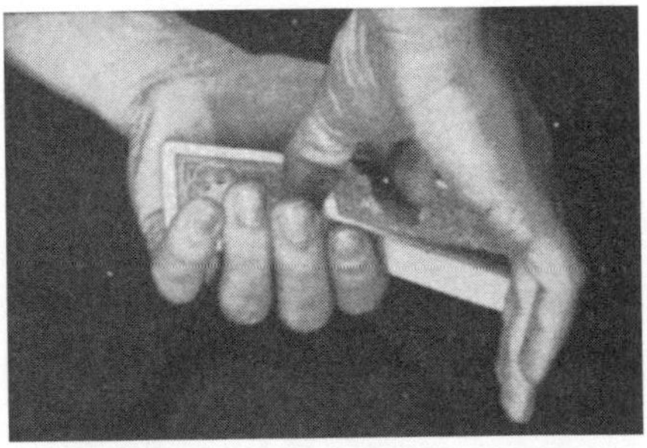

FIG. 27

Palm the cards in your left hand, return your right little finger to its original position (Fig. 27), and carry the deck away in your right hand.

5. FALSE SHUFFLES

You can, if you choose, throw in a false shuffle at some stage of nearly every card trick you do.

The most elementary false shuffles control one card, and are used constantly in chosen-card effects. At the other end of the scale comes the false dovetail, keeping the entire deck undisturbed in its original order. The method given below has never appeared in any book before, and one British magician said it alone would be worth the whole price of any volume that explained it.

There are three regular shuffles in common use by magicians: the overhand, the dovetail (or riffle), and the Hindu, or running cut.

5a. False shuffle: overhand. The most familiar, and the one giving greatest scope to the card operator, is the overhand shuffle, in which the left hand holds the pack by the ends and drops a few cards at a time into the cupped right hand.

The fountainhead of all overhand false shuffling is *The Expert at the Card Table,* by S. W. Erdnase. His definitions of terms in false shuffling are invaluable and I give them here. Any change I made in his glossary would be for the worse, so I reproduce it practically verbatim.

"*Stock:* That portion of the deck that contains certain cards, placed in some particular order for dealing; or certain desirable cards placed at top or bottom of the deck.

"*Run:* To draw off one card at a time during the process of the overhand shuffle. There is little or no difficulty in learning to run the whole deck through in this manner with the utmost rapidity. The right thumb presses lightly on the top card, the left hand alone making the movement necessary to shuffle.

"*Jog:* A card protruding a little from any part of the deck, about a quarter of an inch, to fix the location of any particular card or cards. While shuffling, if the top card is to be jogged, it is pushed over the little-finger end of the deck by the right thumb, the little finger preventing more than one card from moving. If the first card is to be jogged (that is, the first card in the left hand), it is done by shifting the left hand slightly toward either end of the right-hand packet during the shuffle, so that the first card drawn off by the right thumb will protrude a little over the end of the right-hand packet. [Fig. 28 shows the act of making an in-jog.]

"*In-jog:* The card protruding over the little finger of the right hand [Fig. 29].

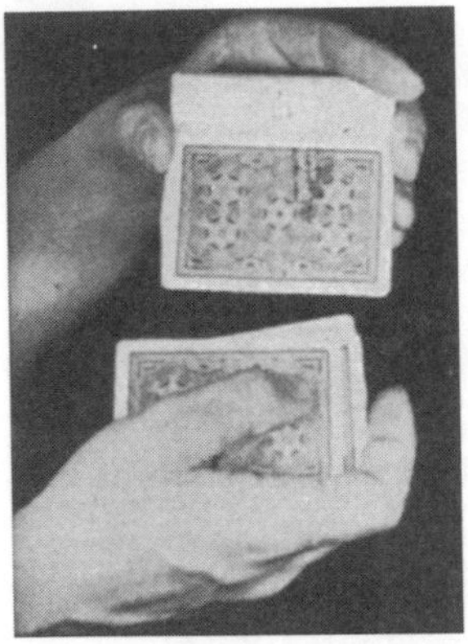

FIG. 28

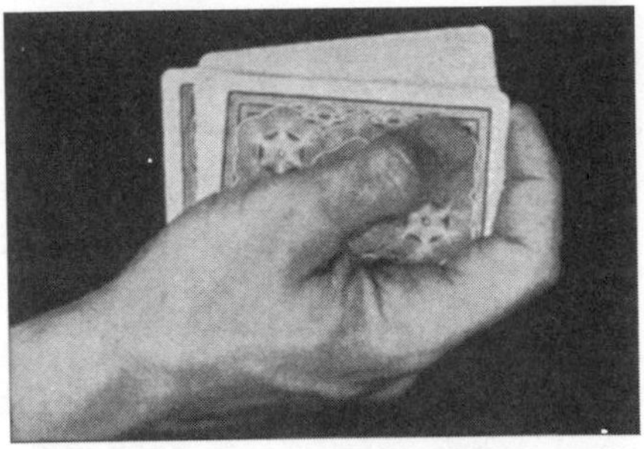

FIG. 29

"*Out-jog:* The card protruding over the first finger of the right hand [Fig. 30].

"The two kinds of jog are often combined in the course of a 'stock,' or arranging, shuffle. [Fig. 31 shows an in- and an out-jog.]

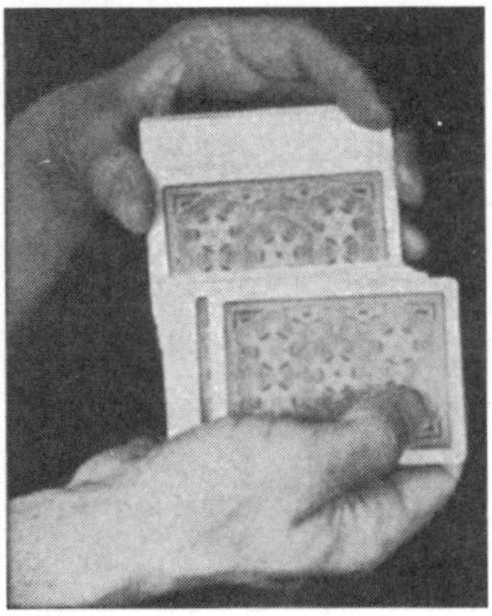

FIG. 30

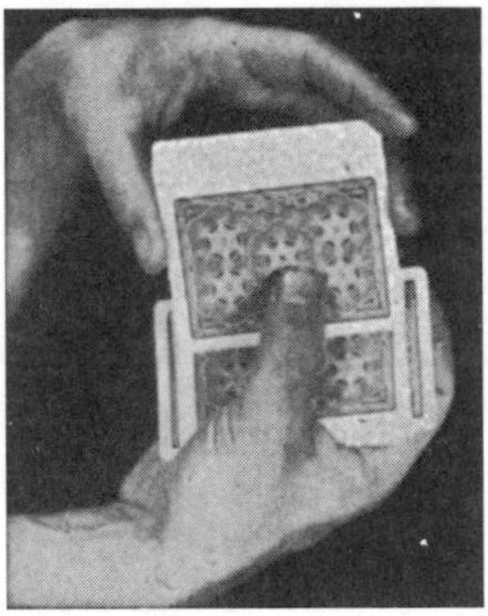

FIG. 31

"*Break:* A space or division held in the deck. While shuffling, it is held at the end by the left thumb. It is formed under the in-jog, when about to undercut for the shuffle, by pushing the in-jog card slightly upward with the left thumb, making a space of from an eighth to a quarter of an inch wide, and holding the space, by squeezing the ends of the packet to be drawn out, between the thumb and the second and third fingers. [Fig. 32 shows the act of forming a break at an in-jog while undercutting to an out-jog.] The use of the break during the shuffle makes it possible to throw any number of cards that are immediately above it, in one packet, into the right hand without disarranging their order.

"*Throw:* To pass from the left hand to the right, during a shuffle, a certain number of cards in one packet, thereby retaining their order. A throw may be required at the beginning, during, or at the end of a shuffle; and the packet to be thrown may be located by the jog, or break, or both.

Fig. 32

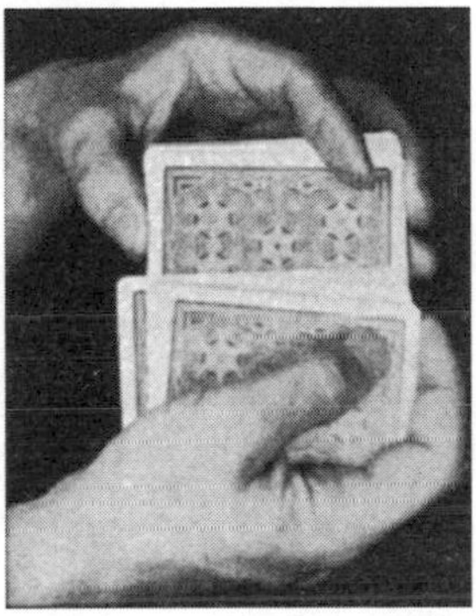

Fig. 33

"*Uppercut:* To take or draw off a packet from the top of the deck.

"*Undercut:* To draw out a packet from the bottom of the deck, during the process of a shuffle. [Fig. 33 shows the act of undercutting to an in-jog.]

"*Top card:* The card on top of the packet held in the right hand, or the original top card of the full deck, which is about to be shuffled.

"*First card:* The card on top of the packet held by the left hand to be shuffled.

"*Shuffle off:* To shuffle without design, in the ordinary manner."

This concludes the essentials of the Erdnase glossary. I will give also his instructions for "drawing from the bottom," which is the oldest and quickest method for the arranging shuffle.

"Seize the deck at the ends between the second finger and thumb of the left hand in the usual manner for shuffling. Run several cards into the right hand, but well down into the palm so that the second and third fingers protrude to the first joints from underneath. Then when the left hand has made the next downward motion, in addition to drawing off the top card with the right thumb, press the right second and third finger tips against the bottom card and let it slide into the right hand. The left hand aids the right fingers by pressing the deck against them and drawing up more horizontally (Fig. 34).

"Suppose for instance that you wanted to bring a chosen card to a position sixth from the top. You would start with the card on the bottom. Undercut about half the deck; run one from the top, drawing one from the bottom; then run five; in-jog the next card; and shuffle off. Undercut to in-jog and throw on top.

FIG. 34

"To keep a chosen card on top of the pack, you may undercut most of the deck, in-jogging the top card; shuffle off; undercut to the in-jog; and shuffle off. The chosen card is now on the bottom. Undercut just a few cards, and run them off, leaving the chosen card on top. You can easily think of half a dozen other ways to do the same thing.

"A combination of in- and out-jogs and breaks will keep a block of several cards intact."

Example of a trick using the overhand stock shuffle: Luis Zingone's Table Spread. This trick will be found described with great thoroughness at page 214 of Hugard and Braue's *Expert Card Technique,* a book you will need if you discover you like this rather ingrown type of card work.

Zingone's Table Spread should never be wasted on an uncritical audience. A jolly, boisterous crowd at a party would far prefer Bertram's Four-Ace Trick, Cards Up the Sleeve (see chapter 4), or some sucker effect. They would also distract you too much to succeed with the Table Spread, whose chief secret is an eagle eye.

When you get a group of hard-bitten poker players, bring on Zingone's Spread, and knock 'em cold.

The whole virtue of the effect lies in the fact that everyone does watch it, and there is positively no chance for trickery. Someone else shuffles the pack thoroughly. You spread it face down on the table (which should be cloth-covered) with a sweep of your arm from right to left. A spectator may do this part too, if he can spread them evenly. It is essential that they be spread evenly and with a fairly wide overlap (hence the need for a cloth table). Particularly in the left half, there must be no bunches of cards sticking together.

Now three different spectators each draw a card part way out—just far enough to turn up the index corners, which they do. Having seen their cards, they themselves push them back into the spread.

One of the three gathers up the cards, squares them carefully, and at last hands them to you. You shuffle them, spread them on the table again, and take three cards from your trouser pocket. These you lay face down on the table. The three spectators name their cards, and sure enough, the three face-down cards are the ones.

Now for the secret. I believe you will find it best to reduce the whole thing to a formula learned by rote, and not bother about the why.

First, you locate the chosen cards by the simple process of counting. For this reason you want the first card to be as near the left end of the spread as possible. An inviting gesture of your left hand will usually accomplish this. Why should they care, since they are having things all their way anyhow? You also want the other two cards as near the first and each other as possible.

The method of counting is to start at the left end of the row, and stop with the first card. Say it is the tenth; your first number is ten. Start again at the adjacent card, and stop with the second chosen card. Perhaps that number is five. Start again at the adjacent card, and stop with the last chosen card. That number might be seven.

Your key numbers are 10-5-7.

From this number subtract the unvarying formula sequence, 1-0-2. This gives you 9-5-5, the numbers you work on in the following stock shuffle.

Undercut a quarter of the pack, in-jog the *first* (not the top) card, and shuffle off. Undercut to the in-jog, run the first number (we are supposing it to be 9), and in-jog the next card. Run the second number, and out-jog the next card. Run the third number and throw on top. Undercut to the out-jog, forming a break at the in-jog; and at the same time in-jog the top card of the right-hand packet with your right thumb. Run the first card, throw to the break, and shuffle off. Undercut to the new in-jog, and shuffle off.

If you care to see why this brings the three chosen cards to the bottom, you may try it with an ace, deuce, and three turned face up in the deck; but the main thing is to memorize your shuffling formula. The actual shuffling takes very little time.

You will hardly need to be told that you now palm the bottom three cards (a couple more won't make any difference) in your left hand by the Erdnase bottom palm (4*c*), and drop them into your left trouser pocket as you respread the cards on the table with your right hand.

The outer (or bottom) card will be the last one chosen, the next the second, and the inner card the first one.

5b. False shuffles: dovetail. I am assuming here that you can do a neat, even dovetail shuffle already, or else you would have no use for ways of falsifying it.

There are, however, two points that not even expert riffle shufflers always know, and both are desirable for the magician.

The first is the proper way of splitting the deck into halves for the riffle shuffle. Normally it should be done as in Fig. 35. The right hand,

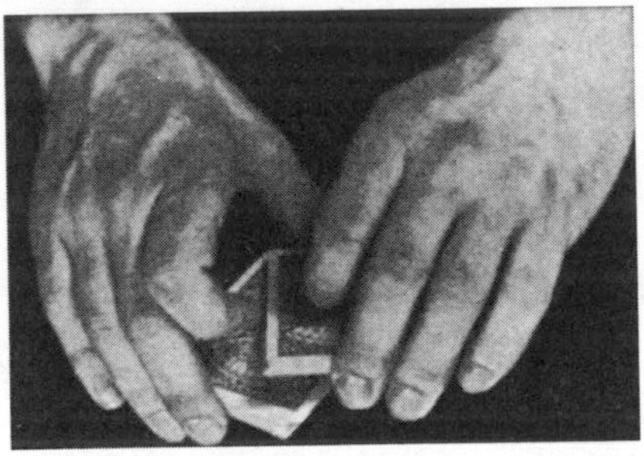

Fig. 35

palm down, holds the face-down deck between thumb and second finger at the *right* near and far corners; the forefinger is curled on top. The left hand takes up an exactly corresponding position on the left. The left second finger, however, reaches only half way down the edge of the deck, whereas the right second finger has a firm grip on the lower part.

The left second finger then pivots to the left, automatically carrying away the top half in the left hand. The two halves are thus separated with one motion, ready for the thumbs to riffle the two inner ends together.

Normally this is the neat way to split the pack. It has, however, the peculiarity that it turns one half end for end. You will learn in head magic about one-way and pointer cards, which must not be so turned. Tricks of that sort require a different means of splitting, as follows: Hold the pack top to palm in your right hand, second and third fingers curled firmly around the far end, thumb at the near end, forefinger curled against the back. By pushing with your forefinger, riffle the cards away from your thumb until about half have escaped.

Then put your left second and third fingers against the upper end of the half you have riffled off. Push this end down until the half is horizontal, and you can clip it by pressing your left forefinger against the top. Then reach out with your left thumb and take the far end.

You now have both halves in exactly corresponding grips, and any one-way arrangement remains undisturbed.

The other point, which you need for my own pet false shuffle, is the waterfall finish—riffling the cards only part way in, then arching the pack and letting them spring square in a sort of cascade.

FIG. 36

Many bridge-players have this knack, the first two stages of which are shown in Figs. 36 and 37.

Once the cards have reached the position shown in Fig. 37, with the two thumbs keeping the dovetailed ends of the cards from unlacing, one's natural tendency would be to push harder with the thumbs.

FIG. 37

Here is the whole secret of the flourish: instead of pushing with your thumbs, relax your fingers, down and out. The cards automatically spring together, finally reaching the position of Fig. 38. For a good waterfall, by the way, you must have the cards quite evenly dovetailed, not in thick bunches.

To keep track of a single card with the dovetail shuffle is so easy that it often happens quite by accident.

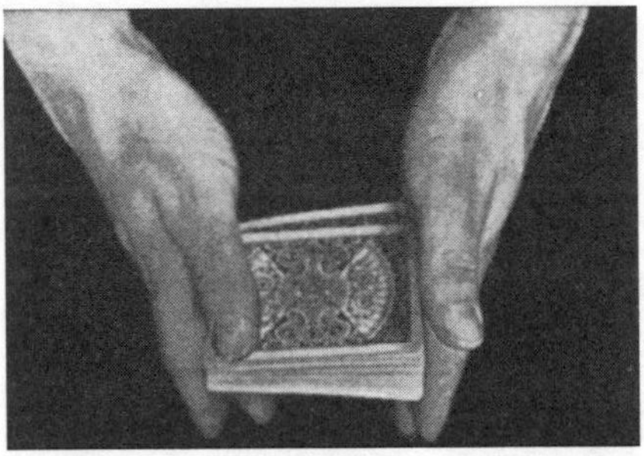

FIG. 38

If the card is on top (and you are using the first method of splitting the deck), simply hold back the last few cards with your left thumb until all the right-hand half has been riffled in. To keep the bottom card, let go of a few from your right thumb before you do from your left.

It is sometimes useful to drop an extra card above or below the particular one you are holding at top or bottom. This you can certainly accomplish without special instructions.

The dovetail shuffle serves as the simplest of all shifts if you hold a break (section 1) at the chosen card, make your split there, and shuffle the card to top or bottom.

There comes a time in every card conjurer's career when he wants to shuffle and yet leave all or most of the pack in undisturbed order. The whole vast range of tricks with a prearranged deck (see head magic) becomes almost worthless without such a false shuffle. With such a shuffle, you can (and I often do) calmly arrange fifteen or twenty cards right before the audience, and then apparently cancel your work by a good shuffle.

False dovetails to leave the whole deck in order are the one weak point in the armor provided by Erdnase. Even the legendary Jack Merlin offers only weird monstrosities in this line. Dai Vernon, another fabled sleight-of-hand king, has produced a sound answer to the problem, but I like my own best—chiefly because it is my own.

Here it is.

Split the deck, carrying away the *top* half in your left hand.

Riffle the two halves in, end to end. But let the far side of the right-hand half overlap half an inch beyond the far side of the left-hand half. And be sure that the top few cards of the right-hand half are the last to be released, so that they fall on top of the left-hand half (Fig. 36).

Keeping your thumbs together at the top of the arch, bend the two interlaced halves into a semicircle, ready for the waterfall (Fig. 37). Relax your fingers, letting the cards spring well together in the normal waterfall flourish.

The two halves are now genuinely shuffled, and they are square *at the ends.* But they are not square at the sides: the left-hand half juts half an inch toward you (Fig. 38). You can show the cards in this position as long and freely as you like. The audience believes the shuffle is over, and they start thinking about something else. (The great flaw in most of the earlier false riffles was that some tricky move came just at this point, while everyone was still watching sharply.)

Without moving the deck from the position in Fig. 38, nip it between your left thumb and second finger so that you can change the grip of your right hand.

Turn your right hand over, knuckles upward, and put your second finger at the far right corner, your thumb at the near right corner.

Squeeze with your right thumb and second finger.

That slides the two interlaced halves into a V shape, with the point of the V at the right.

At the left end is a pronounced corner made by the left far side of the left-hand pack and the left far end of the right-hand pack.

Change the grip of your left hand to match that of your right; but don't squeeze yet.

FIG. 39

Fit your left third finger snugly into the corner I just mentioned. Your two thumbs, together on the near edges, will now serve as a pivot.

Pull *toward* you with your left third finger. You will find this makes a similar corner sprout just to the *left* of your *right third finger* (Fig. 39). By pushing your left and right third fingers toward each other, you could, if you wanted, slide the two halves of the deck almost clear of each other.

But don't carry it that far. Stop pushing when the two halves have about an inch jutting clear at the ends.

Then squeeze together with both thumbs and second fingers, straightening the two halves so that they are square and flush along the sides (Fig. 40). You have now converted a slight sidewise overlap into a big endwise overlap, and are ready to undo the shuffle.

Change the grip of your right hand so that the knuckles are down instead of up, and the palm faces the bottom of the deck instead of the top (Fig. 41). Your left hand hides the projecting left half of the pack from

FIG. 40

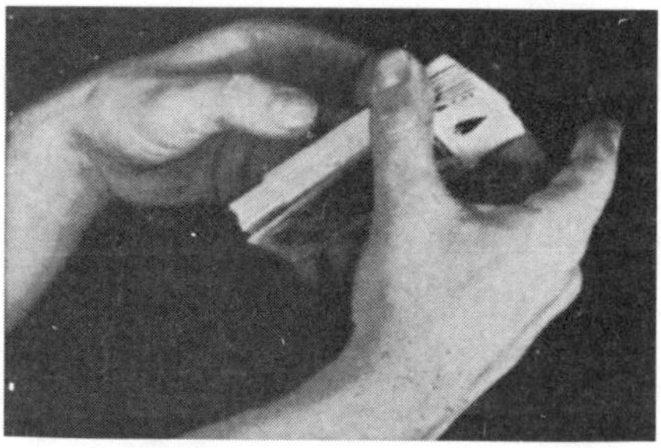

FIG. 41

every conceivable angle. This is why you wanted the top card to belong to the right-hand half.

Your right hand should hold the cards between thumb and second finger at the extreme right end—*beyond* the central overlap.

Your left third finger is on the corner beyond the central overlap at the left end. Pull toward you with this finger; this swivels the left-hand half loose from the right-hand half (Fig. 42).

Draw down with your left hand, as if executing what is called a strip cut (drawing out the lower half of the pack and putting it on top), actually pulling the left-hand half clear of its engagement with the right; then slap it briskly on top of the right-hand half (Fig. 43).

I usually finish off with two more strip cuts as a blind.

To work this at the card table, don't change the grip of your right hand before you strip out the left-hand half, but keep both hands back upward. The moves are still angle proof.

The shuffle positively must be done gently throughout. If you clutch the cards too tightly, they will stick when you try to strip them, probably disarranging the whole order.

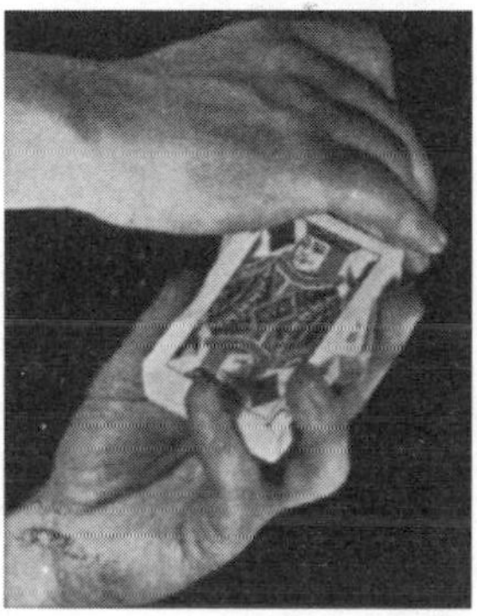

FIG. 42

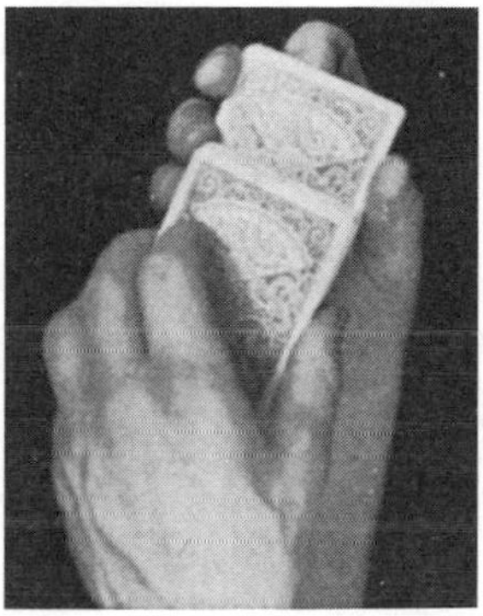

FIG. 43

5c. *False shuffle: Hindu shuffle.* The Hindu shuffle is hardly more than a series of strip cuts. The pack is held in the left hand about as in Fig. 43, the fingers at the right side, the thumb at the left. The right hand undercuts part of the deck, taking it by the edges at the lower end between the thumb and second finger. The left hand drops the remaining cards into the palm; the right hand brings the undercut part over the other cards, and the left thumb and finger tips strip off a few more, while the right hand withdraws again, carrying a remnant of the deck, and finally drops it on top of all.

Since you are already familiar with breaks (section 1) and jogs (section 5), you will see that you can control one card by an in-jog, by a break held with your left little finger, or (the most natural) by a break held with the right second finger tip.

Some performers use this as a location, having a chosen card replaced on the packet in the left hand, jogging it or holding a break, shuffling off on top of it, and finally undercutting to the jog or break and throwing on top.

Facts about shuffling. Never change your shuffling routine—don't do an overhand shuffle for one trick, and a riffle for the next. This disturbs the association of normality with your regular shuffle. You may, as I do, habitually use a dovetail followed by a quick Hindu shuffle.

Two adjacent cards will seldom be separated by a brief overhand shuffle —a useful fact to know in dealing with key cards (see head magic).

A dovetail shuffle often separates adjacent cards, but it *cannot disturb the sequence of the cards thus separated.*

There are many devilishly ingenious tricks based on this fact, which was first exploited in *Thirty Card Mysteries,* by Charles T. Jordan (see head magic again).

An ordinary cut does not disturb the arrangement of the deck in any way. When you dare not let a pack be shuffled, you can almost always let different people cut it again and again, which strikes the uninformed as almost equally impressive.

There are no tricks relying *solely* on a false shuffle. If you tried to do one (for instance, restoring a shuffled new pack to its original order), you would merely spotlight the fact that the shuffle must be false, and so give away your whole secret.

For tricks whose effect is multiplied by a false shuffle, see head magic.

6. CHANGES

Changes are sleights by which one or more cards are exchanged invisibly for substitutes. In this point they differ from color changes, or transformations, where the change is visible, constituting a trick in itself.

6a. The double lift. This is not strictly a change but only the first step in one. The move has become so popular with American card conjurers that the entire first chapter of Hugard and Braue's *Expert Card Technique* is devoted to it.

All it amounts to is picking up two cards off the pack together, and displaying them as one card. You can develop your own moves for doing this. In my opinion the easiest is to hold the pack in your left hand, bring your right second and third fingers to the far end, pry up two cards with the tip of your right thumb at the near end, give a push with the tip of your left little finger to make sure the two cards are together, and then simply turn your right hand palm up, exhibiting the two cards (now slightly bowed crosswise) as in Fig. 50 (6*d*).

Once you have pried up the two cards and taken a little-finger break below them, you may pick them up by the near right corner between your right forefinger and thumb and turn them over to the left on top of the pack. Then take them by the near index corner and turn them back again. The change comes when you deal off the top card, which obviously will not be the one you showed.

The only trouble with this second motion is that, having become hackneyed, it is now almost advance warning of a double lift.

Whatever method you use, you must form the habit of keeping to that motion alone, whether you are picking up one card or two.

Examples of tricks using the double lift. Everybody's Card (3*d*) can be done with the chosen card apparently on top but exchanged by the double lift, instead of done with the card on the bottom and exchanged by the glide.

"The Ambitious Card" (see chapter 4) is probably the most popular trick relying heavily on the double lift.

6b. The top change. This and the bottom change, which follows next, are century-old stand-bys. They have survived strictly on their merits, and you will find many, many occasions to use them.

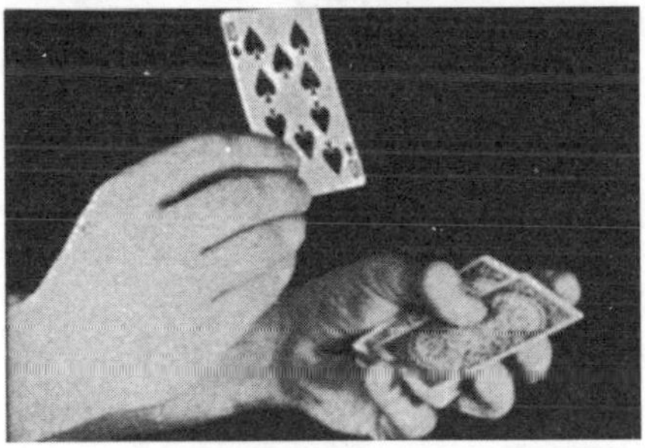

Fig. 44

For the top change, you have one card, *A*—the ten of spades in the pictures—between your right forefinger and thumb, and the other card, *B*, pushed part way off the deck, which is held in dealing position in the left hand (Fig. 44.)

Bring your left hand over to meet the right (not vice versa), and slide

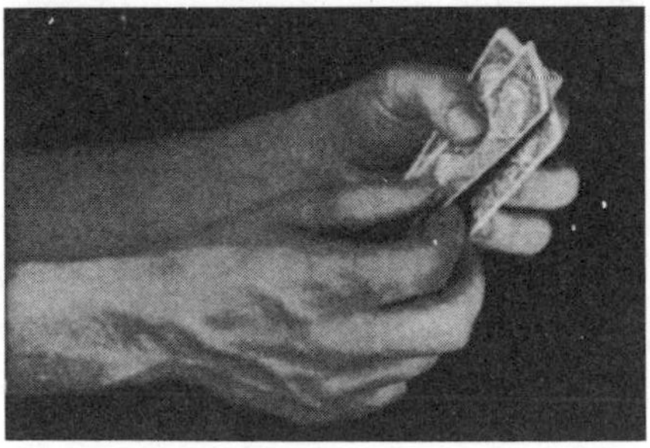

Fig. 45

A under the tip of your left thumb. This brings your right forefinger between A and *B*, and the second finger comes under *B* (Fig. 45).

As you separate your hands again, your right first and second fingers carry off *B*, while your left thumb hangs onto A.

Thus you wind up the change as in Fig. 46, with *B* in your right hand and A on top of the pack.

FIG. 46

You may think this change is utterly obvious, and so it would be if you merely stood still with your hands in front of your stomach and switched cards.

With some slight cover, however, it is perfectly deceptive. The cover that works best for me is to pivot to the right, swing the pack over, and slap the single card with the top of the deck. My left hand goes over, then up to strike the blow; just at this moment A and *B* change places. *B* is the card actually slapped by A when I bring my left hand down, knuckles up.

Another cover is made by pivoting slightly to the left in the act of putting A on the table. In this case the right, rather than the left, hand does the swinging; the change comes as the right hand starts toward the table.

By practice and experiment you can learn to carry the change a step further than I have described. Instead of leaving A on the pack and pulling *B* out from under A, you virtually toss the two cards at each other, releasing them before your hands are quite together. The cards almost seem to float and cross in mid-air, but actually there is not quite that much space between hands.

Once again, gentleness is vital—particularly in the second variation. The talking of nervously handled cards often gives away an otherwise perfect change.

Example of a trick using the top change: Step on It! The effect is perfectly simple: you and a volunteer each choose a card and step on it. The cards change places.

The method is almost equally so. As the volunteer comes toward you, catch a glimpse of the top card of the pack. Now let him choose any card he pleases, taking care that it isn't the top one.

After he has looked at it, take it back from him in your right hand, holding it face down, ready for the top change, so that nobody can see it.

Tell him you want him to hold on to his card tight, so you suggest he step on it. Stoop to drop the card on the floor, and in the process make the top change.

Under his foot is the card you originally memorized; his card is on top of the pack.

Cut his top card to the middle, jogging it or keeping a break. Spread the deck face downward, and draw a card, apparently at random, actually the one you have kept track of.

Look at it without showing it. Put aside the deck. Then drop your card on the floor and step on it.

Go into your build-up. Is your assistant's memory good? Has he got a heavy foot? Is he sure?

"All right, we'll see," you say, naming the original top card. "I had the six of hearts; what did you have?"

"The king of clubs," he may say.

"Was it really? Why don't you look under your foot?"

Naturally he picks up the six of hearts, whereupon you display the king of clubs.

"You must not have stepped heavy enough," you say by way of finishing the trick.

6c. *The bottom change.* Really a minor variation of the top change. The only significant difference is that card A is left under, not on, the pack.

FIG. 47

Start with *A* between right first and second finger tips (Fig. 47).

You make the same swing of the left hand as in the top change, shooting *A* underneath the pack and withdrawing *B* with your right thumb and forefinger (Fig. 48).

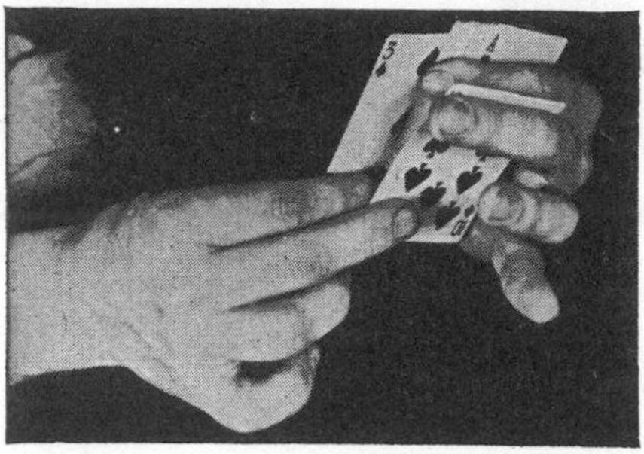

Fig. 48

You finish the change as in Fig. 49.

Fig. 49

The same two-way throw that so greatly improves the top change is equally good in the bottom change, though harder to do.

Whether you use the top or the bottom change depends solely on where you need to leave card A.

6d. The palm change. The rest of the changes are made without the help of the pack, which seems like a great improvement; but actually occasions to use these single-card moves are less common than occasions for the top and bottom changes.

For the palm change, do a double lift as in Fig. 50. The illustration shows the left hand, but either hand will do. Turn your hand downward, so that the visible card faces the floor. Apparently take the card in your other hand, thumb on the back, first and second fingers on the face.

Fig. 50

Actually, you execute a form of side steal (Fig. 51), sliding the front card into palming position and drawing out the back one to display (Fig. 52).

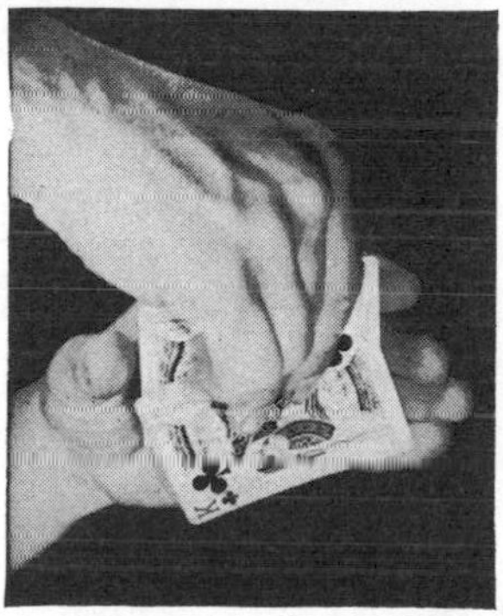

Fig. 51

If you are going to show the change immediately, flip the back of card *B* with the middle fingernail of the hand containing card A palmed.

Fig. 52

6e. The double-palm change. This is a smooth, easy, silent change, fully as good for changing a bunch of cards as for a single one. It is more of a platform than a card-table change because the movements will not all bear detailed scrutiny.

Start with group of cards *B* palmed face outward in your left hand, and group *A* held face downward by the sides between the tips of your left thumb and second finger (Fig. 53).

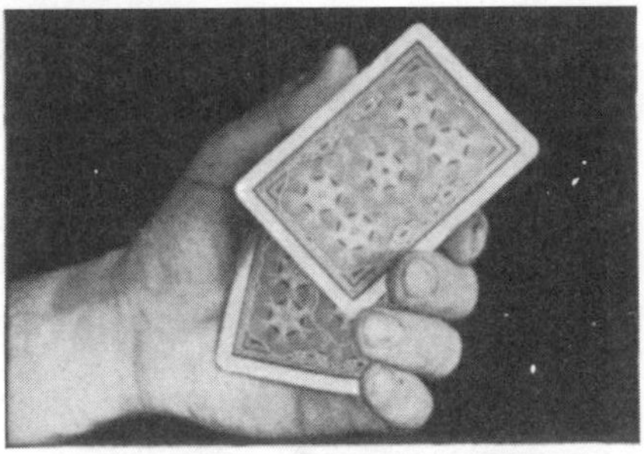

FIG. 53

Boldly cover group A with your right hand (Fig. 54), and palm them there. The partial closing of your right hand makes it perfectly natural for your right second finger and thumb to take group *B* by the long edges and hold them up (Fig. 55), leaving the left hand empty.

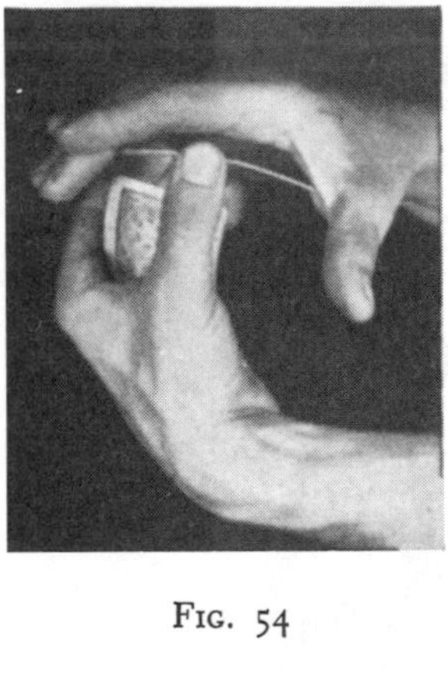

FIG. 54

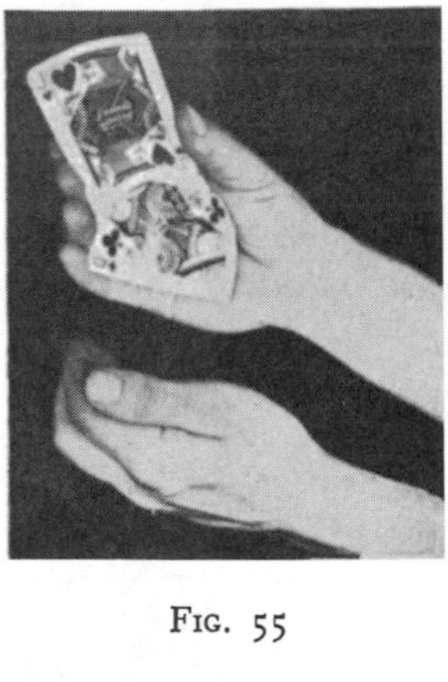

FIG. 55

The point that won't stand scrutiny is when you move to grab A by the ends, and instead come up holding *B* by the sides; but I must say I have used this change for a quarter-century without being detected.

Example of a trick using double-palm change: The Phoney Aces. For disciplining an unruly audience this trick has few equals.

Put the ace of diamonds on top of the pack, and the three next below it. Put the three of hearts on the bottom of the pack, and the ace next above it. A quick false shuffle will do no harm.

Now show the bottom of the pack with one second finger covering each end spot of the three of hearts. As if by accident, contrive to let an index be seen.

Announce boldly that this is the ace of hearts. Make sure you pause long enough for even the dullards to realize that you are cheating. Then turn the deck face down, changing the grip of your left hand in readiness for the glide, which you immediately execute, drawing out the next card and laying it face down on the table. (This, of course, is the ace of hearts.)

By means of the shift, bring the top two cards to the bottom.

Go through the whole routine again with what you declare to be the ace of diamonds, though any fool can see it is an ill-disguised three. Make the glide once more, drawing out the second card—this time the ace of diamonds.

The tumult that invariably follows will give you plenty of opportunity to palm off the two threes in your left hand by the Erdnase Bottom Palm (4c).

Put down the deck and advance on the audience with a rather truculent air, your fists on your hips. This pose gives complete cover for the palmed cards. "What seems to be the matter? Is there anything wrong with those aces?"

Boos. Catcalls. "They ain't aces; they're three-spots!"

Turn them over successively and fling them on the table. "What three-spots?"

Bewilderment, instead of indignation, this time protects you as you pick up the two aces by their long edges in your left hand, ready for the double-palm change.

While you stand enjoying your triumph, make the change.

"What did you say they were? Threes? What ever gave you that idea?" Drop the threes face down on the table, and fold your arms (perfect cover for the palmed cards again).

"Still, it won't do any harm to look again. Sometimes you *can* believe your eyes."

7. COLOR CHANGES

Color changes would be better called transformations, the name given them by Erdnase; but for some reason his term has never caught on, and color changes they remain.

They have nothing to do with color necessarily, being simply methods of visibly transforming one card into another, usually on the face of the deck.

7a. The clip (Felicien Trewey's color change). This is the first of the color changes, and it still has certain advantages of its own. The deck is held in the right (or left) hand in about the position for the Charlier pass (2*f*), but without the little finger barring the near end. The palm of the left hand, flat, is drawn toward you over the face of the pack. As it moves, your right forefinger pushes against the far end of one or more cards at the back of the deck, sliding them into the fork of your left thumb (Fig. 56), which clips them—hence the name.

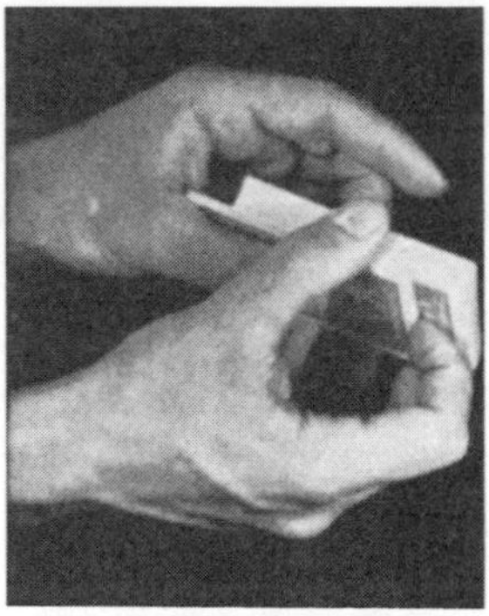

FIG. 56

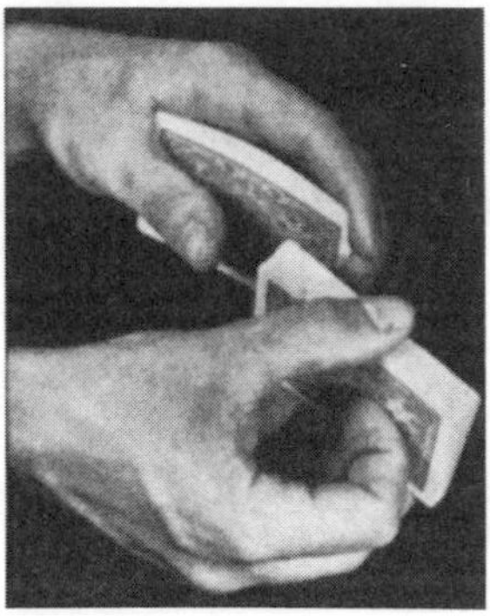

FIG. 57

The left hand carries these cards away and palms them (Fig. 57).

Draw your left hand once again over the pack and leave the palmed cards on the face.

Don't move your hand over the pack any oftener than you must. The impression you want to create is that you display the front card, then change it with one rub, not that you are scrubbing away until you wear off the ink.

The clip color change needs to be practiced with a mirror because the stolen cards have a nasty habit of showing below the heel of your hand just as you palm them.

Another difficulty is that the stolen cards may drag another half way out in their travels. This is cured by pushing the stolen cards out with your right forefinger instead of clutching one card with your left thumb, which was Trewey's original move.

Examples of tricks using the clip color change: Wiping Out the Spot, and a production flourish. The first of these is a brother to the Phoney

Aces. As I have already described it at length in another book of mine, I will only hit the high spots here (pun intended).

You have a three (any suit except spades) on the front of the pack. You declare you are going to wipe off the middle spot. In doing so, you clumsily reveal the corner of a card that you have obviously palmed off the face of the deck. When the audience calls you for it, you finally turn it over, and it is the ace—"Belongs here in the middle," you say, tapping the vacant center of the two-spot.

To set up, put the three-spot on the bottom of the pack, the deuce on top of the pack, and the ace next below it.

You merely steal the top two cards by the clip. In awkwardly rubbing the face of the pack, leave the deuce behind and carry off the ace, pushing out a corner as if by accident. Build-up does the rest.

The other effect is simply a little dodge to be used in a routine of card productions.

You have palmed off a few handfuls of cards and brought them out, spread into fans, from behind elbows, knees, and similar possible but unlikely spots. You have the pack face out in (say) the right hand.

"If I took any cards off the front," you say, momentarily removing a few, "the front card would change."

The moment after you replace these cards, steal a bunch from behind by the clip, and then transfer the pack to a position between your left forefinger and thumb.

"And if I took any off the back, the back card would change."

So saying, you turn the (new) top card crosswise. Straighten it out again, take the pack back in your right hand, and produce another fan of cards with your left. Flash the top card of the pack again to show that it hasn't changed.

7b. The side-steal color change. I think this is the prettiest of all color changes; but then, you must have discovered my weakness for every form of side steal.

The chief thing to remember is the opening position. Hold the pack in your left hand, face to palm, with your forefinger at the extreme edge of the far end, just above the index, and your thumb at the corresponding corner of the near end. Thus both your palm and the pack are fully exposed.

Stand with both hands palm upward. Give everyone plenty of time to realize that your palms are empty. Then turn your left hand over and lay the pack in your right palm, in dealing position.

As you do so, however, your right first and second fingers slide the top card to the left (Fig. 58). This is the regular side-steal move, and your left hand palms the card. No preliminary sweep over the face of the pack

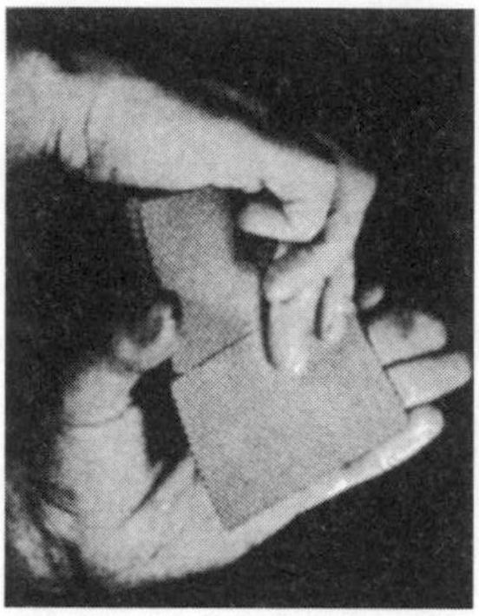

FIG. 58

is necessary—take the deck in your right hand, and bingo, the change is done.

Example of a trick using the side-steal color change: Correcting a Mistake. Have a card chosen and get it to the top of the pack. I wouldn't waste time with a false shuffle in so slight a trick.

Announce that you are going to make the card appear on the front of the pack. Riffle the cards slowly past your ear, then give a loud snap. "Here you are—right on the front."

"No," says the spectator, "that's not it."

You look puzzled and chagrined. Get the pack in position for the side-steal color change, then look at palms and backs of both hands, as if wondering how they could have played you so false.

Turn your hands over, execute the side steal, and palm the card. Then stop, and ask what the card was.

"All right," you say, "if you insist." Pass your hand over the front card, changing it to the chosen one.

Pause. Applause. Then say, "I still like the other card better. If you don't mind, I think I'll change this back."

Show the top card of the pack. "It doesn't seem to be here."

Do a double lift (6*a*) with the bottom two cards, picking them up in roughly the same position that you held the whole pack in at the start of the side steal. "Nor here, next to the bottom."

As you replace the double card on the bottom, you will find it quite easy to side-steal the second one by pushing to the left with your right second and third finger tips. Do so.

"So we'll just have to change it like this"—giving a rub, and leaving the original bottom card back in place.

7c. *Far-end-steal color change.* About the quickest steal for a color change is made from the far end of the deck. Sweep your left hand outward, grabbing a few cards from the top of the pack between your left *first* and *little* fingers in passing (Fig. 59).

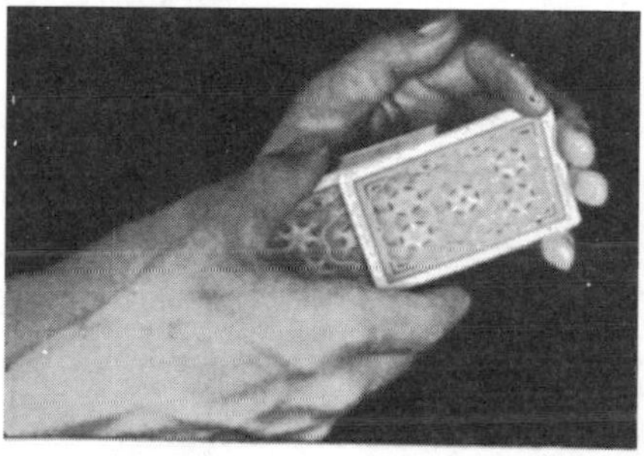

FIG. 59

By a few trials before a mirror you will learn the proper angle to hide the projecting corners of the stolen cards for the instant it takes to shift to the regular palm (Fig. 60).

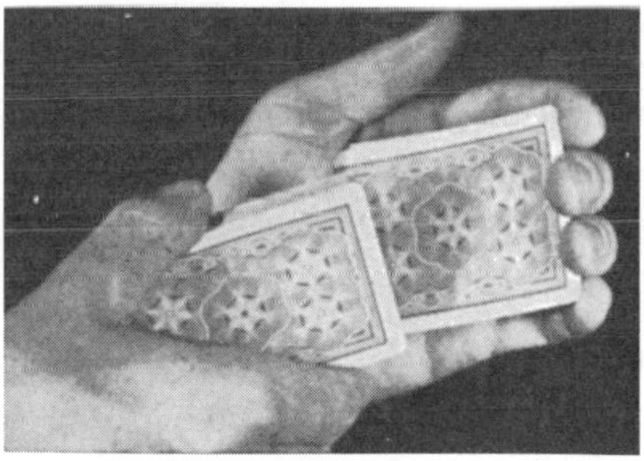

FIG. 60

The right-handed bottom palm (4*b*) may be used as a color change in just the same way.

7d. *The snap change.* Although the most truly magical-looking of changes—for a single card is instantly transformed *in full view*—this has remained a mere curiosity because it left card A in a position that almost no angle would hide.

With a little tinkering, however, I have got very good use out of the snap change. My tinkering consists of pointing the card down instead of up, and retaining the deck in my left hand.

Do a double lift, and show the two cards as in Fig. 61. The peculiarity of the grip is that your right second finger should be as near the *left* edge of the card as possible, while your thumb should be as far as possible to the *right*. Hold the card out slightly in front of the deck, which is in your left hand.

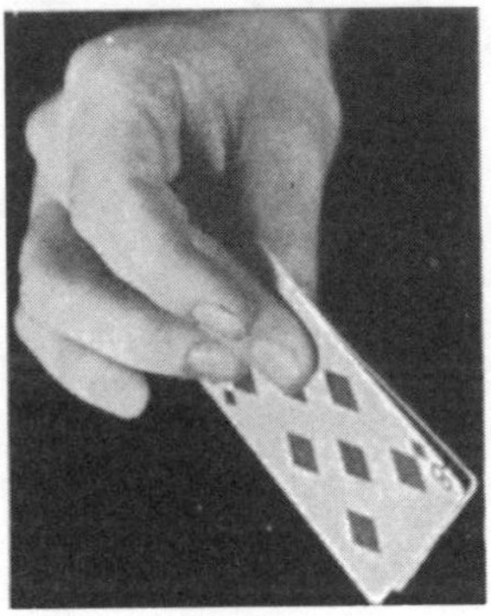

FIG. 61

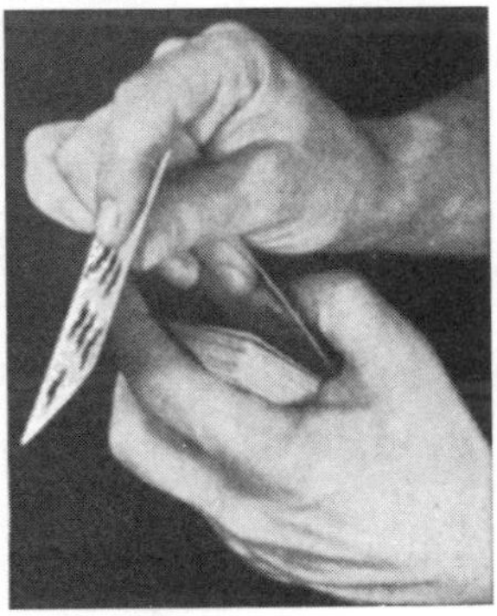

FIG. 62

Make a forward and downward motion of your right hand and simply snap your second finger.

This leaves card *B* between thumb and forefinger, and throws card A back against the heel of your hand, directly over the deck (Fig. 62), where you drop it, carrying your right hand on forward.

I generally use this to correct a "mistake" in finding a chosen card.

8. TRICK DEALS

The second deal and the bottom deal are two of the most famous, simplest, and most difficult artifices borrowed from professional gamblers. You can get through a successful career in card conjuring without them. If you master them, you will find or make dozens of chances to employ them.

8a. The second deal. Of the two false deals, second dealing—dealing the second card when apparently dealing the top card—is the more useful to magicians, whereas Erdnase reports that gamblers prize the bottom deal more highly.

There are several methods of second-dealing. The easy ways are no good, and the good ways take almost endless practice. Probably the easiest good way is illustrated in Figs. 63 and 64.

The only peculiarity in the position of the left hand is that the thumb rests on the extreme far end of the top card. This is to draw back the top card the merest fraction of an inch, enabling the thumb tip to press also on the second card. Now push your thumb to the right, carrying both cards with it (Fig. 63).

That is the only, and almost insuperable, difficulty of the second deal —pushing over not one card, not three, but two. When you have mastered that, you have mastered the second deal.

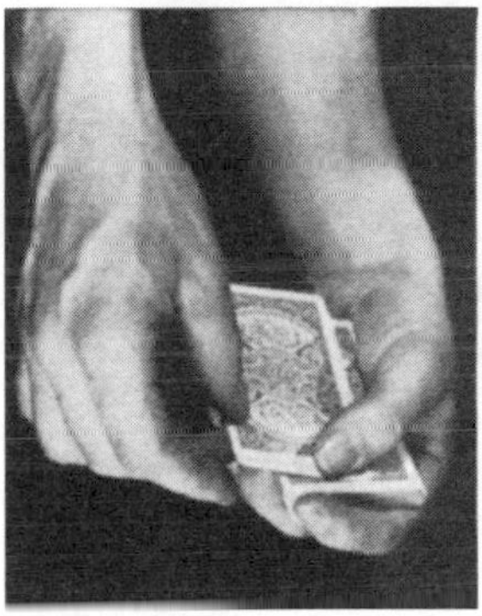

FIG. 63

FIG. 64

As the two cards move to the right, your right hand comes up, and its second finger draws out the under card, while the left thumb pulls the top card back onto the deck (Fig. 64).

Your left thumb then pushes forward the top two cards again.

The second deal should be covered by a slight to-and-fro swing of both hands. Of course, it works far better with new cards than old, and it is less easily detected when the back patterns have no white border.

For the twentieth time, gentleness will do the business.

Example of a trick using the second deal: Five Hands. When the great Nate Leipzig, its inventor, showed me this feat, I had a pretty good idea of how he did it. To me the method was considerably more marvelous than the effect—something that occasionally happens to such superb manipulators as Leipzig.

If you have really mastered the second deal, and have the same kind of sharp eyes needed for the Zingone Table Spread, you can do wonders with this trick.

A spectator shuffles a borrowed pack, then deals five poker hands to himself, you, and three volunteers. Starting at your left, you ask the first assistant to take one card from his hand, memorize it, put it back among his hand, and square up the five cards. You do the same with each of the other three volunteers in succession.

You pick up the cards, shuffle, and deal five more hands.

This time you do pick up your own hand. You ask each spectator to name his card. As he does so, you pull it out of your hand and lay it on the table.

The method, as I hinted above, is simple enough. As the first spectator puts his card back among his hand, you remember the number from the top at which it stands—say third. Just remember the figure 3. The next spectator puts his in second. You now remember 32. The next man puts his fourth. You remember 324. The last man puts his third. All you remember is 3243.

Pick up the hands in reverse order—that is, starting with your own and then going on to the one at your right—and drop them on the deck. A dovetail false shuffle (5*b*) leaves the hands undisturbed.

Start dealing around in the regulation way. The number you are remembering is 3243. When you reach the third card, you second-deal, keeping this card on top until your own turn, when you deal it to yourself.

Your second digit was 2. Hold back the second card for your own hand. And so on for the other two cards.

Thus you have dealt yourself all four of the chosen cards with no fuss or false moves whatever. I won't say this is an easy trick, but it certainly is a puzzler. It lends some point to the infinitely wearisome jape, "I'd hate to play cards with you."

8b. Bottom deal. The general timing and stage management of the bottom deal are just like the second deal; only, instead of having to push forward the top two cards as one, you have to thrust out the bottom card with your left third finger as your thumb draws the top card back.

The position of the pack is what some of the "card detectives" have rendered notorious under the name of the Mechanic's Grip. Essentially you are holding the deck by the index corners between the tip of your second finger and the heel of your hand. If you do that, you will get the correct hold automatically.

As you push forward the top card with your left thumb, your third finger prevents more than one card from sliding. The moment the card is well started, however, the third finger is drawn back under the deck, where its tip slides forward the bottom card (freeing it from the second finger) not quite so far as the top card (Fig. 65).

The right second finger draws out the bottom card as the left thumb pulls back the top one.

The bottom deal can be made perfectly deceptive, but it takes a lot of work. Eliminating noise and keeping the pack from slipping toward

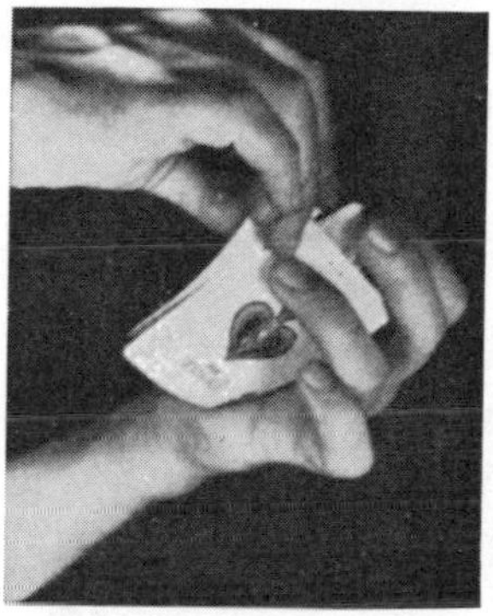

Fig. 65

your wrist are the greatest difficulties. An up-and-down swing in dealing helps cover the moves.

This is the classic method taught by Erdnase. A quite different one, in which the right second finger hooks out the bottom card, will be found in Hugard and Braue's *Expert Card Technique*.

You can see why the bottom deal is so useful to gamblers: it allows them, having collected what cards they please at the bottom of the deck, to deal those cards at will to themselves or to anyone else.

For conjuring purposes, I have always felt that you should think twice before you put into your act any trick that involves much dealing. If you agree with me that constant dealing and counting slow down an effect and tire the spectators, you won't need the bottom deal very often.

9. FLOURISHES

These are the airs and graces of legerdemain—feats of skill that ai pretty and showy, whether or not they mystify.

Flourishes are not a thing you can take or leave alone. The more solemn school of card operators claim that you should have no apparent skill at all—that any flourish, even a waterfall shuffle, kills the mystery of your tricks. They fear people will say, "No wonder he could bring the four aces together—look at the way he handles the cards." The other school of card conjurers, entranced (as who is not?) by Cardini and

LePaul, feel that fanning and back-palming are the acme of card magic. Considering how difficult some of the flourishes are, it is quite surprising how many performers have succeeded in making some sort of card act with very little else.

Obviously common sense lies between the extremes. For my part, I think it is idle to conceal all your skill. The only card worker who can successfully pretend downright clumsiness is the man who does a routine of straight mind reading, apparently using cards simply as a convenience. Very few card tricks are such grand affairs that they must be above the sacrilegious touch of the card manipulator.

Flourishes, on the other hand, are often more juggling than magic, and they become with some performers a nervous habit that subconsciously distresses the audience.

Very few of the flourishes can be truthfully caught by the camera, so you will have to put up with my descriptions, watch other performers when you can, and study the few specialized books on the subject.

9a. The riffle. The riffle, made by running your thumb over one corner of the deck, I mention chiefly by way of warning. It will serve to signal the high point of a trick, instead of the ancient "abracadabra!" or "pass!"

But it all too easily becomes a constant habit, a nervous tic that can drive an audience distracted.

9b. Springing the cards. This is the oldest, the easiest, and the most ostentatious of all the flourishes. If you want to do card tricks instead of playing with strangers, spring the pack a couple of times, and you'll have an audience.

The flourish consists of squirting the pack in a stream from one hand to the other. Don't try to learn it with either stiff or sticky cards.

Hold the pack with your thumb at one end and all four fingers at the other. Bend the cards *in* crosswise—*toward* your palm.

Hold the other hand palm upward, close to your stomach.

Now squeeze your thumb and fingers together until the cards begin to squirt away.

At first they will go in bursts, some forward and some back, all over the floor (or, if you want my advice, a bed).

The secret of success is to let all the cards escape from your thumb, or else all from your fingers. Then a very little practice with soft cards will teach you to squeeze evenly, curing the abrupt bursts. If the cards slide off your thumb rather than your fingers, your stomach will help catch them—a labor-saving consideration at first.

Don't try to spring the cards any distance. Three inches is plenty at first. Once you learn to spring the cards in an even stream, you can spread your hands a foot or more with no extra trouble. In springing from your right hand to your left, pivoting to the right makes the distance look greater.

When you have thoroughly learned this flourish, you can proceed to an elaboration called the Waterfall Drop. Instead of springing the cards, you let them fall in an unbroken ribbon from one hand to the other.

To do this, hold the pack in readiness for springing, but as far back in your hand as you can. Then squeeze until the cards slide forward—this time along both thumb and finger—and are on the verge of springing away. Turn the deck on edge, hold your other hand below, and simply relax the upper hand. The preliminary squeeze has spaced all the cards in the pack, and they now drop in an even cascade.

9c. *Fanning.* More than any other flourish, fanning has to be taught by example rather than precept. Goodlette Dodson's *Exhibition Card Fans* and Lewis Ganson's *Expert Manipulation of Playing Cards* are the standard books on the subject, and I refer you to them for a full treatment. What follows is merely the rudiments that will be useful to the performer who does *not* intend to specialize in these showy moves.

Although you may quite properly be impressed by the skill of the fanning specialist, don't be swept off your feet. All specialists, whether in card fanning or in radio repair, have a great head start simply because they use adequate tools. Even Cardini could not make a very dazzling show with the dog-eared deck on which you practice shifts. And you, conversely, can produce some quite impressive fans if you follow the specialists' rule: a pack of brand-new, thin, glossy, flexible bridge cards for each performance; no shuffling or palming.

Your hands must be clean and dry; keep a towel handy to wipe off perspiration before you open.

Zinc stearate powder is sold by magic dealers, at a slight increase in price, under the name of "fanning powder."

One-handed fans are a necessity if you want to produce palmed or back-palmed cards. The quality of the cards is almost more important than the motion, which is simple.

For a right-handed forward fan, hold the deck with your thumb near the lower left-hand corner of the face, and your four fingers flat at the lower end of the back. Instead of attempting a curved motion, push your thumb straight to the right and your fingers straight to the left; then the fingers continue in a sort of smearing motion down the heel of the hand.

You can learn to make two-thirds of a circle with half the pack in this way.

A right-handed backward fan is made by closing the fingers into a fist and clipping the lower right corner of the cards between the thumb on the face and the knuckle of the forefinger on the back. The thumb then travels to the left, and the fingers are opened, so that the cards are spread across the four finger tips.

Left-handed fans, of course, are the other way around—to make a left-handed forward fan, you must copy the motion for a right-handed backward one.

Thumb fans need a very slick pack. Nip the deck upright between left thumb and second finger at the bottom center. Then just smear your right thumb from left to right, carrying your rear cards around in a circle.

Fundamentally the pressure fan is a variant of springing the cards. The theory is that you revolve the deck around your thumb, springing the cards away from your fingers and so depositing them in an evenly spaced fan.

With practice it might be possible simply to lay out a fan in this fashion on the table, but normally your left hand is a big help.

For a forward fan, hold out the pack upright in your right hand, thumb on the lower end, fingers on the upper. Put the root of your left forefinger slightly above the index of the bottom card and slope the rest of your finger down to the far bottom corner of the front card. This brings the left edge of the deck quite near the fork of your left thumb. Don't press down yet with your left thumb, though.

Pivot your right hand to the right around the thumb (which remains stationary at about the fork of your left middle fingers), springing the cards off your right finger tips as you go. At the same time, swing your left hand counterclockwise.

You probably won't make a very pretty fan the first time you try to follow these directions, but they are about all I can offer you. Keep trying until the fan is unbroken, and with time you can make almost a full circle.

The only difference in making a *backward* pressure fan is in the starting position. This time hold the deck out with the thumb end up. Lay your left third and little fingers across the upper end of the face, once more bringing your right thumb near the fork of the left middle fingers. Keep your left thumb entirely out of the way until the fan is finished.

Spring the cards as before, but revolve your right hand counterclockwise, your left hand clockwise.

It is not very difficult, comparatively speaking, to make such an even backward pressure fan that all the cards except the bottom one look blank. I have a habit of doing this with a borrowed deck, quickly laying my right hand over the bottom card, and saying, "I'm afraid I can't do much with a pack of cards that are all blank." Another way of using this same move is explained in chapter 4.

The famous trick of the Diminishing Cards (see chapter 4) was originally done by simply making smaller and smaller pressure fans. An extension, or perhaps a reversal, is the *giant fan.* The neatest way to make one is first to master another form of springing: the right hand holds the deck by the *side* edges near the top, springing the cards by bending them lengthwise instead of crosswise. The relative motions of the two hands are about the same as for an ordinary pressure fan.

To make a giant fan, you must divide a new deck quite accurately in half, and riffle the ends together very evenly, taking care that both the bottom and top cards in the shuffle come from the left-hand half. This, obviously, nearly doubles the length of the pack, which is then simply fanned as just described.

9d. The back palm. At the turn of the century the back palm seemed practically the be-all and end-all of card manipulation. Howard Thurston's *Tricks with Cards* (still a useful pamphlet if not taken too seriously) devotes a grand total of eight pages to the pass, force, change, and top palm; and nineteen pages to the back palm and its uses. For twenty years after its introduction in 1895, the back palm was a craze like a popular song. Like a popular song, it eventually wore everyone down. Jean Hugard's *Modern Magic Manual* does not even mention the back palm with cards.

I think it unkind to turn one's back completely on an old friend, and so I have included the back palm as a flourish instead of as a trick. In point of fact, the time will probably come surprisingly soon when back-

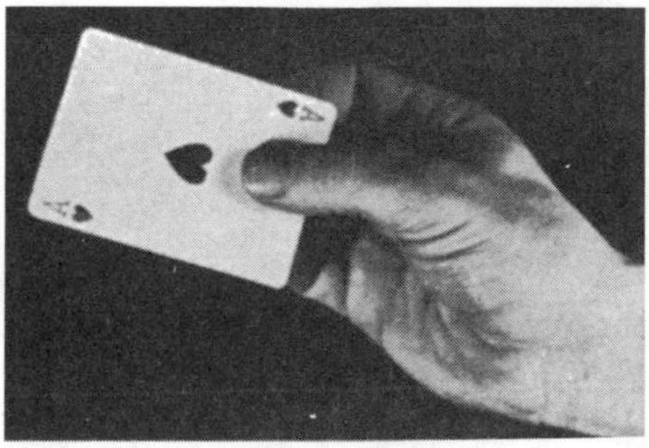

Fig. 66

palming is a novelty again. Individual tricks take on new life every fifteen years or so; I don't think you'll be sorry if you acquire the back palm.

Start with a card held about as in Fig. 66.

Curl in your middle fingers, and stretch your first and fourth fingers around the edges of the card (Fig. 67).

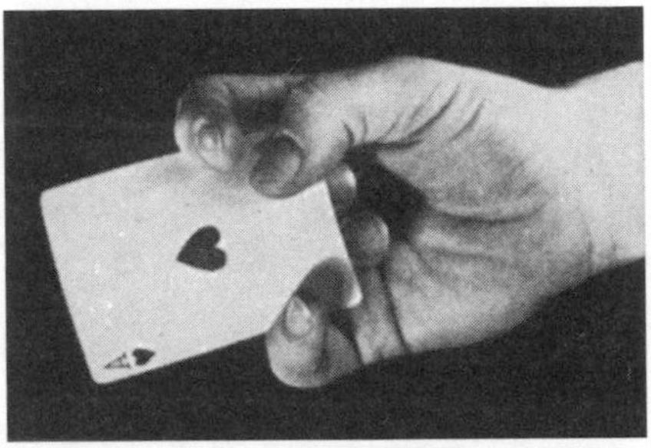

Fig. 67

Straighten your fingers and let go with your thumb (Fig. 68).

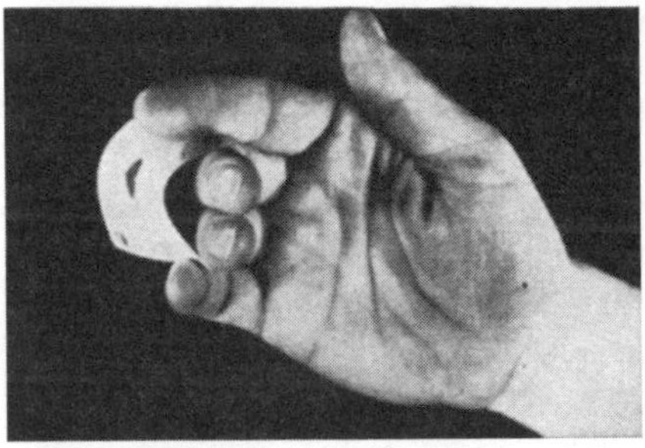

Fig. 68

When your hand is flat, it looks from the back as in Fig. 69.

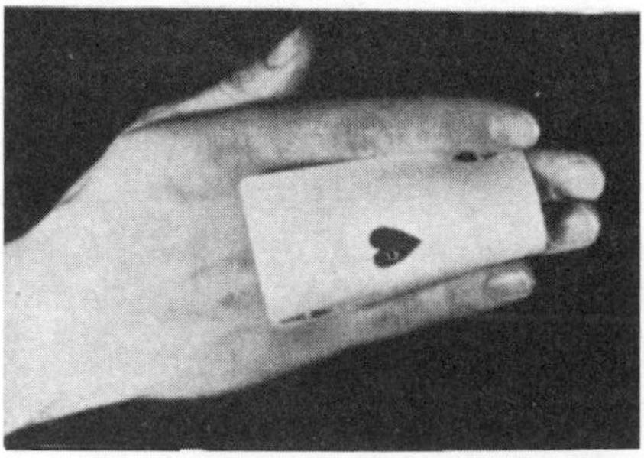

Fig. 69

Thus far the original back palm: a card disappears with a tossing motion, and the palm of your hand is empty. But audiences have grown sophisticated with the years; you are all too likely to hear the ominous mutter, "It's back of his hand." The next step, then, is to turn your hand over.

This you cannot very well learn without a mirror because the angles are the only hard part of the back palm. There is a roll of the wrist, keeping the card pointed straight to the rear, that only experiment can teach you.

The hand motion is simple: close your fist, putting your thumb on the face of the card (Fig. 70).

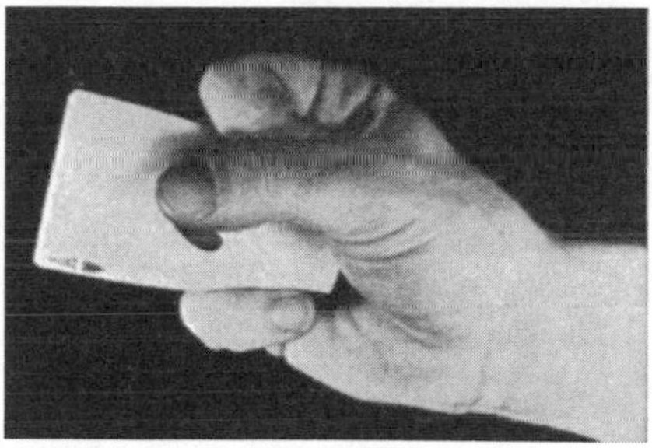

FIG. 70

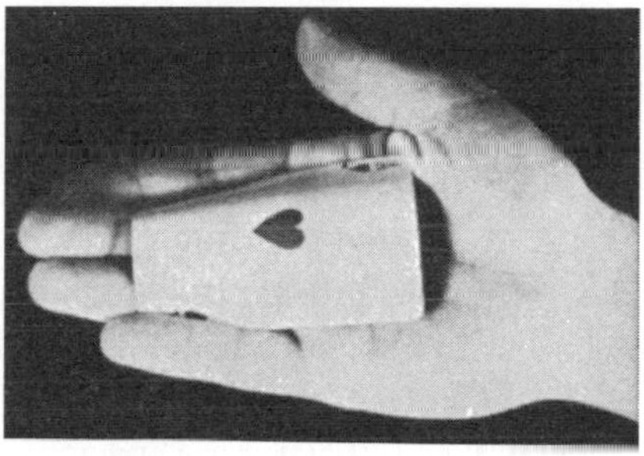

FIG. 71

Open out your hand, but don't let the card escape from your first and little fingers. Fig. 71 shows the result from behind.

The card can be produced at the finger tips from this position (sometimes known as the finger palm); but generally it is more convenient to return the card to the back.

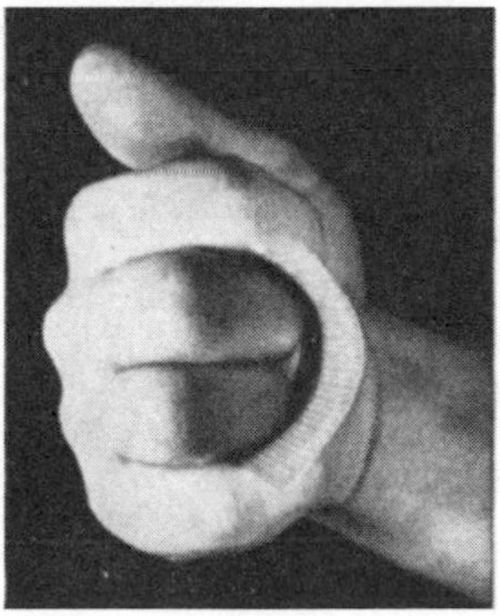

FIG. 72

Simply close your fist again, keeping your thumb out of the way (Fig. 72). Then open your hand, and the card is back-palmed again.

To re-produce the card, close your fingers enough to put your thumb on the index, and let the card snap forward.

You are still, however, in the kindergarten stages of back palming. Real virtuosity consists in doing the above motions with six or eight cards at once. (There have been performers who claimed they could back-palm a whole pack.) You will be surprised how little difference there is between back-palming one and back-palming half a dozen; the only additional risk is that your knuckles may dislodge the card nearest them.

A spectacular flourish is to hold four or five cards fanned. As your hand swoops down, your first and fourth fingers close and square the fan; as the hand goes up in the toss, back-palm the cards. You can show the back of your hand empty, then the front again. Make a snatch at the air, bring the cards forward, and instantly fan them.

The next step in proficiency is to vanish and reproduce the cards one at a time. Back-palm one card. Take another in the position of Fig. 66, and close your fingers, bringing the back-palmed card up behind the new one. Back-palm both together. Except for the noise, you shouldn't have much difficulty.

When they have vanished that way, you want to reproduce them one at a time. Close your fingers. Put your thumb on the near index corner of the front card and spring it over your forefinger (Fig. 73).

FIG. 73

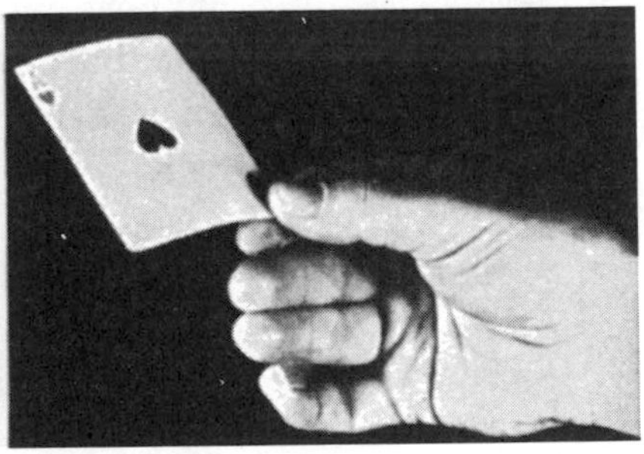

FIG. 74

Straighten your fingers, and the card snaps up as in Fig. 74 (which intentionally exposes the remaining back-palmed cards).

If you want to do back palming on any scale, you need soft, unglazed cards with no white border on the backs. Denver Plaids and 999 Steamboats have been the back-palmer's friends for half a century.

Example of a trick using the back palm: Vanish and Recovery. Neat and easy though it is (for a difficult sleight), the back palm is not truly magical. One glimpse behind the scenes blasts the illusion; and the motion of turning over the hand, though it may well be indetectable, is never natural.

So we put ingenuity to work and do a back-palm trick with just as little back palming as possible. Cardini's card act is almost entirely a back-palming and fanning routine; yet notice how small a part back palming really plays in it, compared to the effect produced. Cardini can do his act four-fifths surrounded on a night-club floor—a marvelous lesson in mastering angles.

You have just learned the means of back-palming five cards one after another, constantly showing the front and back of your hand, and then reproducing the cards. But as I say, this is a futile enterprise. Instead it should be done as follows:

Stand with your left side to the crowd, and the five cards fanned, faces forward, in your left hand.

Stretch out your right hand. Look at it. Close it and open it; turn it to and fro. People think you are just limbering up; but in addition, you are building up an association of moving your hand any way you like, uncramped by the restrictions of the back palm.

Take the nearest card from the fan, and toss it away by the back palm. Give people time to appreciate the empty right hand.

Take the second card and back-palm it also.

Then bring down your right hand to adjust the fan in your left. In doing so, leave the two back-palmed cards behind the present nearest card of the fan, clipped for the moment between your left first and second finger tips, behind the fan.

You have naturally withdrawn your right hand from the fan to survey the effect of the rearrangement. Now take a look at the right hand, spread the fingers slightly, and turn it over.

Come down with your right hand, and pick up together the near card of the fan and the other two hidden behind it. Back-palm them.

Take and back-palm the fourth. This one time you may do a back-and-front reverse with the four cards.

Come down to take the last card; and in the act, bring the back-palmed cards around to where you can palm them all in your left hand, which you do before the right hand moves away with the fifth card.

Back-palm that. You can do another reversing movement if you think best.

Pause. Look around as if hunting for the cards.

Reproduce the one card in your right hand.

Then reach behind your left knee with your left hand, and bring out the four palmed cards in a fan.

Even with absolute perfection of back palming on your part, people have a shrewd idea that something fishy is going on as the cards vanish. But when they suddenly reapppear in the wrong hand, the surprise is complete. Used after this fashion, the back palm ceases to be labored manipulation, and becomes magical again.

9e. Scaling or throwing cards. One of the best-remembered features of Howard Thurston's show was the hundreds of cards he hurled (often by twos and threes) all over the house, including the back of the second balcony. Of course every child in the theater clamored for a card. Thurston improved the opportunity to throw advertising cards, which were also heavier than playing cards and had correspondingly more range.

The flourish itself is probably two hundred years old—at least.

Clip the card by the upper right-hand corner between your right second and third fingers. Curve your hand back toward the wrist, then straighten it with a jerk. This sends the card out, spinning in a horizontal plane. (Caution: don't aim it straight at the audience—the edge of the card can inflict an unpleasant cut in the face.)

To give the card a reverse movement, yank your hand sharply back as the card takes flight. With a little practice, this will bring the card out and then back to you like a boomerang, and you can either catch it in a split you open in the pack, nip it between thumb and forefinger, or cut it in two with a pair of scissors.

If you turn it face up before throwing, you can make it dart back into the pack just below a selected card where you have been holding a break.

4. *Give Them a Rest—*
Tricks Where No Cards Are Chosen

THIS chapter may please experienced magicians more than its does learners. After two or three decades of conjuring, one begins to think, "If he has another card chosen, replaced, and shuffled, I shall scream out loud." In fact, this chapter very nearly got an independent start as a professional reference book for magicians.

So long as having cards chosen is still a novelty to you, it will probably please your audiences. It does give them a certain sense of participation, and the actual choosers always go away much impressed. You can have cards chosen to your heart's content in the next chapter; here, however, is a round-up of tricks new and old in which the conjurer does the work.

Incidentally, this is the only sort of card effect suited to an audience of children, because the cards are objects and not individuals. Even these tricks, obviously, vary in their suitability for a children's show.

You have already, in mastering the sleights, encountered four of these tricks: Charles Bertram's Four-Ace Trick; the Phoney Aces; Wiping Out the Spot; and the Vanish and Recovery. You will find a number of other beauties under head magic.

Meanwhile, here are some more.

1. *The Four Aces.* This ancient trick has several forms with different effects and many methods for each effect. Downs's *Art of Magic*, Hilliard's *Greater Magic*, and Hugard and Braue's *Expert Card Technique* each have a chapter devoted entirely to the four-ace trick.

There are two main effects: dealing out a row of aces with three indifferent cards on each, then magically gathering the aces into one pile; and dispersing the aces throughout the pack, then reassembling them somewhere.

Of the first type, Charles Bertram's method, already described, is at least as good as any other.

Here is a variant, from *The Art of Magic.* A spectator puts the four aces on the pack. You shift three to the bottom, then deal the remaining ace and three odd cards on the table.

Deal three more indifferent cards on each of the three alleged aces.

Shift the three real aces from the bottom to the top. Now, pretending that you want some particular card, do a quadruple lift with the three aces and the odd card below it; give everyone a casual glimpse. Pick up two or three more cards, and glance at them. Drop the whole handful back on the deck and deal the three aces on the tabled ace.

The build-up follows much the same lines as Bertram's, without the by-play of loading cards into the spectator's pocket.

A very neat and clean-looking method is the one ascribed to the English magician, Stanley Collins. You deal the four aces face up, and three indifferent cards face up on each ace. Turning each packet over, you draw the cards from the bottom, and again lay them face up on the table. The aces have vanished completely. You then deal four heaps of four off the pack, and the aces reappear in the chosen pile.

The chief special difficulty of this trick is to get the knack of dealing two cards as one. It is a close relative of the double lift, which can in fact be made to do duty for it.

Pick out, or have someone else pick out, the four aces. Drop them in a row face up on the table. On the first ace, deal two cards face up as one, then two more, fairly. Apparently there is an ace partly hidden by three indifferent cards.

Do the same with the other three aces.

Now pick up the first pile and hold it face down in your left hand, ready for the glide. Honestly draw the bottom card and lay it neatly face up on the table; the same with the second card.

Draw back the third card, and take the remaining two cards as one, laying them also on the pile. The hidden one is the ace. Finally turn over the last card (the one you had drawn back a moment before) and lay it down. The ace is gone.

Repeat with the other three piles.

Gather up the piles, and put them on the pack.

You can now choose between automatic working and strict consistency. If you deal the first *five* cards face down in a row, and keep on dealing until you have five heaps of four, the middle heap will contain all the aces.

If you insist on four piles, you must shift every fifth card to the bottom during the deal, in which case the aces will be in the second pile from the right.

You can then force the ace pile however you like.

The other branch of the four-ace family will be represented here by three specimens.

The first and oldest, the *Red and Black Aces,* is still spry after a century or more.

The aces of one color—say black—are put at the top and bottom of the pack, and the aces of the other color in the middle. You challenge people to remember which is which; a moment later, the blacks are in the middle and the reds at top and bottom.

You do it over again, to see if they can't remember by trying very hard; and all four aces appear in the middle.

The only sleight involved is a smooth and quick two-handed shift (chapter 3, section 2*a*). Give someone the aces, and ask him to put one on the bottom of the pack, its mate on the top, and the two of the other color in the middle of the pack, which you cut at that point to help him.

Then drop the upper half on the aces. Fan the pack slightly, leaving all the aces sticking out at the far end; hold up the fan so that everyone can see the aces are where they purport to be.

This slight fanning makes it easy for you in closing up the cards to get a little-finger separation between the middle two aces.

"All right, now: where did we put the black aces?" When you say this, people glance first at your face, giving you a brief but sufficient opportunity to make the two-handed shift, and then back at the deck, which by then should look undisturbed.

"On the top and bottom," they tell you.

"And the red ones in the middle," you add. "Are you sure? If you can't remember any better than that, I'm afraid I shall have to start over."

So saying, you fan the deck face up, showing that the aces have changed places.

Have someone take the aces out of the fan again, and put one pair back on the top and bottom. (For some reason the volunteer usually reverses the original arrangement—a point that might by ingenuity be worked into a routine of your own as a surprise element.)

Make the shift, bringing the two (probably red) aces to the middle. With your right thumb and second finger, holding the ends of the upper half, lift the top ace from the lower half.

Hold out your left hand to have the black aces put on top of the lower half. Then drop the upper half on these; but drop the lower red ace first, then get a little-finger separation *between* the red aces, which of course are above the black aces.

Make the pass with rather a flourish of your hands: just this once you want people to suspect that something is going on.

"Now this time let's see if we can't remember. Where were the red aces?"

People are quite likely to say, "They *were* on the top and bottom," or even straight out, "In the middle."

"That's right, they are on the top and bottom," you say. Turn up the top card, a red ace. (The black aces are right under it, so you do *not* do a double lift.) Put back the top ace, and in the act get a little-finger separation about the middle of the pack with your left hand.

Grasp the pack with your right hand in readiness for the standard shift. Then turn both hands over, exposing the bottom card of the pack —the other red ace. In turning your hands back to the normal position, you have complete cover for the shift, which you execute.

"Now just once more: what's on top and bottom?"

"Red," they tell you, reassured at last.

Turn the deck over, and fan it out. The aces are all in the middle. "Well, I'm afraid we'll have to give this up for a bad job."

Nate Leipzig's "Slap" Aces is the late master's development of the preceding effect. He asked for two volunteers, to each of whom he handed two aces as he sorted them out of the face-up pack. The right-hand volunteer put his aces on the top and bottom. The left-hand man put his two in the middle. Leipzig then slapped the pack, and all the aces vanished; he ran over the entire deck, and there were no aces.

Then he slapped the face of the deck and brought back one ace; another; and another. Finally one of the volunteers brought back the last ace by tapping the face of the pack himself.

If you have paid attention to the previous chapter, you can figure out your own working. Leipzig's actual routine was to have the first two aces put on the top and bottom. Then he showed them in position, for emphasis. He made the shift, and picked up the top ace of the lower half with his right hand as in the preceding trick, holding a right thumb break below this ace, and taking the entire pack in his right hand. He then asked the man on his left to put the two aces in the middle. By way of giving a perfectly free choice, he dropped a few cards at a time into his left palm until he hit the break. Then he stopped, and the man put in his aces. Leipzig next dropped the ace he had picked up, closed the deck, and made the shift. So far, his moves were substantially the old ones. He then showed the right-hand man the top and bottom aces, put them back, carelessly fanned the pack a little, and said to the man at his left,

"And your two are in the middle." The fact that no one saw them made not the slightest difference.

He next offered to make the aces vanish from the pack by slapping it. As he spoke, he brought the bottom two cards of the pack to the top. If you have perfect control of the side steal, you can steal the bottom two cards instead of one; the clip color-change steal (chapter 3, section 7*a*) will also do the work; so will the Herrmann pass (2*c*), made a few seconds later, though this is a less favorable moment. At all events, any move you use brings all four aces together, with one indifferent card on top.

Leipzig slapped the top of the pack with his right hand, then turned up the top card—not an ace. He stuck this card carelessly into the middle, leaving the aces on top. He turned over the pack to show the bottom (this is the time for the Herrmann shift, only for it you will have to show the bottom card before you show the top).

While everyone was stunned at the disappearance of the top and bottom aces, Leipzig palmed off the top five or six cards—not less than four—in his right hand. He took the pack face outward in the crotch of his right thumb and fanned it a card at a time with his left thumb, showing that the aces were indeed all gone. This position gave perfect cover to the palmed cards.

He brought his left hand across the face of the fan, and with his second finger pulled the cards square from right to left, then took the pack in dealing position. In squaring up with the right hand, he left the palmed aces on top.

Turning the deck over, Leipzig now reproduced three aces in succession by "slapping the pack," using the side-steal color change. After the second card, he would stall, holding his right hand (with which he had been making the slaps) half closed and stealing covert glances at it. He would whisper to the right-hand volunteer to grab his arm. Finally, reluctantly, Leipzig would turn over his hand—empty. A moment later he would make his side steal undetected and bring back the third ace.

He then brought the fourth ace to the bottom, but kept the deck face downward as he told one of the volunteers that the trick was quite easy—the assistant himself had only to tap the cards, so. The volunteer obeyed, and sure enough, there was the ace on the bottom.

Cardini's Ace Trick (which I learned from the excellent description at page 545 of Hilliard's *Greater Magic*) is the quickest and perhaps the most novel of the lot. It can also be done over and over, giving great scope for the comedy of repetition.

The effect is that the four aces are stuck into different parts of the fanned deck, which is closed and shuffled. The aces thereupon reappear at the bottom.

There are two secret moves, both peculiar to this trick, though they can also be put to other uses. The first is a form of push-through that leaves the four aces in-jogged. The second is a diagonal-jog move that strips the aces out during an overhand shuffle.

Make a wide pressure fan with the cards faced toward the audience. Then insert the four aces, well separated, into the fan, leaving perhaps two-thirds of each ace projecting. Give everyone time to appreciate this. Close the fan, with the aces still sticking out, and hold the deck in Charlier-pass position (chapter 3, section 2*f*) in the left hand, only get your little finger out of the way. Cover the pack with your right hand, thumb at the near left corner, all four fingers on the far end of the aces. Apparently the fingers push the aces square. Actually, your first finger, on the extreme left corner of the aces, twists them to the left and travels down past the far left corner of the deck, pushing the aces before it. The near left corners of the aces thus clear your right thumb, and the aces are projecting diagonally from the pack under cover of your right hand.

With your left little finger, push against the projecting edges of the aces. Take your right thumb away, and the aces will be square along the sides, but in-jogged—the same principle as the false dovetail shuffle (chapter 3, section 5*b*).

At this point you can, if you like, depart from Cardini's routine by turning to the Hindu shuffle and simply stripping out the jogged aces, slapping them on top, then undercutting, holding a right second-finger break, shuffling off to the break, and throwing on top. Run four and shuffle off. The aces are at the bottom.

Cardini's own method is less bald. He puts the pack in his cupped right hand, ready for an overhand shuffle. He puts his left thumb against the upper near corner of the in-jogged aces and pushes up and away from him. This reverses his original move, jogging all the aces again diagonally, and his thumb catches both the corner of the pack and the jogged corners of the aces. He shuffles off to the first ace, then picks up all four by the upper corners with one motion between his left thumb and second finger, strips them out of the pack as it sits in his right hand, and throws them on top. He then runs four and shuffles off.

The necessary shuffling is very brief, and the reappearance of the aces at the bottom when the deck is fanned is a complete surprise.

2. *The Cards up the Sleeve.* This is another old-time stand-by, and a classic test of a competent performer. The name describes it: cards ap-

parently pass up your sleeve from your left hand, arriving (in most modern versions) in your right trouser pocket.

The trick is a test of ability because the method—ordinary top palming —is the first thing an audience would naturally look for. Misdirection, backed by smooth, effortless palming, is your only safeguard in this effect.

You will undoubtedly develop your own routine, which will serve you far better than any I offer here. Let me warn you merely that the earliest form of the trick was comparatively poor for two reasons: the effect was complicated by introducing a chosen card; and the whole pack was passed up the sleeve and inside the waistcoat, which tended to grow rather tiresome. On the other hand, you may well like to show the trick with more than the now customary ten or twelve cards, giving the effect of profusion without its tedium.

There is one new sleight to learn—the false count—and one very useful ruse—the top-of-pocket dodge.

The purpose of the false count is to prove that you hold more cards than you actually have. First get the habit of making an honest count in the appropriate fashion: hold the cards (usually just a few) in a modified dealing position in your left hand, all four finger tips at the right edge, the thumb tip just above the second finger tip. Slide forward the top card. With your right second finger and thumb, take the card near the right edge and draw it off the pile downward, with a snapping sound.

Bring your right hand back, lay its card over the end joint of your left thumb, and pinch the second card of the pile with your right second finger, under the card you already have in your right hand. Draw the two together off and down, again with a snapping sound. This motion is simply repeated, each time adding one more card to the bottom of the stack in your right hand.

The snapping noise is the key to the sleight. When you want to false-count, simply draw back with your left thumb the card you have just pushed forward. The snap and the motion of the right hand are perfectly deceptive. If you keep the backs of the cards toward the audience, there is simply no way to tell that you have not taken another card.

The top-of-pocket gag means simply that if you poke any moderate-sized object into the upper far corner of a trouser pocket, the pocket can be turned inside out and still seem empty.

For the sake of example I shall give a routine with ten cards. You can improve it to use twelve or twenty, with any variations you think good. Anyhow, here is my own way.

Count ten cards off the pack, and put the pack aside.

Count them over again with the false-count motions, but slowly, with the faces toward the audience. Ask people if they care to remember a few of the individual cards.

In counting, in-jog the fourth card (chapter 3, section 5*a*).

Take the cards in your left hand, square them with your right, and palm off the three above the jog. Take the cards in your right hand, and stretch out your left, as you explain that the cards will go from this hand up your sleeve, around your back, and down to your right trouser pocket. Take the cards back in your left hand.

Reach into trouser pocket, stuff the palmed cards into the upper corner, and pull the pocket inside out.

If you *must* make a joke at this point, see that it is a good one.

Push the pocket back in, quietly letting people see that your right hand is empty.

"Now we'll make the first one go." Stretch your left arm out straight.

Snap the lower corner of the cards with your left third finger. "There!"

Pursue the supposed flight of the card with your right hand. Again let everyone see that your palm is empty; then plunge your hand into your pocket, and bring out one card.

"One gone leaves how many?"

Actually you have seven, so you false-count at about the third and fifth cards, apparently counting nine.

Another card goes. Hand empty again. Another false count.

The same sequence again.

This exhausts the three cards in your pocket. In counting the remaining seven, in-jog the fourth, palm off three, and follow the motions for passing the previous cards. Plunge your hand straight into the pocket—don't wince or hesitate because of the palmed cards!—fish around in the pocket, look puzzled, and finally bring your hand out empty. No card has passed.

Dawn of intelligence: "They sometimes catch at the elbow." Give a hitch to the elbow of your left sleeve with your right hand. "Yup! There they go! The line was clogged."

This time you do show your right hand empty before bringing out a card. You will notice that no cards have been produced immediately after palming; the hand has been empty just before each card came out.

False-count the remaining four cards as six.

This time make an extra loud snap with your third finger. "I think I got two that time." Sure enough, even though your right hand is empty, out come two cards.

Spread the remaining four, and call attention to which ones they are. Close up the fan and palm off two.

"Sometimes if I'm very quick I can stop them up in here," you say, thrusting your right hand inside the left shoulder of your coat. Leave the palmed cards behind.

Make the third-finger snap, and instantly slap the shoulder of your coat from outside with your right hand, as if to check the flying cards.

"Got 'em!"

Instead of reaching in, draw back your coat with your left hand. Two cards thus come forward on their own.

You now have only two left. Call attention to them, turn them face outward, and side-steal the back one. Make your snap; show some doubt about where the card went; and finally reach for your trouser pocket, whence you produce the card.

The disappearance of the last card is so difficult that it must be carried off by sheer gall. You can hold the card by the edges at your left finger tips, quickly palm it in your right hand, slap your left palm with your right, and make a tossing motion with both hands (don't forget to look up as you do so). Then you produce the palmed card from your pocket.

You may apparently take the card crossways with its face to your left palm, actually back-palming it in your right hand. Reverse the card to the front under cover of the distraction as you stretch out your left fist to the left, with a crumpling motion as if to wad up the card.

You may prefer to pass two or three instead of one at the last.

There are other passes for the same purpose (see C. Lang Neil, *The Modern Conjurer*; Jean Hugard, *Modern Magic Manual*; and Camille Gaultier, *Magic Without Apparatus*), but I have never thought them altogether convincing.

Here are a few variations.

You can let a spectator take some of the cards from your pocket after you have loaded in a batch.

You can palm off several cards, turn and engage in talk with some spectator on your right, gesturing to him with the cards in your left hand, and under this cover slide the palmed cards into your right sleeve. Then you offer to pass some cards up one sleeve and down the other, which you make good by shaking the cards from your right sleeve.

If you can do it without confusing the effect, you may pass cards alternately up both sleeves, using the Erdnase bottom palm (4c) for some of your steals.

You can load a few cards under the right edge of your vest by changing from the palm position, sliding the cards toward the heel of your hand, and clipping them with your bent second finger. This frees the upper ends of the cards, which slide easily under the vest.

So long as the effect is straightforward and the method reasonably devious, you can count on a big success with the Cards Up the Sleeve however you perform it.

3. *The Diminishing Cards.* I have already mentioned Robert-Houdin's method of doing this trick with the whole pack by simply reducing the size of the fan he made. That is still a useful dodge today, when the pack has been pared down to half a dozen cards.

Originally the diminishing-cards effect was almost always shown as a sequel to the Cards up the Sleeve, by way of explanation. You say your secret is to make the cards small so that they will go easily up the sleeve.

Whether or not you adopt this time-honored presentation, the trick should really follow on some other feat, rather than be shown baldly for its own sake.

Again there are several methods of working. Most of them properly belong under apparatus magic in that they require specially prepared sets of small cards. Some of these sets fold in order to grow smaller; others have a sort of pocket at the back to hold successive smaller sets; still others merely have one corner fastened with thread.

If you want to buy such an outfit, the dealer will show you how to use it. All I am going to give you here is a homemade method that I used for years when I was quite young, which required no store-bought apparatus, and never gave me any trouble.

You *will* have to buy two packs of miniature cards, one of them half the standard poker size, the other a quarter the size. If you can't buy them, you may have to manufacture them. You also need a small black elastic band.

As you may have gathered, the effect is that you display a fan of cards, close it, squeeze it, and fan it again, whereupon the cards prove to have grown smaller. You do this six times in all, and at last the cards disappear completely.

Take five or six cards—a mixed lot, an ace on the front is a good idea —from your half-sized pack. Take the same cards from the smallest pack, and arrange them in the same order. Finally, take the same cards from a regular pack. If you are planning to use the trick to follow Cards up the Sleeve, you should take care that these are among the cards you make pass.

Square up the smallest cards, and put them face upward across one end of the face of the half-sized cards. Then put the elastic lengthwise around the center of the smallest cards, which is to say crosswise around the end of the half-sized set. If the elastic is very tiny, it need go only once around; an ordinary small rubber band goes twice around, holding the bundle of cards snugly but not tightly. The elastic must not slip off; yet you must be able to push it off easily when you wish.

With this bundle of cards, face outward, smallest cards across the lower end, in a left-hand pocket, and your normal cards at hand, you are ready to begin. There should also be a number of cards scattered at random, partially hidden, on the table.

Either as you stand talking or as you gather up the appropriate cards with your right hand, palm the bundle in your left hand, the smallest cards at the outer end. You will find this puts the latter in a position where you can hold them against the third joints of your middle fingers by simply bending those fingers. As yet you need not do this.

Take the regular cards in your left hand, thumb on the back, fingers on the face. Fan the cards widely with your right hand, then display them at the extreme finger tips of your left.

Explain that you can make them shrink by squeezing them. Give people a chance to see that your right palm is empty as you close up the fan. Cover the cards with your right palm, slide them part way down into your left hand, and make the gesture of squeezing with your right fingers.

Don't remove your right hand and expose the cards until you have fanned them again, much less widely than before. Then take your hand away, giving just a glimpse of the empty palm.

The cards are half way down in your hand, and barely fanned, so they look smaller; you say they are smaller; and people begin to believe it. Reach over to the table, pick up a card, and poke it part way into the fan by way of comparison. It projects, apparently proving your point. Drop the card back on the table.

Now, with your left forefinger, work the elastic off the bundle of small cards. You can drop it on the floor or not; it will be unnoticed in any case.

Close up your fan, go through your squeezing motion, and palm the full-sized cards in your right hand.

Before you take your right hand away, grab the half-sized cards between forefinger and thumb at the upper left corner (next to the root of your left thumb), and so twist them to an upright position at your left finger tips. Fan them. (You can't make a pressure fan without showing the palmed cards; so just spread them out by pushing with your thumb.)

This, of course, leaves the smallest cards secured in the bend of your left middle fingers—the position known as finger-palming (see chapter 6, section 2). Don't lose them; it takes almost no grip to hold them.

Reach over to the table again for your comparison card and, in doing so, drop the palmed cards from your right hand out of sight. If your body comes between the table and the audience at the moment of dropping, the cards will afterward be indistinguishable from the others scattered on the table.

Stick in your comparison card (naturally it mustn't be a duplicate of one in the fan).

This time the cards are smaller beyond all question. Give people time to get it. After you put down the comparison card, run the little ones from hand to hand. This is where you have the advantage over the prepared outfits, which can be fanned only mechanically, and tend not to look like real cards as they grow smaller.

Close up your fan, squeeze, and repeat your earlier bluff of half fanning. Pick up and use your comparison card; toss it back on the table; close the fan.

Squeeze, palm the half-sized cards, and lift the smallest ones straight to your left finger tips with your right forefinger and thumb.

Spread the smallest fan wide; then get rid of the half-sized cards in picking up the good old comparison card. This time you do need a crumpled handkerchief, book, or other obstacle to hide the medium set, unless you are lucky enough to buy miniature cards whose backs blend pretty closely with the regular deck you are using.

The next reduction—a bluff—is just like the previous one.

Finally, close up your tiny fan, and finger-palm it in your right hand. Hold up your left hand with the fingers bunched, as if the cards were still there. Reach one last time for the comparison card, unloading the miniatures in the act.

Look intently at the "fan" behind your left finger tips; wave the comparison card at it.

Turn your left hand around, palm to the audience, tips of second finger and thumb pressed together.

"That's as small as they'll go." Part your finger and thumb.

That's all.

4. *The Thirty-Card Trick* (also called *The Twenty-Card Trick*). This is another classic effect in which the cards are simply pieces of pasteboard

rather than identities. The trick is so simple that it has never impressed me as anything very startling, when you consider what a magician *can* do. But I know I am wrong, because after a long, long life it is still a show piece. Blackstone and Mulholland performed it; so did Nate Leipzig, and it remains a great favorite with audiences.

Two spectators help you. They count out thirty cards (or twenty), and each man takes half. They may hold the cards between their palms, wrapped up in handkerchiefs, or buttoned into inner pockets. Anyway, you make several cards pass from one man's custody to the other's.

The traditional method of doing this feat seemed to give considerable latitude in the number of cards passed, and further made the division of the thirty at random instead of into exact halves. I think the modern simplification is much better because the one weak point in the original effect is the constant dealing, counting, adding, and subtracting.

It is quicker and more striking, as well as easier, to have two piles of fifteen; then bing, bing, bing—three cards pass. One more count, and the trick is done.

In method you have a choice: the plain palming that was good enough for Robert-Houdin (and is good enough for me); or the steal recommended by Blackstone.

First I will give the traditional routine, then Blackstone's.

Bring two volunteers forward.

Rapidly deal off fifteen cards to one man, then fifteen more to the other. Have each man pick up his cards. Ask them to count together, dealing their cards down as they do so—one, two, three, up to fifteen. This counting is for emphasis because the number used is really important. When the two men count together, it saves even the simple arithmetic of dividing thirty by two, and takes just half as long.

Ask the man on your left to empty his inner breast pocket. As you speak to him, pick up his heap of cards and palm off three in your right hand. Hand him his pile; ask him to put it in the now empty breast pocket, and button his coat.

You have one contingency to face at this point. Just possibly your right-hand assistant may be of such a quick and eager disposition that he empties his pocket without being told. Unless he also seizes upon the cards, there is no grave harm done.

If he has taken up the cards, make him take them out and tell him that you want *him* to hold them between his palms, *so*. That, of course, adds your palmed three cards to his fifteen.

If you think he looks eager, you may keep him out of mischief by having him count his cards again.

At all events, you add your palmed cards to the fifteen in charge of the right-hand man.

The whole value of the feat lies in the build-up from here on. Of course the dirty work is all done; now it rests with you to challenge your assistants—bet them they can't hold tight, bet them they can't see the cards go, bet them they can't feel them arrive. Point out that each volunteer counted his own cards and put them into his own pocket. Point out that you aren't coming near either man, much less his cards.

Well, then, here we go: first card, plunk. Second card, plunk. Third card, plunk.

Standing well back, ask the men to take out their cards, and count them in unison.

The left-hand man has twelve. The right-hand man has eighteen.

Blackstone's routine uses twenty cards, ten in each heap. The first volunteer counts ten cards into your left palm, and takes up his post on your left. You stretch out your left arm, and throw a handkerchief over the elbow.

The second volunteer counts ten cards into your right palm, and stands on that side.

Push forward the top three cards of the left-hand packet, rather as if you were dealing thirds instead of seconds.

Turn your left side forward, and hitch up your left elbow to call attention to the handkerchief, at the same time asking the man on your right to take it.

This brings your hands together, and allows you to toss or drop the three projecting cards from the left hand on or under the right-hand packet (like half of a good top change).

The moment the volunteer takes the handkerchief, separate your hands widely. Give him the right-hand packet, and have him wrap it in the middle of the handkerchief.

In this version you start by keeping the left-hand cards yourself. Riffle to make the first card go. False-count (section 2) your seven cards as nine.

Another riffle, another false count.

The last time, you give the cards to the man on your left, and he finishes by counting seven himself. The other man opens up the handkerchief, and counts out thirteen.

A striking and logical variation is to give one man red-backed cards, the other man blue-backed cards. In the traditional routine, use the

Erdnase bottom palm (chapter 3, section 4*c*) instead of the top palm, and add the palmed cards to the bottom of the right-hand packet. In Blackstone's version, your right thumb must pick up a card or two from its pile before you make the steal or else simply drop the three cards under instead of on top.

This variant needs more nerve than the usual method because you must still let the volunteers handle the cards. If all the motions are made carefully but casually, the wrong-colored cards will never show too soon; however, you may be some time learning to believe this.

5. *More flourishes.* These two pranks are the last I shall give in which the cards have no identity.

One you are already familiar with. Perhaps no one who did not see it done by the late Nelson Downs has any idea how irresistibly comical it can be.

Stand with your right side to the audience, holding eight or ten cards fanned face forward in your right hand.

Close the fan by snapping it into the fork of your left thumb, and with the same motion palm the cards in your right hand. Slap your left palm, then move both hands up in identical tossing gestures. This, combined with your quick upward gaze, somehow makes people quite forget that they can't see your right palm.

Stand for a moment with uplifted hands, gaping ceilingward. When I say gaping, I mean let your mouth hang open.

Bring both hands to your mouth, the right a trifle in advance. Thrust the upper end of the cards into your mouth, and then instantly start sliding them into a downward ribbon with both forefingers on the face and both thumbs on the back, the front cards descending first.

The display made by even half a dozen cards in this fashion is amazing.

The next flourish is a brief startler known as the Fan Away.

If you care to use the misdirection explained in chapter 3, 7*a* for stealing cards from the back of the deck, do. In any case, palm about three-quarters of the pack with its face to your right palm, leaving the remainder face outward in your left hand. Produce the palmed stack in a nice, smooth one-handed fan from behind your right knee or left elbow, and plant yourself with your right side to the audience.

Make a few fanning motions, turning your left hand thumb downward as you do so.

Turn your left hand over once more, showing that its cards are still there. More fanning; turn your left hand again. You will find it easy to arrange your hands so that for just an instant the left hand ducks behind the fan as the left thumb moves down.

This is the moment when you drop the cards from your left hand face forward against the back of the fan, to be caught by your right third and little fingers.

The left hand, of course, turns straight on over as if it still held the cards, and your eyes follow it.

Make two or three more fanning motions, at the same time spreading the stolen cards as best you can toward your right wrist.

Whoops! Your left hand is empty, and an extra-wide swing of the fan shows no extra cards in front or behind.

In the earliest method of doing the Fan Away, the cards fell into the crook of the extended second finger, and the back of the fan had to be hidden.

Try this way a few times before a mirror, and then try it on your friends.

6. *The Ambitious Card.* This effect is often shown with a chosen card, but I see no advantage in it. The trick is a made-to-order opener, especially for an impromptu routine. All opening effects should be quick and striking, putting you at once on the footing you are going to maintain with your audience. Some conjurers treat their audience more pompously than others; accordingly one performer may have to begin solemnly with the Vanish and Recovery, while his colleague sets a mood of horseplay with Wiping out the Spot.

The Ambitious Card, done without too much patter, falls between these extremes. (As a general thing opening effects should not have much patter; it slows them down. And they should never need *any* volunteer help from the audience, for the same reason.)

If you want to show the effect with some particular, conspicuous card —such as the joker—find it and cut it to the bottom of the pack.

The original plot of the Ambitious Card, which strikes me as unnecessarily labored, is that certain cards are ambitious of eminence and will always rise to the top of the deck. Personally I prefer to assert that the pack is made up wholly of one card, and wherever you look, you find another joker (or whatever it is).

I give my routine because I know it works, but you will soon see that every move in the book can be made to serve for the Ambitious Card. Build your own routine and have something nobody has ever shown before.

Your card (call it the joker) is at the bottom of the pack. Make a backward pressure fan, showing a blank expanse with the joker on the front. "Why, the pack is all jokers!"

Close the fan; get a little-finger separation; make the shift in turning the deck face down, and hold the break below the joker. Cut the pack at the break, turning the upper half face upward with your right hand: another joker.

Replace the upper half, side-stealing the joker in your right hand; drop it on top. The top card: another joker.

Turn it up honestly, but with your double-lift motion. Slowly and ostentatiously slide the joker under the next card. Square up. Double-lift (chapter 3, section 6*a*): another joker.

Replace the double card, then take off the actual top card, and push it slowly into the pack half way down. Remaining on top is another joker.

Make the two-handed shift (chapter 3, section 2*d*), holding the break. Cut off the upper half with your right hand, and turn over the top card of the lower half between the tips of your right first and second fingers: another joker.

Turn it back in the same way, holding a little-finger break *below* it. Replace the top half and make either the standard shift or the Herrmann pass. The bottom card is a joker.

Another backward pressure fan shows the deck still "all jokers."

If you want to get rid of the joker, do a double lift with the bottom card (turning the deck so that no one sees its face card, which is not a joker), and then make the snap change (chapter 3, 7*d*).

You will notice that I haven't even touched on what you might do by second-dealing, standard changes, or palming.

7. *The Three-Card Trick.* This famous effect is like the rabbit from the hat in that it is practically considered synonymous with card conjuring, yet very few magicians show it any more. It is the direct opposite of chosen-card tricks: you nominate a card, and defy the spectator to find it.

Some operators use a queen and two odd cards; this version is called "Find the Lady." For one clever bit of misdirection you must use a black ace and the two red aces. One inferior method with prepared cards uses the ace, deuce, and trey of diamonds. Those cards have the advantage that anyone who has bought a set of the prepared cards will suspect you of the same—until you hand him your cards.

The methods are many, the routines innumerable. Camille Gaultier's *Magic Without Apparatus* devotes fifteen pages to the trick. Ever-reliable old Erdnase gives nearly as much useful information in eight pages.

The standard method is to show the three cards as in Fig. 75, two cards (one of them the ace) in the right hand, one in the left. Both hands are palm upward. It is customary to crimp the cards lengthwise rather more than is shown in the photograph, simply so that you can pick them up easily by the ends.

Turning both hands over, you lightly fling down the ace, instantly shifting your right second finger to the corner of the card behind it; then you throw the other card from your right hand, meanwhile dropping the third (the trey in the picture) from your left.

Fig. 75

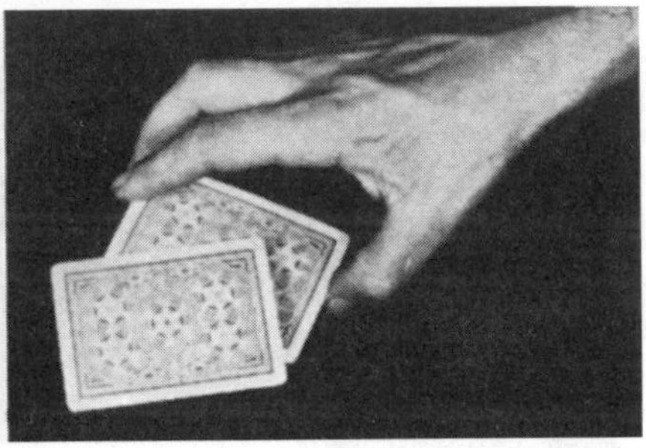

Fig. 76

It is now perfectly easy to spot the ace, which of course is the middle one in the row of three cards you have laid down. Pick the cards up again in your starting position; then throw them down again.

The one secret move that you introduce is to throw the top instead of the bottom card from your right hand (Fig. 76). The moment either top or bottom card is thrown, shift your right first and second fingers, so that in either case there will be no difference in how you hold the remaining card.

You need not always lay the cards down, even apparently, in one-two-three order; you should introduce some confusion by varying the sequence. You may also throw the cards two or three times without turning them up to show the ace. This should mingle them quite beyond the spectator's capacity to follow.

Incidentally, I have found that for some reason if I lose track of the ace, the spectator usually finds it; if I know where it is, he doesn't.

The misdirection move with the red aces follows after a couple of throws in which you do not show the cards. You must wind up with one red ace in your left hand, the black ace on top in your right, and the other red ace below it.

"Here, I'll let you watch," you say. "One red—" and you turn your right hand, giving the barest flash of the bottom ace.

Throw the top (black) ace. "The other red—" giving another flash of the original red ace in your right hand. Drop that a little distance away from the first.

"And the black." Put the left-hand card between the other two.

The great knack of doing the three-card trick this way lies in the tempo —a prompt, unhurried, rhythmic swing that makes the moves thoroughly deceptive.

Some performers hold all three cards in the right hand, switching their fingers around as nimbly as if they were playing the accordion. I can't tell you about this because I have never tried it.

The effect can also be accomplished by the glide, and I presume by a good second deal. Lang Neil in *The Modern Conjurer* gives a very deliberate method requiring an extra card.

In all these methods the spectator has a chance to win, if only by pointing to the card he knows is not the ace. You have one final recourse, a table change called the *Mexican Turnover*, by which he loses no matter what card he picks.

In this version you simply lay the cards out, with no fancy throw. When the sucker (of course the Three-Card Trick was originally a gambling game) makes his choice, you pick up one of the other cards by the near right corner, slide it under the edge of the indicated card, and flip that card over on the table. It is never the ace, because you can substitute another card at will in the act of turning it over.

It is absolutely essential that the table be covered with a cloth, or the cards will slide around, and you can barely turn them over at all, let alone do the Mexican Turnover. Indeed, Victor Farelli, in his useful *Card*

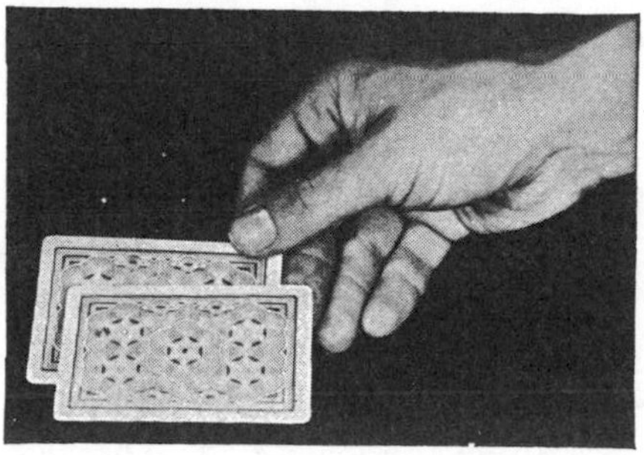

FIG. 77

Magic, advises carrying your own cloth with you and always using the same cloth.

This necessity once attended to, you will find the motions of the Turnover utterly simple. Say the sucker has spotted the ace. Pick up the deuce by the extreme corner between forefinger and thumb. Slide it under the ace, not square, but projecting a quarter of an inch forward (Fig. 77).

Swing your hand up and to the left. In the motion, you will find your second finger tip against the free corner of the ace. Switch your thumb from first to second finger tip (Fig. 78).

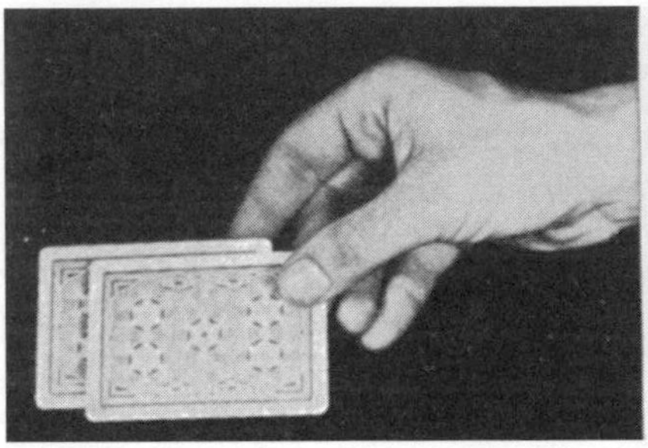

FIG. 78

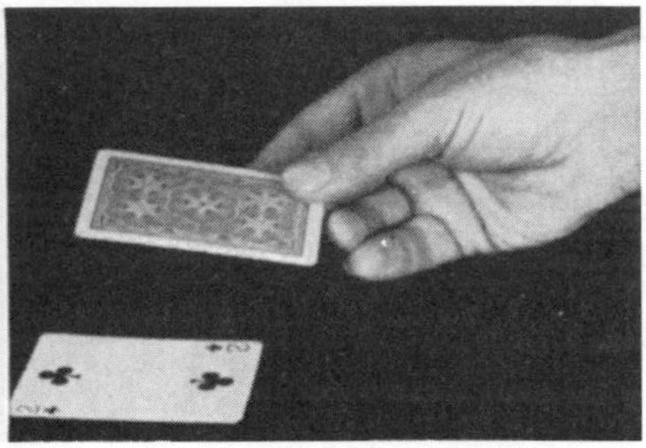

FIG. 79

As your hand travels onward to the left, the forefinger flops the deuce over, while the thumb and second finger carry off the ace (Fig. 79).

By this time I need hardly tell you that you must use the Mexican Turnover as seldom as possible, but must always make the honest turnover with exactly the same motion.

8. *Reading the Cards.* Being able to tell any card in the deck without seeing its face is popularly considered the one essential accomplishment for gambler and card conjurer.

With marked cards it becomes a reality. A prearranged deck, too, allows you apparently to do the same thing. But if you depend on such ruses, how are you to manage when someone shuffles his own cards, hands them to you, and defies you to name just one?

Well, for one thing you can palm a "shiner"—a small concave mirror. With this you can see the reflection of the bottom card as you rub it with your finger tips, or you can glimpse the index of the top card as you deal it.

But you can do both of those things without any shiner. To identify the bottom card, hold the pack bottom outward in your right hand, fingers on the upper end, thumb on the lower end. The face is toward the audience, and you rub the front card with your left finger tips to "feel the ink."

This gives you cover to bow the pack toward your palm, exactly as if you were going to spring the cards. By holding the deck about chest high you will find that the bend gives you just a glimpse of the lower index of the front card as you glance down.

You can then name the card, remove it with your left hand, and in the very act bow the deck again to glimpse the second card.

Naming the cards as you deal them is harder, but also harder to detect. Give the deck a lengthwise downward crimp, and then take it with your left hand in position for the Charlier pass (chapter 3, section 2*f*). Lay your forefinger across the far end, gripping the pack between your first and little fingers, with no support from the thumb. This is the elementary position; as you learn the knack, you can come closer to a normal dealing grip.

Apparently you just push off the top card with your thumb, deal it face down, and name it. In pushing it forward, however, you catch the left edge near the inner corner with the flesh of the second joint of your thumb, bending the index corner up just a trifle. Since the pack is not horizontal, but approaches a forty-five-degree angle, you can get a flash of the index as you deal. Nelson Downs, who showed me this ruse, could glimpse two or three cards simultaneously; one at a time is plenty for me to contend with.

There are various other methods, among which I shall mention only the homemade shiner provided by a bright silver table knife. If you hold the deck in dealing position in your left hand, and poke such a knife through diagonally from near to far index corner, a slight twist of the blade will show you the reflection of the near index so that you can name whatever card you cut to. A little practice should render it almost equally easy to have a spectator insert the knife; the tip instead of the heel of the blade would then give the reflection.

5. *Please Take a Card—*
Standard Card Tricks

TECHNICALLY speaking, the great majority of card tricks consist of a location—some way of finding an apparently lost chosen card—and a revelation. The location is what tends to fascinate conjurers; the most appreciated present you can offer a card operator is some diabolically ingenious new location. I shall give you several beauties below.

Three times out of five, however, the revelation is what gives all the scope for showmanship. A man telling about a trick generally begins, "He had someone pick a card, and then . . ." In short, the revelation is usually what turns a trick into an effect.

If you want to collect locations instead of stamps or antiques, it can do you no harm and may do you some good. But don't try out your whole collection on an audience of laymen. One or two tricks such as Zingone's Table Spread (chapter 3, section 5*a*), where a perfectly baffling location is the whole effect, are about enough in your public repertory.

For entertainment purposes, I suggest that you look over the field, then adopt and completely master one all-purpose location. My own strong preference is the side steal. Some professionals rely on mechanical locators like short or cornered cards (see under head magic), others on breaks and false shuffles. Hilliard's *Greater Magic* devotes eighty-six pages to locations by skill, mechanics, and ingenuity.

Having decided on your habitual working location, you can add two or three more as an anchor to windward, reserved for use in fast company. Here you will probably find the approximation method most helpful.

When it comes to revelations, naturally each one is a trick by itself, and you will simply have to acquire the ones you think your friends will like.

In chapter 3 were several effects that are hard to beat: one form of the Spelling Trick; Rosini's Location; the Stabbed Pack; "You Must Be Wrong"; "Everybody's Card"; Zingone's Table Spread; "Step on It"; "Correcting a Mistake"; "Five Hands."

1. Locations. You learned the groundwork of almost all locations two chapters ago—the shifts, side steal, break, jog, false shuffle, and crimp. You also learned moves that were on the borderline between location and force.

Here are two more methods with their own special merits.

1a. The tap. When a chosen card has been actually removed from the pack, you may take the deck in your left hand with the fingers on the right edge and the thumb on the left. Riffle the front end with your right hand for the spectator to return his card.

Don't let him get it all the way in.

He leaves it sticking out, and you drive it square with two or three taps of your right middle fingers.

Hold the pack gently and be sure your taps are delivered straight and at the center of the end. The last tap is just a trifle harder than the others.

Almost without knowing it, you will find you have driven the card clear through, and in-jogged it. The only danger is in driving it too far.

What you do with the in-jog is your business. (You are in a very natural position for a Hindu shuffle.)

1b. The side crimp. This again is used when a chosen card has been withdrawn altogether. Hold the deck in dealing position in your left hand. Either riffle the front end of the pack or simply let the spectator poke his card in.

As he does so, when the card is pushed about two-thirds of the way home, bend your hand a trifle toward you. This makes the card go in diagonally, and the near right corner (from your point of view) sticks out at the right side of the deck. You will find it almost bumps into your second or third finger tip.

For an instant push that projecting corner ever so slightly up or down with the finger tip; then relax your grip, and let the spectator shove his card square.

With a new pack, even the tiniest corner crimp still shows up after prolonged shuffling by the audience. You are far more likely to make your crimp too sharp than too slight.

1c. Approximation. This dodge really deserves the name of a principle. I first met with it in *The Art of Magic* many years ago, and I am tempted to say that skill in its use makes the difference between a good card man and a very good card man.

Two things you must have to work by approximation: steady nerve and a good eye. Relying on these, you can almost always find a card that someone has chosen ***while the pack was in his own hands.***

With a new, clean deck, spring the cards to remove any downward bend they may have; square them up very carefully, but don't call attention to it. For this first method you need not even fall back on approximation if you can put the spectator in a haphazard mood. He should feel that you have simply tossed the pack on the table; whereas actually the edges are almost like glass, and you deposit the pack without marring them.

Hoping for the best, ask him to look at one card. If he simply cuts off part of the pack, that is what you prefer. If he withdraws one card, you may as well use some other, cruder location. If he bends back the end of the upper half, that will also serve your purpose.

Let us assume he has cut off a handful. You must be casualness itself. "Know what it is? All right, put 'em back."

Unless he takes special care, he can scarcely help leaving a step where he broke the pack. The step may be quite tiny; it may be at an end, a side, or two corners. Spotting it is your whole job.

Hold up your palms for an instant. "All done? Remember, you did it for yourself. I haven't touched the pack. Are you satisfied with the card you got, or do you want to try again?"

He is almost sure to be satisfied, but the question brings his eyes to your face. Just then you casually pick up the deck. There are no rules because I don't know where he left the step; you do.

Get a break below the step as you square up the pack. Hold it, make the glimpse, the shift, the side steal, a false riffle or overhand shuffle (chapter 3). Then square the pack again, ostentatiously. You are ready to do anything that can be done with a located card.

Next let us suppose that the man simply bent up one end of the upper half of the deck.

He will probably leave a step anyhow; but if not, he will have bridged the upper half, and by squeezing one end you get a break—in the pack, I mean. Also in the trick.

So far, you have been trading on the good nature of the audience, hustling the volunteer into being careless. Now imagine you meet a worthy adversary, who picks up the deck from the table, gently opens it to look at a card, then squares it up as carefully as you could have yourself.

Are you stuck?

Not by a jugful.

Watch where he breaks the pack.

When he gives it back, you can afford to look at it closely in squaring it up just once more. That is your cover. Break the deck as nearly where he did as you can.

An expert should hit the spot within three or four cards; a beginner, within not more than a dozen.

Make the shift at that point.

Even though you are quite new to the game, you can rely on having his card among the first six on top or the last six at the bottom.

Give a false shuffle. Then you can fan the deck, face toward you, quite openly. See what the possible cards are, and ask an elimination question. "I take it your card was red?" is a frequent gambit. The particular assortment of cards may suggest instead that you ask whether he chose face or spot, or one suit or another.

At very worst, one question will bring you down to six possible cards, and two questions may bring you down to two or three. The questions should be asked in a fishing sort of way, as though it doesn't matter whether you get any answer. Your morale may be better if you realize that it actually doesn't.

The fewer the cards left by elimination, however, the easier your last step. Calmly separate out the possibilities and put them together at the top or bottom, remembering the order they lie in.

Another false shuffle can do no harm. Then palm off the cards you have memorized. I usually put them in my trouser pocket. Or if there aren't but two or three, you may leave them on top of the pack.

Ask the man straight out what card he had.

Since you know where it lay in the series, you can produce it instantly by counting in your pocket or thumbing off the top of the deck.

The optical fan location, invented by John Mulholland, and which I print with his kind permission, is hardly accurate enough to count on without approximation yet so good that I am certain you will want to try it.

You make a wide, even pressure fan, face down (chapter 3, 9*c*). You swing the fan deliberately over and back, asking a volunteer to remember one of the cards he sees. He never touches the cards, and a good pressure fan should expose at least twenty for his choice. Yet you find the card.

As I say, the fan should clearly expose the indices of twenty or thirty cards, and there should be no prominent break.

The factor that narrows the choice down to three or four cards is the motion of the fan as you turn it over. Your left fingers are on the face. Make your second finger tip the axis on which you pivot the fan. Turn the cards over sidewise with a twist of the forearm—deliberately over, then back just as deliberately, but without a pause. You will find that the cards at the center of the fan (the axis of motion) stand practically still, while those at the outer ends are always moving.

It is thus practically certain that the volunteer can identify only the few cards at your second or third finger tip, and usually one or two of these will be a bit more prominently displayed than the rest.

You can easily check on this because you too see one card much better than any others. When you turn the fan face down again, you will find that the back of one card somewhat to the left of the center is more exposed than its neighbors.

The chances are about two to one that this is the volunteer's card.

In any case, bring your right hand forward to close the fan. Put the tip of your forefinger on the far right corner of this exposed card; a very little experience will teach you to hit it automatically, almost without looking at all. Lift up the forefinger, thus dividing the fan in two. Tilt the entire upper, or right-hand, fan about a quarter of an inch to the left, and then take your right hand away.

Close the whole fan with a sweeping motion of your right hand from right to left; you needn't be in the least careful about it.

The result of this move is to jog the card you have spotted along the left edge of the deck. Undercut to the jog, and throw on top (chapter 3, 5*a*).

You are now in the same situation as when a spectator has cut the pack under your watchful eye. The odds-on probable card is at the bottom, followed by two or three weaker contenders, with a couple more of these at the top.

Warning: Tell the volunteer not to think of the bottom card, "because you know what it is." Otherwise he may quite likely choose it, with ruinous results.

You should also make an express point of fanning evenly, lest people suspect you of "only letting him see one card." Indeed the real difficulty of the move lies in timing the turn over and back fast enough to work your force, yet slow enough so that the choice seems quite free. It is probably better too slow than too fast.

If the worst occurs, and you miss the card entirely (some people, slow-witted or malicious, just imagine a card at random without bothering to see it), you fall back on the card conjurer's old reliable alibi. To begin with, you will very often have in your pocket the next card in sequence, or the corresponding value in the same color. You can gain time by producing this near miss, saying, "The three of hearts? Oh, I was sure you had a diamond."

Next, fan the cards with their faces toward you, and quite openly look through them. The moment you spot the chosen card, look puzzled. "It doesn't seem to be here."

Either jog the card in closing the fan, as I have just taught you to do, or get a little-finger break at the card.

How you want to finish up from here is your own option—double lift and snap change, bottom palm and production from a left-hand pocket, color change, palm off and produce from the volunteer's own pocket.

This is one of the great developments in modern card magic—more of an attitude than a method. You crowd your luck to the limit, but are ready to dodge if it fails you. Some very startling tricks cannot be guaranteed to work every time. In a set public performance you will not use these tricks because they too easily break up your time schedule. In private and impromptu work (which leads to public engagements!) they can make you an awesome reputation.

Such effects depend largely on your nerve, and your nerve depends on how many ways you know how to get out of trouble. An excellent investment in peace of mind is a copy of Charles H. Hopkins' *"Outs" Precautions and Challenges.*

Those are enough locations to keep you busy for a while. There are more in the section under head magic, the various books I have mentioned, and Hugard's *Encyclopedia of Card Tricks,* Blackstone's *Modern Card Tricks,* August Roterberg's *Card Tricks,* and Arthur H. Buckley's *Card Control.*

You will also notice that several of the following effects carry their own location.

2. *Card at Any Number.* This is perhaps the most obvious way to show off your control of the cards: you put the chosen card at whatever position people ask for.

You should not find it very hard to invent your own method of putting a particular card at a particular number. One accomplishment that will be a big help is the art of *thumb counting.*

Hold the deck in both hands, in position for the standard shift, only with no separation. Bevel the deck slightly toward you.

A small number, perhaps up to six, can be picked up one at a time from the top by a single slow forward motion of your right thumb.

The conventional thumb count, however, consists simply of riffling from the bottom with your right thumb, mentally keeping count. When you have riffled as many as you need, take a break with your left little finger.

Obviously, then, if you bring the chosen card to the bottom, and ask for a number, you can quickly thumb-count to the number, and make the shift.

Another excellent method is to start by side-crimping (1*b*) a card at random. After a spectator has drawn a card, cut your crimp card to the middle and fan the deck out for him to replace his card. See to it that he does so to your left of the crimp card, and keep count of how many cards to the left it is. Fifth from the key card is a handy position, though any small number will do. Close up the fan and make a complete false shuffle.

Then take a break above your crimped key card and ask someone to name a number. If the number is five, you simply make the shift and hand the deck to the person who named the number. If it is less than five, you thumb-count off the necessary subtraction from the top of the lower half and make the shift. If more than five, thumb-count off the proper number from the bottom of the upper half.

The easiest and boldest method of doing the trick has become rather famous, but maybe you can get away with it. Bring the chosen card to the top. Ask for a number. Deal off that number of cards "to show the card isn't there yet," or simply have a spectator do so without explanation. In the latter case, obviously he fails to find the chosen card.

Put the cards back on the pack. The next time you count, the chosen card is in its proper place. If you had a spectator try the first time, either have another spectator do it now or say boldly, "Let *me* try."

I am saving some other methods for use in the next trick, which is fundamentally an improvement and extension of the Card at Any Number.

3. *Stop Me.* I trust you will not keep doing this feat until you become known to your friends as *Try* and Stop Me. There are enough methods so that you run this risk.

The effect is that the magician, or a spectator, deals off cards until the spectator says stop. The chosen card, needless to say, is right there.

If you deal, you can bring the chosen card to the top, and hold it back by the second deal; or to the bottom, and hold it back by the glide. In either case the chosen card is the next one after they stop you.

The most generally foolproof way, which I have always used since I saw the great Nate Leipzig do it, is to bring the card to the top; then hand a volunteer the deck, and ask him to give you cards one at a time until he feels like stopping.

This puts the chosen card at the bottom of the pile you receive, which you hold in your left hand. When he stops, ask him whether he means the card he has just given you or the one he still holds. Whichever he wants, put it on top of your pile, side-steal the chosen card, and drop it on top of all.

Ask him whether he thinks you hypnotized him into stopping there; finally, turn up the chosen card.

A different presentation is to put the deck in a hat; you pick out one card at a time, carry it across the stage, and drop it in another hat. People stop you between hats, and you are holding the chosen card.

This can be accomplished with a "Svengali deck" (see under head magic), or by picking up the chosen card, carrying it across, and palming or back palming it as you pretend to drop it into the second hat. You take "another" card, actually the chosen one again, out of the first hat, and so on until they stop you.

With this method, you must load a few cards into the second hat beforehand, just in case anyone should look.

If I were showing the effect, I'm inclined to think I would bottom-palm the chosen card in my left hand, and use the double-palm change when they stopped me. The really deceptive way in that case would be to take each card out of the left hat, transfer it to the right hand, and drop it into the right hat.

4. The Spelling Trick. You have already learned (chapter 3, section 1*b*) one way of doing the Spelling Master, so you realize that it is just the Card at Any Number in a new disguise. The cleverness of the disguise (which is one of the few twentieth-century contributions to the classic card repertory) lies in the fact, first, that only a certain few positions in the pack can be required of you; second, that you aren't supposed to know the card beforehand, and so you have the added mystery of a Stop Me effect.

The version you learned was done with the spectator's name; the great bulk of spelling tricks use the name of the chosen card itself.

You could, of course, resort to either thumb-counting or the run-through ruse of As Easy as Spelling Your Name.

But beyond this, the lucky accidents of the English language have furnished you with a far superior recourse. The name of each card in the deck except the joker contains ten, eleven, twelve, thirteen, fourteen, or fifteen letters. You will save yourself a lot of work by studying the following diagram until you understand it, after which memorizing it is a trifle; it serves to classify the cards according to the number of letters in their names.

LETTERS

	1	2	3	4	5	6	7	8	9	10	11	12	13	14	15	
A-C	A	C	E	O	F	C	L	U	B	S						
2-C	T	W	O	O	F	C	L	U	B	S						10 Group
6-C	S	I	X	O	F	C	L	U	B	S						
10-C	T	E	N	O	F	C	L	U	B	S						
4-C	F	O	U	R	O	F	C	L	U	B	S					
5-C	F	I	V	E	O	F	C	L	U	B	S					
9-C	N	I	N	E	O	F	C	L	U	B	S					
J-C	J	A	C	K	O	F	C	L	U	B	S					
K-C	K	I	N	G	O	F	C	L	U	B	S					
A-H	A	C	E	O	F	H	E	A	R	T	S					
2-H	T	W	O	O	F	H	E	A	R	T	S					11 Group
6-H	S	I	X	O	F	H	E	A	R	T	S					
10-H	T	E	N	O	F	H	E	A	R	T	S					
A-S	A	C	E	O	F	S	P	A	D	E	S					
2-S	T	W	O	O	F	S	P	A	D	E	S					
6-S	S	I	X	O	F	S	P	A	D	E	S					
10-S	T	E	N	O	F	S	P	A	D	E	S					
3-C	T	H	R	E	E	O	F	C	L	U	B	S				
7-C	S	E	V	E	N	O	F	C	L	U	B	S				
8-C	E	I	G	H	T	O	F	C	L	U	B	S				
Q-C	Q	U	E	E	N	O	F	C	L	U	B	S				
4-H	F	O	U	R	O	F	H	E	A	R	T	S				
5-H	F	I	V	E	O	F	H	E	A	R	T	S				
9-H	N	I	N	E	O	F	H	E	A	R	T	S				12 Group
J-H	J	A	C	K	O	F	H	E	A	R	T	S				
K-H	K	I	N	G	O	F	H	E	A	R	T	S				
4-S	F	O	U	R	O	F	S	P	A	D	E	S				
5-S	F	I	V	E	O	F	S	P	A	D	E	S				
9-S	N	I	N	E	O	F	S	P	A	D	E	S				
J-S	J	A	C	K	O	F	S	P	A	D	E	S				
K-S	K	I	N	G	O	F	S	P	A	D	E	S				
3-H	T	H	R	E	E	O	F	H	E	A	R	T	S			
7-H	S	E	V	E	N	O	F	H	E	A	R	T	S			
8-H	E	I	G	H	T	O	F	H	E	A	R	T	S			
Q-H	Q	U	E	E	N	O	F	H	E	A	R	T	S			
3-S	T	H	R	E	E	O	F	S	P	A	D	E	S			
7-S	S	E	V	E	N	O	F	S	P	A	D	E	S			13 Group
8-S	E	I	G	H	T	O	F	S	P	A	D	E	S			
Q-S	Q	U	E	E	N	O	F	S	P	A	D	E	S			
A-D	A	C	E	O	F	D	I	A	M	O	N	D	S			
2-D	T	W	O	O	F	D	I	A	M	O	N	D	S			
6-D	S	I	X	O	F	D	I	A	M	O	N	D	S			
10-D	T	E	N	O	F	D	I	A	M	O	N	D	S			
4-D	F	O	U	R	O	F	D	I	A	M	O	N	D	S		
5-D	F	I	V	E	O	F	D	I	A	M	O	N	D	S		
9-D	N	I	N	E	O	F	D	I	A	M	O	N	D	S		14 Group
J-D	J	A	C	K	O	F	D	I	A	M	O	N	D	S		
K-D	K	I	N	G	O	F	D	I	A	M	O	N	D	S		
3-D	T	H	R	E	E	O	F	D	I	A	M	O	N	D	S	
7-D	S	E	V	E	N	O	F	D	I	A	M	O	N	D	S	15 Group
8-D	E	I	G	H	T	O	F	D	I	A	M	O	N	D	S	
Q-D	Q	U	E	E	N	O	F	D	I	A	M	O	N	D	S	

Notice that the shortest suit is clubs, the shortest values ace, two, six, ten. Notice that *hearts* and *spades* have the same number of letters; notice that *diamonds* is two letters longer than they.

At need you can gain leeway by spelling either *two* or *deuce* and *three* or *trey*. Some methods require you to omit *of* or add *the* on certain cards.

In setting up cards for the Spelling Trick, all you need usually is to put them in their proper groups; the *of* doesn't matter to you.

Notice still further that the ten, fourteen, and fifteen groups are small. The eleven group contains thirteen cards; the twelve group, fourteen cards; and the thirteen group, twelve cards. This last fact is of no great interest in setting up for a thought force, but it does put the odds in your favor in the version I shall now give.

4a. The Automatic Speller. Though automatic, this is rather chancy. The alternative version is sure-fire.

Have someone shuffle the pack, and then cut it as accurately as he can into halves. Have him cut one of the halves as accurately as he can into halves again, look at the bottom card of the topmost quarter, replace it, and put that half on top of the other. You have not touched the cards so far, and if luck is with you, you may not have to touch them at all.

The point is simply that perfect cutting would make the top quarter consist of thirteen cards. Since the spectator puts the heaps down on the table side by side, you can tell pretty well how close he has come. With practice you should be within three of judging how many cards are in the top quarter.

Then, when the pack is put together and squared up, you ask the name of the card.

With good luck, the number you think were in the top quarter and the group number of the card will coincide. You then have nothing to do but sit back and see if your luck holds. You still have three cards' leeway because you can squeak by if the chosen card turns up one letter early, lopping off the final *s*; and it seems legitimate for it to arrive one letter late, a sort of period after the name.

If you think the man has taken sixteen cards on his last cut, and his card falls in the ten group, obviously you will have to take the deck long enough to shift six cards to the bottom; and if you think he has cut only twelve, and the card was the queen of diamonds, you must thumb-count —quick, how many?—and shift them to the top.

That is leaving as much as anyone dares to chance, in fact rather more than I dare. But there are ways, as the French would say, to correct Fortune.

A bold method is to use the crimp. Take a spectator who you have noticed habitually cuts the pack by the ends. Cut or shuffle until a card from the twelve group comes to the bottom of the pack. Thumb-count twelve cards, crimp them upward lengthwise, and shift them to the top.

The chances are now excellent that the spectator will cut right into the crimp, making your 12-grouper a force card. From here on the trick is automatic and infallible. If he doesn't cut into your crimp, you at least have it to guide you in judging the depth of his cut.

An alternative method is simply to thumb-count and crimp the bottom eleven cards, and leave them at the bottom.

Have the spectator draw a card from the pack as it lies on the table, put it back on top, and bury it by cutting. If he wants to go on cutting, you end up by making the shift above the crimped group. In any event the chosen card is twelfth from the top, and you can make any needed adjustment with certainty.

A step in another direction (which really ought to come under head magic, but head and hands are forever overlapping) is to set up six cards ranging from the ten group, on top, to the fifteen group, at the bottom. Put these on top of the pack, and nine indifferent cards on top of those. The rather dangerous chance you took by the first method is now reduced to practically nil: with any care at all, the spectator is almost bound to cut into your set-up, and all six cards in the setup will spell out automatically.

You will have to judge from your own experience whether a false riffle shuffle helps or weakens the effect.

4b. The Mental-Selection Speller. There are several "improvements" on the basic method of doing this stunning trick; I can only warn you to shun them if you know enough to leave perfect alone.

Run up six cards on the bottom of the deck, starting with a fifteen-grouper (the queen of diamonds is probably the best), which you must memorize; then a fourteen, a thirteen, on down to a ten, preferably the ace of clubs. Neither of these cards is important enough to make a long search for.

Clear the part of the pack just above the setup of any naturally conspicuous cards—aces or face cards. Grab six or eight inconspicuous cards at random, avoiding any that could be confused with the bottom card of your setup, and put them below the prearranged six.

I often make this setup quite openly during a breathing spell between tricks, and then give two or three ostentatious false dovetail shuffles (Chapter 3, section 5*a*).

All that remains for you to do is execute the thought force described at chapter 3, section 3*b*, making sure that one of the six prearranged cards is chosen. You memorize the bottom card of the setup simply to help your timing in the force.

By any means you like, cut the pack nine cards above your setup. What I usually do is to make the shift above the setup, run nine, in-jog, and shuffle off, under-cut to the in-jog, and throw on top. Just to make sure, I often boldly run through the pack, at intervals fixing the victim with a hypnotic eye. One more false dovetail shuffle to confound the confusion, and I hand over the deck, asking the victim to spell out the name of his card.

Once in a great while you may miss on the force and have to resort to some stratagem to get out; but when the trick works, I don't see how it can possibly be detected.

5. *Reversed Cards.* An old effect that has been a good deal developed in recent years is that of having chosen cards reveal themselves by mysteriously facing the wrong way in the pack. The original method (secretly reversing the bottom card, then turning the whole pack over before the chosen card was returned) now belongs in the parlor-magic class, along with the Twenty-One Card Trick and the Broken and Restored Matchstick.

It is possible, though not exactly neat, to bring the chosen card to the top, then slip it to the bottom, turning it over in the process, and finally bury it by a running cut.

Much cleverer is the version given in *Greater Magic*. Have two cards chosen (or peeped at). Bring them to the top, and get one indifferent card on top of them; a riffle shuffle is the easiest way to do this.

Announce that one swift flip (make a riffle) will bring the first chosen card to the top. With an air of triumph, you turn the top card face up on the deck, which you hold in dealing position in your left hand.

Imagine your chagrin when the card is wrong!

Now do a double lift (chapter 3, section 6*a*), picking up the indifferent card and the first chosen card back to back. "You're *sure* this wasn't yours?"

Turn the *pack* face upward by revolving your left hand; open a split at the corner with your left thumb; and disgustedly stuff the double card in at the split. Square up, and turn the pack face down again.

This time you decide to try a card from near the middle. Pull one out at random, and drop it face up on top of the deck. Wrong again!

Another double lift; again you turn over the deck and shove in the double card.

"If that's the best I can do, I may as well give up." So saying, fling the cards on the table with a scattering motion that spreads them in a ribbon, revealing the two chosen cards faced up among the line of backs.

Reverses are the subject of a chapter in Hugard and Braue's *Expert Card Technique.*

6. *The Card in the Pocket.* This effect was invented, around 1900, by an English conjurer named C. O. Williams, and the two variations are also British. At one time the trick was worked almost to death, but it always served me well even in its heyday, and I think the carousel is coming around to it again.

Hand someone the deck. Have him shuffle it. Ask him to think of a number—not a card, a number from one to fifty-two. Explain carefully (and at least twice) what he is to do next: count down to the number he thought of, remember the card at that number, then square up the deck carefully.

While he is doing this, you turn your back or leave the room.

Coming back, you skim through the deck, look him searchingly in the eye, take out a card, and put it in your trouser pocket.

So far not a question has been asked. Now at last you ask the volunteer how far down his card was. You count down slowly and carefully, and turn up the card at that number: it isn't his.

Naturally not, because you triumphantly pull his card from your pocket.

Here acting is everything; the manipulation is almost childish. In running through the pack, look as much like a genuine mind reader as you can manage; slide the bottom card across to the middle of the fan, and draw it out with your right hand in such a way that no one can quite see what part of the deck it came from. Put it into your right trouser pocket, and immediately palm it and bring it out again. "At the first favorable opportunity" (*i.e.*, when they aren't looking) deposit it on top of the pack.

This automatically brings the chosen card one place lower than the volunteer left it. Ask him what his *number* was (be careful that he doesn't blurt out his *card* instead, which for some reason often happens), and count down to the number. Suppose the number is eight; put the eighth card face down on the table. Ask him to look and see if it is his.

While everyone is watching him, palm off the top card of the deck, which of course is his. Producing it from your trouser pocket is not a very difficult task now.

This trick is so good that people very often want you to do it again. With most effects you must side-step; this one you can indeed do again —and again.

On the first repeat, put not the bottom but the top card in your pocket, and *leave it there.* This moves the chosen card up one place instead of down one. Put the deck on the table; then ask what the number was.

Pick up the cards off the pack one at a time until, by rights, the chosen card should be on top; actually it is on top of the pile in your hand. Ask the spectator to see if his card is still there, and under this cover palm off the chosen card.

Introducing it into your pocket, slide it inside the card already there, and bring the two out as one, the chosen card.

If they ask you to do it yet again, make some show of wanting to get on with the next trick. Then say, "All right, I don't mind. Just to save time, suppose you don't take a very big number."

When you get the deck back, palm off the top eight or ten cards; take the next card openly in your right hand, and put it in your pocket, leaving the palmed cards there too.

Put down the deck. Stand with your hands in your trouser pockets. Ask the man what number he had, and quickly count down to it in your pocket. Or simply tell him to see if his card is still there, and count in your pocket as he deals on the table.

You may either produce the card without more ado, or palm it out, steal a glimpse of it, and say, "Oh, yes—the five of clubs. That's what I thought."

And you bring out the chosen card.

7. *The Rising Cards.* This is pre-eminent among card tricks, both for antiquity and for its appeal to the audience. No one has ventured to guess how old the effect is, except that Robert-Houdin thought it as recent as the eighteenth century, while I have heard that one method (still in use) was explained in a seventeenth-century Dutch book. Knowing how to do the Rising Cards is part of every magician's education, even though he may not want the trick in his act.

The Art of Magic gives thirty pages to the Rising Cards; *Greater Magic,* fifty-nine pages. If you really want to become an authority on the trick, go to those volumes; much of what I know about it I learned from them anyway.

The title describes the effect: a chosen card or cards, replaced in the deck, rise into view under their own power. In one of the very oldest methods, repopularized by the late Howard Thurston in his card-manipulating days, the cards not only rose from the pack, but floated up into the air, and were caught in the performer's right hand.

First let me give you the sleight-of-hand methods. In the first two, you begin by bringing the chosen card to the top.

For an unassisted rise, hold the pack in your right hand, facing forward, the hand, likewise palm to the front, with the thumb on the left edge, the third and little fingers on the right edge, the tips of first and second fingers on the back. By a walking motion of those fingers you can make the top card rise steadily almost all the way out of the pack.

The trick in this form is not very hard to figure out and should be dressed up with a bit of comedy rather than seriously offered as a great mystery. I can usually get a laugh by holding my left hand above the pack as the card rises. When it has reached nearly the full height, I swing my left hand to the left and then to the right, and make the card tilt from side to side, following it.

A second card you cause to rise by having it cling to your right forefinger, which is laid across the top of the pack. The pack is held in dealing position in the left hand, and turned upright with its face to the audience. Close your right fist except for the pointed forefinger. Rub the forefinger briskly on your sleeve by way of generating electricity; then put it across the top of the pack. On the first two or three attempts you raise your right hand alone; the card refuses to follow. Rub up some more electricity, replace your forefinger across the pack, and straighten your little finger to press against the top card near its lower end.

The next time you raise your right hand, the card comes up dangling from the forefinger.

Watch your angles with this method.

The plunger rise, devised by a magician named Jack McMillen, requires an almost new deck. It is certainly the most magical-looking sleight-of-hand method; the card actually rises from the middle of the pack, and there are no secret devices to get rid of.

Bring the chosen card second from the bottom of the deck. Undercut about a third of the pack, shuffle off down to the last few cards, and end up by running until you have just three cards left. In-jog the third card from the bottom, run the second, in-jog the last. Undercut half the deck, and shuffle off (chapter 3, 5*a*).

The result of this is that you have the chosen card in the middle, with an in-jogged card above and another below it. Take the pack in dealing position in your left hand. Press your little finger against the projecting near right corners of the in-jogged cards. Take the upper end of the deck by the edges between your right thumb and second finger; with the forefinger, bow the end of the deck slightly.

Now tilt your left hand a little to the right and slide it down almost to the near end of the deck; pressure between your little finger and the heel of your hand carries the two jogged cards down until four-fifths of their length is drawn free of the pack, while the bowing at the upper end keeps the chosen card from following them.

You now have the pack in your left hand in very much the position for the Erdnase bottom palm (chapter 3, section 4*c*), except that the pack is upright instead of horizontal.

With your right hand, grasp the pack from the rear by the edges between forefinger and thumb; your right second and third fingers fall outside the fingers of your left hand. Reach down with your right little finger and press it across the lower ends of the two jogged cards.

Push up with your right little finger (which is perfectly hidden by your left hand), and the chosen card ascends startlingly from the deck, pinched between the two jogged cards.

All the classical methods of doing the Rising Cards rely on some form of black silk thread or human hair, either of which is invisible by artificial light at a very short distance. In the days when all magicians had assistants, one of the assistant's prime duties was to pull the thread for the Rising Cards.

Modern conjurers, even more prejudiced against the use of assistants than they are against steamer trunks full of paraphernalia, have devised means for pulling the thread themselves. They have also eliminated the once-customary threaded packet of duplicate cards.

The standard method of threading the cards was to fasten one end of the thread at the middle of the upper end of an indifferent card; then to carry the thread under the lower end of a duplicate of a card to be forced, up over the top end of an indifferent card, down under the bottom end of another duplicate, and so on. Pulling the free end of the thread brought up the rearmost of the duplicates first, followed in turn by the others.

Here is a way of accomplishing the same purpose right during the show.

You need a glass big enough to set the pack in—either a high-ball glass with perpendicular sides (no taper) or a goblet with a foot. You also need a length of 000 black thread with a tiny black bead at one end. The other end is tied to a thumbtack, which is stuck into the rear edge of your table. You will have to determine by experiment how long the thread should be for the number of cards you want to have rise. To avoid getting tangled up in the thread, lay it in neat zigzags from the back edge of the table to a spot just behind the empty glass, where you put the bead end.

Supposing you want to use three cards, pass the deck around and have three different people take out cards. Retrieve the pack, and drop it, face forward, into the glass on the table.

Then collect the chosen cards on a plate. Back at the table, hold up the last card chosen in your right hand, so that everyone can see it. Your left hand, meanwhile, picks up the bead.

After everyone has had a good stare at the chosen card, you stick it into the top of the pack, and push it down. Your left forefinger opens a break for the purpose in the end of the pack, and pushes in the bead. The bottom edge of the chosen card catches the bead, and pushes it down with it, drawing the thread after it.

Show the second card chosen, and stick it into the pack to the rear of the previous one. Your left forefinger keeps this previous one from rising, while your right hand pushes down the second card, which again carries a loop of thread with it. The process is repeated with the first card chosen.

So far as mechanics is concerned, you are now practically done. You have only to pick up the glass and walk forward with it until the thread is drawn taut. After that, the slightest further advance will bring up the first chosen card from the middle of the deck.

Finally, I borrow from *The Art of Magic* a description of what is known as the Alberti method, which has been used for over a century, but probably never surpassed in its combination of simplicity and surprising effect.

The only apparatus used is a human hair about fourteen inches long. The exact length may be greater or less, as the performer finds most convenient. The hair is threaded into a needle and passed through the performer's coat just under the right lapel, near the top button. The end of the hair inside the coat is tied to an ordinary button. The opposite end carries a minute pellet of magician's wax. (This can be bought from dealers, or simply cut from the center of a stick of the diachylon or lead plaster sold by drug stores, and kneaded between the fingers until it is sticky.)

When not in use, the hair is drawn down inside the coat until the waxed end is concealed under the lapel. The button and hair are kept in the inside breast pocket, where the hair is out of the way and cannot be inadvertently broken. Thus arranged it may be worn for months without breaking, if the performer is reasonably careful.

This preparation made, the performer advances to the company and requests three members to draw cards. When the cards are returned he brings them to the top, palms them off, and hands the deck out to be shuffled. The pack being returned, he replaces the three cards. In walking back a few steps he has ample opportunity to find the wax pellet under the right lapel and draw the hair out to its full length, the button keeping the end from pulling through the coat. He presses the pellet of wax against the upper part of the back of the hindermost card, which was the last card replaced.

The right hand now makes a number of passes above and below the pack. As the right hand sweeps underneath the pack it encounters the slack hair, which is allowed to pass between the first and second fingers and is drawn up until the right hand reaches a position about ten or twelve inches above the pack.

Turning to the person whose card is to rise, the performer inquires the name of his card. Say it was the jack of hearts.

"Jack of hearts, rise," commands the performer, and the card obediently rises to the fingers of the right hand, when it is immediately handed to the person who drew it.

This rising is accomplished by a slight upward outward movement of the right hand, which is absolutely indetectable, and which will be mastered after a few trials, although it is rather difficult to describe. The second card rises in the same manner.

To vary the method for the third card, the performer presses the wax pellet against the upper part of the back of the card, and then drops the deck into a glass, turning the pack so that the pellet is at the bottom. He hands the glass to a spectator to hold, waves his hands above the glass, and orders the card to rise. The slightest movement of the body will cause the card to rise, the edge of the glass acting as a fulcrum. If the performer stands directly in back of the glass, so that his coat forms a dark background, the hair is absolutely invisible to the person holding the glass. When the card has risen nearly to its full height above the pack it is removed by the performer, who secures the wax pellet with his right thumbnail and hands the card to the chooser. In replacing the glass on the table he draws down the button inside his coat, thus removing both hair and pellet from sight.

The Rising Cards is not at its best without a certain amount of selling. You must build up the excitement as people wait for the cards to rise, and remember to allow time for realization and applause after each card comes up.

A variety of gags are used with good effect to vary the simple rises. You may call for "the seven" to rise, without result. Then ask for the seven of spades, and the card answers immediately. A king or queen declines to rise until addressed as "Your Majesty." Tell a spectator to make his mind a complete blank, then to concentrate on his card. The next card that rises is blank. Either remove it or stick it back near the front of the deck, and make the correct card rise next. A card rises with its back to the audience; this too you poke back near the front of the pack, and the card "turns around" before rising again.

In short, you can make of the Rising Cards almost whatever you please, from an utter bore to a magical masterpiece.

This remains true, perhaps more than ever now that electronic remote control has placed such effects within the reach of any seven-year-old with a TV set. The trick itself is no longer magic.

Victor Jamnitzky Astor (a dealer doubly dear to me because he taught himself English in his native Hungary with a copy of my *Cyclopedia of Magic* as his text, and because he will sell you just the instructions for almost any trick in his catalog at a nominal price, so that you know what you're buying before you get involved) passes on a warning about the electronic rising cards (see Appendix, Electronic equipment): "You're out of luck if a police patrol car on the same wavelength happens by."

6. *Hand Magic with Coins*

COIN manipulation is unquestionably the hardest branch of sleight-of-hand. It is also (unless, like me, you happen to have a passion for it) the least rewarding. Theoretically you can do the same things with coins that you can with cards—produce, vanish, change. In practice you are limited pretty nearly to production and vanishing. The occasional change of a half-dollar into a cent does not form a real category. Very seldom indeed do you distinguish individual coins, the way you constantly do with cards.

On the other hand, money is something everyone understands and is attracted by; the coins have a pleasant sparkle and jingle. And a good coin manipulator comes close to real magic because of the very simplicity that he can't get away from. Mercifully, there are almost no mathematical coin tricks.

Again, some of the sleights that you learn with coins are basic for all other small objects except cards. No competent coin manipulator ever has the slightest trouble with billiard balls or thimbles.

For decades the standard and only book on the subject was T. Nelson Downs's *Modern Coin Manipulation.* It later came out as a paperback under the title *Tricks with Coins.* This is worth having, but it was written to advertise the skill of Nelson Downs, not to encourage learners. It omits many of the little tips that make all the difference. Jean Hugard's *Coin Magic* and Eddie Joseph's *Coin and Money Magic* are better. Best of all is J. B. Bobo's *New Modern Coin Magic.*

The coins you use are important. For impromptu close-up work, it is practically obligatory to use real coins, and these will be either half dollars or silver cartwheels. You can also use foreign coins of corresponding sizes. A good many people would find seventy-five-cent pieces (if only there were such things) better to handle than halves or dollars. Some foreign coins are about that size.

If you are a bred-in-the-bone coin manipulator, as distinguished from a magician who sometimes shows coin tricks, you will want at least five coins just alike, and all fairly new. If one or two are very much worn, they will slip out of the stack and give you endless trouble.

John Mulholland was the man who first pointed out to me how much real coins impress an audience. I always carry six silver dollars, five new and one old (for Coins Up the Sleeve, see chapter 7, section 17). The only trouble I have had is that people on the eastern seaboard quite often remember my silver dollars when they have forgotten my magic.

If you want to do coin tricks on the stage, you may prefer to use "palming coins," which magic dealers carry in stock. You have a smaller investment than you would have in the same amount of real coins; the palming coins are thinner, and likely to be more sharply milled than the genuine article. They make less noise in handling, and are rather lighter.

Against these advantages, they have what Robert Benchley called "a flat, mocking laugh, like a counterfeit quarter." If the audience get a good look at palming coins, they tend to feel defrauded. Finally, there is great variation in the merits of the palming coins your dealer may have available. Some are reasonably good, but not milled or knurled around the edges. These you must take to a machine shop and have specially milled before you can use them at all. The last batch I had treated cost five times as much for the milling as for the coins. You then have to rub them down on emery cloth so that they will stack without rocking and slide without catching. After this it is often desirable to have them freshly nickel plated.

Another type of palming coin has sharply milled edges and nothing else to recommend it; it has no design and looks more like a disk of mirror glass than a coin.

Occasionally you can get brass palming coins, which have their use in "silver-and-gold" effects.

Let us assume that you are already wearing holes in your pockets with the coins of your choice. We now begin with the basic sleights.

1. *The tourniquet* (or *French drop*). The oldest and easiest of sleights with small objects, this is also one of the least perfect because at best it is by definition an unnatural motion.

As you are about to discover, nine times out of ten the magician who wants to make a coin disappear must pass it from one hand to the other, secreting it en route. Almost never can he use the genuinely natural motion of taking a coin between forefinger and thumb and removing it with the other hand in the same position. Accordingly, even when no monkey business is intended, he must put the coin from forefinger and thumb on the flat of the other palm, and clap that fist shut.

In handling cards you have already learned how to manage your eyes, and the same knack is equally vital with coins.

Getting back to the tourniquet, hold the coin by its edges between left thumb and second finger. Your right hand moves to take the coin, thumb below, fingers above (Fig. 80).

Just as your right hand closes on the coin, your left finger and thumb let it fall into the hollow of your left hand.

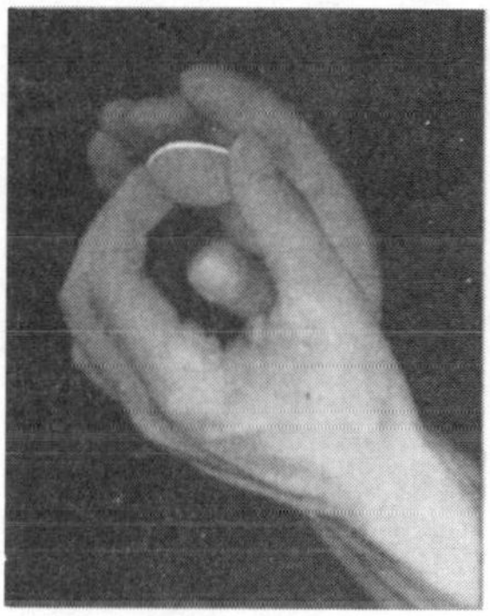

FIG. 80

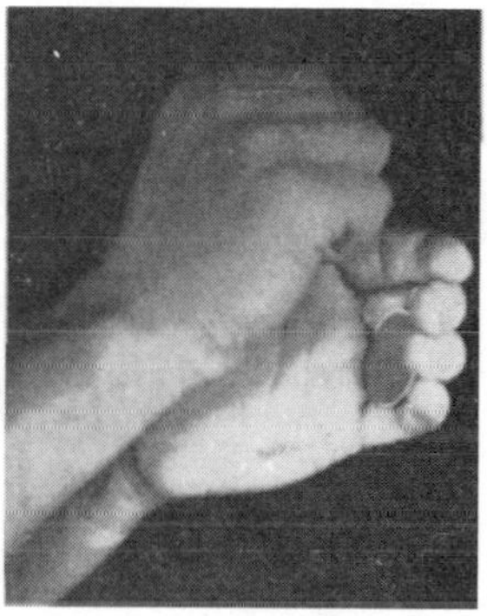

FIG. 81

Your right hand closes into a fist, and moves on, followed by your eyes, while your left hand remains loosely open (Fig. 81).

You will generally need to transfer the coin to some more secure palm. The tourniquet is not itself a palm, but the most elementary form of pass. A coin pass is a move by which a coin is apparently passed from hand to hand, but actually held back.

2. *The finger palm.* The normal, almost automatic palm to follow the tourniquet is the finger palm (Fig. 82). This is so easy it needs no further description, and it has a thousand uses with small objects.

FIG. 82

Some performers claim the results are better if the coin is held by third and fourth instead of second and third fingers.

3. *The flat thumb palm.* This is only a shade less easy than the finger palm. To use the flat thumb palm as a pass, show the coin lying flat on the tips of your right first and second fingers. As your right hand moves to put the coin in your left, the first and second fingers bend inward, turning the coin over and leaving it in the fork of the thumb (Fig. 83).

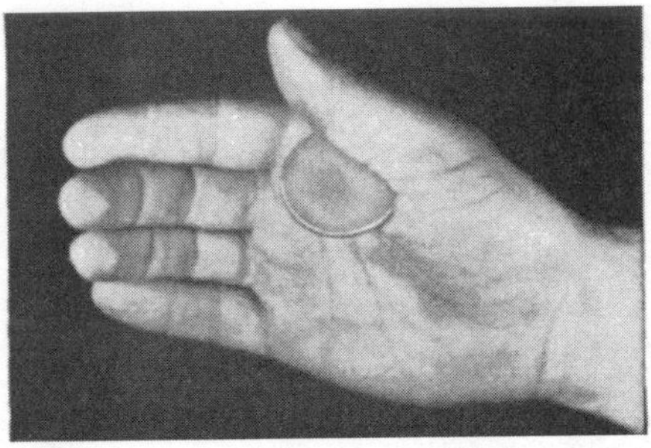

FIG. 83

The right hand continues its motion, the left fist closes on the supposed coin, and the left hand moves away, followed by your eyes.

The only drawback to the flat thumb palm is that it rather cramps the position of your thumb and it cannot be used for more than one or two coins.

4. *The regular thumb palm.* Fig. 84 tells all you need to know about this one.

5. *The regular palm.* Here is the original, classic grip that has given its name to all other ways of concealing small objects, even cards. Here also your troubles begin.

In every hand is a spot where you can hold a coin by contracting the

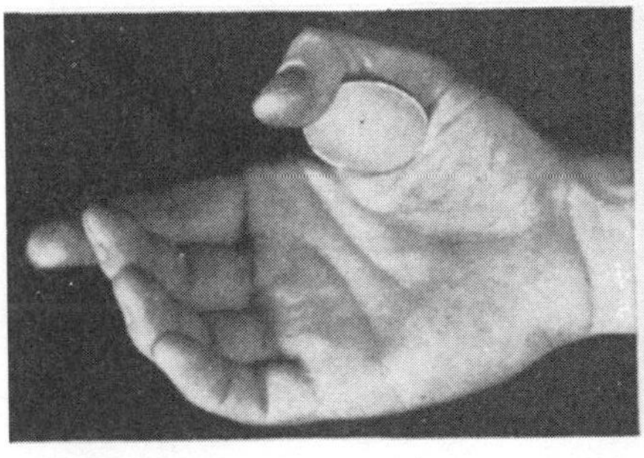

FIG. 84

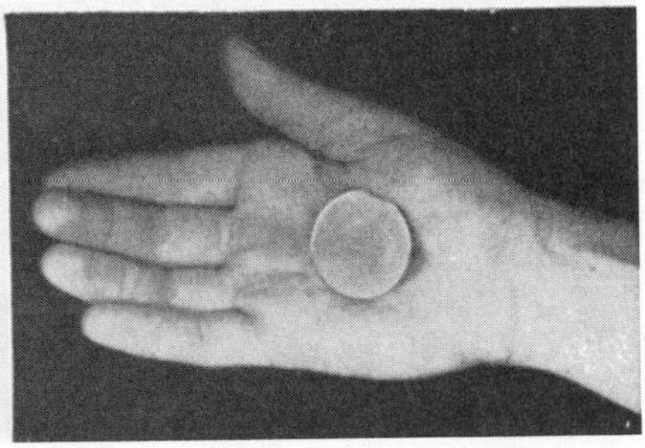

FIG. 85

muscle at the base of your thumb. There are two muscular cushions forming a V, one at the base of your thumb, the other along the heel of your hand. When you find the right spot, these two cushions will hold a coin securely without any cramped and frenzied contortions of thumb or little finger (Fig. 85).

If you have to twist your thumb and little finger inward, you haven't found the spot. I can't tell you where the place is; you will have to discover it by feel.

Remember that you need not grip the coin in a clutch of steel; this would, in fact, merely squirt it out of your palm. Gently, gently, gently.

Once your muscles have memorized the location, you can easily learn to put the coin in place with one motion, as for a pass. Hold the coin flat between your thumb and your second and third fingers. Move your thumb aside, and close your fingers into your palm. Try not to waggle your thumb (Fig. 86).

6. *The edge, oblique, or Downs palm.* When Nelson Downs invented this palm, he took the step that divided ancient from modern coin manipulation. Robert-Houdin boasted of his uncommon ability to palm two

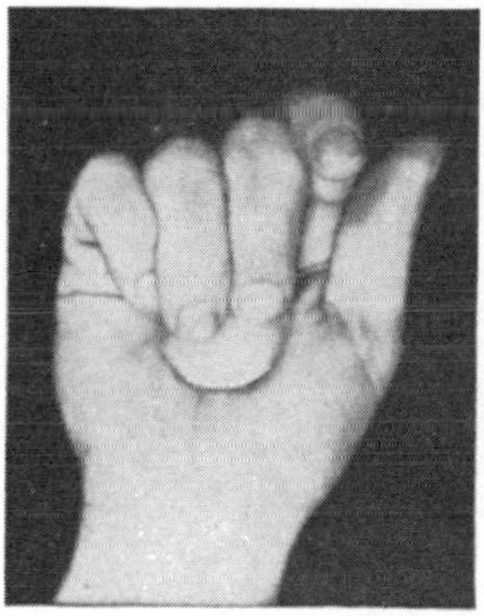

FIG. 86

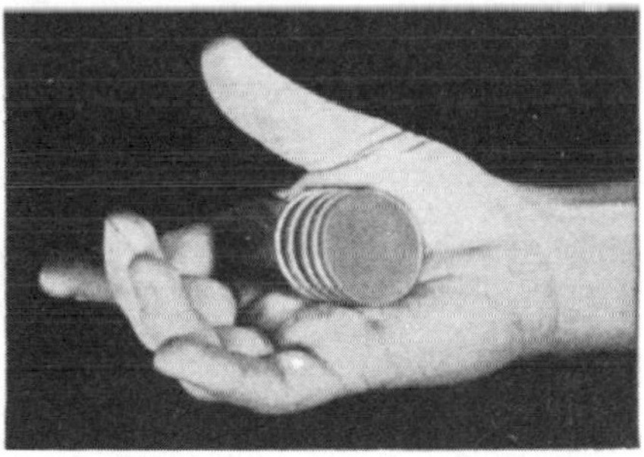

FIG. 87

silver dollars, or even five, by the regular palm. Downs had the most precise control, by his edge palm, over any number up to perhaps a dozen. To get beyond the cradle stage with coins, you start by learning the edge palm.

The fundamental point is the position (Fig. 87). To put one coin there, instead of laying it flat on the tips of second and third fingers, as you would for the regular palm, balance it on the end of your third finger, steadying the edge with the tip of your second finger. Then your third finger bends more sharply than the second. The third finger settles the coin in edge-palm position, and the second finger, pressing against the edge, shoves it home.

The next step is to palm coins one after another. Each new coin is slid *outside* its predecessor. There is a moment when you relax and let go the entire stack; then you repalm all the coins, including the new one.

Even the utmost gentleness will not keep the coins from talking without thorough practice. Noise is your indomitable adversary every step of the way in coin manipulation. The great thing about the edge palm, however, is that talking *can* be stopped. With the regular palm, talking is almost inevitable.

Having learned to edge-palm several coins one at a time, you next learn to reproduce them the same way. Bend your third finger down to the face of the outside coin and slide the coin up until your second finger tip can nip the edge by pressing against the third finger tip.

Nelson Downs had the habit of producing coins one after another to make a fan, his middle fingers sliding each new coin below the previous ones that were held between his thumb and forefinger (Fig. 88). I should

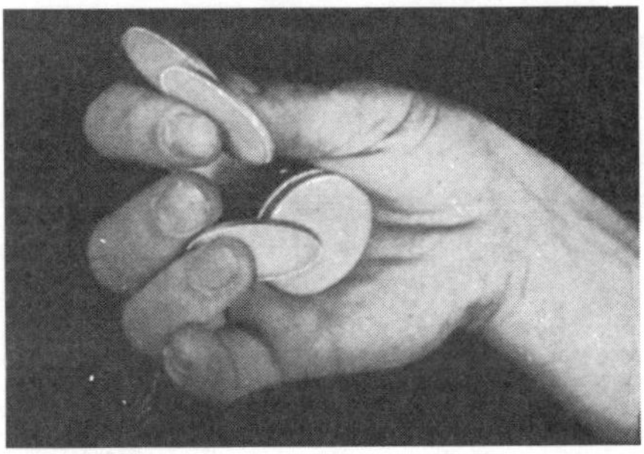

FIG. 88

say it is just a little easier to reproduce coins without talking than it is to palm them.

If you don't want to make a fan, but merely to bring the coins one after another to your finger tips, say for the Miser's Dream (Chapter 7, section 1), I have developed a method that works almost better than the conventional one. Possibly it takes a little more practice.

Edge-palm your coins, then let them fall flat against your palm by relaxing your hand with the palm turned slightly upward. You will now find that after a week or two of practice you can drop coins singly from the face of the stack by progressively loosening your thumb muscle. As your hand moves forward to "catch" a coin, you let one fall from the stack to the curled-in tips of your middle fingers. Your thumb then pushes the coin into view

7. *The change-over palm.* One of the moves to which the edge palm is essential is the change-over. This enables you to show both hands successively empty, keeping a stack of coins palmed all the while. Fig. 89

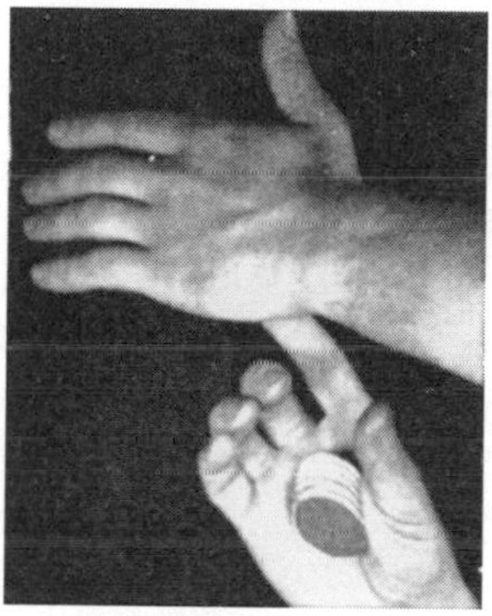

Fig. 89

shows a rear view of how you start—your left palm shown empty, your right forefinger pointing to it.

You pivot from left to right, and your left palm slides over your right palm. As it touches the palmed stack of coins, you relax your right hand, and so tilt the stack until it is in edge-palm position for the left hand (Fig. 90).

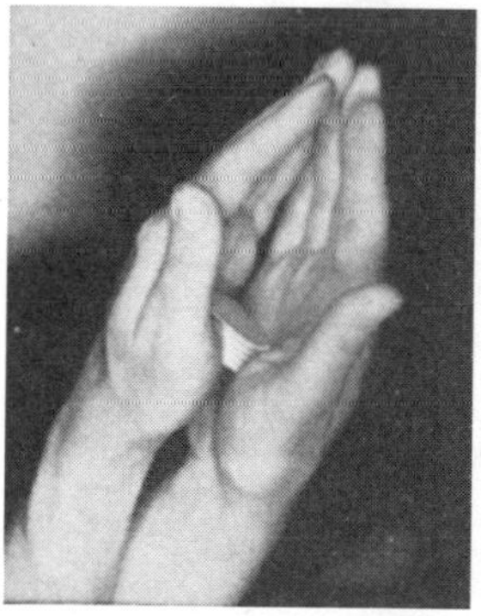

Fig. 90

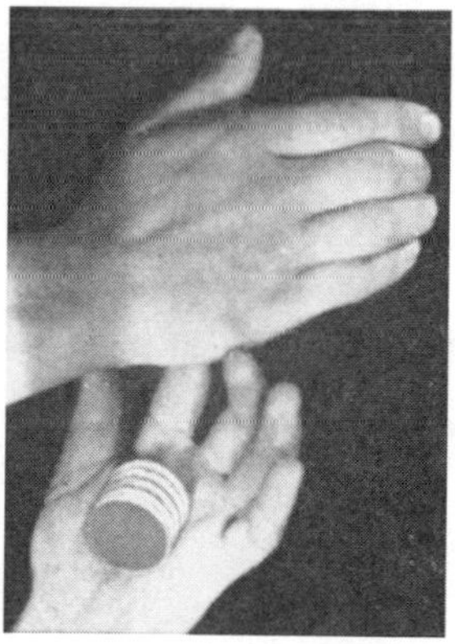

Fig. 91

With one smooth, gentle motion (it has to be gentle, or the coins will talk), your left hand palms the stack and points to the empty right palm (Fig. 91).

Next to noise, your biggest problems are spilling the coins and waggling both thumbs as you make the change-over.

The change-over palm is not really very difficult, and the temptation is to overwork it. I would never venture to use it except at the start of a trick, where people don't know what you may be hiding. In that case the stylized motion—nothing in this hand, nothing in that hand—seems fairly natural. But after you have made the coins vanish, people know they must be somewhere, and this renders the change-over palm mere transparent shuffling.

8. *The back palm.* The same objection may be raised with somewhat less force to the back palm, the showiest of Nelson Downs's contributions to the art. If one were to take seriously the preposterous directions given with figures 6 through 8 of the back palm in *Modern Coin Manipulation,* the results would be ludicrous. Downs himself was far too great a conjurer to do anything of the sort. Like Cardini, he had a back-palm routine with almost no back palming.

To learn the back palm, hold a coin flat near the lower edge between your thumb and middle fingers. Curl those fingers until the coin rests against the nails. Then bring up your first and little fingers to press against opposite edges of the coin. Make sure you don't press on the face, but against the edges.

Take your thumb away, and straighten your fingers. The results should be as shown from behind in Fig. 92.

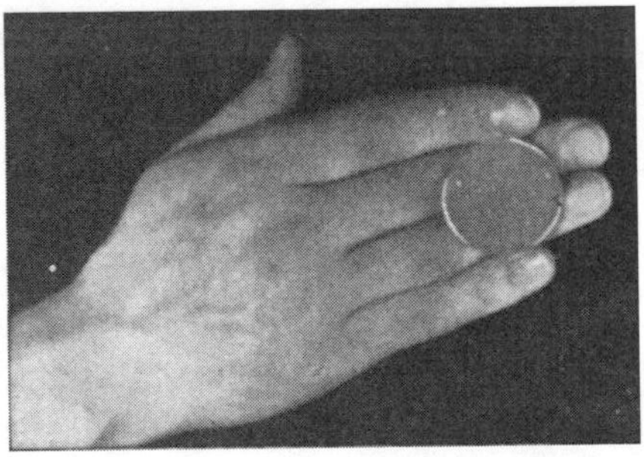

FIG. 92

I say should be, because when the knuckles of your middle fingers slide up under the coin, you are practically certain to drop it on the first three or four attempts. The point to remember is that the coin must be held behind your hand between the first and little fingers; you should be able to bend your middle fingers clear of the coin without losing your grip.

As in the back palm with cards, the next move is to show the back of your hand. The wrist roll that you learned in order to hide the transfer of the card will also serve you here, but it need not be so pronounced. As your hand turns over and your knuckles come up, bend down your middle fingers, draw them to the rear, and straighten them again, pivoting the coin by pushing with the finger tips (Fig. 93).

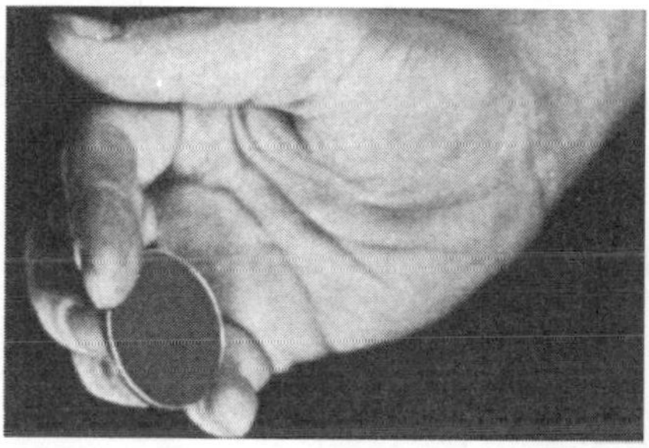

Fig. 93

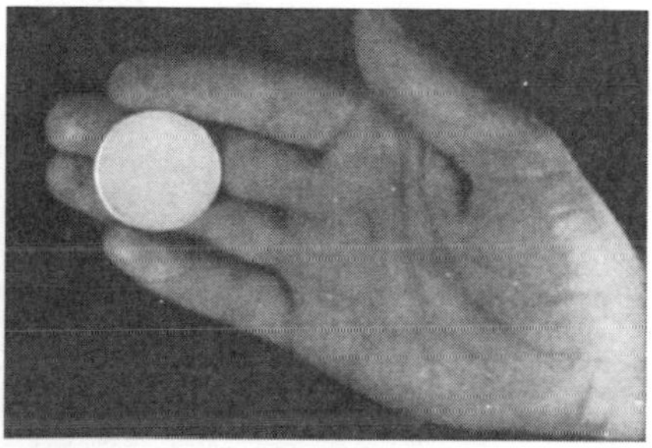

Fig. 94

This brings the coin to the position shown in Fig. 94.

The exact reverse of this motion transfers the coin to the back again.

Even an experienced operator will find himself dropping the coin during these maneuvers, so don't be discouraged—and don't be overconfident!

The necessary wrist roll is so slight that you can actually afford to stand there, show your palm empty, turn your hand over quite slowly, back again, and finally produce the coin. You must be dead sure of yourself, though, or you will merely expose a useful sleight.

Downs himself rarely bothered with the reversing motion. The instant he had back-palmed the coin, he would let go with his little finger, holding it in what some writers call the rear pinch (Fig. 95). This gives the hand

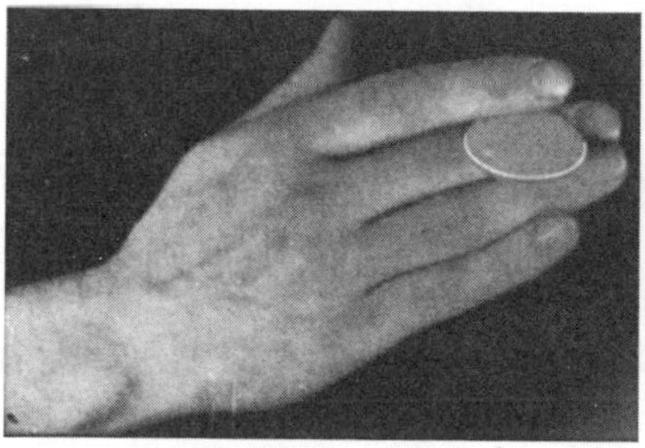

Fig. 95

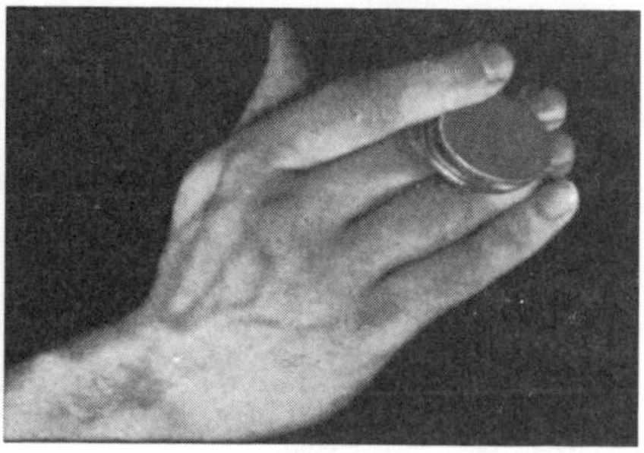

Fig. 96

a much more natural, relaxed look, and does not greatly increase the risk of angles.

As Fig. 96 shows, even then you are not limited to one coin.

Just as with cards, several coins can be back palmed and reproduced one after another. It is undeniably hard work, especially to keep it quiet. You will have to accept my assurance that it can be done if you stick at it.

Instead of the conventional reversing movement to show the back of your hand, you may prefer the following sequence, starting from the forefinger grip. Begin rolling your wrist. When the coin is covered, lay your third finger behind it and straighten your forefinger (Fig. 97).

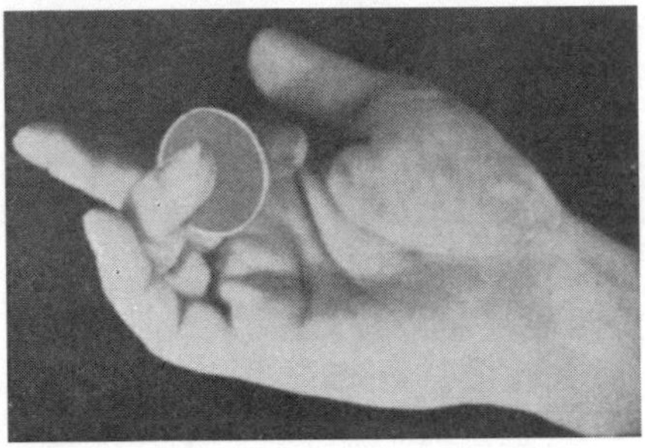

Fig. 97

Close your middle fingers and so plant the coin in the edge palm (Fig. 98), after which you straighten your fingers.

Reversing these motions carries the coin back to the forefinger grip.

Finally, let me give you a little detail that makes a great big difference in the back palm: the best way to reproduce a coin. Most coin manipu-

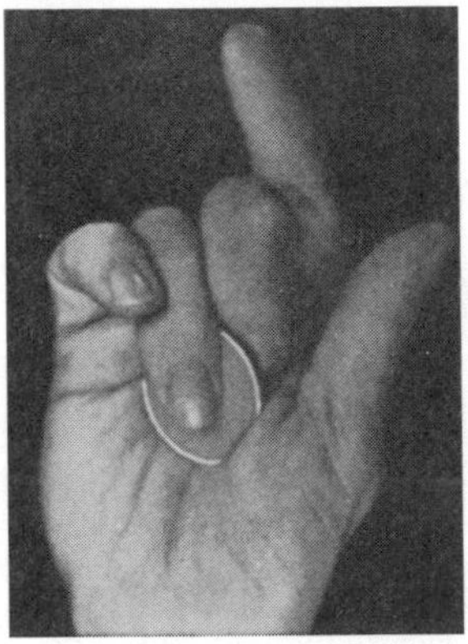

Fig. 98

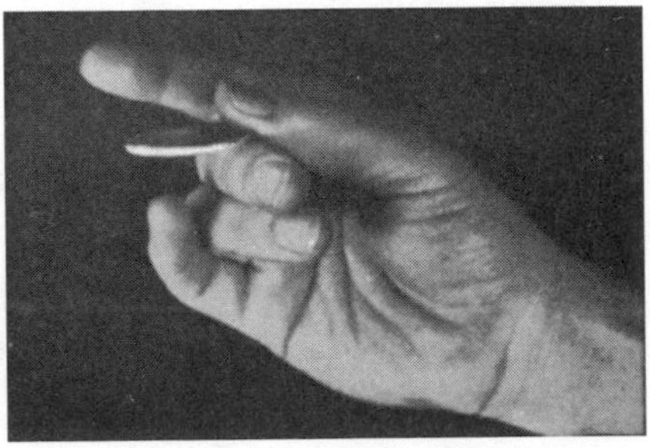

Fig. 99

lators, including the master himself, have brought the coin into view by just reversing the back-palm motion. Instead, you can make the coin spring from nowhere in a flash like this: support the lower edge against your little finger, which you raise until the upper edge of the coin projects slightly above your second finger. Press down on this edge with your thumb (Fig. 99). The coin automatically snaps up sidewise, and you then support it from behind with your forefinger.

9. *The crotch palm.* This sleight produces the same effect as the back palm but has, so to speak, no moving parts to get out of order. The compensating drawback is that even though you are careful the audience may too easily get a flash of the coin.

Hold a coin between the tips of your first and second fingers. Bend the fingers, and leave the coin in the crotch of your thumb. Fig. 100 shows

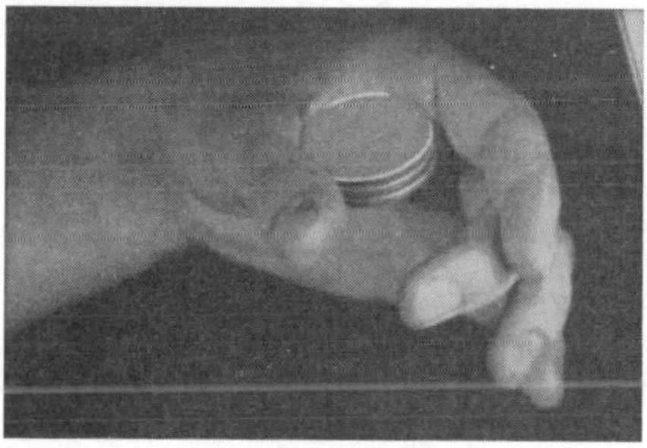

FIG. 100

three coins crotch palmed. If you put the tips of your thumb and first and second fingers together, and keep your hand level, the coins are hidden from every angle.

In handling several coins, put each new one below its predecessor.

Fig. 101 shows the act of reproducing one coin, and Fig. 102 shows this move completed.

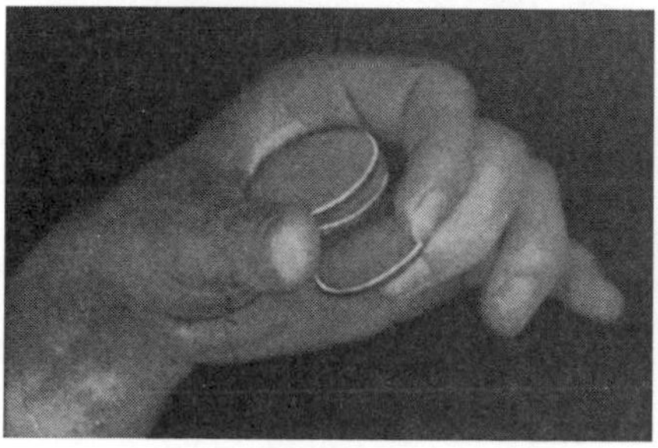

FIG. 101

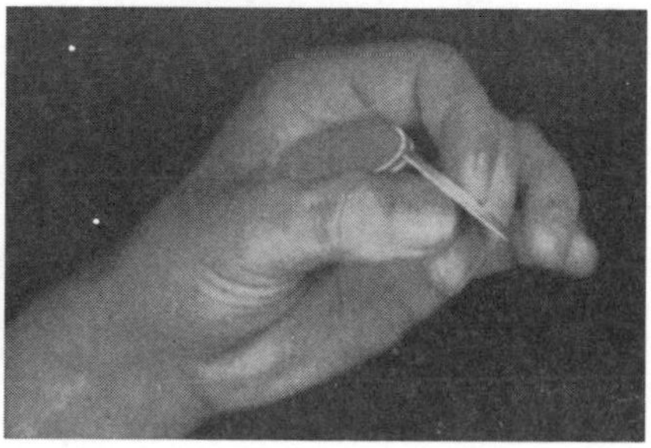

FIG. 102

By gentleness it is comparatively easy to execute the crotch palm without noise.

10. Sleeving. "It's up his sleeve" is a fatuous cry that by now almost turns a magician's stomach. Nevertheless "sleeving" is a recognized expedient in coin magic. Very few other objects can be successfully sleeved; with coins you have a choice of three methods.

Perhaps the most often useful works by inertia. Hold the coin so that nothing will obstruct its passage, and simply stick out your arm. The coin stands still; the cuff moves out and swallows it. You will have to experiment until you learn where the loose part of your cuff is; otherwise the coin will go outside, and fall with a crash.

The coin may also be thrown or snapped up the sleeve. A small coin is held between second finger and thumb; snap your middle finger and the coin spins up your sleeve. Or put the coin on a table top, cover it with the tips of your middle fingers, and whisk the fingers shut. The coin shoots horizontally inward, up the sleeve.

A two-handed method, which might be called a pass, is to hold the coin horizontal by opposite edges between forefinger and thumb. The other hand, palm down, covers the coin and pretends to take it. Just at that moment, squeeze your thumb and forefinger together hard. This squirts the coin clear up to the elbow of the *opposite* sleeve.

11. The Downs click pass. Any form of palming will combine with a pretended transfer to make a perfectly acceptable pass for one coin. In handling several coins together, you must go back once again to Nelson Downs.

Take the coins in your left hand as shown in Fig. 103.

(Probably you will find it easier to do with your right hand; but it is

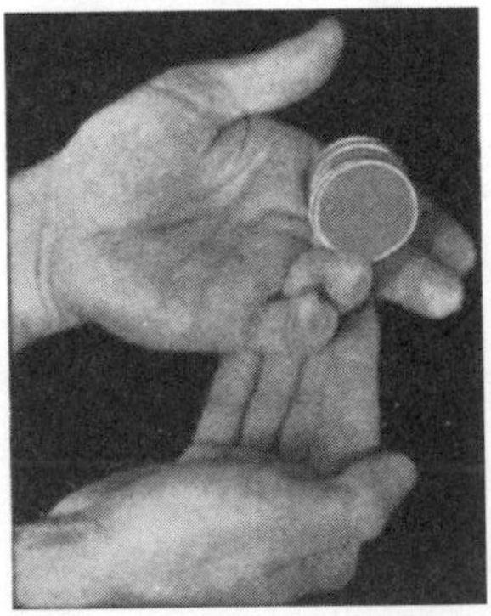

Fig. 103

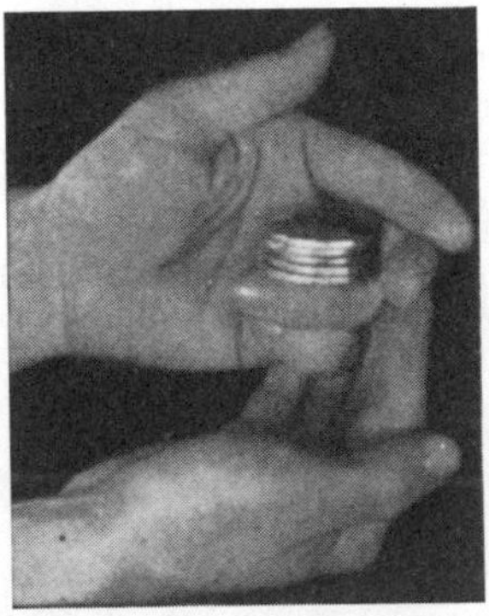

Fig. 104

true of coin manipulation, more than of cards, that the performer who cannot do the palms and passes equally well with either hand is a magical cripple. And you will be pleasantly surprised to discover how much more easily your left hand learns a move once the right hand has mastered it.)

Apparently you dump the coins into your cupped right hand, which closes and moves off. Actually, though, they stack up on your curled left third finger (Fig. 104).

As the right hand moves away, the left middle fingers ease the coins into an edge palm (section 6), while the forefinger points to the closed fist (Fig. 105).

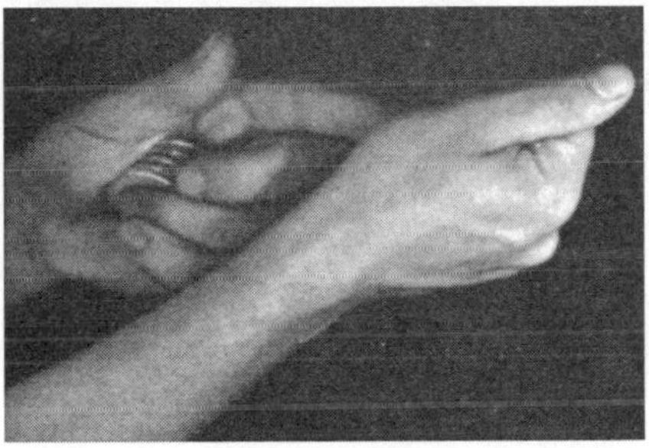

FIG. 105

The noise of the coins as they pile on your third finger is almost as loud as it would be if they fell into your right palm. And since our sense of hearing is not directional except in a very crude way, no one can possibly tell that the coins have not reached your right hand.

12. *The Downs fan pass.* This serves the same purpose as the click pass; use whichever one suits you better.

Show the coins in a fan in your left hand (Fig. 106). Slam the bottom

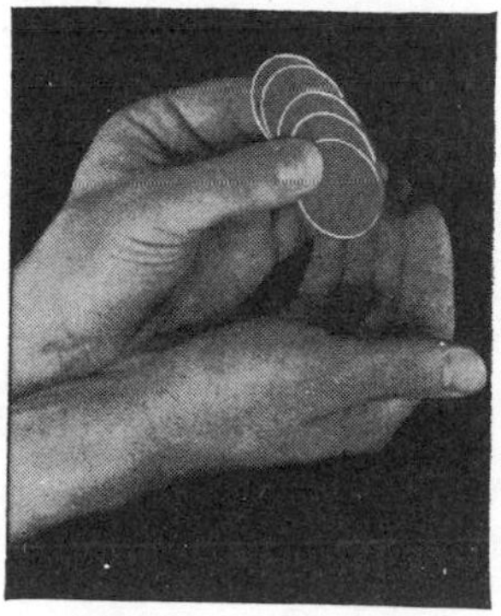

FIG. 106

edge of the fan into your cupped right palm. The fan closes up with a loud jingle, forming a stack which you nip between your left thumb and middle finger (Fig. 107).

Once again your right hand closes and moves away, while the left hand, as in Fig. 105, above, edge-palms the stack.

In all palming you should try to keep your forefinger straight while the other fingers do the work. The pointing gesture is somehow less suggestive of trickery than a closed, convulsively working fist.

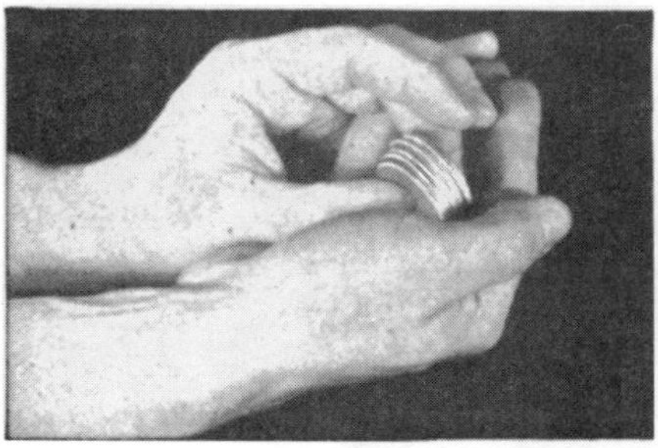

FIG. 107

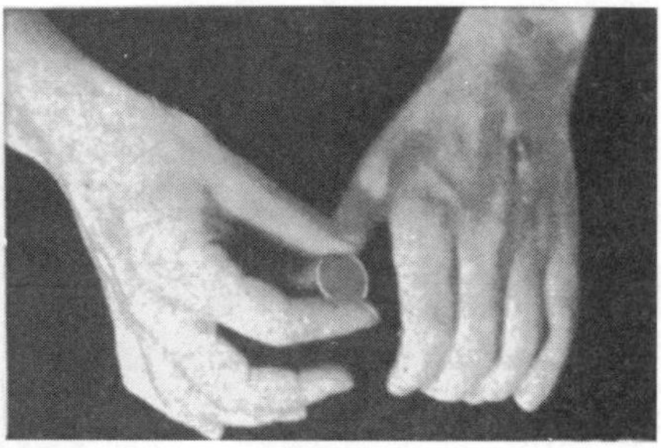

FIG. 108

13. *The squeeze pass.* Here is a deceptive little dodge for one small coin—not bigger than a quarter. Hold it by the edges as in Fig. 108. Your left hand covers the coin in the act of apparently taking it away.

Under this cover, squeeze the coin so that it slips off sidewise from your forefinger and is caught by its upper edge between forefinger and thumb (Fig. 109). From the front, the forefinger and thumb seem merely to be pressed together, empty, because your left hand has "taken" the coin.

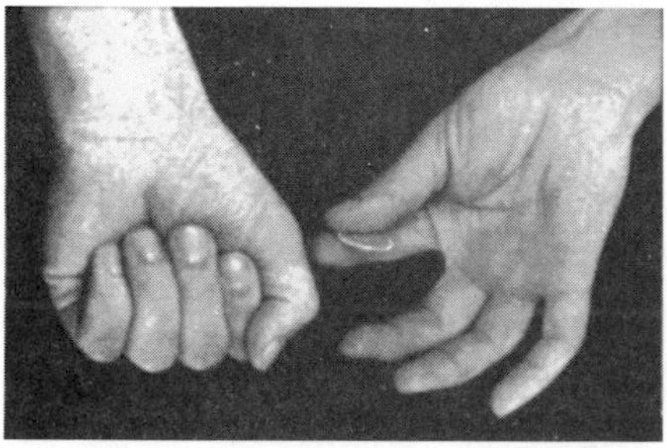

FIG. 109

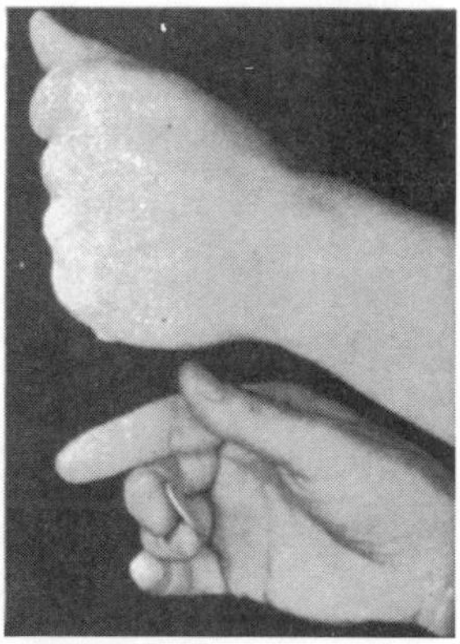

FIG. 110

As the left hand moves off, carrying the eyes of the audience away from the danger spot, you drop the coin to your right middle fingers (Fig. 110), and palm or finger-palm it.

This is the end of the coin passes. As a general rule in making a pass, let me urge you to palm the coin well before it supposedly touches your other, open hand—at the very start of your swing. I have seen beginners frantically try to palm the coin just as their two hands met, when of course the audience was watching them most keenly.

The same thing is true in pretending to toss an object away. Your hand goes down, then quickly up. Palm on the downswing, never on the up.

Some passes, on the other hand, are delayed: don't palm until well *after* your hands separate.

14. The DeManche change. Almost any combination of palms, passes, or even sleeving will make a deceptive coin change, particularly when the switch is an unsuspected one between apparently similar coins (say a substitute of your own for a marked half dollar).

The DeManche change, however, is a special move ideal for the purpose. It is made with one hand, the two coins cannot possibly talk, and the palm may be seen empty almost throughout. It can even be used as a visible change.

You start with the intended substitute coin finger palmed, the original displayed as in Fig. 111.

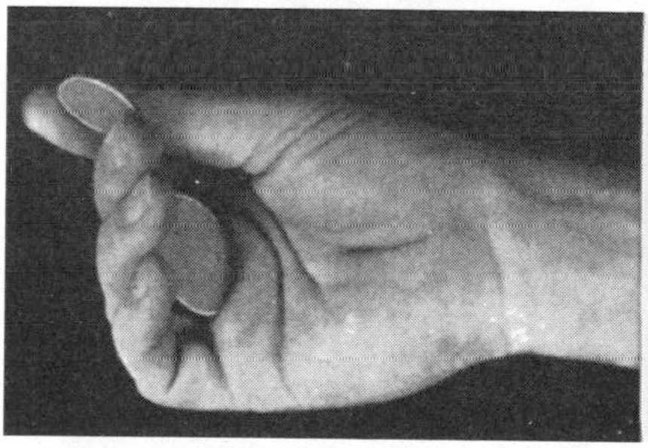

FIG. 111

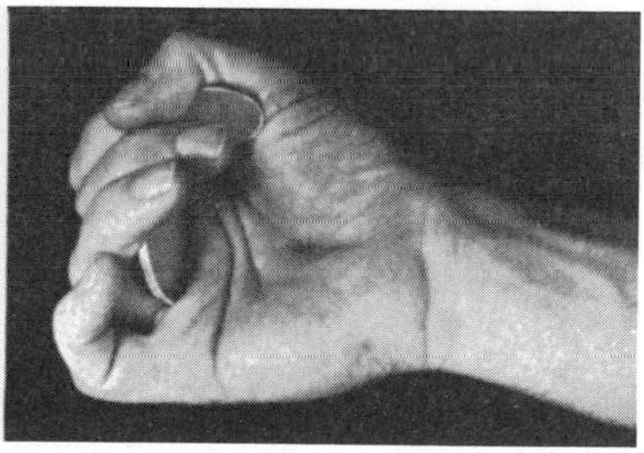

FIG. 112

Your forefinger pushes the original coin into the regular thumb-palm position (Fig. 112). Now put your thumb on the substitute coin and slide it toward the finger tips. This causes the original coin to turn over (Fig. 113) into a position where it in turn is finger palmed, while the substitute coin is displayed at the finger tips (Fig. 114).

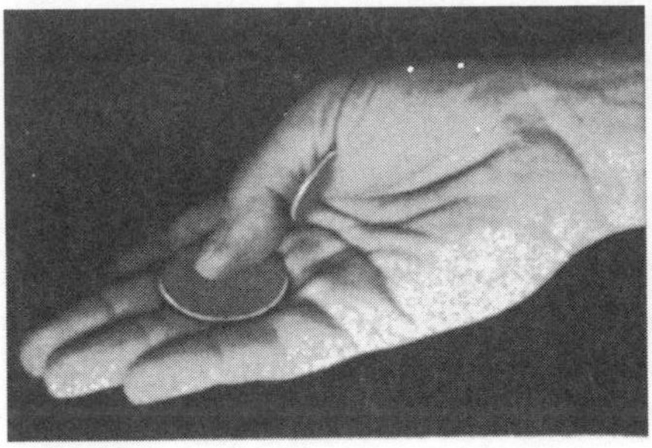

FIG. 113

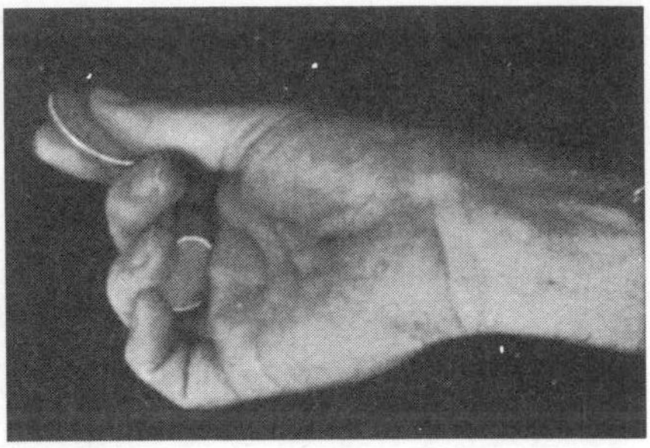

FIG. 114

15. The handkerchief fold. This move apparently wraps a coin in the middle of a handkerchief, but actually leaves it outside, to be either vanished or "pulled through the center" of the kerchief.

Hold a coin upright in your left hand and spread a handkerchief over it (Fig. 115).

Stretch out your right hand, palm up, and catch the coin through the handkerchief between the tips of your first two fingers. Turn your right

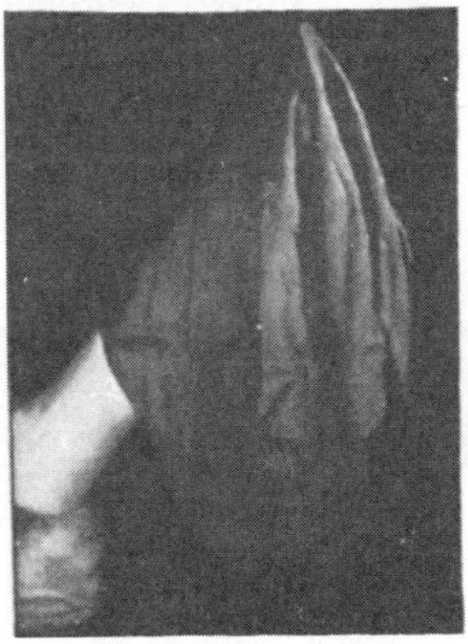

FIG. 115

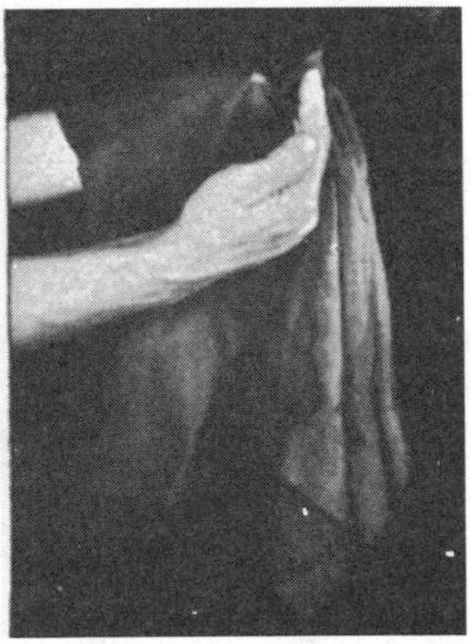

FIG. 116

hand toward yourself, and nip the coin through two thicknesses with your left thumb (Fig. 116). The purpose of this is to put an extra fold of handkerchief underneath the coin.

Now you say (or gesture as if you were saying), "Oh, yes, it's still there." With your right hand pick up the front corner of the handkerchief, revealing the coin (Fig. 117).

Finally, still holding the coin through the cloth between your left

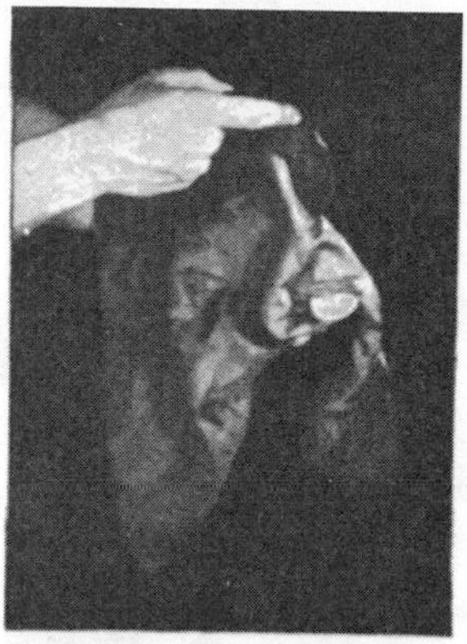

FIG. 117

FIG. 118

forefinger and thumb, shake down the whole handkerchief (Fig. 118). The catch is that the handkerchief has been turned inside out: your left hand was originally under it, but is now above it, and the coin too is outside, hidden from the audience by the fold you have contrived to make.

The handkerchief fold can be used with several coins, and makes a good introduction to the Coins to Handkerchief effect in the next chapter, either in plain form or as Mardo's Shaker Penetration.

16. Flourish: the coin roll, or steeplechase. This small and easy juggling feat has become a sort of badge for magicians. There is nothing very startling about it, but it seems to draw attention and stop conversation if you want to be asked to do tricks.

Hold a coin as in Fig. 119. With your thumb, tilt it over until it lies on top of your first finger. With your second finger, catch the projecting edge, and by pressing down on it turn the coin over to lie across your second finger (Fig. 120).

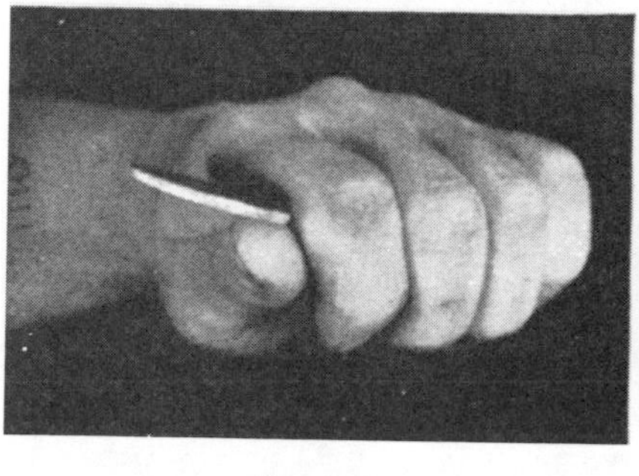

FIG. 119

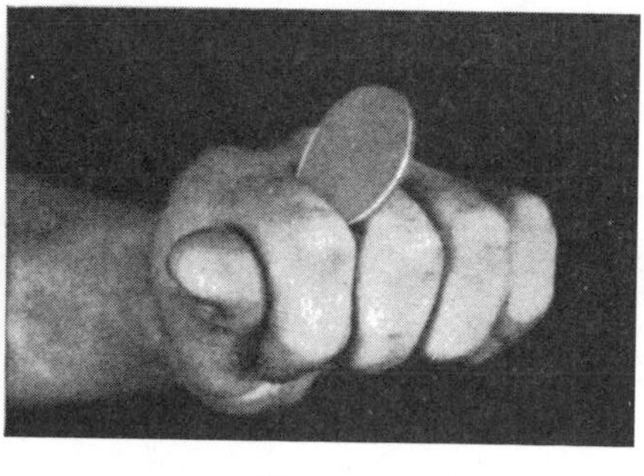

FIG. 120

Repeat this motion with third and little fingers. When it reaches the fork of third and little fingers, work the coin down through (Fig. 121) until you can balance it on your thumb, and carry it out to start the roll over again (Fig. 122).

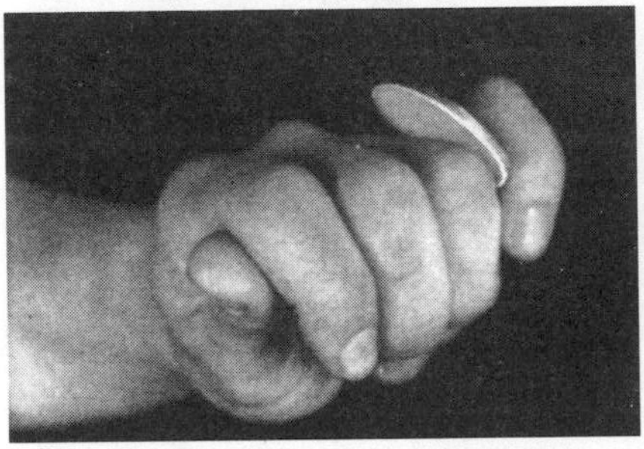

FIG. 121

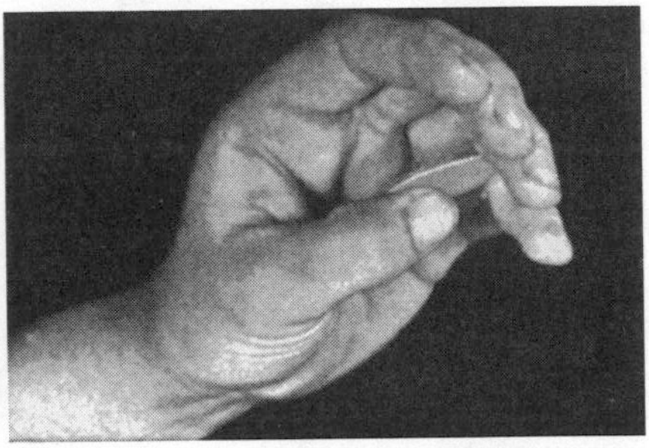

FIG. 122

At first this will be a slow and painful progression. After a while, as the motions become a habit, the coin will almost spin across your knuckles. Naturally the roll may be done in either direction; in fact I generally do it the opposite way from what I have described, and roll it across the inside of the fingers as well. Further elaborations are to roll a pile of three coins as one, and to keep three going one after another—a favorite pastime with John Mulholland.

7. *The Miser's Dream, and Other Great Coin Tricks*

PERHAPS the title of this chapter, like "Wine, Women, and Song," presents an anticlimax. By nature the Miser's Dream is the greatest of all coin tricks; the man who could do it by real magic would never bother with any other feat in the whole range of conjuring.

But even so you must do something for the audience with the money you find. Watching you spend it is not entertainment; hence the other tricks with coins.

1. *The Miser's Dream (Aerial Treasury, Aerial Mint, Coin-Catching, Shower of Money, Rain of Silver, Fortune-Hunt,* or *Coin Chase).* As our local auctioneer says, call it what you like, and use it for the same purpose. You produce a vast number of coins from nowhere, and collect them in a hat, pail, or other receptacle.

The effect was ancient in the days of Robert-Houdin, who remarked in 1868, "This pretty little trick . . . is complete in itself." I should hope so! He did it with seven five-franc pieces (the size of silver dollars); Professor Hoffmann, the patron saint of magical writers, advanced to the point of suggesting ten half crowns. Then the trick settled back to an easy and respectable existence until 1895. That was the year when Nelson Downs (a born showman who had developed the sort of skill that usually precludes magicians from developing their showmanship) opened in vaudeville with his new coin act.

The act was nothing more than the good old Shower of Money, worked on the same principle that had no doubt served Fawkes the elder. The technical innovations, though brilliant, bore only an incidental relation to the success of the act. Downs the actor had a quality of infectious mirth that kept you forever chuckling at the preposterousness of Downs the manipulator. Anyone who does the Miser's Dream (Downs's new name for it) now has something to live up to.

Mechanically speaking, the trick rests on methods of apparently dropping one coin after another from your right hand into a receptacle, but actually palming just one coin and dropping a series of others from the left hand.

Simply to accomplish this, however, even undetected, is hardly to make a beginning with the trick. Real accomplishment lies in the neat and startling way you produce each coin, in your delight at your own success, and in the effect of endless abundance that you create with perhaps two dozen coins.

Now that tall silk hats and even opera hats have become curiosities, you are faced with the problem of a proper receptacle to carry in your left hand. A hard felt hat is fine. Nothing as soft as a fedora is very good, because each coin must make a sharp, distinct sound as it falls in. The makeshift of putting a saucer into a soft hat strikes me as a poor one.

Any sort of small pail or deep bowl will do if it has a pronounced rim that you can engage with your thumb; otherwise your left hand soon grows cramped from clutching the smooth edge.

Every performer has his own routine; in any case, this is not a trick where routine matters much. I give you just one sequence; a score of others might be better for your special purpose.

Start with a stack of twenty-five or thirty coins in your left trouser pocket. Standing on the table is an Oriental brass bucket with a beaded rim.

Put your left hand in your pocket and quite casually steal your load of coins. Pick up the bucket with your right hand, look at it, turn it around, and flip it over in the air.

Then take it in your left hand, with the thumb outside, the fingers and the stack of coins pressed against the inner surface. Go gently; you can't afford talking yet.

Hold out your right hand; look at it; open and close it.

Then shift your eyes to a spot somewhat higher and further away from you. Gaze at it intently; poise your right hand, palm forward, ready to snatch whatever it is.

All this is build-up—the magnet to pull them to the edge of their chairs. When you are sure everybody is awake and breathless, snatch at the imaginary "it," and catch it. Open your hand enough so that you alone can see inside. Look. Smile. *Smile.*

A nod of satisfaction. as if to say that the hard part was done: you have managed to catch something nice. Now that the strain is over, tossing this something into the bucket is a mere afterthought. You make the motion with your right hand, instantly followed by a loud clank in the bottom of the bucket (produced, of course, by one coin dropped from your left fingers).

Start hunting for more where the first came from—and suddenly remember that no one else knows what it was. Take the coin out of the bucket and show it around with smug Harpo Marx satisfaction. Then, content with making your point, drop the coin back into the bucket.

Instead, of course, you palm it in your right hand, at the same instant dropping another from your left.

From here on, almost everything depends on the deftness with which you produce the coins. You must not be vague; you must perceptibly catch sight of a coin in a particular spot, reach your hand out empty, and pluck it back with a coin. I don't mean you must always use the back palm; you need never use it at all. A relaxed hand with its back to the audience is empty so far as that audience knows until you show some sign of its being full.

To produce a coin properly from the flat palm, simply let it fall forward to the tips of your bent middle fingers, and then slide it up with your thumb until you can catch it by the very lower edge between thumb and finger tips.

To produce from the edge palm, pick up the coin between the tips of your middle fingers, then put your thumb under it and tilt it upright.

To produce from the finger palm, slide the coin into view with your thumb.

To produce from either thumb palm, pick up the coin between the tips of your first and second fingers and straighten the fingers.

You already know how to reproduce from the crotch palm (chapter 6, section 9).

If you are among the happy few who have really mastered the back palm, don't let it master you. In the normal version of the Miser's Dream I would never use a reverse from back to front. Once every third or fourth time I would back-palm the coin when apparently dropping it into the hat; stand with my visibly empty hand poised just long enough so that skeptics could see I was not palming anything; and then nip the coin out of the predetermined slot in the air by snapping it upward as described in chapter 6, section 8.

The air as a place to catch coins from soon wears out its fascination; what people remember long afterward is the money you take from their hair, ears, and sleeves. Neatness in producing the coins is even more important now. Unless you are using the back palm (which you must be chary of when you mingle with the audience), advance your hand with knuckles upward toward the spot where you espy a lurking coin. Point your forefinger slightly. Just before your hand reaches the spot, bring the coin to your finger tips. Turn your hand over, carrying the coin out of sight under the lapel, fold of cloth, or whatever the cover is; then draw back your hand, holding the coin at the extreme finger tips.

Because it is *possible* to produce coins by a clumsy grab at the vicinity of someone's elbow, many magicians spoil the magical effect of the Miser's Dream. Neat reproduction is very easy to learn, but it does need rehearsal. Once you know how, you can do it quite slowly, and yet people will actually be puzzled at how the coin could have got to where you took it from.

Perhaps three or four times during the trick, just as an afterthought, you may play pranks with the way you put coins into the bucket. You can apparently swallow one, and pursue its course with your right forefinger down your throat and along your left arm to the bucket, where it lands with a clink. I will not insult your intelligence by explaining this, except to reiterate that you should palm the coin as your right hand starts toward your mouth, not at the last moment.

Using either front or back palm, you can poke a coin through the bottom of the bucket. You can toss one way, way up in the air, run a step or two like an outfielder getting under a high fly, and catch it with a clink.

These are all fun, liven up the routine, and are moderately mystifying; but remember that your ability to make a clink without dropping a coin from your right hand is the vital secret of the trick. Don't be like Camille Gaultier's French performer who proudly passed all thirty coins in succession through the side of the hat, and never dropped any in at the top.

By now the stack of coins hidden in your left hand will be pretty well gone. Stop dashing about among the audience. Shake the bucket. Scoop up a fistful of coins in your right hand, and pour them back into the bucket. Scoop up some more and this time finger-palm as many as you can get hold of.

You may produce one or two singly, or go straight toward some portly spectator, beg his pardon, tuck your fingers under his vest, and bring out a fan of coins.

Let the fan slide back into your cupped hand, jingle the coins, and thus shake them into finger-palm position (chapter 6, section 2). You apparently bung them into the bucket; really the heel of your hand jolts the rim, jingling the other coins, while you retain the finger palm.

Produce some more coins from another unlikely place.

The great difficulty about a satisfactory presentation of the Miser's

Dream lies in managing to telegraph the end of the trick, to ask for the final burst of applause. There is no logical ending: if you had sense, why on earth would you stop finding money?

You will have to think of an excuse or at least a conclusion to suit your own personality. You might, for instance, set down the bucket, and scoop up coins with both hands, carrying on like a really crazed miser. Or you might say airily, "After all, what is this stuff? Nothing but money."

When you have created a finish for the Miser's Dream, you may consider that trick learned.

2. *Catching Five Coins (Downs's Eureka Pass).* As described in *Modern Coin Manipulation,* this was hardly more than an ingenious flourish. As Downs himself did it, it was a trick that gave in a minute or two nearly as much effect as the whole ten minutes of the Miser's Dream.

He picked one spot in the air before him, delicately caught a coin from it in his right hand, and put the coin in his left hand. From the same spot he caught another coin, and another, and another, and another.

Sometimes he went on to do tricks with the five coins; sometimes he poked them successively back into nothingness, where they came from.

The principle is allied to that of the Vanish and Recovery with cards; the method, neat and unostentatious back-palming combined with edge palming and a special steal.

Edge-palm four coins in your left hand and have one in your right, ready to back-palm. Do so just before you start.

You may, if you think it necessary, do one reverse, ending with the coin again at the back.

Then pick your spot in the air and deftly snap the coin out of it.

As you do this, with your left third finger draw off the face coin from the palmed stack. The first two times it is vital that there be no sound. Let the coin sit on your curled third finger.

Put the coin from your right hand between your left forefinger and thumb (Fig. 123). This brings the coin that is balanced on the left third finger directly behind your right hand, in the exact position for a back palm, which you execute, then casually withdraw your right hand (Fig. 124).

You are thus loaded to produce the next coin. You continue this sequence throughout the series, ending with the five coins fanned in your left hand.

To make the coins disappear, you reverse the process, each time stealing the back-palmed coin from behind your right hand with your left third finger, and edge-palming it.

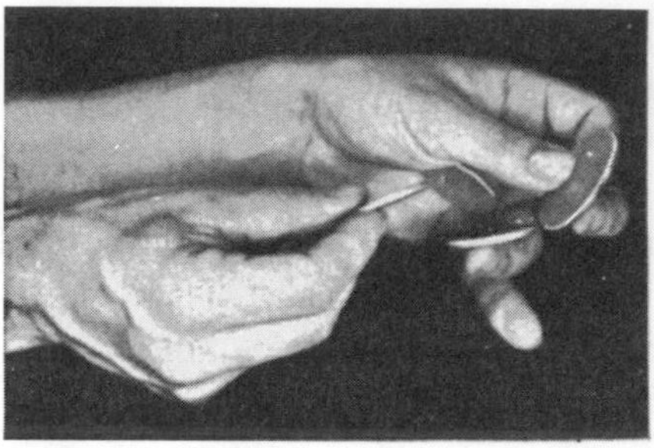

Fig. 123

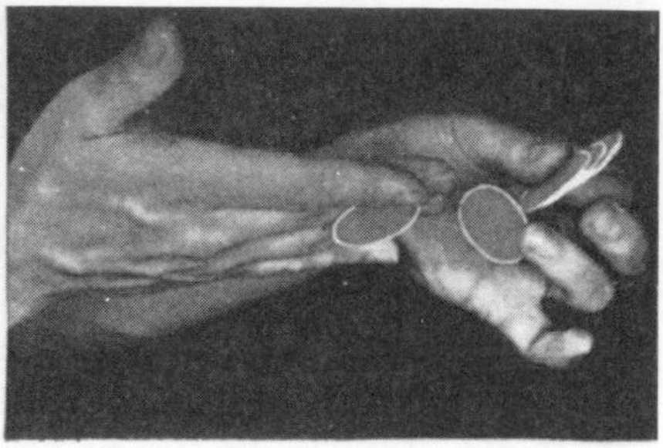

Fig. 124

The fourth coin to disappear is the critical one because up until then any talking as you palm the coins can be explained by the scraping of those still fanned in your left hand. Repalming the coins is harder to do noiselessly than stealing them in the first part of the trick.

Once you have mastered this vest-pocket Miser's Dream, you will have always on call one of the best coin tricks it is possible to show.

3. *Manuel's Thumb Gag.* Nelson Downs was not the only skillful coin manipulator the art has known; he was just the only skillful coin manipulator who was a great showman. Thomas Manuel could also do incredible things with coins and cards, and this little sucker gag is one that he used.

Sucker gags with coins are very scarce indeed; you may have some fun with this one.

Manuel would hold out his left hand flat and stiff. He would display a coin in his right hand against the tip of his left little finger (Fig. 125).

Fig. 125

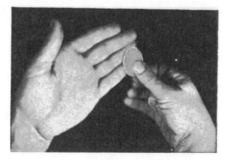

(Never mind the coins palmed in the right hand; we haven't got to them yet.)

Then he would turn the coin over, poke it into the fork of his left thumb (Fig. 126), and close his left hand. A moment later he would open his left hand, and the coin was gone. His left thumb, however, was held tight against the side of his hand.

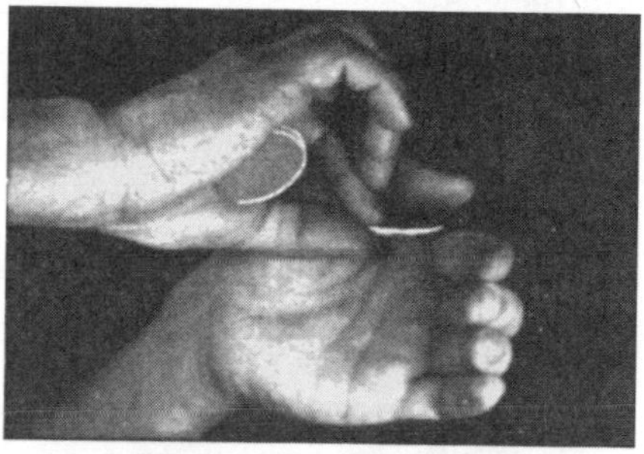

FIG. 126

He would pick up another coin and go through exactly the same motions, after which it would disappear.

If you are using this to follow the Eureka Pass, you will do it five times.

By the end of the series, with his left fingers spread wide apart and his thumb held close, even unsuspicious onlookers began to wonder about what you or I might call reverse thumb palming.

"That?" Manuel would say. "Oh, no." And he would stick his thumb straight up, and waggle it derisively.

The secret is chiefly in the position of your hands as you lay the coin in the fork of your left thumb. The coin is then covered by your right hand, which simply withdraws it again and edge-palms it on the way down to pick up the next coin. Naturally you don't turn your hand over far enough to show the edge-palmed coins, which are seen from an intentionally revealing angle in Fig. 126. The move is repeated with each new coin.

Obviously, noiseless edge palming is the absolute prerequisite for Manuel's Thumb Gag.

4. *Nate Leipzig's Slow-Motion Vanish.* Nate Leipzig was a great showman at close quarters, and a great manipulator of coins and anything else he could wrap his hands around. There was less irresistible drollery about him than about Tommy Downs, and hence his personality did not carry across footlights quite so well. It may be a century before another performer appears who can equal Leipzig in a private gathering. I shall give here two of his small coin tricks, one simple but difficult, the other trickier and easier.

The first is the slow-motion vanish. Leipzig remarked that he could deceive the eye even without quickness of hand; in fact he would do it in slow motion. He passed a coin from his left hand to his right fist, all in slow motion as he had promised. His left palm faced the audience. Very slowly he opened his right fist, and now both palms were empty, his fingers a little apart. Then he turned both hands to show the backs, and finally reproduced the coin between the tips of both thumbs and forefingers.

The whole trick depends on smoothness and a keen study of angles. The angles are why I call this a difficult trick. Start with the coin in your left hand and cover it from the front with your right palm (Fig. 127).

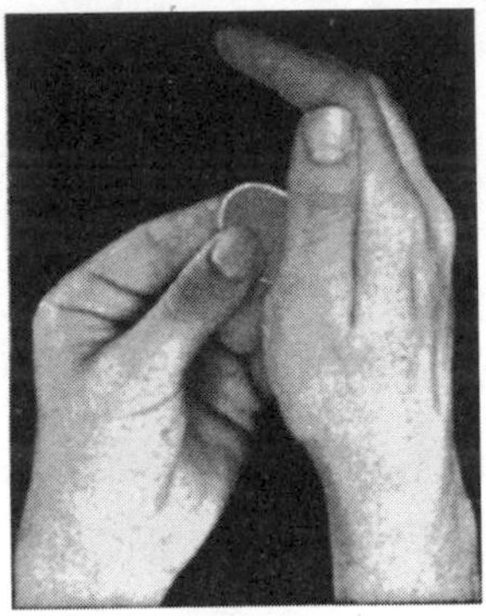

FIG. 127

As your right fingers apparently close over the coin, flat-thumb-palm it in your left hand (chapter 6, section 3). Your right little finger then closes over your extended left forefinger (Fig. 128).

Keep your left hand perfectly still; revolve your right fist, bringing the knuckles to the front, with your left forefinger tip touching the fork of your right thumb (Fig. 129).

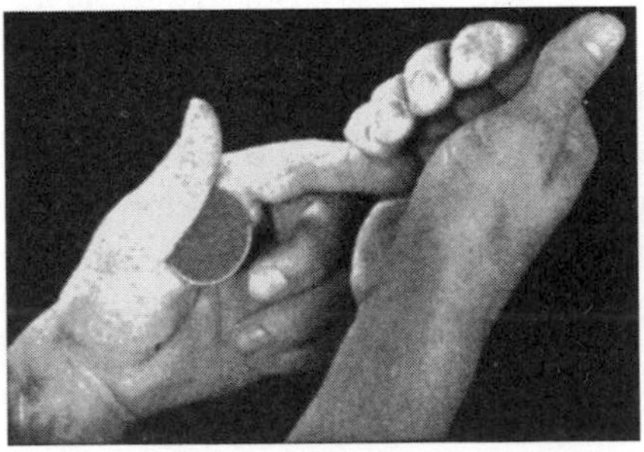

FIG. 128

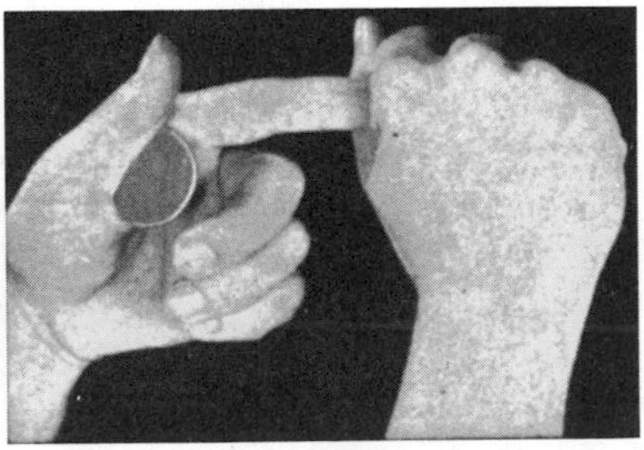

FIG. 129

Bend your left forefinger down around the inner edge of the thumb-palmed coin, which you then push to the rear. Move your left thumb forward so that you can end by hitching the coin clear back out of sight in a reverse thumb palm. As you are finishing this move, turn your left palm toward the audience (Fig. 130). Hold this pose.

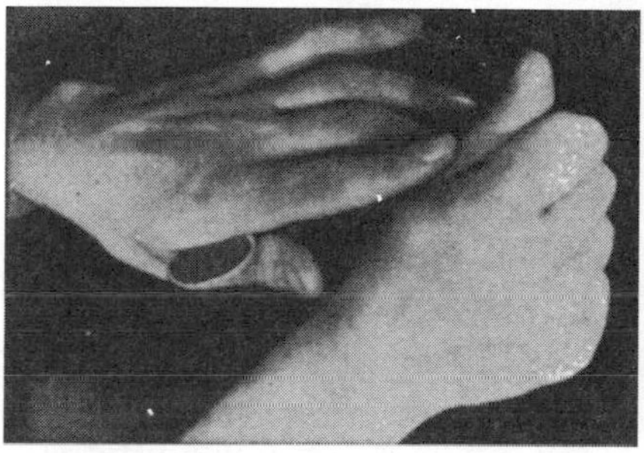

FIG. 130

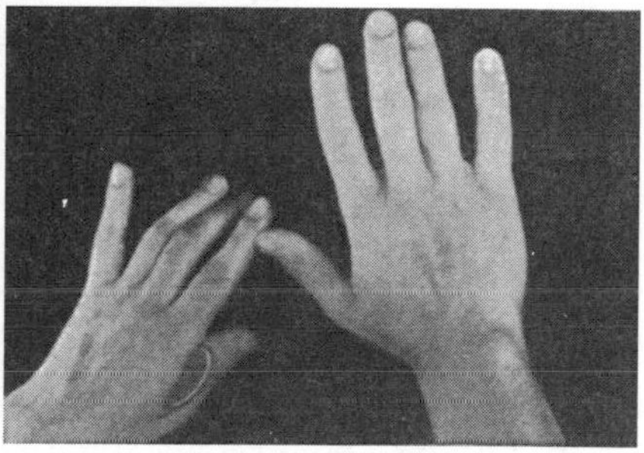

FIG. 131

Then open your right hand (Fig. 131). The coin is gone and both hands are empty.

Bring your right thumb to the rear edge of the thumb-palmed coin (Fig. 132). Now turn the hands with the palms facing each other, the fingers of the right hand partly enveloping the fingers of the left. When

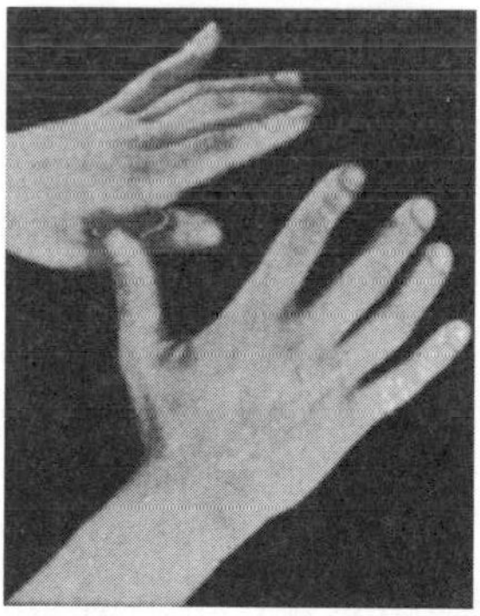

FIG. 132

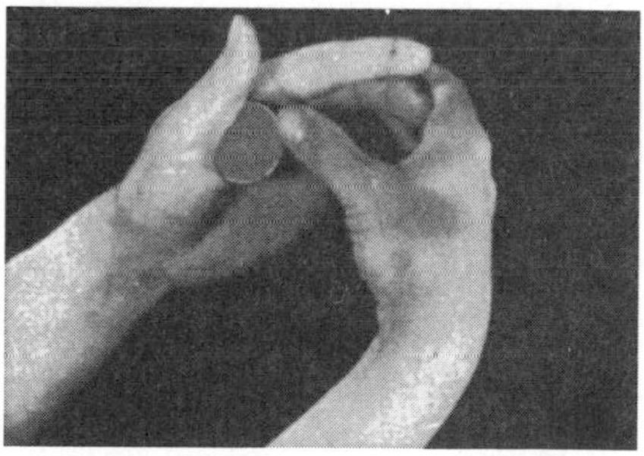

FIG. 133

you do this, it is perfectly natural to roll the coin to the inside of your left hand (Fig. 133).

Pause, holding both hands, back to the audience, in an inverted V, with the third finger tips barely touching.

Finally, slide the coin to the position of Fig. 134, thus reproducing it.

FIG. 134

Try this out on your mirror before you brave a live audience. The angles are killers.

5. *Leipzig's Coin from Hand to Hand.* This is the other little trick by the late Nate Leipzig that I promised a moment ago. The basic effect —a coin passing from one hand to the other—is so commonplace that I shall merely scratch the surface by giving three other methods hereafter; but this version has the true Leipzig touch.

Lying on the flat fingers of your left hand are two conspicuously different coins—say a half dollar and a quarter. Your right hand picks up the half dollar as you step close to a spectator. You seem to tuck the coin under his left coat lapel, which you tug gently twice to start the machinery turning. The next moment, you hold your left hand under the right point of his vest; there is a clink, and the half dollar drops out onto the quarter.

In describing the presentation I have virtually explained the trick. You will find that if you have the quarter in about fingerpalm position, and the half dollar overlapping it toward your finger tips, it is quite easy, when the right hand affords cover, to back-palm the half dollar without disturbing the quarter. Somehow when you remove the larger of the two coins, no one ever dreams that you might really have left it behind. The misdirection is perfect.

Leipzig, like Downs, always released the back-palmed coin with his little finger; this is particularly important here because for a moment or two everyone is looking closely at your left hand, which must not appear cramped.

To reproduce the half dollar, slide the four fingers of your left hand under the edge of the victim's vest, letting the quarter repose in your cupped palm. Stick your third finger behind the half dollar, and so pull it through between second and third fingers. It falls with a clink on the quarter.

6. *Coin from Hand to Hand (three methods).* In all these methods more than one coin is shown. Of course it would be perfectly simple to make a lone coin travel from one hand to the other by any of the passes; but the extra coin provides misdirection, and the clink when the two coins meet is a good part of the effect. Besides, few performers do any pass well enough to lean on it safely as a trick by itself.

The first method is used in another book of mine as the school example to illustrate presentation, timing, and misdirection by imitation and intensity. There I described a rather elementary pass; you, however, are sufficiently advanced to skip the lecture and to use any pass you like.

Hold up a coin in each hand. Put the right-hand one between your teeth. Hold out your right hand and apparently put the left-hand coin in it, actually palming the coin.

Either take the coin from between your teeth with your left forefinger and thumb, or drop it thence into your cupped left fingers, taking care not to expose the palmed coin or let the falling one clink against it.

Stretch out your right fist; look at it, look back at your left hand (which you hold down and to the left), and then once more at your right hand. Snap your right fingers and open the hand.

Just about as quickly as you can swing your eyes from right hand to left, drop the palmed coin on the one in your left fingers—clink!

This is one of the small effects that rather gain by repetition. It is safe enough to use the same move, or you may follow my example in ostentatiously reversing hands. I put the left-hand coin between my teeth, and apparently take the right-hand coin in my left hand, actually *back*-palming it. I quickly switch from back to edge palm, take the coin from between my teeth with my right hand, and apparently make the other one pass through my body this time, instead of merely separating my hands.

The Second Method is the only piece of hand magic I know of where quickness actually does outrun the eye.

It must be worked at a table (though I have sometimes toyed with the idea of practicing until I could do it on my knees as I sat). You show a small coin (not bigger than a quarter) on each palm; your hands are held flat on the table, six or eight inches apart.

With one quick motion you whip over your hands, slamming them on the table top.

When you lift them, there are two coins under the left palm, none at all under the right.

The method is perfect in its simplicity: you throw the coin. Although I said you showed a coin on each palm, actually the right-hand coin rests on the third joints of your middle fingers. Your right hand turns over a split second before your left; the position of the coin gives you leverage to shoot it across, whereas the left-hand coin, in the hollow of your palm, merely falls into place. The thrown coin drops on the table just under your left hand.

I may mention that copper cents are less likely to give a revealing flash than bright coins. The other troubles you may have are a tendency to bring your hands together, and next (in avoiding this) a tendency to move both hands to the right, merely dropping the right-hand coin and covering it with the other hand instead of throwing it across as you should.

The trick is sometimes shown as a transposition, with a cent in one hand, and a nickel in the other. Each hand throws its coin to the other hand.

The third method, I understand, was the favorite coin trick of David Devant, the king of English wizards. It is generally used as a follow-up for the second method, to throw people off the track.

Instead of two coins, you need four. They must all be alike, but need not be small.

Shut one in each fist. Lay your fists, backs down, on the table. Have a spectator balance the other coins, one on the knuckles of each hand.

You spin your hands over, as people have learned to expect from the previous version. Nothing happens, however, except that you lose the two outside coins and have to ask the spectator to replace them.

On the second attempt you succeed: one coin in your right hand, three in your left.

Naturally the failure was part of the act. As you whirl your hands over, open your left fist just enough to admit the outside coin. Simultaneously your right hand secretly spills both outside and inside coins on the table. When the spectator once more balances a coin on each of your fists, he unwittingly transfers one coin for you.

So far as presentation goes, the first method depends on everyone's realizing (by your pantomime more than your talk) what is going to happen, what is happening, what has happened. The second method speaks for itself once people have grasped the elementary fact that you have a coin on each palm. In the third method, you want to give an impression of difficult juggling (just what you *don't* want to do in the second method), so that they will forget your initial failure. None of these tricks alone, or even the three in combination, is solid enough to stand up under much patter.

7. *Silver and Gold.* This is my version of the routine called Winged Silver in *Dai Vernon's Select Secrets.* Dai Vernon is known for his fabulous card tricks, but excels many of his fellow card stars in being skillful with coins as well.

The effect is that you take three gold coins (presumably brass palming coins) in your right fist, and three silver coins in your left. There are no "failures"; the silver coins pass one after another to join the gold coins in the left hand. Each silver coin clinks loudly on arriving.

The method is not remarkably difficult, except that I found the routine confusing to learn. Once you have it memorized, you will be all right.

In addition to the six coins (which you carry in a right-hand pocket) you have a fourth silver coin. Palm this in your right hand as you take out the six from your pocket. The six should be stacked in your right hand with the silver coins under your thumb.

Stretch out your left hand, and shove the first silver coin off the stack with your right thumb. Put the coin exactly in palming position in your left hand. Push off the second coin and lay it on the first, overlapping away from your wrist. Then a third, fourth, fifth, and sixth. You count as you lay them out in this ribbon fashion. All this time your right hand keeps the extra coin quietly palmed.

So much for the first step.

With your right hand pick up the three silver coins in a stack, held by the edges. Plunk this stack down on the table to your *left.*

That is the second step.

Make the motion of dumping the silver coins from your left hand into your right. Actually, hold onto the first coin, which you carefully placed in palming position, in your left hand. The original palmed coin in your right hand adds in to make three.

The moment the silver coins are in your right hand (this is where I always forget and hesitate), plunk them down on the table to your right.

That is the third step.

Now your left hand picks up the gold stack, your right hand the silver. Close each fist, but don't let go of the palmed silver coin in your left.

As you close your right fist, fingers underneath, separate off the top coin of the silver stack, and palm it.

That is the fourth step.

Hold your hands fairly well apart, fingers underneath. This is the build-up, the warning of magic to come. Pause. Your left palm drops its silver coin with a loud clink on the gold stack held by the fingers.

Promptly slap the two free silver coins from your right hand on the table, keeping the third palmed.

Open your left fist, letting everyone see the silver newcomer among the gold. The coins should lie on your open hand in such a way that the silver coin is once more in palming position. (I do the trick with silver dollars and smaller brass palming coins, which makes it much easier.)

That is the fifth step.

As soon as the audience on your left has seen the four coins, give the people on your right a chance: dump the three gold coins into your right hand, palming off the silver one in your left. The silver one that was palmed in your right makes the count correct. Show the four to some people on your right.

That is the sixth step.

With your right hand drop the four coins into your cupped left fingers and close your left fist.

Pick up the two silver coins from the table with your right hand, palming off the top one in the act of closing your fist.

That is the seventh step.

Another clink in your left hand. Your right hand slaps down just one silver coin; your left hand opens to display three gold and two silver, one of the silver again in palming position.

From here on the routine is the same: dump four coins from your left hand into your right, palming off one; drop the five back into your left hand, closing your left fist; and pick up the solitary silver coin in your right hand.

Either in taking this coin from the table or a moment later, sleeve it.

Another clink in the left hand. Your right hand is empty; your left hand pours out three silver and three gold coins.

8. *The Sympathetic Coins.* This was described by John Northern Hilliard, perhaps with a bit of the sponsor's partiality, as "the classic coin trick." It is certainly the king of table effects. An Italian conjurer who adopted the odd name of Yank Hoe invented it, and it was first described in Downs's and Hilliard's *The Art of Magic*; since all authorities agree that the trick has never been improved, I borrow this standard description.

"Effect: A handkerchief or napkin is spread over the table. Four half dollars are laid on the handkerchief so as to form the corners of a square, which we shall call *A*, *B*, *C*, and *D*, reading from the performer's upper left to his upper right, thence to the lower left and finally the lower right.

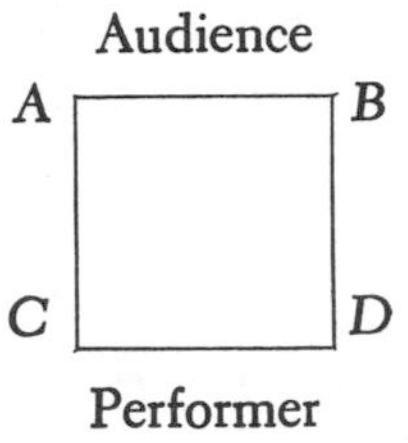

Two of the coins are temporarily covered with small squares of paper or playing cards. The four coins eventually come together under one of the papers.

"Two squares of stiffish paper about four inches by four make perhaps the best covers.

"The effect of the trick will be enhanced if a handkerchief of dark color is used, as the silver coins show up better by contrast.

"Presentation: The four coins are at positions *A*, *B*, *C*, and *D*. The performer exhibits the two squares of paper, calling attention to the fact that the experiment is more in the nature of an optical illusion than a feat of magic. The successive covering of the coins, hereafter described, may thus be accounted for by means of patter based on the science of optics.

"Standing behind the table and holding a square of paper in each hand, revealing the hand otherwise empty, the magician covers coins *A* and *B*, *A* with the paper in the left hand and *B* with the paper in the right hand.

"Observing that by covering these two coins, the other two coins are made visible, he quickly shifts the papers so as to cover the coins *C* and *D*, observing at the same time that the two front coins are visible.

"He now covers *C* and *B*, calling attention to the fact that *A* and *D* are visible; and then, quickly shifting the papers, covers *A* and *D*, the paper in the left hand covering *A* and the paper in the right hand covering *D*.

"Now while the left hand holds the paper over *A*, the right hand shifts the paper from *D* to *B*, and while he is talking to, and looking straight at, the audience (asking them, for instance, if they can see the two rear coins), the fingers of his right hand (under cover of the paper) pick up coin *B*.

"This movement, it must be understood, is made without moving the paper; nor should there be the slightest visible movement of the right hand. The sleight will be facilitated if the right thumb presses down on the left edge of the coin, slightly tilting the right edge up to the finger tips. The performer's eyes, it is scarcely necessary to say, must never for an instant glance at the right hand during the picking-up movement. Should he forget himself in this respect, the audience will instantly suspect the removal of the coin.

"Now comes the crucial move of the trick. It is not a difficult move; and, if it is made properly, the whole operation is covered.

"While the right hand holds coin *B* under the paper, the left hand removes the paper from over coin A and holds it squarely in front of the right hand.

"Under cover of this paper, the right hand carries paper and coin away; and, as the right hand moves away, the paper in the left hand is allowed to fall on the table, where coin *B* is supposed to lie.

"The right hand moves over to the left side of the table, and in the act of covering coin A with the paper, the coin in the right hand is laid on the table near A. Of course you must not let coin *B* clink against coin A in this operation.

"At this stage in the experiment, you have two coins under the paper at A, although your audience believes that there is one coin under each of the papers. It will be understood that all these moves are made quickly and to the accompaniment of lively patter.

"Now for the second part of the trick. Grasp the lower left corner of the handkerchief with the left hand, the *fingers well underneath* and the *thumb above*.

"Take coin C in the fingers of the right hand. Hold it up high, so that all may see that you actually hold a coin. The left hand lifts up the corner of the handkerchief, and the right hand carries the coin under the handkerchief and apparently pushes it toward the front of the table until it is directly under the paper at A.

"A slight upward movement is made with the fingers of the right hand; there is an audible clink of two coins coming together; and, removing his right hand from beneath the handkerchief and showing it unmistakably empty, back and front, the performer daintily picks up the paper at A, and exhibits the two coins.

"If these movements are made as described, and the clink of the coins is audible, the effect to the audience is that the coin really passed through the cloth.

"Of course, it did no such thing. As you passed the right hand under the handkerchief, you left the coin between the first and second fingers of the left hand.

"There must be no hesitation in the execution of this movement. The right hand must transfer the coin to the left without pausing a fraction of a second, and the fingers of the right hand, held as though they contained the coin, push slowly forward until they are under the paper cover at A. Now, if an upward movement is made with the fingers, one of the coins will be thrown upon the other, causing the illusive clink.

"The right hand is now withdrawn and lifts the paper cover.

"At the same moment the left hand, holding the coin between the first and second fingers, releases the handkerchief and takes the paper cover from the right hand.

"The coin is now concealed under the paper in the left hand, which replaces the paper cover over the two coins, being careful not to allow the coin to clink as it is released from the fingers.

"As there are three coins now under the paper at A, the process is repeated with coin *D*. When the paper in the left hand is again placed over the coins at A, there are four coins under the cover, although the audience is convinced that there are only three.

"In order to pass the coin *B* (apparently) under the paper at A, you must vary the procedure. Simply bend over and blow briskly under the paper at *B*. The effect is as if you blew the coin from *B* under the paper at A.

"Lift up this paper and exhibit the assembled coins.

"Invariably an encore is demanded when this trick is shown, and unlike most sleight-of-hand effects, it may be repeated before the same audience. As a matter of fact, its performance by means of a second method leaves the audience more mystified than ever.

"In this method the magician uses five coins instead of four; but of course the audience is unaware of the extra coin.

"Conceal the fifth coin in your left hand, and arrange the four coins as before. In laying the papers over A and *B* you do not take away *B*, as in the first method, but allow the extra coin in the left hand to join the coin at A.

"The trick now proceeds as before, except that after passing the last coin, *B*, under the handkerchief you must get rid of it in some manner. It is easy enough to slip the coin into a pocket while lifting up the paper at A because all eyes are attracted to this part of the table.

"We have been at some pains to describe this trick in detail because it is really worth the attention of the most fastidious sleight-of-hand artist. It is simple in theory, but the amateur will discover that it must be worked with a delicacy of touch and breezy patter, in which case the illusion produced is perfect. Don't be misled by the apparent simplicity of the trick and present it without the requisite amount of practice, or you will regret your temerity."

The same effect has been extended, since the above description was written, to use lumps of sugar and bare hands (Nate Leipzig did this, palming the lumps), crumpled paper under saucers, and the like. It is still hard to beat the original version.

9. *Coins Dissolving in a Handkerchief.* If you have shown the Sympathetic Coins with your own handkerchief, you can pass on very naturally to this little trick, which depends on a special form of click pass.

You spread the handkerchief over your left hand. Pick up one coin with your right hand and put it in your left hand, which you close, handkerchief and all. You then put the second, third, and fourth coins also in your left hand, the accompanying clink growing louder each time.

With your right hand you catch a corner of the handkerchief and yank it away from your left hand. The coins are gone.

As you put the first coin into your left hand, you make a normal pass, flat- or edge-palming the coin (chapter 6).

When you pick up the second coin, let it rest fairly well back on the tips of your right middle fingers. Then just as they touch the inside of your cupped left hand (which is helpfully obscured by the handkerchief), drop the palmed coin on top of the one at your finger tips and retrieve both of them, holding them much as you would after the reverse in the back palm.

In reaching for the third coin, edge-palm the first two.

The third coin in turn appears to go into the left hand, and there is a smart clink as the two palmed coins fall and pile up on the third.

In reaching for the fourth coin, you edge-palm the first three. Of course three palmed coins falling on the fourth make a still louder clink.

You have time to edge-palm all four coins as you reach for the corner of the handkerchief.

Done briskly and with almost no patter, you will find this pass perfectly deceptive.

10. *The Shaker Penetration.* This ingenious new twist (and twist is what I mean) to an old trick appeared in Señor Mardo's excellent pamphlet, *Routined Magic.*

You wrap a coin (or with a little experimenting you can safely use the four from the Sympathetic Coins) in a handkerchief, twist the handkerchief a few times to seal off the coin, and stick this twisted part between two highball glasses, held mouth to mouth, with the corners of the handkerchief hanging out between the rims of the glasses.

Hand this improvised shaker to a spectator, and tell him to shake himself up a Hi-Yo Silver cocktail. After a few shakes, the money falls out of the handkerchief into the lower glass.

Señor Mardo's presentation is everything; the secret is merely the handkerchief fold (chapter 6, section 15) plus a few twists of what we may call the neck of the handkerchief, which serves to hold the coin in place until it is disturbed by the shaking.

11. *Coins to Handkerchief.* This trick, one of the very few that I can actually claim as my own, is the reverse of Señor Mardo's: you pass several coins from your hand into a handkerchief held by the spectator. The two effects make a fine combination—first pass the coins in, then get them out. The two sets of moves are different, so you will be quite safe.

Mine rests on a smooth and ingenious steal whose originator I do not know. Instead of using the steal for my trick with a handkerchief, you may fall back on it to confound the wise guy who once heard about a coin pass and wants to see the coin really in your left hand before it disappears.

Shake out the handkerchief and hold it flat in front of you for a moment; then spread it over your right hand. Try inconspicuously to get your right hand as nearly as may be under the exact center of the handkerchief.

Take the four coins in your cupped left hand. Jingle them and show them around until people have forgotten the handkerchief and the right hand.

Turn your left hand over, knuckles upward, so that the coins stack up on the curled-under tips of your fingers.

Turn the stack gently over toward your wrist (Fig. 135). This leaves

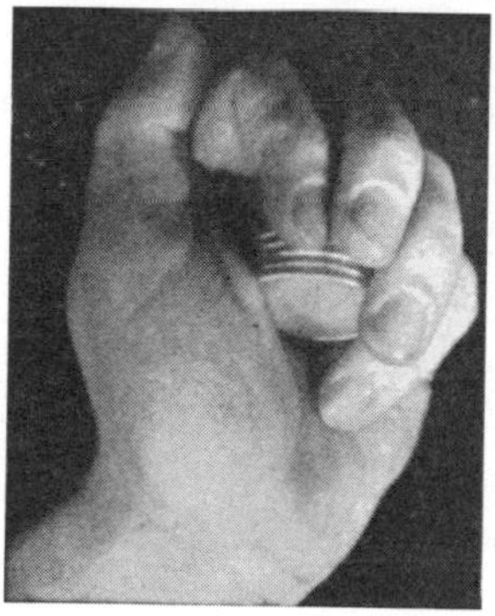

FIG. 135

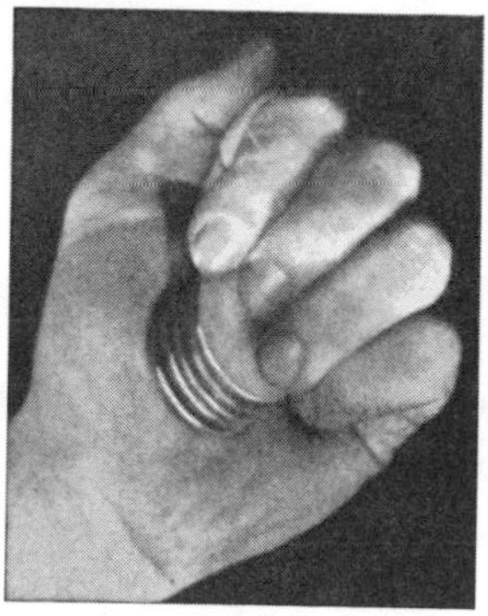

FIG. 136

the coins projecting beyond the finger tips, which press the stack against the heel of your hand. (Fig. 136).

Underneath the handkerchief, your right hand now has its forefinger pointing and the other three fingers curled in.

The crucial moves that follow are all made by the right hand, *through the handkerchief*. If you are using the steal simply as a pass, the moves are just the same, only without the handkerchief.

Draw back your left sleeve a little.

"The coins are shut in here," you say, tapping the upturned back of your left hand with your right forefinger.

Turn your left hand over, bringing the knuckles downward.

As the left hand turns, the projecting stack of coins comes into a position where you can nip it flat between your right thumb and the side of your second finger, through the handkerchief.

When you make this steal, the right forefinger continues to point and you carry your left hand on out toward the audience (Fig. 137). If you

FIG. 137

are gentle, the coins won't talk anyway, and if they do, the handkerchief muffles them.

Turn toward a spectator slightly to your right; and, as you do so, shake down the handkerchief.

The coins are now inside the kerchief, held snugly and silently between the right thumb and second finger.

Say to the spectator, "Just grab right around the handkerchief halfway down." He does so.

Bring your closed and bulging left fist to the bottom of his hand so that your thumb touches his little finger. "Nothing can get through *there* without your feeling it, I suppose?"

He says no, and looks at your left fist, quite forgetting that you have never let go of the handkerchief with your right hand.

"Ready? Hold tight! One, two, three, *four* half dollars!"

Jingle! Open your left hand and drop the coins with your right.

Let the spectator remove them from the handkerchief himself.

12. *Coin from Handkerchief to Handkerchief.* This time you need only one coin, but two handkerchiefs.

Lay one handkerchief on the table; put the coin in the exact center. Lay two diagonally opposite corners one over the other, reducing the handkerchief to a triangle; and, starting from the folded edge, roll it into a tube with the coin inside at the middle.

Pick up the rolled handkerchief by the opposite ends and raise the left end just a very little. This slides the coin to your right hand.

Now explain that you are going to knot the coin into the middle of the handkerchief. Make a plain overhand knot at the center, where the coin is supposed to be, and hang the handkerchief by its left end over the back of a chair.

As an alternative, with a large handkerchief, you can use the handkerchief fold (chapter 6, section 15), followed by a knot, and steal the coin in the act of hanging it up.

In either case, you are left with the coin finger-palmed in your right hand.

Take the other handkerchief by diagonally opposite corners, your middle fingers underneath, your thumb, first, and little fingers on top at each end. This, of course, brings the finger-palmed coin underneath the handkerchief.

Swing the handkerchief skip-rope fashion into a tube, rolled around your middle fingers.

Bring your hands toward each other to make a knot, and in the act let the coin slide down to the middle of the tube, where it rests safely until you make the knot that ties it in.

Hang up the second handkerchief on another chair.

You can now step well away from both handkerchiefs and still cause the coin to pass impressively from one knot to the other.

13. *Trouser-Leg Vanish.* Here we have something between a single sleight and a trick: you lay a fold of your trouser leg over a coin, let someone feel the coin, and then just drop the cloth. The coin is gone.

You need two coins, one to show and one to keep in your right trouser pocket as a dummy.

Lay the one that shows against your right thigh just below the duplicate, and hold it there with your right thumb. With your four fingers gather up the cloth below the coin. Draw the cloth up and under the coin, so that your middle fingers press against the coin (through two thicknesses of fabric) opposite your thumb.

Now pull your hand upward, turning the coin right over, and covering it with the fold of cloth that your fingers picked up.

Withdraw your thumb and second, third, and little fingers, leaving the extended forefinger to hold the fold—and supposedly the coin—in place. Actually your thumb simply draws the coin up into your palm, and the three fingers curl around it. Continuing the same motion, straighten your thumb. Two or three trials will show you that this steal is simplicity itself, and perfectly deceptive.

Now ask someone to feel the coin. Your upward movement has brought the fold directly over the coin in your pocket, and of course that is what the spectator feels.

Step back, lift your forefinger, and whoosh!

14. The Dissolving Coin (no disk!). I have mentioned that sucker gags with coins are scarcer than hens' teeth. Possibly you will not consider the following feat a sucker gag but only an improvement on a too-well-known trick. Whichever it is, certainly magicians are always searching for methods like this—tricks that squelch the fellow who once had a magic set.

You cannot have reached your time of life without reading of the trick in which the magician covers a coin with a handkerchief, then gets a spectator to drop the coin into a glass of water. The handkerchief is removed, and surprise, surprise—no coin! You will also have read that the coin is secretly replaced by a glass disk of the same size, which doesn't show in the water. If ever a trick was completely ruined by popularity, this is it.

Now put a rubber band in your left vest pocket, get a handkerchief, a small tumbler perhaps a third full of water, and borrow a half dollar.

First have the owner mark the half dollar on both sides.

Put the half dollar under the center of the handkerchief. Hold up the tumbler in your left hand, your fingers pointing upward past one side of the bottom, your thumb ditto on the opposite side. Your palm is thus below the bottom of the glass.

Hold the coin, through the handkerchief, in your right hand three or four inches above the glass. Of course the handkerchief hangs down around the glass and hides your left hand.

Say you are going to count three, and then drop the half dollar. Do so.

At about the count of two, however, tilt the glass away from you just enough so that the falling coin hits the outside of the glass with a clink, and glances into your left palm.

Let the glass settle down right over the coin on your palm.

Lift up the handkerchief, holding your left hand quite low down, and let people look down at the half dollar. It seems to be in the water, all right, and the mark still shows.

Cover the glass with the handkerchief again, and reach into your left vest pocket for the rubber band. Leave the half dollar behind in the pocket. Put the rubber band around the lower part of the glass outside the handkerchief, and hand the whole business to the man whose half dollar you borrowed.

You can reproduce the half dollar by knotting it into a handkerchief (see section 12) or in any other way you like.

If you are working on a spectator who you know from the first is suspicious, I suggest that you do *not* show him the coin "lying on the bottom of the glass." Just drop it, put on the rubber band, and then let him look for the glass disk.

15. Finding the Chosen Coin. About the only way in which coins can be used, like cards, as identities is by the dates they bear. For such tricks cards are generally much better, but you may want to vary your coin work. Or you may be one of the people meant by the reviewer of a popular magic book some years ago, who said, "Stunts with playing cards are included in one chapter, but the discriminating Christian leader will of course omit them from his repertoire." The next two tricks are borrowed, with some changes of working and many acknowledgments, from Eddie Joseph's admirable volume, *Coin and Money Magic.* Mr. Joseph, who has lived all his life in India, has skillfully blended the best in western and East Indian coin conjuring, creating a new style more different from the Downs tradition (though Tommy Downs would have loved it) than you might suppose possible.

Get a hat and a large handkerchief or scarf. Borrow and collect in the hat as many coins as you have time for.

Shake up the coins vigorously. Cover the hat with the handkerchief as you explain that you have a large number of coins, which can be distinguished only by their dates.

Stir the coins up with your left hand, finger-palm one, and take the hat in that hand with your thumb outside—the regular Miser's Dream move.

Ask a spectator to reach under the handkerchief and pick out any coin he likes.

You can have him mark it, but I agree with Mr. Joseph that the trick will drag less if you simply have him remember the date.

Take the coin back from him, put it under the handkerchief, and promptly drop it among the coins—people think. Really you palm the chosen coin, and drop the one from your left hand in the familiar fashion.

Go to another spectator, and have him take over the job of shaking. Finally you say you can hex him into finding the chosen coin among all the loose change in the hat.

Have him reach under the handkerchief, take a coin, and hand it to you, still under the handkerchief.

You promptly make a DeManche change (chapter 6, section 14), at the same time asking the first volunteer the date on his coin.

Sure enough, the one you toss him is his.

You are now left with a coin finger-palmed in your right hand, ready to do the whole trick over again, which you should; it needs more weight than a single showing will give it.

16. Date Detection (Eddie Joseph). The stage setting is exactly the same as in the last trick—a hat full of borrowed coins covered by a handkerchief. Instead of finding a particular coin, you read the date on one after another before you bring it out. If you use what Mr. Joseph calls the "mental" presentation, you announce the date first, then produce a coin to match. If you use his "sensitive-touch" presentation, you feel of the coin under the handkerchief, then say what the date is.

By way of explaining what you propose to do, take a coin out of the hat, hold it up, and calmly read off the date aloud. Toss it aside. "Instead of just reading it off," you say, "I am going to . . ." (then follows whichever story you use).

When you picked up this first coin, you also finger-palmed the first other one you could get hold of.

In raising your hand to read off the coin you display, catch a quick glimpse of the finger-palmed coin. If its date side is toward you, remember the date. If away from you, instantly flop the coin over out of the finger palm on to the palm of your hand, and *then* note the date. Mr. Joseph insists that this glimpse and the turnover (if needed) must be made as your right hand moves up, *before* it stops for you to read off the unconcealed coin.

Toss aside the latter, and reach for another one.

This is a very clever employment of the "one-ahead gag," which you will meet again in head magic and mental magic. Your next move is to dip another coin at random out of the hat, at the same time announcing the date of the coin you have palmed as the date that you will bring forth. While your hand is still covered by the handkerchief, make the DeManche change.

Reading off the coin you now display, to verify the date, you also learn the date of the new finger-palmed coin; and so you are set to go right through every coin in the hat, if people have the patience to listen to you.

Mr. Joseph gives a number of important twists to break up the monotonous sequence of palming and reading, but having helped myself to a piece of his cake, I shall send you to him for the frosting, merely observing that he suggests various ways of leaving a secretly known coin where you can retrieve it, while having spectators shake the hat, and letting your hands be seen altogether empty.

17. *Coins up the Sleeve.* Magicians are constantly trying to do with cigarettes or thimbles tricks that ought properly to be done with coins and rings. An overingenious wizard has even adapted the Sympathetic Coins to cards. I plead guilty to the failing, with the excuse that the Cards up the Sleeve is more dramatic with coins, which can be heard arriving, and the misdirection is quite as good.

With a helpful suggestion from Walter Gibson, I devised this trick for myself about 1928, and have used it with great satisfaction ever since. The first flush of my inventor's pride was damped by word from Tommy Downs that the Australian coin manipulator Allen Shaw had been doing the effect for years. I never saw Shaw work but once, and the trick was not in his act, so I don't know how he did it.

Be warned by this when you make an invention: the invention is yours, to be enjoyed as such; but very likely it must go down in the books as your *re*-invention of the Great Blotto's original masterpiece.

In the present case I have acknowledgments to make both going and coming. My friend Alexander Adrion, probably the busiest German professional performer and writer today, saw me do the trick in the early 1950s, and made a radical improvement that I am proud to pass on. And more by good luck than good management I stumbled on a mechanical expedient to eliminate the test of nerve originally involved at key moments.

To show the Coins up the Sleeve as I do, you need five silver dollars, four about alike and one noticeably different. I have four dating from the

1920s and one dated 1883. The other way around would serve just as well. The trick can also be done with half dollars.

In addition you want a shot or liqueur glass whose mouth is somewhat wider than the diameter of your coins (Adrion advises having a spare in case one should break) and an elastic web tennis belt. Mine is 1⅛ inches wide.

You must wear a vest or sweater. Draw the belt snug but not taut around your waist just below the regular belt, thus catching the tops of the trouser pockets. This avoids the tricky business of wedging a coin in the pocket perpendicular to the body, which sometimes made the original version of the trick a bit nerve-racking for the performer.

The effect, as you have already guessed, is that the coins pass one at a time from your left hand up your sleeve and into your right trouser pocket, where they fall with a loud clink into the glass. (This was Adrion's above-mentioned radical improvement.)

Take the five coins in your left hand, with the odd one anywhere but on top of the pile. Hold out your right hand palm up and count the coins into it. Put the first coin in palming position, as you did in Silver and Gold (chapter 7), and the others overlapping it outward, not too closely, in a ribbon.

Dump the coins back into your left hand, but palm the convenient one in your right. Pick up the glass in your right hand with the thumb inside. "And we'll put this in the pocket so that if anything arrives here we'll hear it."

Put the glass into the pocket, then stick the palmed coin under the belt zone at the top of the pocket. You can legitimately finger the glass to make sure it's right side up. (Actually, this is desirable but not vital. A coin hitting the side or bottom will still clink.) Then withdraw your hand.

Start the build-up for the first coin to pass. Hold your left fist out at arm's length; get set as for a feat of skill. Clink the coins in your left hand once. Straighten up, throw back your shoulders, trace the course of the imaginary coin with your right forefinger up your sleeve and down toward —not clear to—the pocket. Right hand clearly empty.

Draw in your stomach and the wedged coin goes down with a bang.

Stop for applause.

Open your left hand, showing four coins left. Count them slowly into your right palm, again planting the first in palming position. Dump them back (minus one) into your left hand.

"Four. And one in the pocket makes five."

Take out the coin and show it, leaving the glass in the pocket. In returning the coin, wedge it and drop the palmed one into the glass.

Next coin up sleeve and to pocket as before. Clink.

"One, two, three left." (Count out, palm one.)

"And two make five." Show, wedge one, drop two into glass.

Hold the two coins remaining in your left hand flat between fingers and thumb, the back of the hand toward the audience. Push the top coin up into view, and apparently stick it into your mouth, actually just drawing it back with your thumb. Poke your tongue into your right cheek. Chase it from side to side once or twice with your right thumb and forefinger, then crowd it to the center, and finally swallow.

Down comes the wedged coin. Let everyone realize your right hand is empty. Show just two coins lying on your left palm; without bothering to count them, put your right hand in your pocket. Bring out the three coins; show them around. "And three make five."

Drop them back into the glass, wedging one of them.

Now point out that you have an old coin and a new one left. Which shall go first, old or new? Make it very plain which is which.

When they decide on one, pick it up from your palm by the edges between your right second finger and thumb, and show it around once more. Then lay it back on the other coin, but overlapping somewhat to the right, and pick up the two together, separating them ever so slightly. Once more turn your hand over, this time exhibiting the reverse of the coin that is to be left behind.

Turn to the left and drop both coins on your left palm. Owing to the slight separation, they clink loudly. The next instant, your left hand moves off, carrying the lower coin; the upper is retained between your right second finger and thumb and palmed a moment later.

Hold out your left fist; more build-up. Drop the wedged coin.

Open your left fist, showing just the one coin that was to stay behind.

Reach calmly into your trouser pocket, and bring out four coins. "There it is, right on top."

In replacing the four coins, wedge one.

The last coin can go from your left hand by any pass you like. For myself, this is one time when I want to meet all objections. I lay the coin plainly in my left palm, close my fingers over it, and work it back toward my wrist, ready for the steal you learned in Coins to Handkerchief (section 11). With my right hand I pull my left sleeve *down*, ostensibly so that the coin can go up it better. At that moment I make the steal.

Another clink as the wedged coin comes down. Left hand empty, five coins from the pocket.

HEARTBREAKERS

The tricks that follow are the reason that I began by saying that coin manipulation is the least rewarding branch of sleight of hand. You may think you have mastered some pretty tough assignments, but until you look at the next few pages you haven't even begun. "Months of practice" is usually a figure of speech. This time I mean it.

And when you get through, you probably won't impress people half so much with your Coin Stars and Heads-or-Tails as with Catching Five Coins or Date Detection.

Yet if you have coin-manipulating fever, as I have, you won't be able to rest until you can do them all. I won't rob you of the pleasure, Mr. Embryo Downs, but don't say I told you it was good showmanship.

18. Heads-or-Tails. This I take on the good and sufficient word of Eddie Joseph. He explains how it is possible to flip a borrowed coin, and call heads or tails correctly *every time.*

No trick to it—just mechanical uniformity of action. It is obvious (when pointed out) that which face of the coin comes up depends simply on the number of revolutions the coin makes; and this depends on the weight of the coin, the height of the flip, and the force of the spin.

By always using one denomination of coin, you fix the weight. The uniform flip of your right thumb comes with practice. To get a uniform height, pick some marked point on the wall, and practice until you can toss the coin just that high every time.

You must also catch the coin on your left palm at exactly the same height each time—your waist, naturally, is the easiest.

Once you attain true uniformity, you will discover that the coin always comes down showing the same face that went up, or else always the opposite face. Experiment with different heights of toss, keeping track of the way the coin comes down. Never vary the force of your thumb flip because that is the hardest to judge.

In performance, pick a mark such as a molding or picture frame on the wall of the room where you happen to be, make one trial toss to that height, and see whether the coin comes down the same as it went up, or opposite. Every time you toss to this mark afterward, the result should be identical.

About the only way to use this as a trick is to announce that you will flip, say, five heads in succession, then five tails. Then let people call what they like, and bring it down wrong every time.

This is the sort of easily described knack often acquired by one-trick men, whom you find tending bar or peddling gadgets on the sidewalk. They don't know any magic, but they have one move that you could scarcely copy in a lifetime.

Mr. Joseph gives an easier alternative method—catching the coin in your right hand, getting a flash of it, and flopping it over or not, as necessary, in the act of slapping it on the back of your left hand; but without the first method to break the way, I don't believe the second would be terribly impressive.

19. *Coins to Glass.* This little beauty, which Nelson Downs tossed off as just another palming trick, is without doubt the hardest nut I have ever attempted to crack.

The effect seems to puzzle and please people, which is some compensation. You take some coins (Downs said ten, but five is plenty for me, and you can start with three) in your right fist, and hold a tumbler by the rim in your left hand, fingers on the front edge, thumb toward you. You pass the coins one at a time from your hand to the glass, where they arrive noisily in plain sight. Just before the last coin is due to go, you say, "Oh, yes, there *is* something in my right hand!" and show the coin to prove it. It, too, then flies into the glass.

You will scarcely need any explanation. You have an extra coin finger-palmed in your right hand; you make the Downs click pass with your left hand and edge-palm the coins (chapter 6). (The subsequent release works a little better if you let the stack flatten out on your palm, as I mentioned in the alternative method of reproducing from the edge palm at chapter 6, section 6.)

That's all. Pick up the glass in your left hand with the palmed coins directly over the mouth. And every time you make a tossing motion with your right hand, you can just try dropping only one off the face of the palmed stack.

It can be done.

When I complained to Tommy Downs that it wouldn't always work for me, he suggested helping them down with the tip of the third finger; but I noticed he never had to.

The last coin, of course, disappears by the back palm. You can get by with dropping two at a time on the left until the last one, but if that goes too soon, your goose is cooked.

I still wonder how I had the nerve to use this professionally in my act at the age of fifteen.

20. *The Coin Star (one hand).* In his last years Nelson Downs had the sleight-of-hand world crazy with his trick of balancing five coins on the finger tips of one hand, gathering the coins into the other hand, tossing them through his body, and reproducing them balanced once more on the five finger tips.

With more help from Walter Gibson, I managed to learn this with four coins. As for the fifth, J. B. Bobo discovered after the master's death that Downs had not been reluctant to use a gimmick: the thumb coin had a dime-sized cavity filled with wax.

All right, with four coins: use dollars. They sit steadier. Balance them as in Fig. 138.

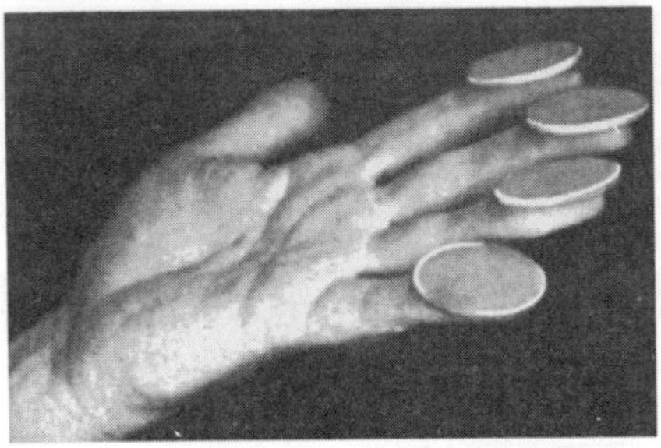

FIG. 138

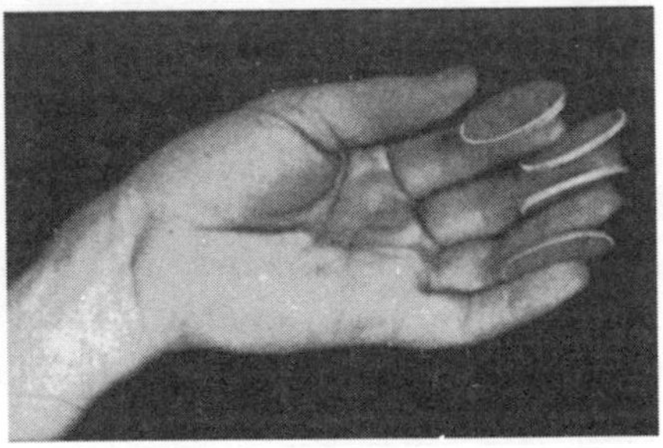

FIG. 139

Make the motion of sweeping the coins off with your right hand. Under this cover, lay your left fingers together (Fig. 139). This brings the top coin into thumb-palm position, enabling you to stretch out your forefinger (Fig. 140) (which, as I have already mentioned, looks much less tricky than a closed fist), while the other three fingers curl in and clip the coins.

With all eyes on your right fist, carry your left hand behind you. Your right hand seems to slap the coins through your stomach, while your left thumb replaces the thumb-palmed coin on your forefinger, and all four fingers then gently, gently straighten out and level off (Fig. 141).

If you are lucky, you bring your left hand out with the coins as they were at the start.

21. *The Coin Star (two hands).* Who first performed this I have never been able to learn, but it was made famous among magicians by Manuel. The effect is that the two hands are suddenly placed finger tip

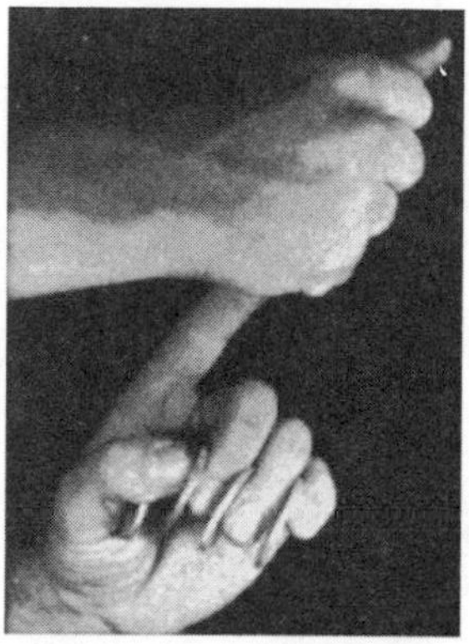

FIG. 140

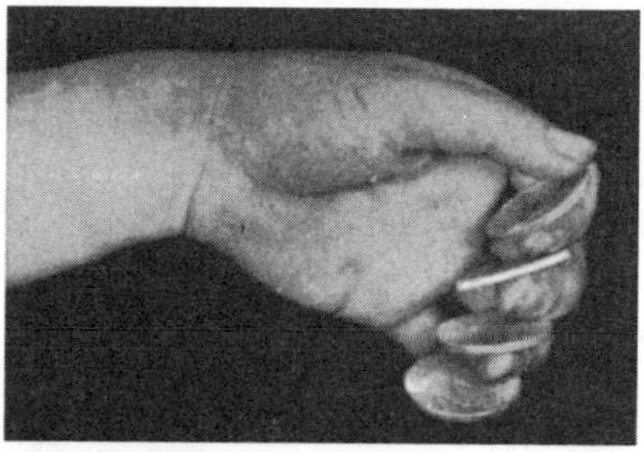

FIG. 141

to finger tip, and a coin appears between each pair of fingers, as if you had done a one-handed star and then put your other hand on top.

I do not know Manuel's routine because I had to devise my own from descriptions before I saw him work. Mine has served me well enough, and here it is.

I show five coins fanned in my left hand, then do the fan pass, and edge-palm them. I walk toward a spectator on my right, pretending to hand him the coins in my right fist.

Meanwhile I am shifting the palmed coins to a regular back palm. (Five silver dollars are too many to hold without the support of your little finger.)

I open my hand, giving the spectator a big bunch of nothing, then whirl to the left, stretch out my left hand, and lay my right fingers across my left fingers, thus showing both palms empty but masking the otherwise inevitable flash of back-palmed coins.

Then I bring the coins to the front and grasp them with my right thumb and second finger (Fig. 142).

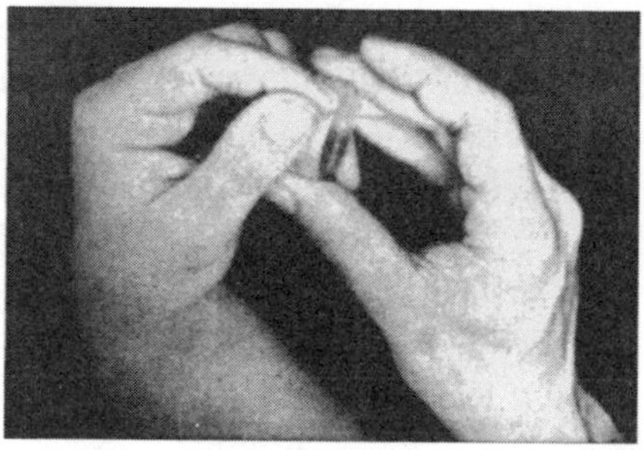

FIG. 142

The right hand simply steadies the stack until the left thumb can fan the coins evenly toward the little finger. Each finger tip must get a bite of one coin; this is the real difficulty of the move.

When the coins are evenly fanned, your right hand swings into a position exactly matching your left (Fig. 143). You will discover, when you

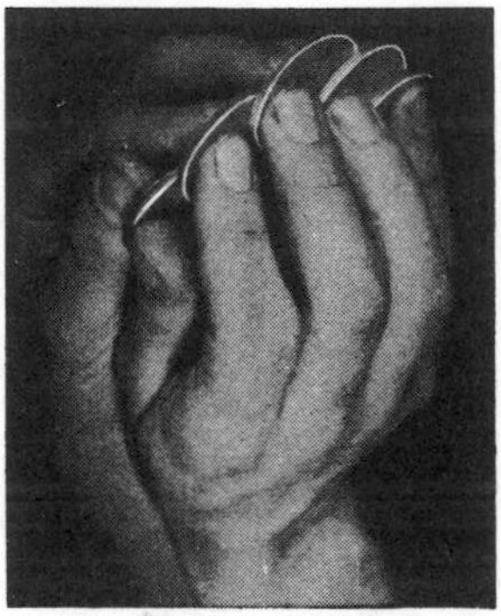

FIG. 143

have successfully arrived at this point, that each coin is held separately by two opposing finger tips, and you have only to straighten and spread all ten fingers to complete the star.

By sliding the coins together again (reversing the fanning motion) it is possible to vanish the star, transferring the stack to a right edge palm or right or left crotch palm.

A third variety of star is described in J. B. Bobo's *New Modern Coin Magic* under the name of "Roll Down Flourish with Four Coins." It consists essentially in holding the stacked coins by their opposite edges at a right angle between thumb and fingers; splitting the stack into halves held respectively between forefinger and second and between second and third fingers; and then rolling out single coins with thumb and little finger after the fashion of Multiplying Billiard Balls (see chapter 9) so that you wind up with the four coins held crosswise between four fingers and thumb. See Bobo for details.

This looks difficult and is difficult, but have a care: done with skill and speed it creates a fluttery, fidgety impression quite unlike what I call real magic.

By the time you have learned this assortment of honeys, you should be able to write a magic book yourself.

8. *Hand Magic with Billiard Balls*

BILLIARD *ball* is just a conjurer's pet name for the little spheres he manipulates. Although Maskelyne and Devant in *Our Magic* advocate real ivory balls because they sound more convincing, I have never met a performer who took their advice.

Magical billiard balls are made of wood or plastic in one and a quarter, one and a half, and one and three quarter inch sizes. Inch and a half is usual, one and three quarter inch is showier and harder to handle. The traditional color is bright red; white can often be had. The sets of three, sometimes four, balls come with a half-shell for the Multiplying Billiard Balls, treated in the next chapter.

Alas, the old plaint that "they don't make 'em like they used to" is really true of billiard balls. What you want is balls and thin shell turned out of seasoned boxwood and French-polished. What you'll probably get is something roughly spherical of green wood, the shell thick and clumsy, the finish a hard, slippery plastic lacquer; or else plastic balls, shiny and unbreakable but maddeningly light, with the shell likely either to stick like glue or to rattle. You may find it necessary to glue a small flannel patch inside the shell to forestall either threat. The current sets of three sealed in plastic packages are deplorable: you can't test the shell for fit, and the only way to get a fourth ball is to buy a second set.

Cardini's trick of climbing billiard balls (p. 185 below) is almost impossible to do with modern balls.

Now that you have learned coin palming, billiard-ball manipulation will be a breeze. The chief danger, in fact, is that you will find it too much of a breeze. There are many fewer useful and natural sleights with billiard balls than with coins; yet billiard balls are such easy and delightful objects to handle that magicians have devised scores of intricate moves—nearly all of them good only for the conjurer's own entertainment.

Allow me to quote from *Our Magic* by Maskelyne and Devant: [1]

[1] Reprinted by permission from Our Magic, by Nevil Maskelyne and David Devant, second edition (1946), published by Fleming Book Company, York, Pennsylvania.

"In Billiard Balls we have a moderate sized object, dear to the heart of manipulators. . . . The manipulator finds the temptation strong upon him to linger lovingly over sleights, passes, and palms galore, whilst losing sight of the ultimate effect on the mind of his audience. We do not remember ever to have seen an illusion with billiard balls in which the effect was not blurred by this sort of thing instead of being made to stand out in relief like a clearly cut cameo. On being asked afterwards what the conjurer did with a billiard ball the spectator probably replied—'Oh, all sorts of things.'

"Now, one does not wish to hear a criticism like that if one has been displaying a feat of magic; rather would one hear a greatly exaggerated description. At present, manipulation pure and simple will not carry a conjurer very far if he is using billiard balls and eggs. Let us suppose that a modern conjurer was in the power of some cannibal savages and that his very life depended upon proving to them that he was a real magic man. Even the cleverest sleight-of-hand performer would stand a very poor chance of living if all he had with him was, say, half a dozen ivory billiard balls and the same number of eggs. He would not know one cumulative feat of magic with them, simply because no genius has as yet invented one. But give the same conjurer twenty silver coins and a top hat and he would know what to do. The natives will be astounded to see him catching money from the air, picking coins from all sorts of places, and throwing them into the hat. Even if the savages were so happy as not to know what money was they would wonder at this medicine man who created those shining disks at his finger tips. If, instead of the money and the hat, the conjurer had three cups and a few cork balls of different sizes and three oranges or apples he might still convince his audience that he was a genuine magician because his play with these articles would have a plot—a beginning, a middle, and an end. It would be a satisfactory effect."

Maskelyne and Devant then go on to point out that with the shell you can do a satisfactory effect. Without it, you are limited to palming.

What I am trying to emphasize is that pure manipulation of billiard balls is great fun for you, but with the audience a little of it goes a long, long way.

And one thing more: billiard balls are easy to palm but hard to hide. Angles are tricky with coins, bothersome with cards; with billiard balls they are almost an insuperable obstacle.

I hope you are now sufficiently warned about billiard-ball sleights.

1. *The palm.* This is done exactly as it would be with a coin, except

that you may choose to roll the ball from your finger tips instead of slapping it into your palm. The previous warning holds good about trying to hold the ball by moving in your thumb and little finger. And don't go to the other extreme, displaying your ability to stretch out all five fingers in an ostentatious "starfish" or "goose-foot" attitude.

Just hold the ball gently as in Fig. 144.

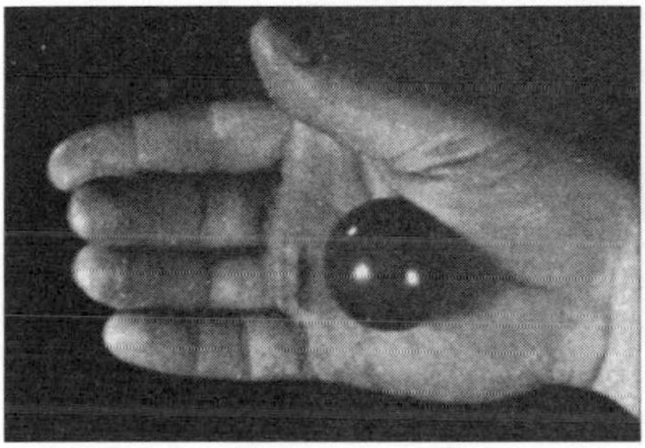

Fig. 144

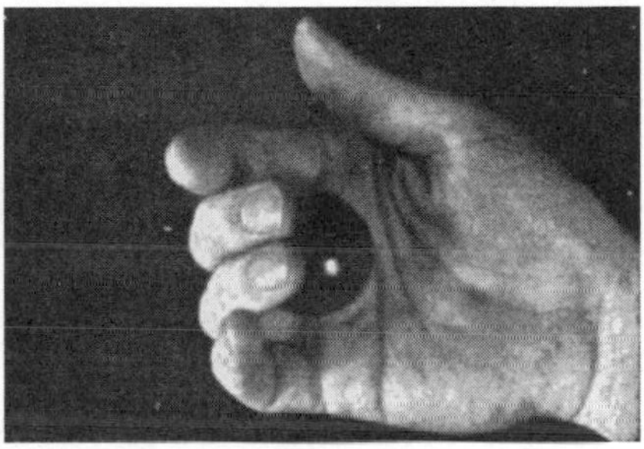

Fig. 145

2. *The finger palm.* Fig. 145 tells all anybody could want to know about this. Don't hold your first and little fingers rigidly straight, and don't stick your thumb out like a sore thumb.

The power to shift a ball from finger palm to regular palm or vice versa is useful, and can be acquired after about one attempt.

3. *Simulation.* Simulation has in magic the special additional meaning of *acting as if an object were present when it is not.* Young manipulators, particularly of billiard balls, often fall down here. They make a smooth and beautiful palm, and then close the other fist down to a size that wouldn't house a marble.

Silent Mora was one of the few magicians who possessed what I earlier described as slow-motion-camera perfection. He handled billiard balls like quicksilver. And the great point about his sleights was the simulation.

He knew that when you grasp a billiard ball (Fig. 146) you can't get your fist all the way shut. With one coin you can; with five coins you can barely.

Those facts were in Mora's subconscious, as they should be in yours. When he was really holding a ball, he knew how his fist looked; when he had palmed the ball, and was just simulating, he held his fist exactly the same way (Fig. 147). He kept his knuckles turned toward the audience, so as not to reveal the void where the ball ought to be; but the shape of his hand was flawless.

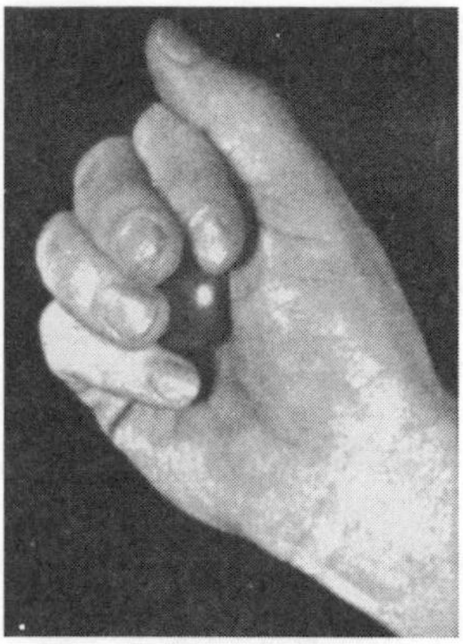

FIG. 146

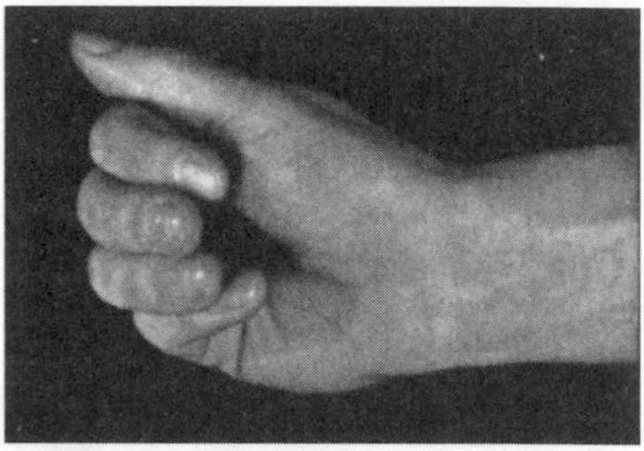

FIG. 147

4. *Standard passes.* Once you have mastered simulation you have nothing more to learn about the ordinary ball passes. You can palm a ball, finger-palm it, or use the tourniquet. Simulation and misdirection are all there is to it.

One pass that would not show off so well with coins may be called the pick-up pass. Show a ball on the flat palm of one hand. The other hand seems to pick up the ball. Actually you just palm it in place, turning the back of that hand to the audience as the other hand, bulging, moves away.

5. *The trap pass.* Used in a repeating routine, this move can be amusing. Close your left fist, the forefinger more tightly than the little finger, and set a ball on top of the fist.

Your right hand closes on the ball and apparently carries it away (Fig. 148).

The moment the ball is screened by the right hand, open your left fist enough to let the ball drop in, and promptly palm it (Fig. 149). Immediately relax your left hand as if it were empty.

The pass gets its name because it works like one of the traps that nineteenth-century magicians built into their tables.

You will usually find yourself told to turn your right hand over, thumb down, and apparently take the ball with an outward sweep. This strikes me as a fine sample of the "artistic manipulation" that ruins billiard-ball tricks. It is not altogether natural to stand the ball on the top of your fist in the first place; why go quite literally out of your way to emphasize this with contortions?

In order to use the trap pass as a comedy repeat, you must learn the

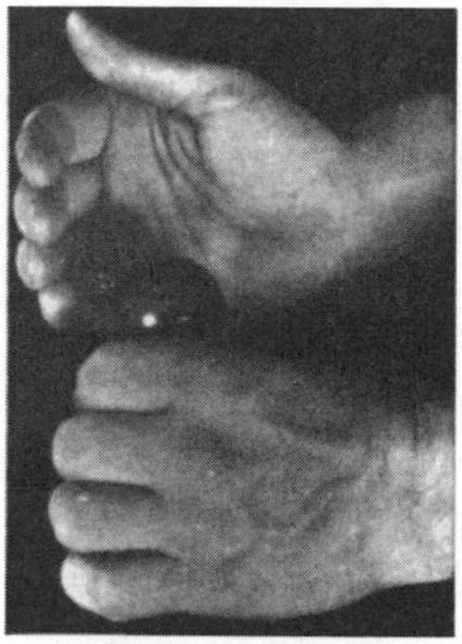

Fig. 148

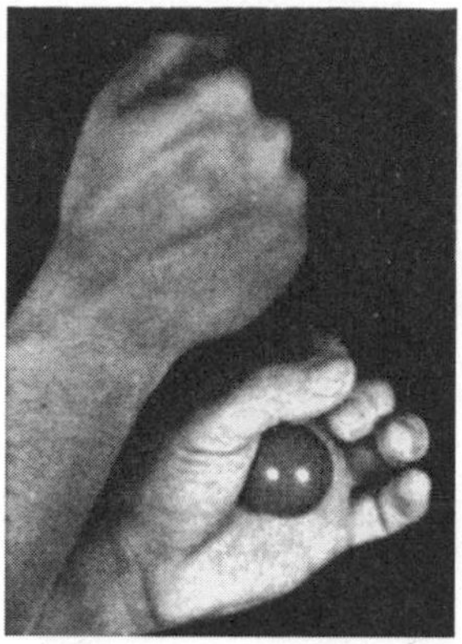

Fig. 149

knack of bringing the ball from your palm back to the top of your fist with one quick, gentle squeeze. You seem to take the ball in your right hand and rub it away to nothing. Your eyes are still fixed on the empty right hand when the ball suddenly jumps to the top of your left fist again. Give them time to get this; then take the ball away and swallow it. Back it pops. And so on, as long as they still laugh.

6. *The kick pass.* This comes fairly close to being one of those sterile devices, magician-foolers. The motion exactly simulates a trap pass, only you stand with the palm of your left hand forward, and both hands are quite empty when the ball disappears.

You must hold your left fist fairly close to your stomach, your left elbow against your side, and stand with your right side squarely to the audience. The position is everything.

When your right hand seems to take the ball, it kicks or tosses it along your left forearm so that it comes to rest in the bend of your left elbow. Your right hand should not actually pass out of sight; your right forearm screens the motion of the ball.

After the ball has disappeared, of course you can show both hands empty. Then drop your left hand to your side, and the ball falls into it unseen, to be palmed and used at pleasure.

7. *The change-over palm.* To one who has already mastered, or even attempted, the change-over palm with coins, the photographs tell the whole story except that with a billiard ball the move is incomparably easier. The ball rolls between your palms instead of having to be accurately transferred from hand to hand.

Fig. 150 shows the start of the move from the front; Fig. 151 shows it from the rear.

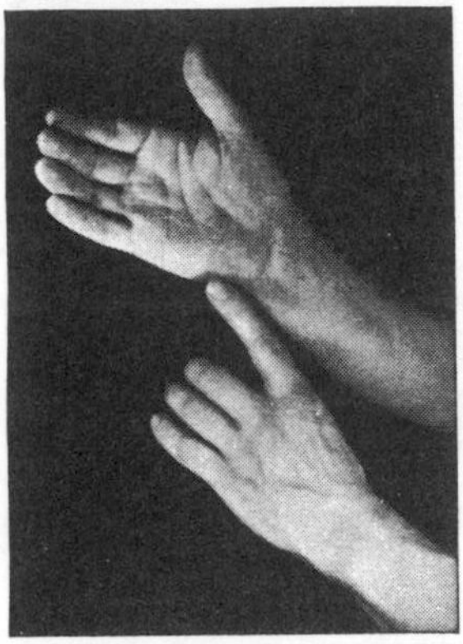

Fig. 150

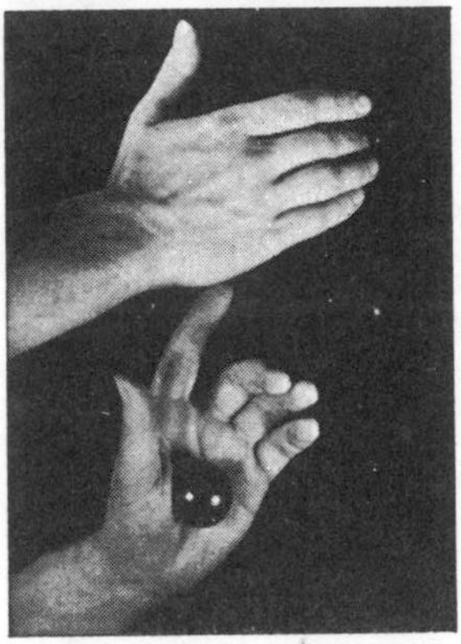

Fig. 151

In Fig. 152 the hands are face to face, and the ball is actually being rolled from the left to the right palm. Don't waggle your thumbs.

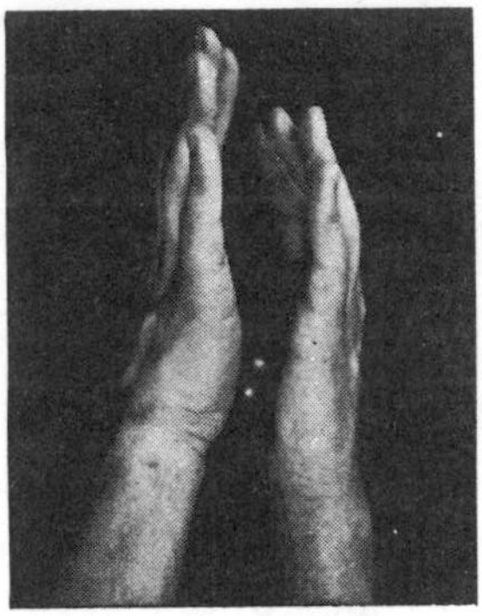

Fig. 152

Fig. 153 and 154 show the front and rear views of the completed move.

8. *Color changes.* Naturally one is very seldom called on to switch billiard balls invisibly. Visible color changes are one of the few variations you can introduce into billiard-ball manipulation.

Methods like palming a red ball in your right hand, and then executing a trap pass with a white ball on your left fist, will occur to you at once.

Two methods done in plain sight are as follows. Palm the red ball in your right hand. Show the white ball about in palming position in your left hand. Pass your right hand over the white ball from above down-

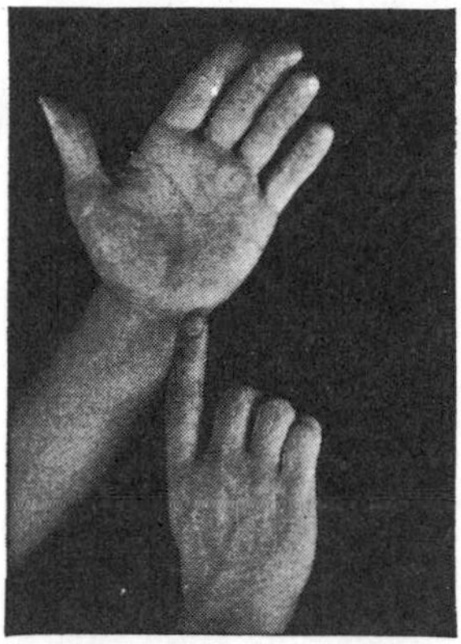

FIG. 153

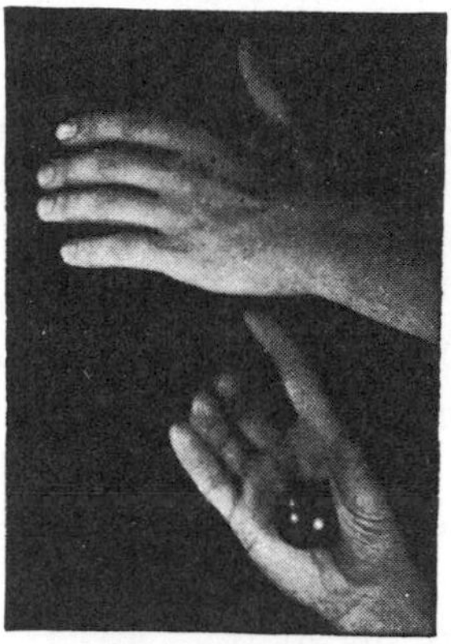

FIG. 154

ward. In the act, press the red ball against the root of your left forefinger, and so let it roll into view, while your right hand palms and carries away the white ball.

The starting position for the second method is the same, except that your right forefinger holds the ball against your vertical left palm. Pivot to your right, rolling the white ball out along your left fingers, then down your right fingers until it comes to rest in the center of your right palm, held by your left forefinger. In making this transfer, you do the change-over with the red ball.

Reverse the motion, pivoting back to the left. The ball is still white.

Finally, pivot to the right, but instead of rolling either ball, palm the white ball in your left hand. When you complete your swing to the right, your left forefinger naturally comes to rest on the red ball, which thus replaces the white.

Anyone who has ever seen Cardini will remember how he uses a color change for comedy. After he has changed a ball back and forth two or three times, he tosses the visible one in the air, and when he catches it, there is a telltale click. In dumb show he expresses his chagrin at having thus given himself away and shows the two different-colored balls. But a moment later he is well into his multiplication routine, and the spectator's smug, "Oh, of course," has turned to a bewildered, "Where did they all come from?"

9. *Flourish: Cardini's climbing billiard balls.* This is one of the moves that most impress people with Cardini's uncanny skill. I was impressed too, until I went home and tried it.

He holds a ball in each palm, then presses the balls together, holding his hands parallel, fingers pointing straight up. He squeezes, and the two balls climb straight up inside his hands to the very tips of his fingers, clinging together as if by magnetic attraction. He relaxes his hands, and the balls sink down almost to his wrists.

There is nothing to this except that the balls must be fairly heavy, and in squeezing the hands together you must not let one ball climb faster than the other. Of course the heels of your hands are brought closer together than the finger tips, which is why the balls climb. The cracks between your fingers make a channel to keep the balls from slipping sideways. Try it a few times, and you, too, can astonish the multitude.

There is nothing to it except that the balls must be fairly heavy and not too slippery; this, as I remarked a moment ago, rules out those now commercially available. In squeezing the hands together you must not let one ball climb faster than the other. Of course the heels of your hands are brought closer together than the finger tips, which is why the balls climb. The cracks between your middle fingers make a channel to keep the balls from slipping sideways. Try it a few times with suitable balls, and you, too, can astonish the multitude.

9. *The Multiplying Billiard Balls*

THE Multiplying Billiard Balls, Twentieth Century, Chicago, or One-to-Four Billiard Ball Trick is very nearly the only effect depending on billiard-ball manipulation that has what Maskelyne and Devant called a plot. Indeed with astonishingly few and unimpressive exceptions it is the only billiard-ball trick.

In addition to some skill, as I indicated in the last chapter, it requires you to have a hollow half shell, which will fit snugly over any of the three or four solid balls in the set.

I have already bewailed the low estate of modern magical billiard balls and shells; I hope your dealer can help you do something about it.

There are various alternatives to the classical red sets—gold balls, rhinestone-encrusted or soft surfaces. With the latter you are deprived of the essential excuse to knock the balls together while loading the shell.

As you undoubtedly realize, with the Multiplying Billiard Balls you are up against nearly the worst accidental handicap a trick can have: it has been included in every magic set since the 1930s. The number of people who know that you have "a hollow ball" must be greater than the population of New York City. Yet the trick remains intrinsically beautiful, and it can still be handled well enough to fool or at least surprise even the boys who once had a Mysto Magic set.

The moves are not difficult; just learn a routine so that you have no pauses or fumbling, and I believe you and your audiences may still enjoy this sorely tried effect.

Where to hide the balls until you want them is a question that can be answered in various ways. You may "vest" them—tuck them under the lower edge of your waistcoat; this was the old-time magician's reply to every stowage problem. You may distribute them in your side pockets. When I was in the Marine Corps, and had nothing but shirt or trouser pockets, I managed all right with one ball and shell in my left trouser pocket and two solid ones in my right.

You will prefer to work out your own routine; I give mine merely as a starting point.

Steal and produce one of the balls that were originally in your right pocket. Do one or two sharp, clear-cut passes with it, finally palming it in your right hand.

When it disappears from your left hand, reproduce it proudly from your left trouser pocket—actually the ball and shell together.

You are now ready to start the multiplication. On the stage it is conventional to stretch out your left arm, with the back of your hand to the audience, holding the ball and shell as shown from the rear in Fig. 155.

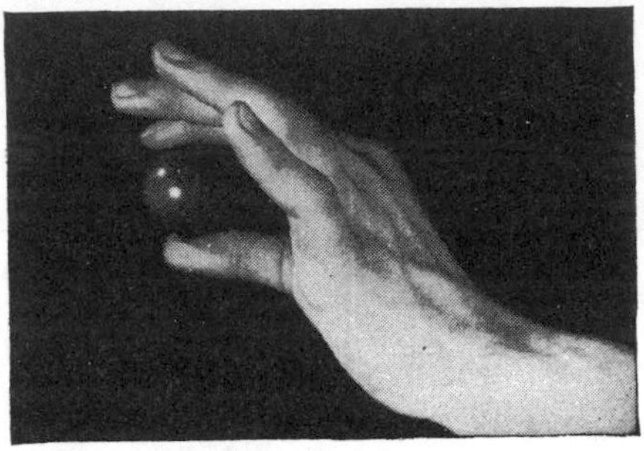

FIG. 155

At closer quarters, you may do better to hold your hand with your palm in front of your stomach. The only difference this makes is that your stance is less constrained, and that your hand is thumb upward instead of thumb downward.

Turn the ball around, looking at it from all sides—and helping the Mysto Magic contingent to forget about the "hollow ball."

Bring down your second finger below the ball as shown in Fig. 156.

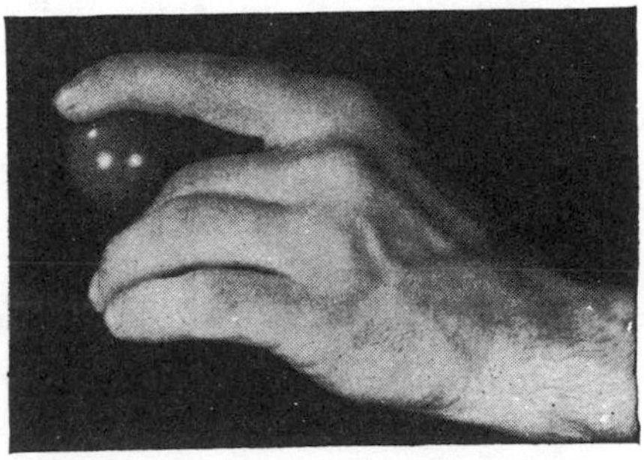

FIG. 156

One is usually taught that the shell must be toward the audience at this point. If you are working in front of your stomach, however, it is quite as successful to have the shell and the back of your hand toward you, and then deftly turn your hand thumb uppermost as you roll the ball out of the shell.

In either case, your second finger does this, bringing your left hand into the position shown in Fig. 157.

FIG. 157

You have been left all this time with a ball palmed in your right hand. and this you now proceed to load into the shell. Finger-palm the ball (chapter 8, section 2), then reach up with your right hand to take the solid ball from between left first and second fingers. This puts the palmed ball right next to the shell (Fig. 157), into which you slip it in the act of knocking the two balls together.

When you replace the ball that you have taken with your right hand, put it between your left *second* and *third* fingers, not back from where you took it.

Once again you turn your left hand every which way, admiring the balls. Keep your second finger either against the side of your forefinger or down across your thumb—not, at any rate, where the empty space between first and second fingers will be conspicuous.

Meanwhile, you must quite lazily steal the last ball (next to last if you are working with the four and a shell) from your pocket.

Bring the second ball out of the shell; in knocking the "three" together, simply remove the one from between first and second fingers, simultaneously reloading the shell; tap the other two balls, then put the one that you have removed between *third* and *little* fingers.

A smooth, brisk worker will probably not have too much trouble with the wise boys. There is, however, a pivoting move that should stop the noisiest of them in his tracks. At any time when the shell is empty and you have no ball between your left first and second fingers, you can swing your hand slowly from side to side, showing first the back and then the palm, and no sign of a hollow shell. Fig. 158 shows the pivot: by revolving

FIG. 158

the shell with your second finger on the axis formed by your thumb and forefinger, you can keep the good side constantly to the front, in time with the slow swing of your hand.

When you have brought out the last ball, and all your fingers are occupied, you may decide that the trick has reached its climax, and stop. (Incidentally, the difficulty of multiplying in the later stages increases disproportionately if you use the large plastic balls. With wooden inch-and-a-half balls it is perfectly easy.) In that case you need a fourth solid ball, which you load into the shell. Some shells will stick to a ball if given a good squeeze, and you can retire in triumph like that. Again, you may do as Cardini does—fling the balls on the floor, where they roll off into the wings. This means you must palm off the shell.

The traditional routine calls for the balls to disappear singly, as they came. If you do this, vary the procedure as radically as you can. "Take" one ball away in your right hand (actually rolling it into the shell, of course), and swallow it. Tap the remaining three together, stealing the one from the shell; then rub your left hand against the front of your right thigh, and pass one ball into your trouser pocket, whence you produce it. When you are down to two balls, one with a shell over it, take the ball and shell into your left hand, the ball alone in your right, and stand with your right side forward.

Toss the right-hand ball way up, and catch it again in your right hand.

As you do this, quietly drop the left-hand ball and shell into a pocket. Make another toss or two. Finally, as your right hand descends for another toss, zip the ball over and back into your left hand. Complete the toss with your right hand, and that ball is gone.

You now come out boldly with the remaining ball in your left hand, and vanish it by palming.

10. Other Hand Magic with Balls

BILLIARD balls are the showy members of the spherical family, but as Maskelyne and Devant indicated in my quotation, the best tricks are largely with other kinds of ball.

1. *Cups and Balls.* The ancient fraud that we call the shell game and the British call thimble-rigging is itself only a recent form of Cups and Balls, the ancestor of all conjuring. For anything I know to the contrary, Cups and Balls may go back to neolithic times. Europe and Asia have their own, apparently independent, versions of the same trick. The East Indians are masters at it, and of late years the East Indian method has been gaining followers in this country. You are referred to Eddie Joseph's *Magic and Mysteries of India* for details.

Whoever shows the trick, the plot is always the same. There are three cups and a small ball. The ball travels from cup to cup, is magically extracted through the upturned bottom of one cup, invisibly passed under another, and then it multiplies into several balls. Finally large balls or small potatoes appear under all the cups.

The conventional Occidental cup is made of aluminum and shaped like the ones in Fig. 159. Dealers carry them in various sizes. The small balls can be of blackened cork, but these are not always available nowadays. Other materials are stuffed cloth, rubber, and sponge rubber. The primary requirement is that the balls must not talk against the cups.

In order to prevent talking and to show off the balls, the table should be covered with a thick cloth of contrasting color. Jean Hugard suggests black cork balls and a thick white Turkish towel.

The special cup-and-ball sleights are few and easy. Of course a ball that is not too tiny can be palmed like any other small object. The tourniquet is also a standard small-ball sleight.

The characteristic *small-ball palm* starts as shown in Fig. 159. Then your thumb rolls the ball to a spot between the bases of your second and third fingers, where you catch it (Fig. 160).

The photograph shows the palm being used as you pretend to slide the ball under a cup, but it is often better in a normal pass: pretend to

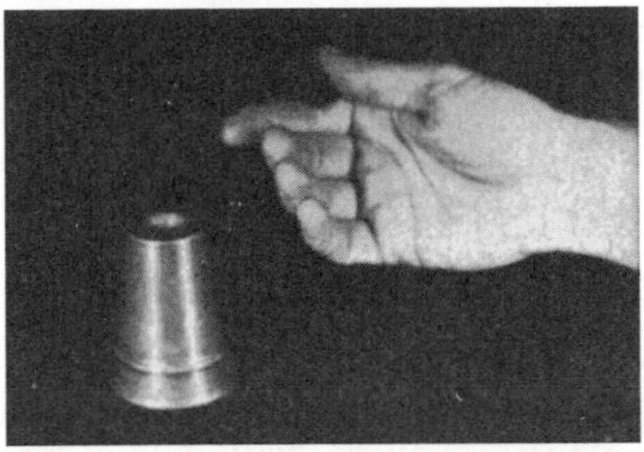

FIG. 159

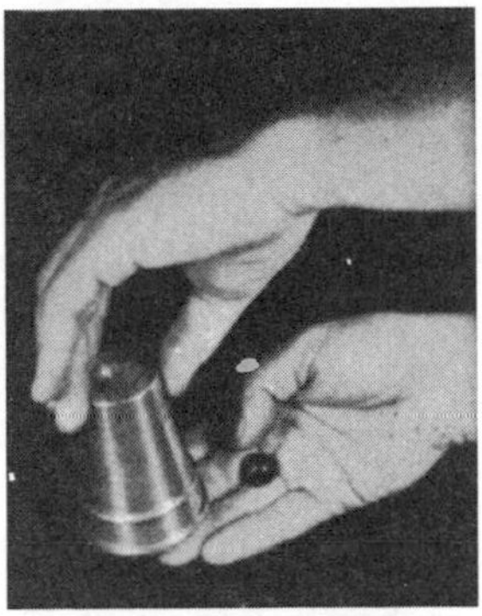

FIG. 160

take the ball in your left hand, palming it this way in your right; then pick up the cup with your right and simulate putting the ball underneath with your left.

The *Bosco* or *little-finger palm,* originally introduced by the great Bartolommeo Bosco for balls somewhat bigger than his predecessors had used, is done in various ways. One is shown in Fig. 161, where it is being

FIG. 161

used to load a ball under a cup in setting the cup down on the table. Bosco himself merely caught the ball in the crook of his little finger. Charles Bertram, a successful English society performer, used to catch a small ball between the end of his little finger and the side of his third—this specifically to load a ball under an apparently empty cup.

Pretending to put a ball under a cup without actually doing so will give a performer of your present attainments no difficulty. Loading a ball under a cup that you have picked up to show the table bare is not hard either; it can be done from the regular, the small-ball, or the Bosco palm. The only point to notice is that you must pick up a cup in a way that will bring the ball under the edge when the cup is set down; and you must *always* pick up the cups that way, whether you are loading or not. Take care not to shift the cup around sidewise in the act of setting it down. My personal opinion is that the Bosco palm allows you to load with the least waste of motion.

To load with a small-ball palm, encircle the very mouth of the cup with your thumb and forefinger, putting your palm almost flat on the table top. This allows you to scoot the ball toward you as you set the cup down again.

The regular palm is more often used in loading Indian cups, which are hemispherical, with a knob on top that is caught between the tips of first and second fingers.

Large balls, potatoes, or tangerines are loaded almost entirely by misdirection. They are carried in the left side pocket. Something interesting (such as a small ball appearing under each cup) happens on the table, and you pick up a cup with your right hand, turning your right side toward the audience as you steal a potato with your left hand. You then transfer the cup from right to left hand, with its mouth to the rear, and simply stuff the potato in as you take the cup. The object you load should be just big enough so that you can wedge it in the top of the cup, though this is not absolutely essential.

That is really the whole necessary foundation of Cups and Balls. A great number of passes, routines, and expedients are given in three books by Eddie Joseph: *A Practical Lesson in Cups and Balls; Advanced Lessons in Cups and Balls; The Last Word on Cups and Balls.* Old-fashioned (and fundamental) routines are given in Professor Hoffmann's *Modern Magic* and Lang Neil's *The Modern Conjurer.*

The whole secret of success with Cups and Balls, as with many other tricks, is to work out one routine and stick to it until it becomes second nature. Pauses and uncertainty will ruin the trick even more quickly than accidents; and accidents seldom happen to performers who know their routine.

Consequently books on magic that treat Cups and Balls always detail at least one routine. But I think you will bring more freshness to the effect if you work out your own, following the general lines I shall explain, which are practically inevitable in the nature of the trick.

First, keep it short. A slow and repetitious cup-and-ball routine seems endless; it is nearly as bad as an amateur card trick.

The pace of your routine should suit your own natural tempo. (This is not a truism because some tricks must be worked fast, and others cannot, no matter who does them.) It is better to err, if anything, on the side of deliberation; there may be some slight danger of confusing people as the balls pass from cup to cup.

Your routine must begin with the production of a ball.

Some performers start with the three cups stacked; this permits you to hide some of the balls in the hollow spaces between cups, which are designed that way on purpose. By taking each cup mouth upward, then turning it over and setting it down with one prompt swing, you can load any or even all of the cups without any sleight-of-hand or any steals from your pockets.

Other men begin with the three cups standing mouth down in a row. They generally steal a ball from a pocket and load it under one of the cups that they pick up to show that the table is bare.

The first ball may be produced from under a cup, or it may be pulled off the end of your wand if you use one (simply roll the ball to the finger tips from any palm).

Next, this one ball will travel. It can be vanished by a pass and reproduced under one of the cups. If you start hunting for the vanished ball, and pick the wrong two cups first, you can load, say, the middle cup with the ball you have just palmed.

When you find the ball, perhaps under an end cup, you pick it up and show it. In replacing it under the cup you palm it. The ball thus travels from an end cup to the middle one. Thence it may pass to the other end cup, which you have had ample opportunity to load.

The next major step is multiplication. Every time you pick up a cup, you load it. As a gag you may pass one ball from cup to cup without showing that it has vanished from the first or second cups; when you are called on this, pick up the cups and produce an endless stream of new balls. One variation is to get a handful of the small balls in your left hand and dump them all into a cup just as you would load in a potato. You hold the cup tilted slightly downward and set it on the table with a swing.

In any case, you lead up to the final stage, which is the production of a potato, onion, tangerine, or large ball under each cup. That is normally the end of the routine.

Eddie Joseph gives many variations with live chicks, liquids, fire, and heaven knows what else. If you become a cup-and-ball specialist, you will have to read his books.

There are two flourishes that always seem to entertain people, though I never could tell just why. The first is to drop one cup through another.

Hold a cup mouth up by the rim between the left thumb and forefinger. Drop another cup into this one with your right hand. You will find it very easy to let the upper cup knock the lower one out of your hand, and to retain the upper one between your left thumb and forefinger instead.

The other is to measure a cup with your wand, showing it to be deeper inside than outside. Stick the wand into a cup held in your left hand. Mark the depth of the cup on the wand with your right thumb. Then put the wand in a corresponding position outside the cup, but slide your thumb an inch or more to the right as you do so. When your right thumbnail comes to a stop against the rim of the cup, this proves that the inside is deeper than the outside.

2. *Sponge balls.* Balls made of sponge are a novelty, as magic goes; they have been used only since the late 1920s. Their compressibility makes them different from any other article a magician handles.

The balls may be bought from dealers, but you can just as well make your own. Get a fair-sized rubber sponge (some performers believe real sponge of the best quality is more satisfactory). With sharp scissors or a razor blade, cut it into inch-and-a-half cubes. Then keep trimming off the corners until the cubes have become spherical. The balls need not be perfectly round, but they must all look alike.

The manipulation of sponge balls is easy and pleasant. The regular and finger palms can be used as with any ball. In addition, the ball may be caught in the fork of the thumb; pinching a very small bit of the rubber will hold it.

The basic special sleight with sponge balls is the mash—showing two balls mashed down to the size of one. One ball lies on the table or in your hand. Get another ball to the finger palm in the other hand. In reaching for the visible ball, slap the finger-palmed one on top, press the two flat with your thumb, and show the result. That's all.

Use of sponge balls, like Cups and Balls, depends very much on routine. Indeed Cups and Balls is often shown with sponge balls nowadays.

Two particularly good effects are a repeat with three balls (actually four), and a method of increasing the balls in a spectator's own hand.

With the three balls you keep putting two balls in your left fist and one in your right trouser pocket but then rolling three balls out of your left hand. Of course you start with the extra ball palmed, do the mash with the second ball that goes into your fist, and palm the third ball in pocketing it.

The effect in the spectator's hand may be worked with two balls showing and one palmed. Do the mash with one of the two, put it in a spectator's palm and close his fingers over it tight. Then vanish the remaining ball by a pass and let the spectator open his hand. Out pop two balls.

If the sponge balls appeal to you, you can have more fun devising your own effects than reading mine. They should be worked quite fast; there is not much danger of confusing the audience, but a good deal of being detected if you give them time to think. Sponge balls depend on shock effect, not on brain-teasing.

Sponge-ball moves and routines are given in *Greater Magic* and in Jean Hugard's *Modern Magic Manual*. The most elaborate treatise is Frank Garcia's *Encyclopedia of Sponge Ball Magic*.

11. Hand Magic with Thimbles

THIMBLE manipulation, which for some mysterious reason hardly came into being before the start of this century, is extremely easy and lots of fun if it doesn't go on too long. Just be warned by the cartoon in *The Sphinx* that showed two men peering down from the second balcony, one with opera glasses. "He just produced another thimble," he explains to his less fortunate companion.

Thimbles can be palmed by the regular palm, the finger palm, or the back palm (the rim caught between first and third fingers).

1. *The thumb palm.* All those methods are mere variants; the thumb palm is the primary thimble sleight. Put the thimble on your forefinger; bend the forefinger and leave the thimble in the fork of your thumb (Fig. 162).

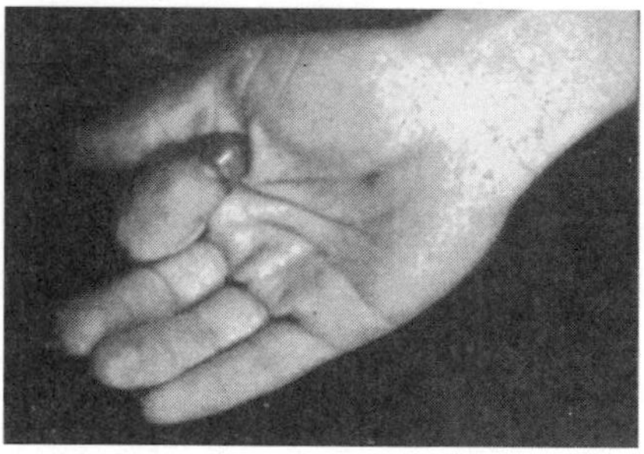

FIG. 162

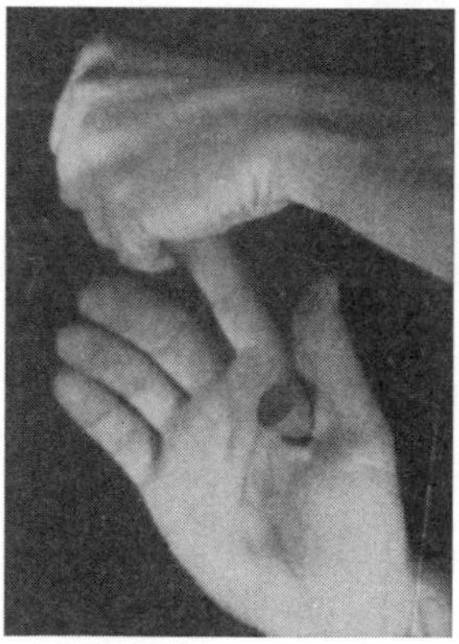

FIG. 163

You are now, as I observed in another book, a thimble manipulator.

Fig. 163 shows the completion of an ordinary pass with a thimble.

In addition to their other pleasing features, thimbles give you little to worry about in the way of angles.

2. *The steal pass.* Thimble manipulation should be worked fast, like sponge balls, not giving the audience time to reflect. Even so, you may

occasionally bump into the man who wants to *see* the thimble in the hand where you claim to put it. If you do, give him this.

Put the thimble plainly against your left palm (Fig. 164).

Slowly close your left little finger around your right forefinger, then close your left third, second, and first fingers. The thimble is definitely shut inside.

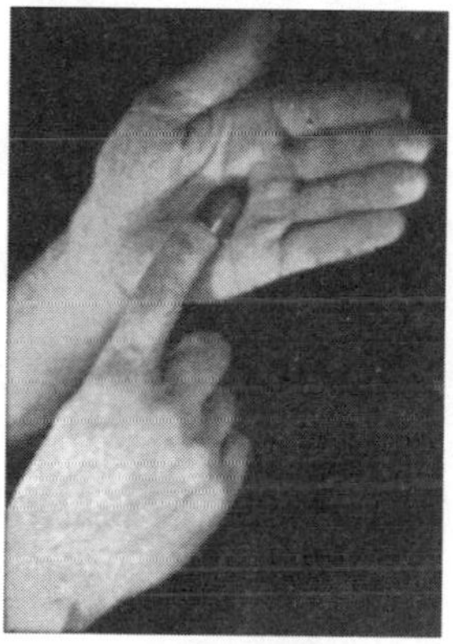

FIG. 164

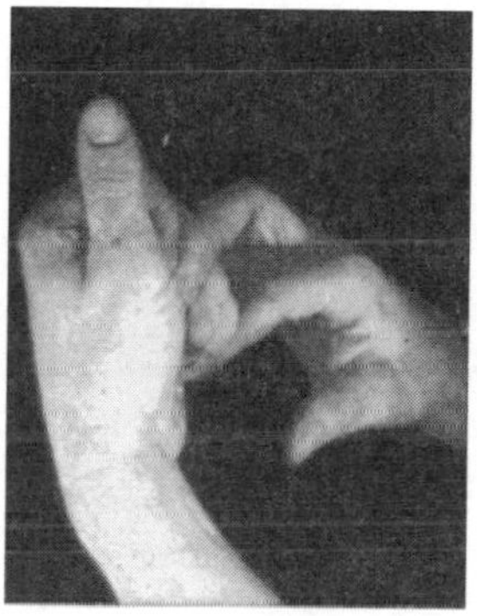

FIG. 165

Move your right hand forward and up instead of simply withdrawing it. This brings the thimble down to the position shown in Fig. 165. The back of your right hand blocks the view, giving you a good chance to thumb-palm the thimble, which you immediately do.

My own custom is to cover this upward motion with a shake of my (now bare) right forefinger, admonishing the skeptic to watch closely.

3. *Thimble changes.* The use of borrowed and marked thimbles has never, mercifully, become general. But it is a peculiarity of thimbles that color changes are hard to make visibly. You have to put a red thimble in your fist, then take it out blue.

Naturally this can be done by first palming the blue one and making an ordinary pass with the other hand.

A bolder, but in some ways neater, change is done by putting the blue one on your right second finger and keeping your second, third, and fourth fingers curled into your palm. Put the red thimble on your forefinger.

In the act of transferring the thimble to your left hand, thumb-palm the red thimble but don't straighten your right forefinger again; straighten your second finger, thus putting the blue thimble in your fist.

4. *The multiplying thimbles.* Thimbles share very much the qualities

of billiard balls in being fun to manipulate, easy to overdo, and in reaching their culmination with one trick—multiplication.

For the multiplying-thimble routine you need some sort of holder that will keep four thimbles secure and release them instantly when you want them. Dealers carry several forms, or you can improvise one with four loops of elastic webbing on a small cardboard panel.

Further you require eight thimbles just alike (red is the customary color), of any material you choose, and other colored thimbles if you mean to include color changes in your act.

Again I shall let you build your own routine, merely outlining the basic stages. You will want to pin your thimble holder either under your vest on the left or inside your coat near the right shoulder. Very likely you will put three thimbles in one of your right-hand pockets.

At the start of the routine you should produce one thimble by poking at the air with your forefinger. It may then travel hither and yon, partly by pure palming, partly by apt use of another thimble. For example, you rub a thimble against the elbow of your left sleeve and thumb-palm it, instantly reproducing a duplicate on your left forefinger.

You may introduce one or two color changes; swallow the thimble; pull it out of your ear; and so on, but not too long.

Your routine must be so arranged that you finally dip into your right-hand pocket, and come out with one thimble displayed on your right forefinger, and the other three out of sight on the remaining three fingers, which are curled in.

"Toss away" the visible thimble from your right forefinger, and reach with your left hand wherever the holder is fastened. Steal all four thimbles from the holder, but produce only one, as you have just been doing with your right hand.

You can now do a brief hand-to-hand sequence, at the end of which you apparently forget yourself by leaving two thimbles in view.

Just as people start to snicker, straighten another finger of your right hand, then of your left, then of your right, until you have eight thimbles —all that your hands can accommodate.

You then have your choice of walking off with a Cheshire-cat grin or vanishing the thimbles, which you do by stacking all eight and making the tourniquet.

Jean Hugard's *Thimble Magic* is devoted wholly to this branch of the art.

12. Hand Magic with Cigarettes

CARDINI and his followers have made such hits with brief cigarette acts that almost every modern amateur who smokes will try his hand at cigarette manipulation sooner or later.

The example of Cardini, too, has fixed all attention on work with lighted cigarettes. Unlighted cigarettes are scarcely used any more except for a few pocket tricks.

Although this chapter is called hand magic with cigarettes, you can hardly do anything without some mechanical assistance. There is only one palm you can use for a lighted cigarette, and only three or four passes. The real surprise of a cigarette act depends on little gimmicks called holders, or tanks, which enable you to keep burning cigarettes safely hidden under your clothes until you need them.

These tanks are made of perforated metal, with some sort of grip inside to keep the cigarette or cigarettes away from the metal walls. You can get various types from any magic dealer.

Dealers also carry quite realistic dummy lit cigarettes, which can be rung in after you have got the stage sufficiently full of smoke, and your lungs ditto.

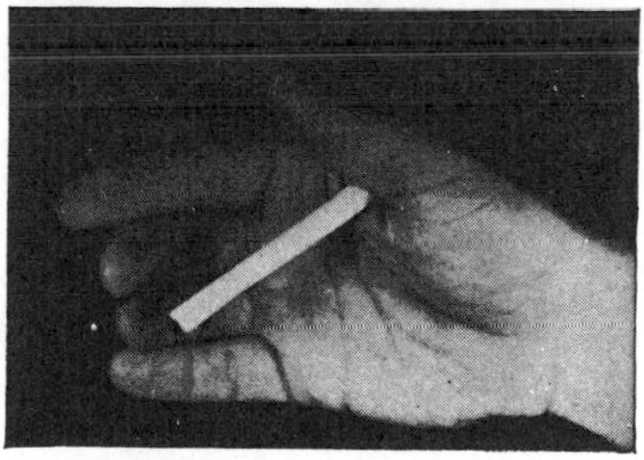

FIG. 166

1. *The thumb palm.* This is shown in Fig. 166. Obviously you will have no trouble at all in either palming or producing a lit cigarette in this fashion between your first and second finger tips. It is the only way in which you can palm a lighted cigarette without burning yourself.

2. *The tip-tilt pass.* Originally devised for an unlit cigarette, this can be adapted for a burning one as follows:

Clip the cigarette near the lit end between your left first and second fingers, with your thumb on the butt end. Cup your right hand, ready to catch the cigarette (Fig. 167).

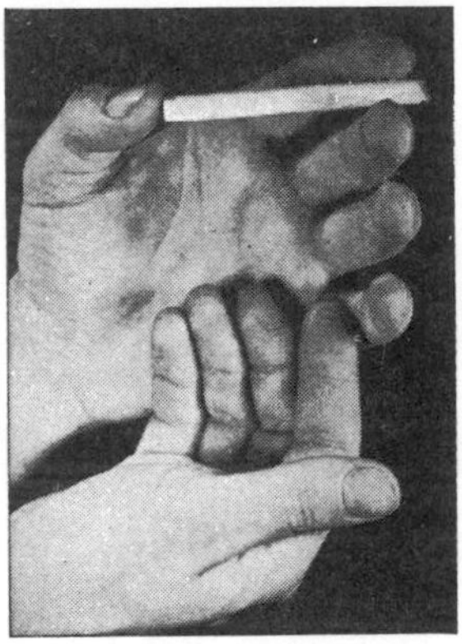

Fig. 167

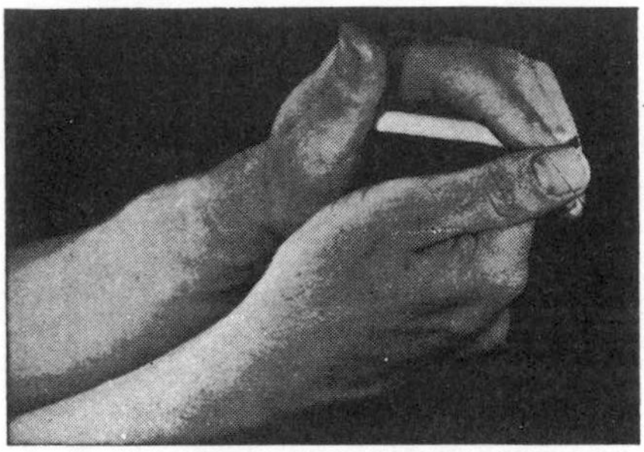

Fig. 168

Turn over your left hand as if dropping the cigarette into the right palm. Really you press it against your right second finger, which automatically tilts the cigarette into thumb-palm position (Fig. 168).

Your right hand immediately closes and moves off, leaving the cigarette behind, as in Fig. 169.

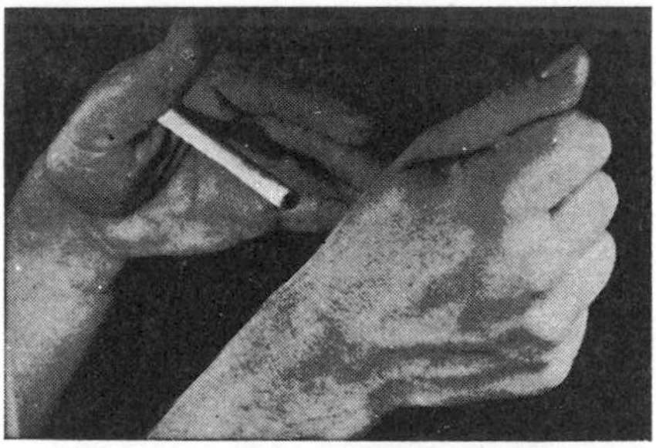

Fig. 169

3. *The poke-through pass.* The peculiarity of this move is that you look as if you were using one of two mechanical devices, the pull and the thumb-tip (see apparatus magic), to vanish the cigarette; but then you are able to reproduce it, which you cannot do with either gimmick.

Make your left hand into a loose fist, smallest at your forefinger and largest at your little finger. With your right hand push the lit end of the cigarette through the curl of your left forefinger. Follow this with a push on the butt end from your right thumb. In a moment the cigarette is gone.

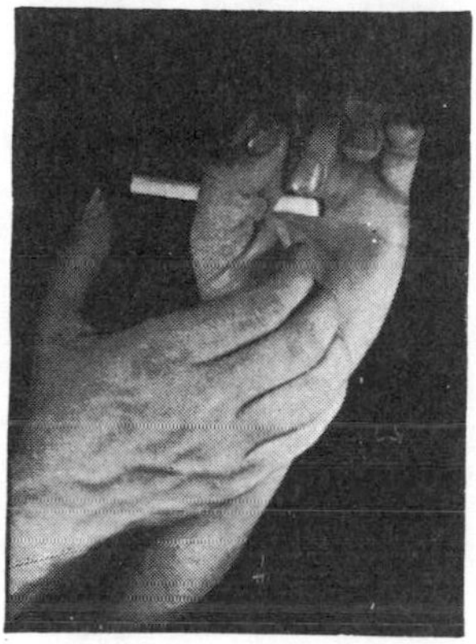

FIG. 170

You start as in Fig. 170. When the cigarette gets in far enough, you steal it between your right first and second finger tips (Fig. 171). With-

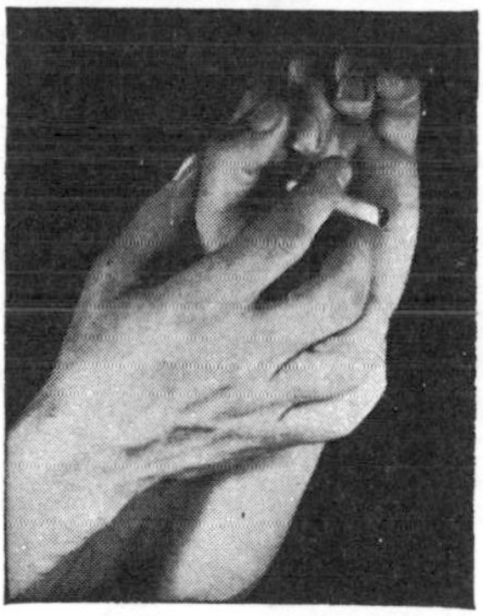

FIG. 171

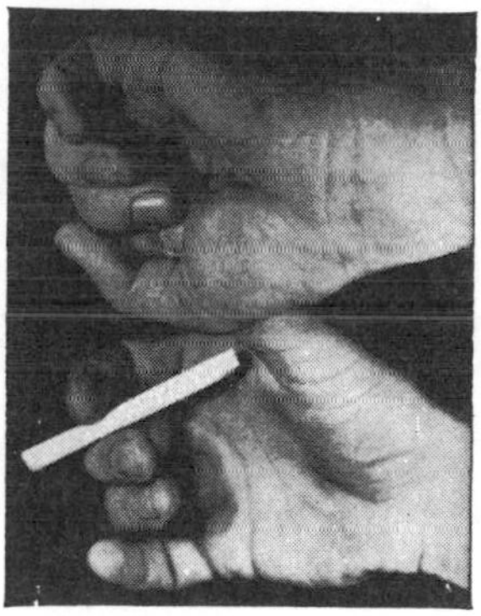

FIG. 172

draw your right thumb, move your left fist away, watching it, and then thumb-palm the cigarette in your right hand (Fig. 172).

4. *The king-size pass.* In order to do this without burning yourself, you need a long cigarette; and since I have never seen the pass described elsewhere, I must give it a name of my own.

Hold the cigarette by the unlit end in your left hand and lay it across your right fingers as in Fig. 173, holding your forefinger back to keep it from getting burned.

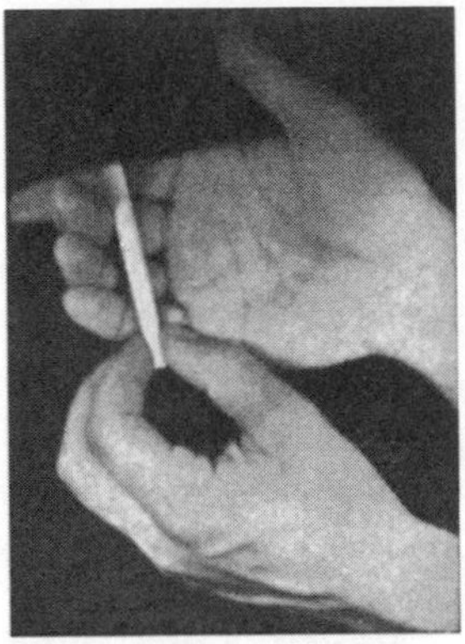

FIG. 173

Close your right second, third, and little fingers around the cigarette as in Fig. 174. The left hand is not shown in the photograph, in order to expose the position of the right; actually, however, the left hand moves

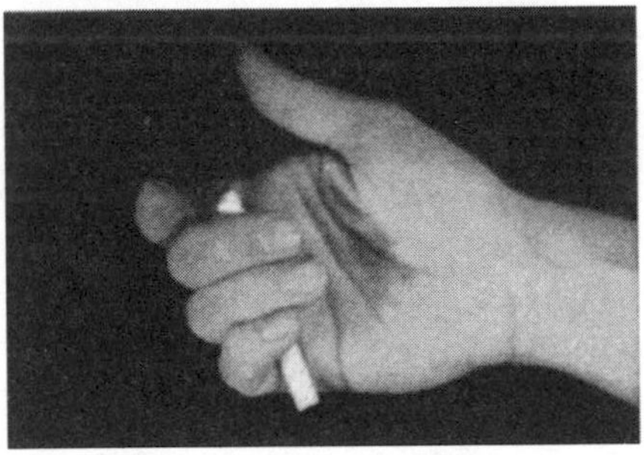

FIG. 174

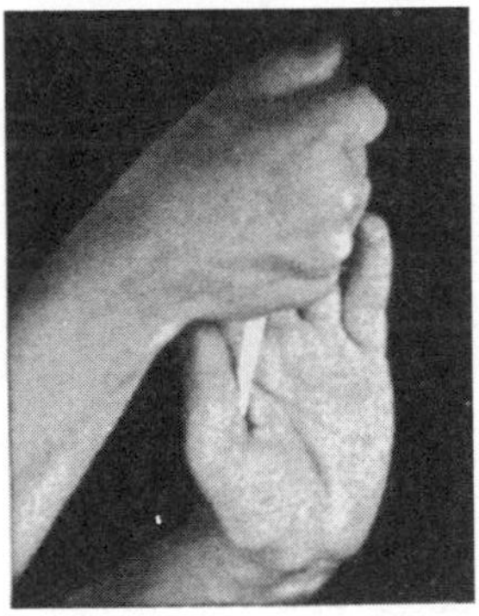

FIG. 175

up, as if patting the right fingers shut, and thumb-palms the projecting lower end of the cigarette as in Fig. 175. The right hand then moves away, leaving the cigarette behind.

5. *Tonguing.* This, along with the thumb palm, is the foundation of modern cigarette routines. It is a method of hiding a half-smoked cigarette butt in your mouth when apparently removing it from your lips in one hand.

The method is simply to lay your tongue tip on the butt end of the cigarette, holding it against your lower lip. Open your mouth and press down with your tongue, turning the cigarette end over end. Keep your tongue slightly hollowed so that the lit end doesn't burn you. The books all say it won't anyhow, but I have heard of once-daring magicians who maintained otherwise.

You reverse the motion to reproduce the cigarette, still burning, between your lips.

With these sleights, and a set of tanks pinned into your clothes (under the vest is a favorite location), you are ready to create a cigarette routine.

Possibly you will begin by producing either an unlighted cigarette or a package of them. An unlighted cigarette may be withdrawn from your ear by holding it flat against the inside of your fingers with your thumb. Put the tips of your middle fingers to your ear, slide the cigarette forward with your thumb, and withdraw the fingers as if pulling out the cigarette, which of course actually stands still until your fingers reach its outer end.

It is also possible to cut a hole in one corner of the end of a matchbox drawer, insert the cigarette, and push the drawer out far enough to hide the end of the cigarette.

In complete pantomime you put a cigarette between your lips; take the actual matchbox from your pocket, take out a match, strike it, and cup your hands to get a light. This brings the matchbox in front of your lips, and shutting the drawer pokes the cigarette into your mouth. You will have to pretend some difficulty getting a light if you really want to start this cigarette on the same match.

You can't very well produce your first cigarette lighted, by palming, because the smoke would give you away.

Next you do one or two vanishes and recoveries, puffing industriously at the cigarette in the intervals so as to smoke it down short enough to be tongued.

A cigarette routine deceives almost wholly by misdirection, as you will realize if you watch Cardini. There is always something going on with one hand while the other makes a steal.

For instance, you pretend to carry away the cigarette in your right fist; actually you tongue it. (Just then your left hand steals a cigarette from a tank.)

The original one vanishes from your right hand, and instantly reappears between your lips (reverse tonguing). Your left hand goes up and "removes" the cigarette, substituting the palmed one, while your right hand steals another from a tank.

Blow smoke at the one visible in your left hand, fling it on the floor, and quickly step on it.

Catch the palmed cigarette from the air in your right hand; just as everyone is watching that, bring the tongued cigarette back outside. (You mustn't do this visibly very often, or the trick of tonguing will be exposed.)

Look around suddenly at the new cigarette in your right hand and people will then realize that you have another between your lips.

That is the moment to make a new steal with your left hand.

Cardini has great fun with his own confusion at an unexpected cigarette in each hand and one or two in his mouth.

The sequence that follows will probably be fast and furious, one cigarette after another caught or produced between the lips, instantly removed, thrown on the floor, and stepped on. Once the floor is fairly well littered, you need not bother to substitute a palmed cigarette for the one you tongued—just do it empty-handed. This is also the moment to use the dummies; no one will have time to notice the difference, and you can steal them from anywhere without worrying about tanks.

Cigarette manipulation is quite extensively treated in *Greater Magic* and Hugard's *Modern Magic Manual; Celebrated Cigarettes,* by Keith Clark, gives exact details of one routine.

From *Greater Magic* I give you one very good trick with a lighted cigarette, which may be done wherever and whenever you can borrow a cigarette, a handkerchief, and a piece of newspaper.

6. *Lighted Cigarette Through Handkerchief.* Have two spectators hold the handkerchief horizontal by the four corners, not too tightly. Lay the piece of newspaper (which should be about eight by ten) on the handkerchief. Borrow a cigarette, have it marked unless it is an unusual brand, light it, and puff at it until it is burning brightly. Take it by the unlit end in your right hand and hold it under the middle of the handkerchief.

With your left hand, thumb on top, pick up the newspaper and draw it toward you, exposing the center of the handkerchief. The burning tip of the cigarette can be seen glowing through the cloth.

Slide the paper forward again, but hold onto it. At this moment your left first and second fingers dip under the handkerchief, and steal the cigarette.

Simulate the continued presence of the cigarette by poking up your right forefinger.

Draw back the paper again to show the raised spot, made by "the butt end of the cigarette," where the cigarette is going to burn through.

Once again put the paper in the middle of the handkerchief, and this time grab the unlighted end of the cigarette through the fabric with your right hand. Straighten it up so that the lighted end comes against the newspaper.

In a moment it burns its way through, and is removed by the left hand.

Finally take away the newspaper in your right hand. Surprise, surprise —no hole in the handkerchief!

7. *Card in cigarette.* Not primarily hand magic, this will serve for a transition (either way) between a cigarette and a card routine.

A card is chosen, torn up, the pieces put in a card box (see p. 263), and one corner given to the chooser to hold. The magician meanwhile borrows a cigarette, but when he lights it, it refuses to draw. He pulls it apart, and finds inside the chosen card, rolled up tight, but lacking the corner held by the spectator. The card box contains nothing but a few grains of tobacco.

The preparation consists of tearing a corner off a card, and putting the corner in an accessible pocket; soaking the card in water until it can be rolled up and pushed into a cigarette or wrapped in a cigarette paper with a little tobacco stuffed in at the end. One compartment of the card box is loaded with a little shredded tobacco.

The performer forces a duplicate of the card that is rolled in the cigarette. He borrows a cigarette, and switches it for the prepared one, which is easy since no one knows why he wants it. The spectator who tears up the card drops the pieces in the card box; the performer, having stolen the previously prepared corner from his pocket, pretends to pick it out of the box and hand it to the spectator. The rest of the working is obvious.

P.S. after a generation. Cigarettes are not what they were when this chapter first appeared. The best evidence I've seen was an enchanting number by the brilliant Dutch professional Fred Kaps. He had a glove puppet of a little boy on one hand. After a brief interchange, Kaps produced a cigarette. The puppet protested. Kaps argued, and got ready to light the cigarette. The puppet pleaded, Kaps used his lighter, the puppet hid under Kaps' coat, coughing. Kaps' better self won out, and the cigarette vanished.

I was so charmed by the story that I can't remember whether he produced the butt magically or from a pocket, nor how the vanish went. It wasn't a trick, it was a moral drama.

PART TWO · APPLIED ART: HEAD MAGIC

IN the next two chapters are the tricks done by ingenuity and prearrangement rather than manual skill—the clever combinations that have always been used (mistakenly, I think) to teach the beginner in magic. I have already pointed out that you can learn the mechanics of these feats *too* easily. The temptation is irresistible to *perform* them long before you have learned to *present* them.

By this stage in the book, however, you will have come to appreciate the showmanship that dresses up a small trick and makes it into a big one. Although you can instantly pounce on the method that will locate a chosen card without your lifting a finger, you are now wise enough not to show the trick until you have memorized it, rehearsed it, and discovered how to make this location impressive, not just puzzling.

Furthermore, you will keep seeing chances to use sleights in tricks of ingenuity. This gives you a shifty offense with which you can even fool fellow magicians at times. And as for the layman who has acquired, say, one card trick, you can show him his own effect, and leave him open mouthed.

I am offering a comparatively small selection of tricks; almost every magic book you open will give others. But let me warn you that many of these books are less particular in their choice than I have been. A great many tricks requiring no skill of hand are feeble efforts.

That, however, calls in turn for the opposite warning: even the sorriest bit of head magic, unless it is just a cheap substitute for sleight of hand, can often be dressed up by manipulation and showmanship into something you will be happy to do.

Included in this section are a few small effects with miscellaneous objects that might at least as logically have appeared under hand magic. But since they are impromptu tricks, and the manipulation is easy, head magic is where you will find them.

13. Head Magic with Cards

TRICKS of ingenuity and preparation with cards outnumber other feats of head magic even more heavily than card sleight of hand outnumbers other sleight of hand. You had better watch your step because this is the one branch of conjuring where social pests have had a field day. Nothing about your work must give the slightest hint of the man who "always insists on doing card tricks."

(If you do always insist on doing card tricks, make the audience insist for you: spring the cards, make a color change, or show some other ostentatious flourish. That will have them demanding more if they are in any mood for magic. You may be surprised to hear how often a group of people could not be pleased by the Great Herrmann himself; at such times it's just no use trying.)

1. LOCATIONS

The most and greatest ingenuity in card magic has been applied to locations. There are methods so refined that no one can possibly detect them unless he is in the habit of using them himself. Sometimes they go a little too far, becoming so ingenious that the performer himself can hardly remember them. You will have discovered by now that far cruder methods sufficiently baffle the intelligent onlooker. If you must acquire these hyper-refinements, save them to surprise other magicians—a hobby that is fun, but the ruination of many a potential entertainer.

1a. Unprepared key cards. In most chosen-card tricks, adequate precautions are taken to keep you from seeing the chosen card itself; that is, after all, the point of the trick. But you can locate the chosen card just as well by keeping track of some other card that will follow the chosen one around.

The most venerable device is to look at the card above the chosen one when it is replaced. Most parlor magicians know this dodge, but they can be fooled just the same if you use it deftly instead of furtively.

For example, pick a spectator who you have noticed always shuffles overhand. Shuffle the pack yourself, overhand, and catch a peep of the bottom card.

Then hand your victim the deck. Ask him to run it before his eyes, and fix his mind on one card while he has the pack in his own hands. This is quite likely to give him the idea that he merely thinks of the card instead of drawing it. So much the better, of course, if it does.

However, you next ask him to take out the card he has fixed on, put down the rest of the deck, and concentrate on his card.

All this has been slow and impressive. Now you speed up a little, growing more casual.

Just so that you shan't touch the cards, ask him to cut off part of the deck. Is he *sure* he has fixed his card indelibly in mind? (The purpose of this is to take his attention off the two halves, so that he won't remember which is which.)

"Now if you'll just put your card on there" (pointing to the original top half) "and put the rest of the cards on top, and cut the pack, and give it a shuffle . . ."

This has brought the original bottom card directly above the chosen card. The cutting, as you know, is immaterial. A brief overhand shuffle will not separate key and chosen card once in ten times.

This trick is so simple that you yourself may not be properly impressed with what you have done: a spectator has chosen (he may say merely thought of) a card while the deck was in his own hands. Then he himself has replaced it and shuffled. You could scarcely give him so much leeway by the most daring approximation and sleight of hand.

All you need now is a good pretext for looking through the deck. (This, incidentally, is a thing the parlor magician usually lacks. Flat-footedly searching through the pack, until by some not very mysterious means you find the chosen card, scarcely comes under the head of magic.) You may look through for a particular card—say the queen of hearts or the joker—that you claim will enable you to attract any other card in the deck. In finding this card, of course, you also collar the chosen one, and then use the other, perhaps, as the indicator in the slip or the Collins force (chapter 3, section 3*d*).

You may also openly search for the chosen card and claim (looking greatly crestfallen) not to have found it. It can then come out of your pocket, or appear in half a dozen other conclusions.

That is the key card at its crudest. You have already seen, in Zingone's Table Spread (chapter 3, section 5*a*), that the key card will serve just as well if it is not next to the chosen one but separated from it by a known number. The subsequent working is exactly the same.

Next we have methods of making the chosen card itself a key.

The most versatile principle is the *one-way deck.* I take this to include pointer cards, which we shall come to in a minute.

First, the back designs of a great many decks, even those apparently symmetrical, are different at one end from what they are at the other. The hunting scenes and vases of flowers are so conspicuously "one-way" that you may not have the nerve to use them. But many of the elaborate scroll and leaf designs show flaws in the engraving—a curlicue thick on one end of the card, thin on the other; a white lozenge that breaks into a white border at one end only; some three-cornered center pattern, plainly but inconspicuously pointing north.

Obviously, then, you can prepare for a card act by arranging the deck with the backs all one way. No amount of overhand shuffling disturbs the arrangement. Riffle shuffling is safe if you split the pack as described for one-way cards in chapter 3, section 5*b*. Again you must work your miracle on a person who habitually uses one of those two shuffles.

Instead of a good excuse to look through the deck, this time you need a natural way of turning it end for end. One method is to fan the cards for the choice, close them up, and then take the deck by its outer end in your right hand, preparatory to making a one-handed fan, which you do as soon as the chooser is ready to return his card. Or you can simply make a backward pressure fan when the card is to be replaced, refraining from turning the pack end for end as you might naturally do in starting the fan.

You can make any fairly new pack into a one-way deck by a mark across one end. This may be put on with a pencil in five seconds, scratched with your thumbnail in one, or (as suggested by William Turner in his excellent little volume *How to Do Tricks with Cards*) made literally at a blow by whacking the end of the deck on the sharp edge of a table top. Mr. Turner suggests an even more ingenious location based on making the mark diagonal instead of perpendicular; if you read his book you will find out about it.

Pointer cards are those in any deck that have one-way faces, owing to the arrangement of the spots.

When you look at a pack you will discover that the pips are not symmetrically arranged on the following hearts, spades, and clubs: ace, three, five, six, seven, eight, nine; the seven of diamonds is also a pointer. Some brands of cards, notably Bicycles, have a one-way king, queen, and jack of spades as well.

A little experimentation with pointer cards will introduce you to the next principle on our list, the *divided deck.* If the cards can somehow be sorted into two roughly equal groups segregated on a principle known only to the performer, the resulting location is *ipso facto* indetectable (though not necessarily worth showing). You need only have a card drawn from one group and replaced among the other.

Returning for a moment to the pointer cards, you will see that you can spot any one of the twenty-two or twenty-five pointers when it is reversed among its fellows. You can also, however, spot one pointer, whichever way it is turned, among the non-pointer cards, and vice versa.

Here is a pointer location that I contrived (probably not for the first time in magical history), which fooled one of the best-informed professionals in the business. I am not particularly proud of this, and indeed I consider the use of locations that mystify conjurers to be among the idlest of pastimes. I give the method simply as a convenient sample of the ways you can combine bits of head magic.

To work this location at its very best, you must choose a victim who is an expert dovetail shuffler, and furthermore who splits the deck by the first method described in chapter 3, section 5*b*. (I nearly came to grief because my spectator was so used to handling one-way decks that he always split by the second method.) Start with all the pointer cards on top of the pack. Hand the deck to your victim; ask him to cut it into two halves as nearly equal as he can. Ask him to take a card from this half (pointing to the top one), look at it, put it back in the other half, put the two halves together either way, and give them a shuffle. Until he is through shuffling, you never lay a finger on the cards, yet of course you find his. If he does not habitually shuffle in the necessary way, you must carry out the steps yourself, but fairly, just as the victim would do if he could.

If you follow my directions—and make sure he does—you will discover that the result is to put a pointer card in the nonpointer half, and then turn one half, so that the lone card is shuffled in end-for-end among the pointers. Of course the pointers are now thoroughly intermixed with non-pointers, but you simply ignore them. Incidentally, your man can also do an overhand shuffle after, but not before, the riffle.

The reason why you need an expert dovetail shuffler is that he must split the pack just about in half. A few nonpointers on the bottom of the pointer half make no difference and are likely to occur because the pointer group is the smaller; but a couple of pointers in the nonpointer half will make trouble. If they do occur, or you think they may have, you must look through and see whether more than one pointer is reversed. The turned card lowest in the pack—or highest, depending on which half the victim puts on top—will be the chosen one.

Other methods of dividing the deck depend on the suits and values of the cards. The most elementary (and accordingly useless) division is into red and black cards. Much more practical is the division into odd and even cards. The ingenious Charles T. Jordan carried this to the furthest point that can be reached short of arbitrary memorizing: he divided a pack into even spades and hearts, odd clubs and diamonds in one half; odd spades and hearts, even clubs and diamonds in the other. If you are going to divide your pack thus elaborately, you will need some practice with it before the sorting can grow automatic.

The late Leopold Figner, a German specialist in head magic with cards, used a divided-deck presentation that he called Division of Labor. He summoned two spectators, one of whom was to deal the deck alternately into two piles, thus making sure that all the cards were there; then the second man was to choose one half, and have several cards drawn. Next the first man had the chosen cards replaced in the other half, and well shuffled in by yet a third volunteer.

Finally Figner ran through and picked out the chosen cards; but then, splashy showmanship was not his strong point. (He had retired on the proceeds of the first linen-supply business in Munich before he devoted his time to magic.) It will be a fitting test of your own ability as an entertainer to devise some better finish.

The method, of course, was simply to start by arranging the deck with odd and even cards alternating. The first spectator's count then divided the pack into odd and even cards, and the routine took care of the rest.

1b. Prepared key cards. I share with many modern conjurers an almost obsessive dislike for prepared cards. From this feeling, however, we who have it are the only sufferers. If unprepared key cards will give us locations that no sleight of hand can duplicate, prepared key cards let us make these locations by touch instead of sight. One quick riffle or a rub of the thumb, and you have it.

One form of key card is prepared in a borrowed deck by sticking a tiny bit of diachylon on the face of the bottom card, cutting the deck, and giving a squeeze. This sticks two cards together. Various means of elaborating this principle are given on pages 104 ff. of Hugard's *Encyclopedia of Card Tricks*. In any case, the two cards stuck together can be detected by feel and by sound in riffling the deck.

Various other methods of thickening or weighting a key card require elaborate preparation in advance. A spot card such as a five or nine may have extra pips pasted on. A face card may have an extra face, minus the white border, pasted on; the same preparation can be made with the back of any card whose pattern has a white border. Some magicians used to split the back off a card, put a piece of silk between, and paste the card together again.

All of these devices, however, have largely given way to key cards whose edges only have been doctored. Probably the oldest version is the *long card,* which may in fact be either long or wide. You have two decks exactly alike, and get a hair's breadth shaved off the end or side of one pack. Remove any card from this pack, and replace it with the corresponding card from the untouched pack. You can then cut by feel to the projecting card.

European conjurers still seem to prefer long cards; American wizards, however, are almost unanimous in choosing the *short card* (which likewise may be either short or narrow). This does not require you to have two decks, since you can trim any one card you please—be sure to round the corners again. But the real advantage is that a spectator can handle a deck containing a short card, whereas he is quite likely to blunder on the long card by accident.

The short card is located by riffling the end of the deck; the card goes by with a perceptible slap or clink. It is quite easy to stop just above the short card, cutting or splitting the deck as may be needed.

The *cornered card* was used with amazing skill by the late Ralph W. Hull in his Tuned Deck series. Instead of shortening the whole card, Hull merely rounded off two diagonally opposite corners a little more than the maker had intended. This enabled him to have two key cards, one rounded at the index corners, the other at the nonindex corners. Chapter XVIII of *Greater Magic* gives his routine. It also points out that you can corner a card in a borrowed deck with your thumbnail. Hull said, "I have had magicians square the deck, look it over critically, seeking for short, long, wide, narrow, thick, thin, double or slick cards and never yet have I had anyone find the true secret after the closest examination."

Another form of key card, known for a century or so before it really grew popular, is the *rough-and-smooth* principle. If you put a new pack on the table, lean on it hard, and twist, it will often break at an ace, because the aces, carrying less ink than the other cards, are not so sticky. With a pack not quite so new, you can generally break at the same card (not necessarily an ace) several times running.

But you will soon find that this does not always work. So instead of depending on nature, you treat one side of one card with Simoniz automobile polish. If you treat the back of the card, you can cut it to the top every time; if the face, it will cut to the bottom.

There is a knack to cutting at a slick card. The actual moves are up to you, but you must press the pack together, then exert a sliding pressure. You don't need to squeeze very hard.

When you have mastered this knack, you can force your slick card by the Collins force (chapter 3, section 3*d*) without holding any break. Give a squeeze with your left thumb, and the top half slides forward, forcing the slick card (which, in this case, must be smooth on the face).

Obviously, prepared locators that can safely be handled by a spectator have another immense advantage over unprepared key cards: you can force the locator (chapter 3, section 3), and then no matter what happens you can always find the chosen card without so much as a glance.

Rough cards, the exact opposite of slick cards, have one face rubbed with the finest emery paper. You can't cut to them (unless you sand the face and Simoniz the back), but if you put a rough card against a chosen card, it will stick almost like glue. Ralph Hull's "Pop-Eyed Eye-Popper" deck, with which many ingenious tricks can be performed, consists of twenty-six duplicate cards roughened on the face and twenty-six indifferent cards roughened on the back. The cards are arranged in pairs and can be fanned without exposing any duplicate cards. Yet any card touched from the back will be one of the duplicates. This is sure-fire fan forcing with a vengeance.

2. MECHANICAL DECKS

This has a creaky sound, but magicians use the cog-wheel name to indicate any pack that has been generally prepared, no matter how simply or unobtrusively.

Passing over the old-fashioned forcing deck (which consists entirely of one or three cards repeated), as being of interest only to complete beginners and hardened professionals, we come to the ultimate in one-way decks —*strippers*. These are cards trimmed diagonally along the side, so that one end of the pack is a tiny fraction of an inch narrower than the other end. Any reversed card can thus be "stripped" out of the pack with one motion.

Normal or side strippers are too well known among the general public to be of great use to the ordinarily skillful card worker. End strippers, in which the ends instead of the sides are tapered, may still be used to advantage. Chapter 15 of the *Encyclopedia of Card Tricks* is devoted to effects with strippers. In addition Hugard and Braue have written an entire pamphlet on the subject: *Miracle Methods No. 1 (Casting New Light on the Stripper Deck)*.

Next we have the *Svengali deck*, which contains twenty-six short cards, all alike, and twenty-six indifferent ordinary cards. They are arranged in pairs, first a short, then a regular. If the pack is riffled through, face to the audience, only the normal, indifferent cards will show. But if a knife is inserted during the riffle, it always goes in above one of the duplicates. You are thus able to force one card, and later show it anywhere in the deck—or out of it, if you have mastered the ordinary top palm (chapter 3, section 4*a*).

The Svengali deck cannot be fanned with the face to the front. The late Ralph Hull improved it, rechristening it the mirage deck, and produced a pack that could safely be fanned, thumbed through, shuffled overhand or riffle, sprung from hand to hand, or spread on the table. You could then force a card by riffling, by counting down to a chosen number, by dealing until a spectator said stop, by ribbon-spreading the cards and having one pointed to, or by letting a spectator cut the pack.

In addition to having its twenty-six duplicates shortened, Hull narrowed them, slicked the faces of the indifferent cards and the backs of the force cards, and sanded the faces of the force cards and the backs of the indifferent cards.

Another mechanical deck using short cards is the *Mene Tekel*. This consists of twenty-six different cards, each with a short duplicate above it.

Both the Mene Tekel and the Svengali deck can be dovetail-shuffled without breaking up the arrangement if you first give the deck a smart tap against the table to settle the short cards at one end.

With a Mene Tekel deck, when the selection is made by the riffle, of course it always falls on the upper of a pair. Then when the chosen card is removed, its duplicate is brought to the top by merely cutting the pack. Hence this pack is sometimes called "self-shifting."

Here is a particularly ingenious effect using such a deck. Your Mene Tekel pack must have backs of one color, say blue, and you use an ordinary deck with backs of the other color—in this case, red.

Have a card chosen from the Mene Tekel deck, cut the duplicate to the top, and take back the chosen card. Drop it on top of the pack, then pick it up and show it. No matter how clumsy you are, you can hardly help doing a double lift (chapter 3, section 6*a*). As the top two cards are duplicates, no one is the wiser. Put the two double-lifted cards as one in a tumbler, back to the audience.

Now have someone draw a card from the red pack, but don't let him look at it. Take it from him, and put it in the glass behind the other two cards, so that its red back shows.

Turn the glass around, and lift out the front card. Its duplicate, the short card, is left behind; yet when you turn the glass around again, the card appears to be red-backed.

3. SETUPS

3a. Systems. One of the oldest principles in magic is the arrangement of the entire deck by some system that looks accidental but allows the performer to calculate or remember the name and location of each card.

The most useful system mathematically, and the least accidental-looking, is known to American magicians as the *Si Stebbins Setup*. The suits usually alternate red and black. The word CHaSeD gives by its consonants one easily remembered sequence—clubs, hearts, spades, diamonds. In value, each card is three higher than the one below. Starting from the face of the pack, you have the ace of clubs, the four of hearts, the seven of spades, the ten of diamonds, the king of clubs, the three of hearts, and so on to the jack of diamonds, the top card of the pack.

The Si Stebbins setup allows you to know the exact position in the pack of any card that the audience calls for. Done as a trick by itself, this would almost irresistibly suggest some mathematical arrangement, and the whole effect of the trick would depend on the perfection of your false dovetail shuffle. But if you help yourself out with shifts, thumb counting, and perhaps up to four strategically placed key cards, you can show a control over the pack that is utterly inexplicable. (Your key cards may be two cornered ones, as in 1*b* above, and two others with tiny bits scooped out at the ends, one at upper left and lower right, the other at upper right and lower left.)

To calculate the position of a given card, quickly glance at the bottom four cards of the deck. Now, if the given card is lower in value than the card of its own suit nearest to the bottom of the deck, subtract the given card from this lowest card of its own suit. Multiply by four. Subtract the number of cards below the one of the given suit nearest to the bottom. The answer is the position of the given card from the top.

If the given card is higher in value than the card of its own suit nearest to the bottom, subtract the given card from thirteen. Add the value of the nearest-to-bottom of this suit. Multiply by four. Subtract the number of cards below the nearest-to-bottom.

All this calculating is required on the assumption that the deck has been cut. If not, you will soon know the bottom four cards by heart, and can calculate like a flash. Presumably your key cards will be the thirteenth, twenty-sixth, thirty-ninth, and bottom cards of the deck. You can then instantly break at any quarter of the pack you like, and find the given card by thumb-counting not more than six, up or down.

Naturally with any setup you can always tell what card has been drawn by glimpsing the card above it. If several cards are drawn in a bunch, you can name them all, just as you can "read" the deck or name every card in it. You can also tell "by weight" how many cards have been cut off. You know that successive cards of a given suit are four cards apart. Cards three apart in their suit are thirteen apart in the deck. If a small number is cut, you can simply run through the missing cards in your head; if a large number, calculate as explained.

(By the way, if you practice a lot, and invariably use one make of cards, you can cut off any number called for by feel. I should imagine you could equally well learn to judge how many had been cut off; but the setup method is less strain.)

Another system is the ancient one suggested by the nonsense line,

> Eight kings threatened to save
> Ninety-five queens for one sick knave.

The sequence, obviously, is 8, king, 3, 10, 2, 7, 9, 5, queen, 4, ace, 6, jack. The suits follow as before.

Then there is the "hungry jackass" sequence given by John Mulholland in *The Art of Illusion:*

> Jackass ate live tree
> King intends to fix
> Several for benign queen.

This is intended to suggest: jack, ace, 8, 5, 3, king, 10, 2, 6, 7, 4, 9, queen.

Finally, there is the Nikola card system, described at the end of Hugard's *Encyclopedia of Card Tricks.* This is the final elaboration in setups because there is no method whatever in the arrangement except that every fourth card is a heart. The system is a mnemonic one, enabling you to memorize an order of the pack originally reached by pure accident.

Apparently European conjurers are partial to this scheme of memorizing a chance arrangement; and it certainly defies detection. In my private opinion it represents an altogether disproportionate development of one small branch in card conjuring; but if you find yourself fascinated by it, as some excellent performers have, that is certainly your privilege.

One of Leopold Figner's better efforts with a stacked pack was an effect he showed under the guise of *Muscle-Reading.* I have dressed it up just a little, and here it is. Start with two or three false dovetail shuffles. Don't cut, or if you do, sight the bottom card so that you know what is on top.

Now start dealing cards in a row, face down. Tell people they can stop you whenever they like. Then let them have their choice of the next card on the deck, the last one you dealt, or in fact any card at all in the row. Have someone take the chosen card, peep at it, put it in his inside breast pocket, button his coat, and put his hand over the card.

You tell him that there will be a muscular reflex, which he can't control, when you mention his card. Lightly hold the wrist of the hand that is pressed against the pocket, and starting reciting the names of cards at random. Not too quickly, but before people get tired, you say, "That was it! Did you feel the tremor? The six of clubs."

All this build-up effectually conceals the fact that you can name instantly any card chosen from the row you deal out. Just run through the setup in your mind as you deal. Instead of having the card put in the spectator's pocket, you may (if you don't mind disturbing the setup) scatter a lot of cards face up on the table and guide the spectator's hand around until you make it hover over the chosen card. (This could actually be accomplished by a good muscle-reader without prearrangement, but your results are surer as well as easier with the setup.)

Behind Your Back is an effective trick with a Si Stebbins deck or any recurring setup. Fan the cards behind your back for a spectator to draw a card. Cut the pack where the chosen card comes out.

Announce that you will draw two cards, still holding the deck behind your back, and one card will show the suit of the chosen one, the next the value.

With any regular setup the fourth card from the top will be of the suit you want, and the thirteenth will give the value. Thumb-count to the fourth card, show it—all this still behind your back, while you face away from the audience—then count nine more, trying to act as if you were fumbling rather than counting.

If you hold a break, you can put the thirteenth card back in place, then go to other tricks using the setup.

The Shuffled Setup, a very bold effect invented by the late Theo Annemann, shows what you can do by crowding your luck with a stacked pack.

You hand a pack to a spectator and let *him* shuffle and cut. He then looks at the top card, sticks it back anywhere in the pack, and hands the deck to you. Until that moment you have never touched the cards, yet you instantly name his.

Annemann says this trick sometimes fails on the first try, but practically never on the second. Your success depends on at once lulling and hurrying the spectator into making a very perfunctory overhand shuffle. Hand him the pack, and the moment he starts shuffling, tell him, "When you have them mixed, square the cards up on your left hand. Ready?"

Have him cut, replace the lower half on top, and then look at the top card and shove it into the deck wherever he pleases.

The secret of your discovery is simply that you act as if your stacked deck had not been shuffled—glimpse the bottom card, and name the next card of the setup. About eight times out of ten you will be right, because a hasty overhand shuffle merely disarranges a few solid blocks of your setup, and the spectator is extremely likely to cut into one of these blocks. If by ill luck he does cut between two blocks, have him cut again and choose another card. The chance of failing again is very tiny indeed.

It was by gambling on methods like this, and by always working out the least complicated and most natural presentation (see chapter 2), that Annemann gained his reputation of being almost a real wizard.

Annemann depended on the inadequacy of the overhand shuffle. Charles T. Jordan's *Thirty Card Mysteries* shows in great detail what you can do with a stacked pack despite an honest dovetail shuffle. You can find out the underlying principle more easily than I can explain it if you will take a new pack (or any one arranged in numerical sequence) and give it one dovetail shuffle. The two halves are intermingled, but neither half has been disarranged at all within its own sequence. If the shuffle is made perfectly—the deck split exactly in half, and the cards released alternately one at a time from the two halves—eight successive times, the pack will return to its original order. Hardly anyone is skillful enough to do this, and it would be too tedious if he could; but see what Mr. Jordan does with a setup deck, letting the spectator shuffle.

He calls this mildly A Novel Detection, but *The Foolproof Card in Pocket* gives a better idea of the effect. You hand someone a pack, asking him to cut, shuffle, and cut again. You turn your back while the victim deals any number of cards he pleases (say from ten to twenty) off the top of the pack into a face-down pile on the table. Then he remembers the card on top of the pack, leaves it there, and puts back on top the heap he has dealt off. Finally he cuts the deck again several times.

You run through the cards, looking him fixedly in the eye, then remove one card, and put it in your pocket. When he tries to find his card in the deck, it is missing. As a matter of fact, you could perfectly well show the card as soon as you remove it, for it is the right one. The pocket business is just build-up.

The location rests upon the fact that dealing cards off the top into a pile face down reverses their order. At the start of the trick you let the victim make one dovetail shuffle, then promptly say, "Now cut, please—several times." His one shuffle breaks your setup into two intermingled series, but they both run forward—that is, in the normal sequence of your arrangement. The cards he deals off the top, however, are in backward sequence. Therefore, when you run through the pack after he has finished cutting, you will find a batch of cards arranged backward, and the next card in sequence below them is the one you want.

It would be equally easy, and I think perhaps more effective, to have the shuffling done after, not before, the card is chosen. Open with a false dovetail if you like; there is no reason for the spectator to think of a setup anyway. After the card has been chosen, one honest dovetail won't disturb the break in the setup.

Another thing to remember is that you need only set up half the deck if the victim is not allowed to count off more than twenty cards. In fact my suggestion is to simplify your own job to the limit by simply running up all the cards of one suit in order on the top of the pack; then ask the spectator, by way of saving time, not to deal off more than ten cards. After that, even two honest dovetail shuffles will not disturb the break in the suit you have set up, yet they will mix in enough cards to obscure the fact that you had one suit prearranged.

3b. Special setups. These are the ones required for individual tricks (see particularly the Spelling Master, chapter 5, section 4). Some of them are merely extensions of the key-card principle.

Such is Leopold Figner's *Sound of the Voice.* Get the four sevens on top of the pack and the four nines on the bottom (or any other two sets of four you like). Have a spectator deal the pack into four piles, one card to each pile in succession. (This leaves each pile with a seven on the bottom and a nine on top.)

Turn your back. Ask the victim to draw a card from any pile he likes and remember it, then to put it on any of the four piles, collect the piles in any sequence he pleases, and then cut the pack several times.

This is a good place to toss in a false shuffle.

Give the victim the deck. Tell him that you are not doing a card trick, but exercising your power of observation. When you turn your back, he is to start dealing off the cards, naming them aloud as he goes. No matter how careful he is to keep his voice on a dead level, you have a sort of lie-detector ability to spot the recognition in his tone when he names his own card.

Of course you demand complete silence and freedom from distraction as he reads off the deck. The amount of concentration you really need, however, is modest—just enough to tell when some card falls between a seven and a nine. The method of reassembling the pack has brought the sevens together with the nines except in the one case where the chosen card separates a pair.

I first came across the *Spot Location* during the 1930s in David J. Lustig's pamphlet, *Vaudeville Magic*. I took an immediate liking to it and have been doing it with great success ever since. Yet for some reason I have never seen another magician show it. It also appeared in a beginners' book some years ago, so possibly it has gained some more followers.

The effect is that someone draws a card and replaces it. No shifts, no breaks, no shuffling. You ask anyone to call a number between five and ten. The instant the number is called, you show a card with that number of spots on it. Then you count that number of cards off the top of the pack, and so produce the chosen one.

Put a six spot (any suit) on top of the pack and a seven on top of that. Have an eight at the bottom and a nine just above it. That is the extent of your setup.

After the card has been drawn, quietly count off seven cards from the top (if you can thumb-count that many from the top, fine) and hold a little-finger break below them.

Casually open the pack at the break for the chosen card to be put back. Square up carefully and then get ready for a double lift (chapter 3, section 6*a*).

Now ask for your number between five and ten. Possibly because of the familiar saying and the popular song, "Take a number from one to ten," half the time somebody pipes up, "Two!" or "Ten!" Then everyone fatuously laughs at him when you reiterate, "*Between* five and ten, please."

If the number called for is six, complete your double lift, showing the six spot. The chosen card was the eighth in the deck; the double lift brings it to the sixth, which is the correct position.

If seven is called for, just show the top card, a seven spot; then count down.

If they want eight, show the bottom card, then count down eight.

If they want nine, draw back the bottom card, pull out the nine, show it, and be sure you *count it as number one* when you deal off the cards.

Got Any Good Phone Numbers? is an effect devised by U. F. Grant to be done with a one-way deck, which brings it into the category of head magic. But I greatly prefer my own method, which logically belongs in hand magic. No matter; the effect is a beauty.

Ask someone his telephone number. Fan the deck face upward, picking out for him four cards that correspond to the digits.

Let him shuffle the rest of the deck; then have him arrange the four cards in the proper order—you don't want to risk a wrong number.

Either take the four cards one by one, and jab them into the pack face up, or break the deck at random in four different places, allowing him to put the cards in, likewise face up.

Finally turn the deck face upward and spread it on the table. The cards forming the victim's telephone number have unerringly located the four queens.

As I said before, Mr. Grant uses a one-way deck and reverses the queens beforehand. I think a corner crimp is much more satisfactory. As you run over the deck to hand out the four cards forming the telephone number, you will also see the queens. Each time you come to a queen, crimp the near right corner downward with your right third finger, which is hidden under the fan.

To all intents and purposes the trick is now done. The deck can be shuffled indefinitely. (Try to hand it to an overhand shuffler with the crimped edge down.) If you jab the number cards into the edge of the deck, of course you do so just under the crimped corners of the queens. If you break the deck at random, have the crimped ends near you; your right thumb, at the near left corner of the pack, quite naturally breaks at the lowest crimp first, then the next, then the next, and finally at the topmost.

The Royal Marriages, another stunner, is by far the best card trick in *Dai Vernon's Select Secrets.* At the risk of lese majesty, I have made what I consider improvements in the routine.

I announce this with a leer as a sex trick. A spectator shuffles the pack, then removes the kings and queens however they happen to lie. They are obviously quite helter-skelter. I gather them together, then pass the top card underneath, deal the second on the table, pass the third underneath, put the fourth beside the second on the table, the fifth underneath, the sixth on the table beside the fourth, the seventh underneath, the eighth on the table beside the sixth, the ninth (there are still four left) underneath, the tenth on the first card (number two) that went on the table, and so on until there are four pairs side by side on the table. Despite the lack of arrangement, the kings and queens prove to have matched themselves.

Next I discard the king and queen of hearts ("too easy!"), and put the three kings face down on the table. The spectator puts the three queens face up on the three kings in any order he likes. Nevertheless the kings and queens match themselves again.

The secret of this ostensibly "self-working" trick lies in a special setup, the peculiarity of the true dovetail shuffle, and careful memorizing by you of every step in the proceedings.

First pick out the kings and queens, turn them face up, and match them by suits as follows, counting from the bottom:

1 and 8 match.
2 and 3 match.
4 and 7 match.
5 and 6 match.

In other words, if it were a rhyme scheme you would express it thus: a, b, b, c, d, d, c, a.

It makes no difference which suits occupy these positions, nor whether king or queen comes first. You can soon learn to make the setup in five or six seconds. Leave the cards thus arranged on the bottom of the deck, with an indifferent card or two below as camouflage. From here on through the first stage of the climax the trick is self-working if you don't go to sleep at the switch. Two dovetail shuffles by the spectator merely distribute the royal pairs through the lower half of the pack without disarranging them.

The spectator then turns the deck face up, and drops each king or queen on the table as he comes to it. This reverses the order of the setup, which is necessary before the trick will work. If the spectator does *not* reverse the cards, you will have to take them and count them down on the table when he is done, "to make sure they are all there."

Now, as long as you start by passing the first card under, dealing the next, and passing the next under, and don't forget to pass the proper cards under, the kings and queens (thanks to Mr. Vernon's ingenious setup) will pair themselves off without further help from you.

When we come to the repeat action, however, you must keep your wits about you. Put away the king and queen of hearts. Toss the other three queens, face down, to a spectator. Put the three kings in a row face down, and be sure you know which king is where. I suggest making a habit of one particular arrangement, such as spades, diamonds, clubs, from your left to right.

Ask the spectator if he is right-handed or left. Whichever he says, tell him to take the queen whose king you privately know to be in the middle, and put her face up on any one of the three kings. The chances are pretty good that he will put her in the middle. Next, if he is right-handed, tell him to take the queen whose king you know to be at your left (his right), and put her face up on either of the other two kings. What you hope, of course, is that he will match all three pairs of his own accord.

If he does so, you step back, and tell him to turn over the lower cards himself. The trick is a miracle.

If he does not, there are only two things he can do. They call for different treatment, as follows.

He may have one pair matching, the other two mixed. In this case, put the matching pair below the other cards. Then pass the top card of the six underneath, deal the next one on the table, pass the next one underneath, and so on as you did at first (only with three heaps). The royal pairs will reassort themselves.

The spectator may have none of the three pairs matching. In that case, pick the pairs up in such a way that the bottom card of each pair matches the top card of the pair below it. Have a spectator cut the pile three times, leaving a face-down card on top by the last cut. Simply take the cards off two at a time, and show them—paired off again.

The Ten-Card Trick must be almost as old as playing cards themselves. I was originally mystified with it (after a ripe experience of three years in magic) by a man who knew only this one trick. Some years after that, one performer was able to sell as a new and baffling "secret" to a number of eager customers a small twist in the routine that turned detection into prediction. On the first occasion I should have been ashamed of myself because the trick was on page 104 of my favorite reading, Professor Hoffmann's *Modern Magic*. When I met the man who was selling the new twist, however, at least I saw what was what, and merely appropriated it without asking for a demonstration.

The chief real improvement in this old stager was first published in *Howard Thurston's Card Tricks* in 1901. It consisted in keeping the cards in a bunch instead of laying them out as a row on the table.

So much for history. Pick out ten cards from ace to ten (all of one suit if you want to use this as an easy way of setting up for the Foolproof Card in Pocket). Arrange them in order, with the ace on top and the ten on the bottom. Show them, not hiding the fact that they are arranged, but also not pointing it out. Then explain that while you turn your back or leave the room, you want someone to move a number of cards from the top of the pack to the bottom, so. To illustrate, you move three cards, one at a time. Charge your victim to think hard of the number he is going to move. Look him piercingly in the eye, then hand him the cards, and turn your back.

When he returns the cards, you turn up the top one, which has as many spots as the victim moves cards.

You repeat this once or twice, and then say you can read his mind the moment he has made it up. As soon as he admits that he has decided on a number to move, you tell him mysteriously, "Very well, *after* you have moved that number, *then* the [say] sixth card will show how many you have just decided to move." Sure enough, it does.

The bottom card of the heap always gives you the key to the next repetition: you shift that number to the top (the equivalent of subtracting it from ten). At the start of the trick, you illustrated by moving three cards to the bottom. The bottom card is therefore a three. This is your key to the next step.

After the spectator has moved his first lot of cards, thumb-count three off the bottom and shift them to the top. The bottom card then shows how many the spectator moved. Say it was a five. After the next moving you will thumb-count five off the bottom and shift there. (Profuse thanks to my friend Richard Hatch, the first reader to spot a blunder at this point in the original description of the trick).

You can probably see why I didn't need to pay money for the "prediction" finish. Before the final move, you already know the number that will indicate how many were moved. Just reveal it instead of waiting to make the shift afterward.

There are very few better card tricks of any kind, and you will not be sorry if you learn to present this one well.

4. CARD READING

4a. By the one-ahead method. In hand magic (chapter 4, section 8) you learned to read cards before you dealt them. By the one-ahead gag you can name them before you pick them up off the table.

In its most elementary application you let someone shuffle the pack. You contrive to glimpse the top card. Then you have the deck cut into several heaps. You point boldly to the top card of the lowest heap and declare that it is (whatever the top card of the pack is). Pick it up, glance at it, and announce that the top card of the next heap is the one you have in fact just glanced at. And so on through the row. When all the top cards are assembled, they are indisputably those you have named.

A more effective and generally better method is to use a one-way deck, with a single known card reversed. Have the pack thoroughly shuffled and let a spectator spread it face down on the table—not necessarily in a ribbon, just spread around.

Card-reading by the one-ahead method should always be worked briskly, and particularly so here. Notice where the reversed card lies. Then start rapidly calling out cards, and as rapidly snatching them off the table. Needless to say you name the known reversed card first, but pick it up last.

This method combines well with other forms of card reading and demonstration of card control; by itself it is a trifle precarious.

4b. The Whispering Queen. This is one of the few perfect self-working card tricks. It has no weak point and no sleight of hand can improve it.

The effect is that someone lays out a number of cards face down, sliding them part way under various objects to hold them. You use the queen of hearts as a tattletale, sliding her face upward under the edge of each card. You withdraw the queen, hold her to your ear, and conduct a whispered conversation, after which you name the card in question. Each card can be shown at once; there is no one-ahead ruse.

Have someone shuffle the pack. For once in your life you don't care whether he shuffles overhand, dovetail, underhand, or with a whisk broom.

You run through and remove the queen. At the same time, memorize the bottom three cards of the pack (or however many you intend to use).

Have your spectator cut off part of the deck. Have him point to one half, and by the ordinary equivoque (chapter 3, section 4*a*), see to it that he is left with the bottom half. Tell him to count the cards he has. Of course the actual purpose of this is to bring the bottom three cards to the top, but you look wise, and say, "I guess that will be about right."

The rest is pure showmanship. You have him put the first three cards around under things, and since you know them already, the queen is telling you nothing new.

Don't be *too* much disappointed that you can make a reputation with the Whispering Queen quite as well as with Leipzig's Five Hands or Zingone's Table Spread. That's always the way with magic.

14. Varied Head Magic

HERE is an assortment of head magic using other objects than cards.

1. *Find the Dime.* This is Al Baker's ingenious little reversal of "Find the Lady"—the spectators hide a dime under any one of three cards, and you find it.

Carry a little salt in your vest pocket. When you lay out the three cards, sprinkle a few grains from your fingernail on the middle and one end card. Invite people to pick up a card and hide the dime under it; by way of illustration you lift the card that is not salted.

Naturally after they have hidden the coin, if they have used the unsalted card, all the salt will be undisturbed; if one of the other cards, the salt will be gone from it.

You have to make this impressive the first time because you can't do it again.

2. *Who Has Which?* A good follow-up for Find the Dime, because it seems to be an elaboration, and actually bears no resemblance to it at all. You put down a dime, a quarter, and a half dollar. While you step out of the room, three spectators are each to take one of the coins. Using cards or poker chips to help you (but with very little stalling), you discover who has which coin.

Here we have a first-rate trick, *if* it is well built up. Hilliard, in *Greater Magic,* suggests that an earnest address on mind reading and telepathy is the best staging. In any case you will have to think the whole routine over carefully and try out your particular plot critically on yourself before you inflict it on an audience. The trick is mathematical, and if you just plod through it, it becomes utterly dismal.

The routine is as follows. Bring out the coins and twenty-four indifferent cards or counters of some kind. Call attention to the coins—dime, quarter, half dollar. If you are showing the trick as an example of mind control, possibly you will distribute the cards before the coins are chosen, claiming that this influences the choice in the direction you want. Or you may have the coins chosen first, then distribute the cards as a step in getting the information. Personally I lean to the former procedure, with the important proviso that all the emphasis must be laid on the coins; the cards must not obscure the plot.

In either case, you give one card to one spectator, and fix him in your mind as Number 1; two cards to the next spectator, and fix him in your mind as Number 2; three cards to the last man, and remember him as Number 3. Then drop the cards on the table.

The coins have either been chosen already, or are chosen next.

Then—again, or still, in your absence—the man who has the dime is to take as many more cards as you gave him. The man with the quarter is to take twice as many as you gave him; the man with the half dollar is to take four times as many as you gave him.

The moment you come back, you know where the coins are; only, as I have pointed out, the whole virtue of the trick is in making it seem like hard work. Hard work for you; a mere trifle to your assistants. Your ideal in showing the effect is that everyone shall forget you used any cards at all. If they must remember, it should be only vaguely.

I will not go into the arithmetic of it, but there are six different ways that the three spectators can distribute the three coins among themselves. When they have followed your instructions about the cards, each of these six ways leaves a different number of cards behind on the table. No doubt you could work this out for yourself, but I suggest that most conjurers will prefer simply to memorize the following table. First let me point out that the coins are identified as *D* for dime, *T* for twenty-five-cent piece, and *F* for fifty cent piece. The sequence of those letters in the words forming the table gives the distribution of the coins among spectators Numbers 1, 2, and 3. The number preceding each word in the table stands for the number of cards left over. There is no combination that will leave four over.

1. DoubTFul: DTF
2. sTeaDFast: TDF
3. DeFeaT: DFT
5. TerriFieD: TFD
6. conFiDenT: FDT
7. FasTeD: FTD

Although it all seems complicated, you will discover that you come to think automatically, "Five cards on the table—terrified. Number 1 has the quarter, 2 the half, 3 the dime." And then you go into your mind reading to-do.

3. *Money Sense.* With this clever routine of Eddie Joseph's you can

"repeat" the last trick, once again by an entirely different method. You use the same three coins, three glasses, and a blindfold (or you can work behind your back). One coin is put in each glass. Some one hands you a glass, and you know instantly which coin is in it. To wind up, you put one of the glasses on the table behind you, and let somebody drop a coin in it. You know instantly which coin it is.

The glasses are marked in a way that nobody would ever dream of: one is dry, one is wet on one side, and one is wet on the bottom. As you collect the coins, remember what glasses they go into. That's all of that.

When the coin is dropped into the glass on the table, you can identify it by sound. A very little practice will teach you to distinguish the clinks made by dime, quarter, and half. Since there has been no noise until now, people are not thinking about that; the routine is perfectly devised to confuse them.

4. *Date Reading (two methods)*. You have already learned a one-ahead method of date-reading that requires you to be fairly nimble (chapter 7, section 16). Here are two more, to throw skeptics off the track.

The first, one of Nelson Downs's favorites, shows that the great man was not above using his head to save his hands. Borrow six half dollars, and read off the dates one at a time as you drop them into the hat. Give the hat a good shaking, then pour the coins into your inside breast pocket. Have some spectator call for a date. You instantly reach in, and come up from the pocket with a coin bearing the date that was demanded. You can go on until all six coins are used up.

Get six half dollars of your own, memorize the dates, and arrange them in chronological order in your upper right vest pocket. When you "read off" the borrowed coins, actually you are just reciting the dates of your own half dollars. After the borrowed coins have been shaken, you dump them into your breast pocket, and turn your right side a little toward the audience. With your left hand you dip for the wanted coin, and nobody can tell whether you are reaching into your coat or your vest pocket.

The second method is Eddie Joseph's. You either borrow or have ready a considerable number of coins. Different spectators take coins, remember the dates, and hold the coins face down.

You then go around with squares of soft, opaque white tissue paper, and have each coin wrapped in paper. The paper bundles are mixed up, and you can call the date of any bundle that a spectator hands to you. There is no one-ahead move; you can really tell.

The secret lies partly in the paper, which must be *soft* tissue. But it needs more body than Kleenex. Let me warn you to experiment at some length with different kinds of paper and different coins. Anything smaller than a half-dollar is very difficult to read, besides which old coins often have the date partly worn off.

The rest of the secret lies in the way the coins are wrapped. Hold your left hand out flat with a square of paper on it, and have the spectator lay his coin (face down, of course) on the paper. Then you gather up the corners of the paper, and twist them so that the coin is wrapped up like a chocolate bud.

This pulls the paper flat against the date side of the coin. When the paper is very thin, you can sometimes read clear through it; otherwise, press your thumb over where the date ought to be and you will get an impression, which can be smoothed out afterward in unwrapping the coin.

Just because this method is simple, don't think it's easy. Furthermore, don't let it look easy. Build up the reading of each individual coin; let there be nothing perfunctory in your actions.

5. *Coin Telepathy.* This, one of the prettiest tricks I know, is much safer to do if you are a thorough master of the DeManche change (chapter 6, section 14); a good false shuffle beforehand does no harm, either.

You borrow a coin—say a quarter—and have someone hold it. Another spectator cuts the pack, takes one half, and deals it into four piles. The custodian of the quarter now reads off the date. He then turns over the piles of cards. The spots on the bottom cards correspond to the date of the coin.

Get a quarter with no zeroes in the date (unless you want to use the joker for zero). Pick out four cards whose values correspond to the date, and arrange them in order on top of the pack. At the start of the trick, finger-palm your quarter and promptly switch it for the borrowed coin. A convincingly offhand procedure is to accept the borrowed coin between your right thumb and forefinger, make the change, and immediately toss the substitute to someone a few feet away, saying, "Catch!"

Then have another spectator cut the pack. Force the top half on him (chapter 3, section 3). When he deals the first four cards in a row face down, he has finished the trick so far as the secret is concerned. The rest is build-up. Make a great point of never touching either the coin (!) or the cards.

6. *Torn and Restored Paper.* Here we have not a trick but a whole class of tricks, some of the best in magic because they are simple, natural, and straightforward. One of the things a real magician might be expected to do is tear up paper and put it together again. Furthermore, he would

do it just about as you do—tear the paper, wad it up in one hand, open it out whole again. No covering with handkerchiefs, no monkey business at all.

Naturally almost every method depends on switching the torn pieces for a whole substitute, but the switch varies according to the paper you use.

What you might call the junior version is done with a cigarette paper. You roll your duplicate up into a tight little pellet and clip it between the tips of your first and second fingers. After you have torn the original paper, but before you complete the switch, press the two wads together like sponge balls, and show them as one. Your hands are obviously otherwise empty. Then, in trying to unroll the (substitute) pellet, you moisten your fingers at your lips and thus contrive to pop the wad of torn pieces into your mouth.

The next version is to tear and restore a paper ribbon. This is normally done with the help of a thumb tip (see chapter 16). Another method, very nearly perfect, except that it is now rather well known, is to use a length of Dennison's crepe-paper ribbon and a pair of scissors. You cut the strip actually in half, and then apparently into quarters, eighths, sixteenths. You must manage, however, to leave one half of the strip intact and confine your snipping to the other half.

In wadding up the cut pieces, keep the undamaged half separate enough from the cut bits so that you can steal the latter in putting the scissors into your pocket, where of course you also leave the cut pieces.

The ingenious part of this method is that you can now stretch the uncut half, by a series of short, quick tugs, to twice its length. The crinkle, which runs crosswise of the ribbon, pulls out, and there you are with a piece just the original length.

It is when we reach the larger sizes of paper, oddly enough, that the matter of marking and identification crops up. Not that you actually have the paper marked—that would be asking for trouble. But if you have some sort of design on the paper, even though it is printed, people never seem to think about substitution. This is why the "Chinese laundry ticket" version is so popular among magicians. When I used to do the trick in my regular act, I had a supply of paper napkins cut into quarters, and printed with an Arabic motto from a linoleum block. If I show it regularly again, I shall use a half-sheet letterhead of cheap typewriter paper with some sort of message typed on it. There will be a word missing, which a spectator who reads the message cannot help noticing. I shall write in the word in ink or crayon, and I will bet any amount that no one ever dreams I might have done the same beforehand with another sheet of paper.

Paper of this size can be handled just about like sponge balls, including the mash when you want to show your hands empty in the middle of a trick.

One way to shed the bundle of palmed pieces is by reaching for a fan with which to fan the paper. Another is to pinch the torn bundle behind the restored piece with one thumb, showing your palms empty, and then crumple everything into a conglomerate ball again.

With paper of this size, too, you have available a sucker routine. After tearing and restoring one piece, you point out that obviously the trick must be done by swapping a whole paper for the torn pieces. So saying, you roll up one piece into a ball and hold it rather clumsily in your left hand. Don't actually palm it—that would be exposing a basic sleight. Just fold your third and little fingers over it. Meanwhile you are stealing another duplicate ball from a right-hand pocket or some convenient hiding place. This one you do palm.

Take up a fresh sheet of paper in your left hand. Tear it up, roll the pieces into a ball with your right hand, and make a switch by taking the palmed ball between your left first and second fingers and thumb, and palming the torn pieces instead in your right hand.

"Now," you explain, "we have the torn pieces here—" pointing to the ball at the left finger tips—"and the whole piece here. All we have to do is trade them around." This you do with your left hand alone, but make quite a chore of it—a clumsy sort of DeManche change. At the same time, "go south" with the palmed ball of torn pieces from your right hand. All eyes are on your left hand, and you should have no trouble.

"Now we unroll the whole piece, and everybody is very much surprised."

Pause. "But if we aren't careful, somebody may see the torn pieces, and then what can we do?"

Pause. "Well, then there's nothing for it but to open up the torn pieces too." Needless to say, the torn pieces are likewise restored.

Another method is shown with a newspaper. Here a pliable metal clip holds the duplicate, folded small, behind the newspaper, and after the sheet has been torn, the clip is bent the other way, catching the packet of torn pieces. This trick can be bought from all dealers.

7. *Paper Pellet Repeat.* An amusing little table trick, exactly the same as the repeating routine with sponge balls (chapter 10, section 2): you make three pellets ot cigarette paper, paper napkin, or anything handy.

Two you put in your left hand, one you pocket or throw away. You open your left hand and out roll three pellets. For a comedy finish you can let a spectator throw away one pellet, and when you open your fist you roll out two pellets and a lump of sugar.

The method too is basically the same, only instead of palming the pellets and doing a mash, you hide your duplicate (fourth) pellet between the tips of your right first and second fingers, as in the Torn Cigarette Paper. The lump of sugar is loaded into the left hand at the proper moment from the right finger palm.

8. *The rubber pencil.* This is not a trick but a flourish that livens up an effect where you use a pencil. You hold the pencil by one end, shaking it, and it appears to bend as if it were made of rubber.

Hold the pencil horizontal, with your right forefinger and thumb near the right end, the palm to the audience. Simply move your hand gently up and down, letting the pencil waggle. The center of the pencil thus stays more or less still, while both ends describe arcs, and the result is an optical illusion that you will see for yourself on the first trial.

This works equally well with a ruler, wand, or other small stick.

9. *The Rising Cigarette.* You have probably seen mechanical cigarette boxes that pop one cigarette at you when you press a button. With a slight preparation of an ordinary cigarette package wrapped in cellophane, you can do the same by magic. Take a pencil and punch a hole through the cellophane at the upper edge of the package. Push the pencil on down, forming a perpendicular channel between the side of the package and the inside of the cellophane. Slide a cigarette into the channel.

When you want the cigarette to rise, you rub your thumb upward along the side of the package, pressing through the cellophane against the bottom of the cigarette.

10. *Restored Matches.* In connection with the Rising Cigarette, you can take a folder of matches from your pocket, tear out all the matches, and stick them in your pocket. A moment later you open the folder, and the matches have come back.

As you have undoubtedly noticed, there are four rows of matches in a folder. Before you start the trick, divide the inner two from the outer two, leaving a slight separation. Open the folder and stick the flap down behind the matches, but stick it in the gap between the second and third rows, not behind all four rows.

Then when you tear out the first two rows, the folder seems empty. After just enough pause to take people's minds off the folder and telegraph your climax, you open the folder, and the matches are back.

11. The Linking Matches. A little trick with the straightforward simplicity of real magic. Each hand holds a wooden match by the ends, between forefinger and thumb. You can pass the matches through each other at will.

Angles are the secret of the trick. When they are properly mastered, you can work it under any conditions, but if you forget about them you will give yourself away.

In holding the matches, put the head against the middle of your thumb tip. The butt end of the right-hand match also goes against the middle of your forefinger tip. The butt of the left-hand match, however, rests not against the middle of the forefinger tip but as far over toward the second finger as it will go without slipping off.

Bring the two matches at right angles to each other, holding your right hand palm upward, your left hand palm downward. Now you seem to lower your left hand, so that the matches pass through each other, and sure enough, they are linked.

Just before the matches touch—or after you have tapped them together, if you prefer to begin with a few practice swings—you lay your left second finger alongside your first, nipping the end of the match. Thus the match stays in position while your left thumb opens a gap and lets the right-hand match pass between the left thumb and match head. You instantly replace your thumb, straighten your left second finger, and turn both hands about so that everyone can see the matches linked.

Then you return your hands to their starting position and unlink the matches with the same moves that linked them.

You will find that all the angle problem amounts to is keeping the back of your left hand in the way while you remove your thumb from the match head. Give your mirror a brief workout, and remember that smoothness comes next to angles in importance.

12. Ring on Stick. The last two tricks in this chapter will be the small masterpieces of the East Indian magician—the really good things, not the labored mummery of mango or basket trick. For the first, I give the description of Major L. H. Branson, Indian Army.

"The magic wand is produced for our next little experiment, that of putting a borrowed ring on to the middle of a stick that is held at both ends. Almost every European in India has seen this performed, for it is the favorite of the Jadoo-wallah, and is the most effective of the small tricks that he can show. It takes up a considerable time and is simplicity itself.

"In case any of my readers have not seen the trick in India, or on their way out at Port Said, I will describe it to you. The performer either borrows or uses his own thin cane, and passes it around to his audience to show that it is devoid of all mechanism. He then borrows a wedding ring, which he also allows to be freely examined. He gets *A* and *B*, two of his audience, to hold the ends of the stick each by one hand. He then boldly proclaims that he proposes to pass the ring on to the middle of the stick without either *A* or *B* letting go of their respective ends. In order, however, not to divulge the secret he must pass it on under cover of a handkerchief. He takes the borrowed ring and wraps it up in the middle of the handkerchief, which he asks someone to hold, and to feel the ring wrapped up in it. In order to let everyone know that the ring is really there, he takes the stick from *A* and *B*, and gives a tap on the ring. He then gets *A* and *B* to hold the stick once more, and persuades *C*, who is assisting with the handkerchief, to hold it over the middle of the stick. The performer holds the corner of the handkerchief and instructs *C* to let go his hold on the word 'three.'

" 'One! Two! Three!' The handkerchief is sharply pulled away and the borrowed ring is seen to be spinning on the stick.

"This is how it is done. The stick is an ordinary one, thin enough to pass easily through a wedding ring. The only prepared article is the handkerchief, in one corner of which is a duplicate wedding ring sewn into a small pocket. It does not matter whether or no it is exactly similar to the ring that is borrowed, as the performer takes care that the owner of the borrowed ring does not get a chance of feeling the duplicate even through the folds of the handkerchief. When the performer takes the borrowed ring to fold in the handkerchief, he folds the one that is already sewn in it, and palms the borrowed ring. He takes the stick from *A* and *B* to tap on the ring folded in the handkerchief, really to slide the borrowed ring over the middle of it. He hands the stick back to be held by *A* and *B*, but keeps his hand over the ring now on it, thus concealing it until it is covered by the handkerchief. When the handkerchief is pulled away on the word 'three' it takes with it the ring sewn into its corner, and as it brushes the stick it makes the borrowed ring on the stick revolve apparently as if it had just arrived in that position.

"For simplicity's sake let us take the various moves as they occur.

"1. Borrow a stick and hand it round for examination.

"2. Get *A* and *B* to hold it at the ends.

"3. Borrow a wedding ring.

"4. Take the handkerchief from the pocket. (The duplicate ring sewn in the corner being held preferably in the right hand.)

"5. Pretend to wrap up the borrowed ring in the handkerchief, in reality wrapping up the corner ring, and palm the borrowed ring in the right hand.

"6. Take the stick from *A* and *B* and tap the folded ring with it, now being held by C. While doing so, slip the borrowed ring into the middle of the stick.

"7. Hand the stick back to *A* and *B* but keep the hand on the stick over the ring.

"8. Get C to cover this hand with the handkerchief, holding the ring over the middle of the stick, and instruct him to let go on the word 'three.'

"A neat little trick that can be performed by anybody who takes the trouble to practice it a couple of times."

There are several related effects using a string instead of a stick. One of the simplest and most ingenious will be found at page 131 of John Mulholland's *The Art of Illusion.* Instead of a ring you use one of your own calling cards, and you take it off the string instead of passing it on.

Fold the calling card in quarters, and tear off the corner that will produce a hole in the middle of the card. You do this on the spot, and then thread the card on a string, which someone holds for you. Like the Indian conjurer, you cover the card with a handkerchief and a moment later pull the card clean off the string without damage to either object.

The use of a calling card serves the same purpose as the design printed on the Torn and Restored Paper: people just assume there can't be a duplicate. Why they should never imagine you might have more than one of your own calling cards I won't pretend to say, but they don't.

You prepare for the effect by folding up another card, tearing out the center, but leaving the card folded. This you palm when the time comes. The card on the string you quite simply tear off, fold, and palm in your left hand, while your right hand unfolds and brings forward the duplicate.

13. *The Potsherd Trick.* Either in its East Indian form, done with a pottery fragment and charcoal, or with a lump of sugar and a pencil, this effect has always struck me as one of the miracles that you read about in Kipling, but don't believe. The plot is truly magical, the misdirection superb.

You give a spectator a small flat piece of some porous substance—lump sugar is the likeliest in Occidental circumstances. You ask him to draw on this object a small design, letter, or figure. The trick is impressive enough so that you can legitimately ask for some cabalistic symbol. (The swastika, which the East Indian conjurers used, has perhaps lost some of its former appeal.)

You drop the sugar on the floor, and ask the victim to grind it to powder under his foot. Alternatively, you may drop it into a glass of water, design side up.

Then tell the victim to stare at his palms. Next he is to hold his hands palm downward over the place where the sugar rests (either in powder or in process of dissolving).

Finally he turns his hands over, and finds his own design printed on his palm. It is an exact, recognizable duplication, in his own handwriting.

Mechanically, the method is child's play. Just before you take the sugar from him to drop it on the floor or into the glass, you get the ball of your right thumb moist. Enough water for your purpose usually condenses on the outside of a glass of ice water. When you take the sugar, you press your wet thumb squarely on the design, and so pick up an impression of it.

The key point of the whole trick is the delay that follows. Instead of doing anything yourself, you have the victim stare at his palm. He must be made to realize that he has seen his palm bare *after* the sugar was destroyed.

Once this point has been tacitly but clearly made, you tell him he is to hold his hands over the place where the sugar was. You take his hands, and show him how, at the same time pressing your moist thumb against his palm. That transfers the impression you got off the sugar. Don't let go of the hands right away, but shift your own position so that you aren't pressing his palm for more than a moment.

Then, with a little more build-up, you are ready for the climax.

Practice this thoroughly, and guard it well; there is no better trick for a small audience.

PART THREE · APPARATUS MAGIC

15. Silks

I THINK I shall hardly be going too far if I begin this section with a quotation from a magic book nearly a hundred years old. Says the anonymous author, "In this account of conjuring, I have purposely avoided such tricks as require expensive apparatus. Such apparatus is either entirely beyond a boy's reach, or at all events he ought not to be encouraged in the notion of spending much money on objects of no real use."

On an earlier page I remarked that apparatus conjuring had fallen into professional disrepute because so many amateurs who could afford the money for apparatus did not think they could afford the time to rehearse with it. To become a really successful apparatus magician you need two scarce qualities—willingness to take endless trouble in learning, transporting, showing, and packing up your trick; and a keen sense of discrimination.

The apparatus in a magic dealer's catalogue runs all the way from 25-cent ball clips to $250 buzz-saw illusions. Within this range are the makings for some of the best tricks in magic, and also an astonishing number of monstrosities that have no purpose except to lighten the pockets of overzealous amateurs.

Several of my friends among the magic dealers are fine performers and storehouses of information concerning the art. But if they want to stay in business they must sell what magicians will buy, not what they ought to buy.

What magicians will buy is to me an endless source of dismay. Who in his right senses would shell out fifteen or twenty dollars, say, for a set of eight three-inch wooden disks, two garishly daubed metal covers, and a suspicious-looking tall tin can, the purpose of which is to make the disks, an orange, and some rice move around among the tinware? Or what about two odd-shaped boxes with gaudy trimmings, whose sole function is to make one of three wooden blocks disappear from one box and be found, for some reason, in the other? Yet I can assure you that magicians buy these contraptions, and once in a while I am afraid somebody even shows them.

The reason why discrimination is so necessary is that far too much magical apparatus simply does not make sense. Coins make sense; strait jackets make sense; billiard balls, though not exactly logical, are simple and perfectly reasonable. Elaborate and hideous objects that can have no possible purpose except to do for the magician his self-imposed job of producing, vanishing, or transposing some other elaborate and hideous object do not make sense. Even though the principle of their construction may not be apparent, they are quite without mystery; they cannot create an illusion. They have no possible association except "magic apparatus—fake."

A few pieces of apparatus, such as the sliding die box (see the appendix: Further Tricks and Illusions), successfully depend on just this spurious look for their whole effect; but naturally they are a minority.

Since I have bought amazingly little apparatus in my many years of conjuring, perhaps I should not pose as an authority. Nevertheless I am going to give you the tests I would apply to any piece of apparatus before I bought it. They are perfectly simple, and I think you will find them hard to quarrel with.

First, can you use the piece for more than one trick? Thumb tips, pulls, and lotas would still be a good buy even if they cost several times what they do: their usefulness is limited only by your ingenuity.

Second, if they are one-trick pieces, does the trick make sense? How close is it to real magic? Which association is inherent in it—ordinary, or fake? The egg bag is a one-trick piece. Though the bag may not be quite like any that people have seen, still a cloth bag and an egg are reasonable and natural things to do real magic with.

Third, does the trick make sense for *me*? Will *I* use it? By this I mean not merely that a pack of marked cards is useless to a discriminating Christian leader, but that every performer has his own style and his own tempo, and so have a good many tricks. In the long run a necessarily rapid-fire trick will not satisfy a leisurely performer. The moves may require some kind of patter that doesn't fit your act. In short, don't be swept away by the fascination of a great performer showing a trick that is made for him. Stop and ask yourself coldly, How would it look on me?

If you're the Cardini type, don't buy a piece of apparatus just because Blackstone knocked 'em dead with it.

Fourth, can I do the same trick without the apparatus? One catalogue that I have before me lists thirty-five pages of card effects. It includes a number of good tricks but surely less than a dozen that you really need the apparatus for. As I said in connection with head magic, don't accept cheap substitutes (or expensive substitutes either) for sleight of hand.

On the other hand, there definitely are times when sleights are the substitutes. You can vanish a silk by sleight of hand, but it doesn't look half so magical as using a pull. Some of the books contain directions for doing the Multiplying Billiard Balls without a shell; the result is labored, difficult, and not very mystifying.

For children's shows (chapter 20) my strictures don't always apply. Here manipulation and deception are at a discount; what matters is primary colors and splash. Above the minimum level, make-believe replaces mystery. Folk-art figures and fairy-tale castles are the ticket: they proclaim loudly that they're not real and it's all in fun. Cartoon figures have their own personalities; take care they don't outrun the trick. (Mickey Mouse can do far more on the screen than on your table.) Anything as big and showy as children's effects must be is often a one-trick piece.

Magic is what you are after; apparatus, kept firmly in its place, can make you more of a magician. Only when it gets out of hand does apparatus spoil the illusion and crab the act.

Most silk tricks take skill, and some of the moves taught in this chapter are downright hand magic. I have put silk tricks in the apparatus class because nearly every effect depends heavily on some sort of container. A silk that is to appear or disappear must be compressed and confined. Palming alone is seldom the answer: the handkerchief must first go into a firm housing.

To begin with, you want the proper kind of silk handkerchief for magic. The silk itself should be thin and elastic; the hem very narrow, to make as little bulk as possible in packing a load. Anything smaller than fifteen inches square is too small; eighteen inches and up is better. The colors should be bright and clear; take care that they don't swear at one another. Multicolored "rainbow" silks were a magical fashion that set my teeth on edge, and I am happy to believe that conjurers are learning better than to use them.

Your silks should be washed and ironed often—certainly before every set performance. Dirty, crumpled silks are worse than a dirty collar because they show farther. John Mulholland had his white silks folded and ironed like ordinary linen handkerchiefs, and brought them out of his pocket in that condition. The resulting association of innocence was too much for the most suspicious audience.

The first general treatment of silk tricks is still probably the best—Chapter VII of Professor Hoffmann's *Later Magic*. I don't pretend I can improve on Professor Hoffmann's treatment except by discarding some of his methods that time has weeded out and adding a few successful new arrivals since his time. At any rate I shall unblushingly borrow his classifications and much of his material.

1. PRODUCTIONS

To produce a single handkerchief you may resort to head magic. Roll the silk into a compact ball, tucking in the corners. You can put this ball in the bend of one elbow or under your arm. In that way it comes naturally into your hand as you pull up your sleeves. You then produce it as you might a coin in The Miser's Dream (chapter 7, section 1), either from someone's clothes or by a simulated catch in the air.

The rolled silk may also be loaded into the empty rear end of a half-open matchbox. You take out a match, strike it, and close the box, which automatically gives you the silk.

Two of the best and simplest mechanical devices are named after their inventors.

The Stillwell ball is simply a hollow ball with a hole in one side. The handkerchief is packed in and the ball can then be treated like a billiard ball. (Maskelyne and Devant's warning about passes and palms holds here more than ever.) George Stillwell used rubber balls. A Ping-Pong ball with an inch hole cut in the side is good except for its tendency to talk. The dealers carry aluminum balls, painted flesh color. Anything big enough to hold your silks will do so long as you can palm it.

The Roterberg vanisher is just as good for productions. It is a small tin box shaped like the heel of a child's shoe, open where the front end of the heel would be. The top and bottom of the box overhang a trifle, and are toothed to give a better grip in palming. Near the round end on each flat side is a pin point slanting toward the mouth of the box (Fig. 176). These "hooks" are also used on various other conjuring properties; they allow you to hang the vanisher anywhere on your clothes, behind a chair, or even on the back of your hand. This cuts down on the number of passes and "acquitments" you must resort to. You can start with your hands really empty, grab at the air with your right hand, and steal the vanisher with your left.

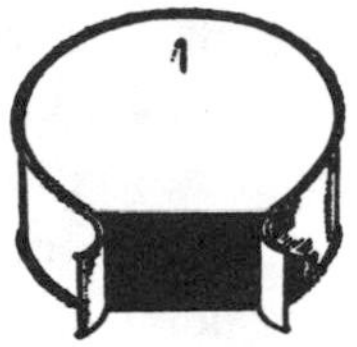

Fig. 176

Both the ball and the Roterberg vanisher (or hand box) can be used to multiply a silk already produced, by stroking the silk. Hold the silk by one corner and stroke it with the other hand, in which you have your gimmick palmed. The hand holding up the handkerchief catches a corner of the silk in the gimmick and draws it out as the stroking hand moves down.

The *false finger*, another production device, shows just how much people notice when their attention is not called. It is simply a hollow metal or celluloid finger, its open end shaped to fit in the fork of your middle fingers. The false finger is loaded with a silk and put in place just before you want to make your production. So long as your hand keeps more or less in motion, no one will ever notice that you have five instead of four fingers. If you are short on nerve, just keep the edge of your hand toward the audience, and then they *can't* see anything.

To produce several silks at a time you may like one of two very similar-looking pieces of apparatus.

The *drumhead tube* (Fig. 177) is a metal tube that is made into a

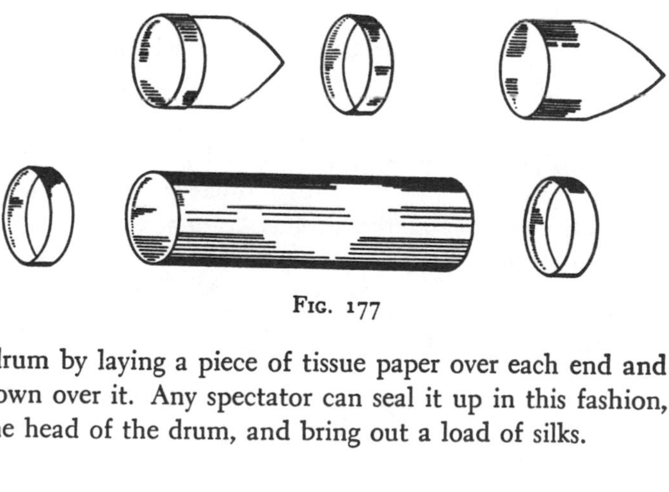

Fig. 177

sort of drum by laying a piece of tissue paper over each end and shoving a ring down over it. Any spectator can seal it up in this fashion, yet you break one head of the drum, and bring out a load of silks.

The gimmick is a container with one pointed end. The other end is covered with a paper drumhead of its own, held in place by a ring that goes snugly inside the tube.

You pack this "torpedo" with silks, put on the tissue paper drumhead, and have the gimmick where you can get at it. Usually it is small enough to palm for the brief moment it is necessary.

After the spectator has sealed up the tube, you receive it in your right hand, and with your left jam the point of the torpedo through the lower drumhead. When the torpedo is shoved flush, both ends look as before, but the lower end, of course, is loaded with the silks.

With the *phantom tube* the rings and paper drumheads are not necessary. You hold the tube up to a light, or look through it at various members of the audience; yet all the while it contains a large load. The secret is a tapering inner tube, which starts full size at one end, and at the other is less than half the diameter of the outer tube. Looked through from the big end, the tube merely seems longer than it ought (Fig. 178).

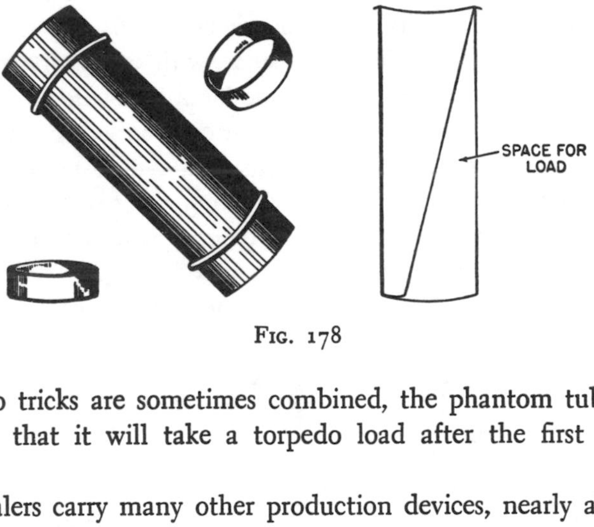

FIG. 178

The two tricks are sometimes combined, the phantom tube being so constructed that it will take a torpedo load after the first load is exhausted.

The dealers carry many other production devices, nearly all of which are unlikely investments. Even the two tubes have a strong tinge of "magic apparatus—fake," and the various "production boxes" look like exactly that and nothing else.

2. VANISHES

There are two sleight-of-hand methods, both of them confined to silks rather smaller than one is likely to use on the stage.

The traditional method is to roll the silk into a hard ball between your hands and then make the pass with it as with any other ball. To do this, let most of the handkerchief hang down over the back of your right hand and bring the upper corner through the crotch of your right thumb so that it falls between your palms. By a circular motion of both hands, roll this corner into a hard nub. Then the rest of the handkerchief will roll quickly and firmly around it, and you can palm or finger-palm the resulting bundle. Moist palms make this move much easier. An even bigger help (though not worth the trouble in my opinion) is to sew a small block of rubber into the corner of the silk.

The second method, the *poke-through vanish,* is my own so far as I know. You poke the silk into your left fist with your right forefinger, whereupon it vanishes. Don't let the silk get down into your left fist beyond the second finger. If you bend your right forefinger and keep the rest of your right fingers closed, you will find it very simple to hook the silk under your left thumb and into your curled right fingers. By straightening your left thumb, you can ram the silk home in your right hand. As I mentioned above, this does not work very well with big enough silks.

Of course either the Stillwell ball or the Roterberg vanisher will serve as well for vanishes as for productions. You can show both palms empty by getting the Stillwell ball on the end of one thumb or by sticking two fingers into the mouth of a hand box, and keeping the other hand in front of the gimmick. These acquitments, however, are but makeshifts. For a complete and magical vanish, nothing comes up to a pull.

Pulls consist essentially of a string that will pull some object up your sleeve or under your coat. You will also find them discussed in chapter 16, below.

The most familiar type is the old DeKolta pull, a metal cup or cylinder closed at one end and fastened at this end to a piece of elastic. The other end of the elastic is pinned to the back of your vest. When you are ready for the vanish, you hold up the silk ostentatiously in your right hand and get hold of the pull in your left. You put your left hand out as far as the elastic will stretch, work the silk into the cup, and then simultaneously release the pull and straighten your left arm, keeping the fist closed. The pull, of course, flies under your coat.

This form of pull can be bought of any dealer for less than a dollar, and is included in most toy magic sets. The necessary motions of "getting down" the pull and working the silk into the cup are unnatural and confining, and elastic has never been known as the Wizard's Friend. On the other hand, the DeKolta pull pins into your clothes in a moment, and a good operator who is careful of his angles can make it serve him well.

The most truly magical and puzzling of all silk vanishes is done with the *lamp-chimney pull.* Conjurers a generation ago worked the lamp-chimney vanish almost to death, and now you can't even buy that kind of pull; you will have to make one. I think you will find it worth the trouble.

The lamp-chimney pull is of the double-action, loop variety. This means that it holds the silk in a loop of gut rather than a cup, and the pull itself is a thin, strong cord, not an elastic. The double-action feature consists of anchoring the fixed end at your waist and running the pull through a ring or small pulley at your left elbow, then around your back, and so down your right sleeve. By shooting your arms forward and spreading your elbows, you can draw the loop up very nearly between your shoulder blades.

When the pull is ready to go, with the silk in the loop, your posture is quite cramped. The fastening at the fixed end is therefore made movable so that you can have plenty of slack until just before the vanish, and can then shorten the pull to its working length.

To make such a pull, you must assemble a catgut violin E string; some very strong, thin, black line such as heavy fishline; a strap with a buckle, long enough to go around your left forearm; a small pulley with some kind of guard to keep the line from running off; and a metal ring perhaps an inch in diameter. Make a loop of the catgut about four inches long and tie it with the hardest, smallest knot you know to one end of the fishline. If the knot is at all bulky, it will catch in your sleeve. Have a cobbler fasten the pulley permanently to the strap. Run the line through and tie the other end firmly to the ring.

You will have to figure out the length of the pull by putting it on. Buckle the strap around your left forearm just below the elbow. Carry the loop end of the pull across your back and for the moment hook it over your right thumb. The pull runs through the pulley and then through some guide such as a belt loop at your waist. You may prefer to sew a smaller ring to the waistband of your trousers for this purpose. The pull should be long enough so that when you put your coat on you can move freely with the large ring up against this guide. In addition you need an anchor, such as a very large dress hook or a suspender button, in such a position that, when the big ring is hooked over it, the gut loop will just about reach to the end of your extended right second finger when your elbows are against your sides.

Arranging the pull and getting it the right length are the most complicated part; working the trick is quite simple. Before the show, loop the gut over your cuff button or over the outermost button of your coat sleeve. A third procedure, ideal for some performers and highly suspicious in others, is to put an ordinary pocket handkerchief through the loop and let the pull draw it just a little way up your sleeve. The ring on the end of the pull, of course, is against the guide, allowing you enough slack to be comfortable.

It was originally customary to show this vanish with a glass cylinder open at both ends, whence the name "lamp-chimney" vanish. All things considered, I believe you will do better with a very tall highball glass.

Put out your glass and the silk that is to vanish. The next step is to get down the pull. Either quietly unhook the gut from the button or draw the pocket handkerchief from your sleeve and wipe your face with it. What you need is to have the loop over the second joint of your right middle finger. Then move the ring end of the pull over to its anchor position. Pick up the silk and draw it halfway through your right hand, contriving at the same time to run it halfway through the gut loop. If the silk is very large, you will have to pick it up by the middle so that the loop catches it and divides it into quarters rather than halves.

Pick up the glass in your left hand. With your right hand crumple the silk and pop it, loop and all, into the tumbler. Put your right palm flat over the mouth of the tumbler, your left palm flat on the bottom. Turn the tumbler horizontal.

Give everyone plenty of chance to see the silk isolated in the glass. You may even go so far as to remark that you are keeping your fingers out of the way. Be very sure you have people on the front edge of their chairs, with their eyes fixed on the glass, because this is one of the biggest things any magician can do.

Ready? Set? Bingo!

Shoot your hands forward and spread your elbows. Relax the pressure of your right palm on the rim of the glass. The pull snatches the silk up to your shoulder. The glass is empty. Not a trace of fraud is left.

By experimenting with the length of your pull, you can even vanish a small handkerchief when your sleeves are rolled to the elbow.

3. COLOR CHANGING

Changing the color of silks is perhaps the prettiest thing you can show with them. There are, of course, various ludicrous contraptions to do the job; but two of the old stand-bys are infinitely the best.

One is a prepared silk, which you can buy from any dealer under the name of the *color-changing handkerchief*. Since you had better buy one rather than try to make it, I will only explain in a general way that the silk is actually two, sewed together into a sort of triangular pocket. A metal ring is sewed into the joined corners in such a way that it will slide up and down. When the ring is up, the red silk is outside; when the ring is down, the pocket turns itself inside out, bringing the green silk into view. A quick sweep of the hand makes the change automatically.

This color change (invented by Dr. Harlan Tarbell) is perfection in its limited way; but you can't let the audience have even a good look at the silk, let alone examine it, and therefore the effect is more of a flourish than an independent trick. You can work up combinations that somehow take people's attention off the actual silk—for instance, tie one Tarbell silk in its red condition by the corners between two white silks, and another Tarbell one in its green state between two other white ones; and have the red and green silks "change places." (In this case you would have to make the color changes unobserved, behind the screen of the white silks.)

For effects where the color change is the thing, the *dye tube* remains the best of all gimmicks. There are two kinds of dye tube, the small one for the hand color change, the large for the paper-tube version.

In the hand change you poke a red silk into the top of your left fist and draw it out at the bottom blue. Your left hand, needless to say, is empty before and after.

The *hand dye tube* is a metal cylinder two inches long and an inch in diameter. A length of tape is fastened by the ends inside the center of the cylinder; it is long enough so that the slack middle of the tape will just reach to either end of the tube. Pack the blue silk into the tube, starting with one corner and finishing with the diagonally opposite corner. Then put the tube in your right trouser pocket with the tape end down and the open end up.

Steal the tube in your right hand, holding it palmed with the tape end against your middle fingers and the open end against your palm. Take the red silk by one corner between your right forefinger and thumb and draw it through your left hand. This silently calls attention to the silk, and also shows your hand empty. Repeat this motion perhaps twice more; the last time, drop the dye tube into your left hand, and pivot around to the right as you draw the silk down. Your right palm is thus seen empty also.

Close your left fist around the dye tube. With your right forefinger, poke the corner of the red silk into the top of your left fist. Give a good hard push, sending the bottom part of the blue silk out of the dye tube. Give one more poke to the red silk, and then leave it for a moment while you tug the corner of the blue silk free from the bottom of your left fist.

Now you keep alternating, poke and tug, until the red silk is entirely worked into the dye tube, and the blue one is almost wholly in view. Nip the very top corner of the blue one with your bent left little finger. (Unless you take this precaution, the blue silk sometimes catches in the bottom of the dye tube, and is pulled back to the top of your fist when you make the immediately ensuing steal.)

The reason for the alternating, almost fussy, poking and tugging is that you want to create an association. After each poke, people must learn automatically to look *down* at the growing expanse of blue. When the red silk is all packed in, grab the rim of the tube between your right thumb and forefinger and lift it straight out of your fist. As your right hand rises, the tube almost of its own accord falls into the palm, where the second, third, and fourth fingers close on it. Another tug at the bottom, and, if you like, another poke at the top. Then you pull the blue silk clear away.

Wait a minute, keeping your left fist closed. Wait long enough so that people realize there should be something in the fist; then open it. They will be far too much surprised to wonder about your right hand.

The *large dye tube* works on exactly the same principle as the hand dye tube, but is often made a little differently. It is an inch and a half in diameter, and four inches long.

(The dimensions of both these tubes are calculated for somewhat smaller silks than professionals use, and packing the last corners in is rather a frantic business. The gimmicks are simple enough so that you might well make your own on a slightly larger scale.)

The large tube may have two crossed tapes instead of the single one in the hand tube. More generally it has a sliding cup three-quarters of an inch deep, which is kept from falling out by turned-in edges on the tube. In loading this type, push the mouth of the cup to the end of the tube and load from the other end with three silks.

The effect is that you roll a sheet of paper into a tube, then poke a silk in at the bottom white and bring it out at the top (say) red. You follow this with two other silks, which perhaps emerge blue and green. When you unroll the paper, it is empty.

The best paper I have found for the trick is an ordinary manila office filing folder. Lay the folder on your table with the fold to the front, and the loaded tube in the fold near the edge closest to you (the right-hand edge if you are working right handed). The open end of the dye tube is away from you, the empty mouth of the cup toward you.

Pick up the paper in your left hand by the upper edge, with your thumb on top. This allows your fingers to grab the dye tube. The lower half of the folder hangs down. Look at the paper as if in search of marks. Then take the lower edge of the folder in your right hand and swing it forward and up. When it is in front of your left hand, drop the rear edge of the folder and take the other edge with your left thumb. The left fingers, of course, still hold the dye tube. Scrutinize the side of the folder now presented. (This is incomparably better than saying the paper is empty; the move with the tube is not subtle enough for that.)

Curl the top edge of the folder to the left and roll it briskly into a cylinder around the dye tube. Take the cylinder in your left hand near the lower end and stick your little finger across the bottom as a stop. Relax your fingers enough to let the dye tube slide down almost to the bottom.

Poke your first silk in at the bottom. A good hard shove will free the top silk from the dye tube, and it can be brought out a little at a time by tapping the upper end of the cylinder against your right hand. Don't let it come all the way before you have got the first silk completely into the dye tube!

What you do with the silks after they are dyed depends on how you mean to go south with the dye tube. My own custom is to hang the silk by the corner from between my left second and third fingers.

You repeat the same moves with the other two silks. My method of shedding the dye tube is to let it slide down behind the silks and catch it with my left thumb just as I remove the rolled-up paper with my right hand. I keep my eyes on the paper, turn it horizontal, then let it unroll.

If you use a servante or a black art table (see platform magic), you will have a ready-made place to drop the dye tube. A box, hat, or other obstruction on the table will serve the same purpose.

4. KNOTS

The other class of effect peculiar to silks involves the mysterious tying and untying of knots. This is pure hand magic—an easy and rewarding variety.

The *dissolving knot* is perfectly easy to do once you understand it, but a shade tricky to memorize. The effect is simply that you tie a plain overhand knot in the middle of a silk; when you blow on it, the knot disappears.

Let a handkerchief hang down from the fork of your left thumb. Roughly the upper third of the silk lies over the back of your hand. With your right hand take the lower end, bring it up behind your left third finger, through between the third and second, and so into the fork of your left thumb, across the end that is already there.

Move your left thumb to the left, so that you are holding only the former lower end, while the former upper end runs free underneath (Fig. 179).

Reach your right hand through the resulting loop; reach away from you. (This is one of the confusing points.) Catch the former upper end in your right hand (Fig. 180).

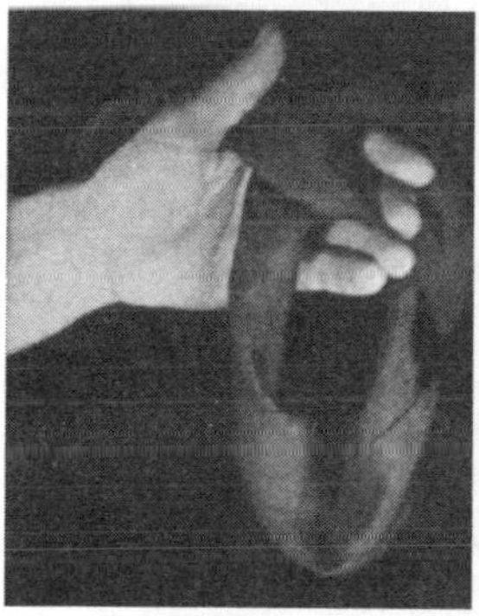

Fig. 179

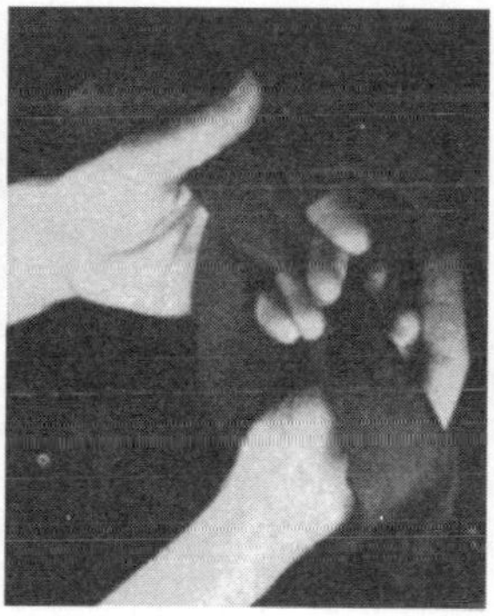

Fig. 180

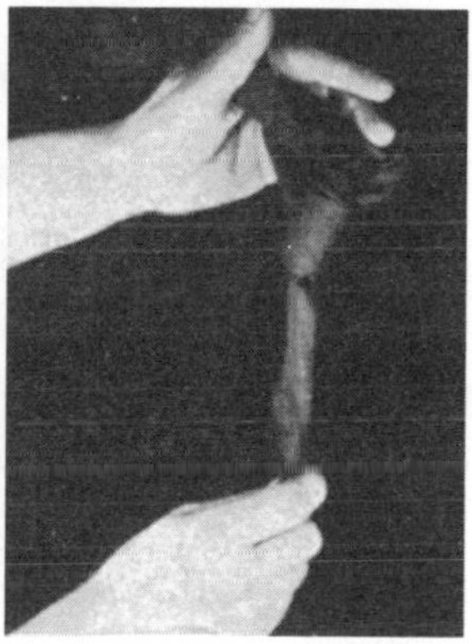

Fig. 181

Now bring your right hand back toward you through the loop. Hold firm with your left thumb and your left middle fingers and pull the right-hand end of the silk snug (Fig. 181).

If you do this without dawdling, it looks like a perfectly fair knot. Actually, the knot is just tied around a kink in the silk. The right-hand end is what you might call the "knot" end, and by it you can shake the silk quite hard without dissolving the knot. The left-hand end is the "kink" end, and a very gentle pull on it will make the knot evaporate.

A dissolving knot can be made not only in a magician's silk, but in a shawl, muffler, or even a ribbon. With a ribbon it is not nearly so deceptive.

The *appearing knot* is an old effect, but the method of doing it with one hand is comparatively modern, and Al Baker's follow-up is a mere infant.

You take a silk by the middle and give it a shake or toss it in the air. An overhand knot instantly appears.

Wind the silk ropewise; then take it in the right hand as in Fig. 182. Swing your right hand up and back so that the front, or lower, end of the handkerchief swings back, encircles your wrist, and falls forward across the front of your hand.

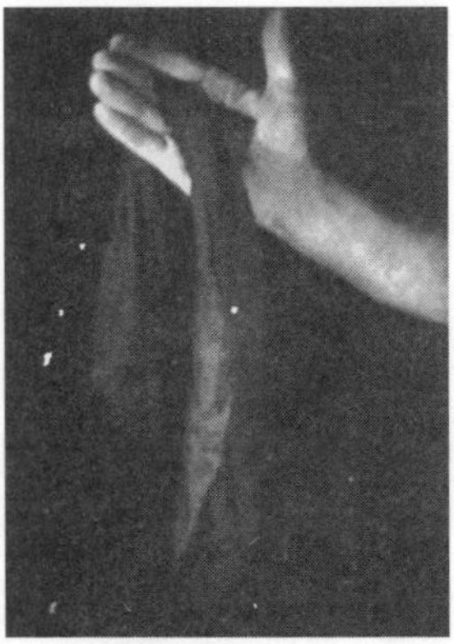

FIG. 182

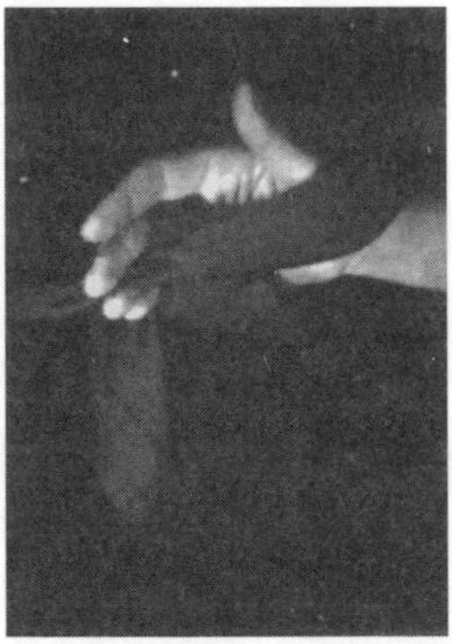

FIG. 183

Nab this flying end between your second and third fingers (Fig. 183).

Shake the silk off your fingers, releasing the part from between your first and second fingers but holding on with second and third fingers (Fig. 184).

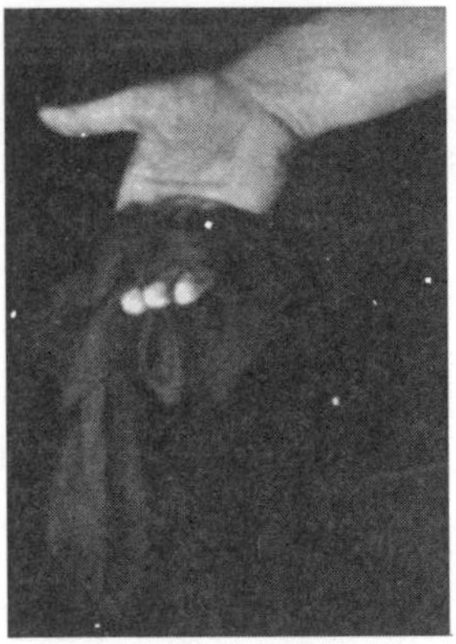

FIG. 184

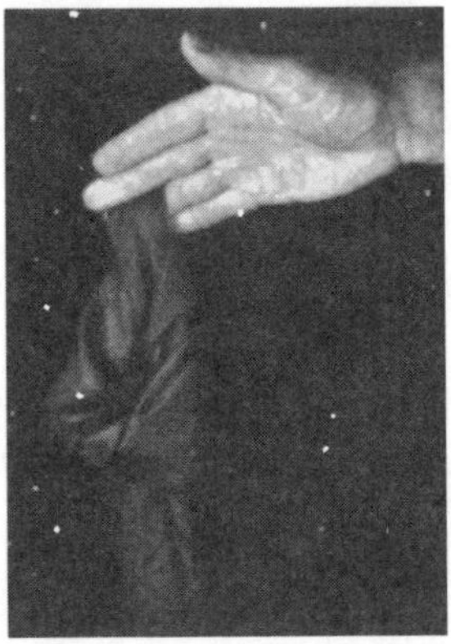

FIG. 185

When you have shaken the silk free, an overhand knot is the result (Fig. 185).

This move is best covered by a down- and then an upsweep of the hand, carrying the silk briefly out of sight behind your thigh.

You will soon learn that the knot is very hard to produce in a small silk. The flying end is hard to catch; and, when you do catch it, the knot will probably fall off the lower end.

Although this knot, properly produced, is indetectable, at best the audience can't help but realize there is *something* going on. To throw them off the track, the ever-ingenious Al Baker produced the sequel that follows.

You snap the handkerchief like a whip, and after two or three failures a small hard knot appears in the free corner.

Seize a moment when they aren't looking to tie a small knot in one corner of a handkerchief (a pocket handkerchief or bandanna is perfectly good for this if you aren't doing a silk routine). Hold the handkerchief up by an adjacent corner in your right hand; run your left hand down the edge to the knot (which of course has been hanging out of sight). Clip the knotted corner between your left first and second fingers, with the knot inside. Lift the opposite corner and put it between your left forefinger and thumb.

Give a snap of the handkerchief, holding onto the knotted corner. Try it once or twice more, until you begin to get impatient; then hold on with your forefinger and thumb and release the knotted end from between your fingers.

Marvelous!

Fake square knots can be either made or converted from real ones.

Converting them is known as upsetting them. A favorite trick with Harry Blackstone, Horace Goldin, and other great performers is to have volunteers tie the corners of a borrowed handkerchief together in several hard knots; and then you magically separate the corners. This you do by upsetting the knots. You can upset any square (or any granny) knot by pulling into a straight line one of the strands that form it. In other words, take one corner of the handkerchief both above and below the knot, and pull hard. After each knot that a spectator ties, you give one more tug "to pull it tighter," and so upset the knot.

The only way you can be stumped is to have someone lay the two corners side by side, and tie them jointly in an overhand knot. To prevent this, offer the spectator the corners of the handkerchief at a wide angle, almost head on. If he insists on making the foolproof kind of knot, you will have to untie it on some pretext and tie it up yourself in a very hard fake square knot, unless you prefer taking your chance with a more obliging volunteer.

As the several spectators tie their knots in the corners of the handkerchief, you keep upsetting the knots, and shortening the straight end as you go. Eventually you put the middle of the handkerchief over the knots, simultaneously drawing the straight end clear out so that all the knots are undone.

There are two ways of making a fake square knot. One was a specialty of Houdini's, and is thus described in Downs's *Art of Magic:*

"Hold an end of the handkerchief between the thumb and first finger of each hand, about three inches from the tip—the natural position for tying an ordinary knot. Now lay the right end across the left, and apparently tie the two ends together. Really, when the two ends are crossed, the right over the left, the two ends are clipped at the point of intersection between the tip of the right thumb and first finger. With a sweeping movement of the right hand back and down, the end is grasped by the tips of the left first and second fingers and brought up in *front.* The movement is simply the reverse of actually tying the right end around the left.

"The student should first tie a genuine knot, closely noting the movements of the hands and fingers, and these movements should be faithfully imitated when tying the fake knot. Deftly done, the keenest eye cannot detect that the right end of the handkerchief is doubled behind the left end instead of going around in front.

"Holding the handkerchief tightly at the point where the ends are apparently entwined, the performer requests one of the spectators to tie the second part of the knot, telling him to pull the ends as tight as possible. Cover the knot with the loose part of the handkerchief and hand it to someone to hold. Grasping one end of the handkerchief, request the spectator to breathe on the knots, and to release his hold. He does so and the knot has disappeared."

This form of knot is now generally used to tie two separate handkerchiefs together, and the magician completes his own knot instead of getting a spectator to do it. The reason is that this is possibly the best knot for the Sympathetic Silks trick, which we shall learn in a moment.

The second variety of fake square knot is upset in the tying. For clarity I shall describe it as being done with a light and a dark silk. Hold the light silk between your left forefinger and thumb, palm to the front, second finger sticking up. With your right hand, bring the dark silk through the fork of your left first and second fingers from back to front, and leave it there (Fig. 186).

Then reach under your left hand and catch the free end of the dark silk. Draw it back and to the right, thus winding the dark silk around the light one (Fig. 187).

Again bring the end of the dark silk over your left forefinger from behind and catch it. Now reach your right hand through the half-formed knot from inside to out, grab the end of the dark silk, and pull it off the same as you have already done once.

Fig. 186

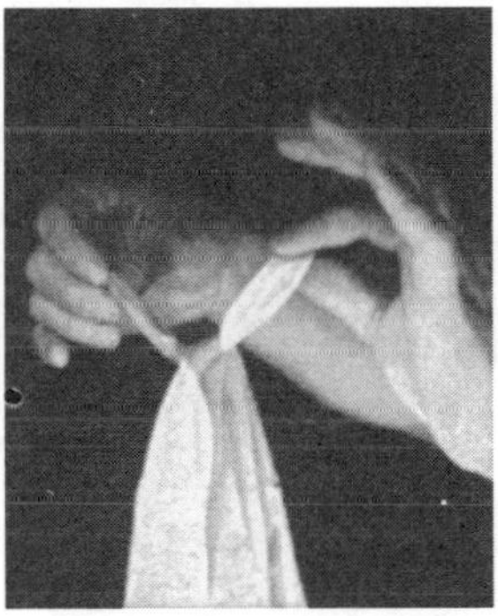

Fig. 187

Fig. 188

At the same time, your right middle fingers grab the lower part of the *light* silk, while your left middle fingers do the same with the dark silk. Pull with your left forefinger and thumb and your right middle fingers only, while pretending to pull on all four ends of the knot.

The result is that the light silk is straight, with the dark one tied around it (Fig. 188).

Obviously, a gentle pull on the light silk will draw it out of the knot.

The *Knot That Unties Itself* is done perfectly by Cardini and a few others, quite badly by many conjurers who should know better. You tie an overhand knot in a silk; the lower corner simply rises back and crawls out of the knot, which accordingly falls apart.

The motive power is a fine black silk thread fastened to one corner of the handkerchief. The thread may be either a couple of feet long, in which case you work it with one hand, or long enough to drag on the floor when the silk is held up shoulder high. In this case you step on the thread.

Either you may hold the silk up by the threaded corner in your left hand, tie an overhand knot around the thread, and then hold the handkerchief up in your right hand by the opposite corner; or you may hold the silk up by the corner opposite the threaded one, make an overhand knot that brings the thread through, and continue to hold the silk in your left hand.

In either case you raise the silk and hold the thread fast below. Naturally the threaded corner crawls snakelike up through the knot.

This is one of the tricks that are too obvious and too slight to stand on their own feet. Done as a slow flourish or interlude, it is hard to beat.

The *Sympathetic Silks*, a comparative newcomer among tricks, has already made its way into the select company that will surely be done by magicians a century hence.

You show six silks, and put three of them, separate, on one side of the stage. The remaining three you tie corner to corner and put on the other side of the stage. You make the knots pass from the tied silks to the loose ones, which are immediately found to be tied.

If you want to lead up to the effect, you can first take two silks, tie a dissolving knot in one, and toss them both into the air simultaneously, one with each hand, shaking in a knot in the other silk as you do so. The dissolving knot snaps out, so that the knot appears to have passed in midair from silk to silk.

To prepare for the Sympathetic Silks, get six just alike. Although it may be less showy, I think it is also less confusing to have them all one color. Tie three of them corner to corner. Pick these up by corners adjacent to the tied ones, so that the two knots will be hidden in the fullness at the middle of the silks. Lay these three together with the other three, keeping the upper ends of the two groups slightly separated. Put them out on a table or over the back of a chair, and you are ready to begin.

Your first move is to count the silks. The simplest way is to take them near the upper end in your left hand, the tied group outermost. With your right hand take the top corner of the first tied silk and lift it up and a little back for a third of its whole length. The tied silk thus moves as if it were free, and does not bring the knot into view. Count one. Go back and pick up the next tied silk with the same motion; count two. The same with the third; count three.

Put the three in a heap on the seat or across the back of a chair well over to your right.

Count the three loose silks with exactly the same motion, just as if you had knots to hide.

Tie the three corner to corner with either kind of fake square knot.

Show them in a long chain; then, while bunching them together, slip out the knots, and drop the three silks on a chair to your left.

So far, the trick can be worked quite briskly; now is the time to be impressive. You can personally carry those knots one at a time across the stage. Don't let anyone miss this: it's good. No wires, no mirrors, just *zip!*

Snatch up the "loose" pile, allowing it to string out. Then pick up the top two silks from the other pile, scattering them to either side.

The knots have traveled.

Some routines wind up by magically untying the newly tied silks. I think this is a mistake. Like extra billiard-ball passes, it confuses the plot. You are not professing to untie knots (which any monkey can do), but to make the knots travel. The Dissolving Knot is much more surprising than any "surprise" ending to the Sympathetic Silks.

16. *Small Gimmicks and Fakes*

HERE are the subtlest aids in the whole bag of tricks. On the authority of John Mulholland, a *gimmick* is a secret device never seen by the audience; a *fake* is a device seen by the audience, but not understood. A dye tube is a gimmick; a bottomless glass is a fake. What class the thumb tip and the mirror glass fall into, I can't say for sure.

The distinction is perhaps logical rather than actual. Magicians call any small device either a gimmick or a fake, or sometimes a gaff, as the humor takes them.

Whatever the name, this is the first kind of apparatus I should buy in your shoes. The pieces can nearly all be used for many tricks; they are close enough to hand magic so that you profit by what you have learned thus far; and by definition there is a reason for them.

True, a wag at one of the magic shops told me they were now supplying nested thumb tips, so that you could steal one and pass the other out for examination; and I have seen magicians whom I thought quite capable of doing it. But the day is happily past when Professor Hoffmann's "pieces of apparatus of general utility" included mainly such items as a tin windmill that would blow coal dust in the face of an obstreperous spectator, and a tin cover with a large plunger in the side that actuated a scoop to produce and vanish articles put underneath. When fakes and gimmicks are seen at all nowadays, their whole merit is that association passes them by without a thought.

Perhaps the most complete maid-of-all-work on the dealers' shelves is the *thumb tip*. This is an aluminum or rubber cap shaped and painted roughly like the end joint of a thumb. In buying one, first make sure you get a comfortable fit; then try to get a color that more or less matches your particular skin. Fit is much the more important requirement because you can buy different shades of flesh-colored paint from the dealer for retouching. Cheap thumb tips show a gleam of bright metal around the edge, which it is well to paint over; good thumb tips are painted inside and out.

As a matter of fact, however, the appearance of your thumb tip makes hardly any difference at all. The art of using one is to keep it from being seen. Al Baker created a furore by his statement that a thumb tip might just as well be nickel plated, and the late Stuart Robson, a dealer, used to amuse himself with a tip from which he had sanded all the paint. For a manipulator of your attainments it is very easy hand magic to keep one thumb out of sight, either behind your fingers or pointing straight away from the audience. Unless your thumb tip is actually bright silver, furthermore, it can safely be pointed straight *at* the audience. A profile view is the only thing they mustn't get.

The uses of the thumb tip are enough to fill a fair-sized book. I will give you just a few of the suggestions that appeal most to me.

Its use as a vanisher for a lighted cigarette tucked into a handkerchief has unfortunately become familiar to the Mysto Magic crowd. But peculiarly enough it is still perfectly good to vanish loose tobacco, poured from a Bull Durham sack into your fist, or a small spoonful of salt. Start with the tip on your right thumb, rub your left palm, close your left hand into a fist, and leave the thumb tip inside. Pour in the tobacco or salt; give one tamp with your right thumb, stealing the thumb tip; and away you go.

You can roll a dollar bill into a tube, leaving the thumb tip just inside the edge of it, and pour yourself a small drink using the bottomless paper tube as a cup. In unrolling the tube you can easily steal the thumb tip again.

I have already mentioned the thumb tip as a method of doing the Torn and Restored Paper Ribbon.

The late Theo Annemann used a thumb tip for a "billet switch." Billets, as you will learn in the chapter on mental magic, are slips of paper bearing a message or question, and folded up. To get them the right size for a thumb-tip switch, use slips about two and a half by three and a half. Fold them beforehand, once lengthwise, making a narrow strip, and then twice crosswise, folding the strip into thirds. You hand them out in this condition, and naturally a person who writes on one will refold it in the same shape.

The switch is accomplished by putting a folded billet in the thumb tip. Get the tip on your right thumb, with the billet against the front. Hold out your left palm, and have the original folded billet laid on it. Promptly put your right thumb on the billet, and as promptly close your left fingers over your thumb. Draw the thumb out, carrying the duplicate billet with it, and carelessly drop your left fist with the original billet and empty thumb tip to your side.

You will find a use for this switch in mental magic.

The *finger tip* is exactly like a thumb tip, but of course smaller. I bought one just so that I could do the trick called *Taps,* at page 103 of Annemann's *Practical Mental Effects.* In general its smaller size rather limits its usefulness, and it cannot be so easily kept out of sight as a thumb tip.

The *thumb writer* is a device—thumb tip or band clip—with a bit of pencil lead attached. It enables you to write (or at least scrawl) on a card or slip of paper unobserved by the audience.

The thumb writer is used chiefly in prediction tricks, where you pretend to write something down beforehand, and then offer a choice of cards, numbers, or whatever. The actual writing is done with the thumb writer after the choice has been made.

Charles H. Hopkins suggests habitually carrying a thumb writer to meet the not infrequent situation where a trick with a chosen card has gone wrong, and you have lost track of the chosen card without learning what it is.

You have already learned in the optical fan location (chapter 5, section 1*c*) how to manage when the spectator tells you what card he had. But suppose he refuses to tell you—"It's your trick, you find it." Then, says Mr. Hopkins, you take out one of your business cards and a pencil. "All right," you say, "I'll make a note of it here before we start, so that there can't be any misunderstanding." You pretend to write on the card and drop it on the table face down. Next, spread the pack face up on the table. Tell the spectator to put his finger on his card. That done, he is to pull it out of the pack.

As soon as you have spread the pack out, you pick up the business card in your right hand, which by now has donned the thumb writer. The moment the spectator touches his card, your right thumb starts scratching out "2 S" or " QH" or whatever it is.

When he pulls his card clear of the pack, you toss your business card face down upon it. The two agree. You knew the card all the time.

Having got back on the subject of card tricks, I will tell you about one very, one fairly, and one occasionally useful piece.

The *card index* (Fig. 189) is simply a pocket filing cabinet. In it you can arrange not only a pack of cards but an assortment of billets or any other paper items that you may want to locate instantly. Card indexes were originally used in pairs for the trick of producing any card called for from a shuffled pack in your trouser pockets. The pack was split in halves, and so each index contained twenty-six prearranged cards. The secret of effective operation is just practice with a loaded index. As you see, each folder in the file contains two cards. If you know where to reach, there need never be more than four finger motions to find any one card: up or down three tabs on the proper side, and take the inner or outer card as required.

Fig. 189

Your own ingenuity will no doubt show you a trick in which this power of immediate selection within a wide range comes out at its best. Just for instance, you might have fifty-two different cards bearing portraits of famous people. You could stand up a blank card beforehand. It wouldn't take much management to see that one of your fifty-two celebrities was named; you could then palm the proper portrait from the index, and change that card for the blank one by the palm change (chapter 3, section 6*d*). This is not a very finished specimen, but it is not meant to be.

Sixteen Card Index Gems, by Max Andrews, is a pamphlet that should be very helpful to all intending users of card indexes.

You can buy a card index from any dealer, or make one yourself out of red manila board. This is one of the cases where the store product is not necessarily better than the homemade.

The *card box* comes in various forms. The best in my opinion, because it might be a cigarette box, is made of chromium-plated metal. It is flat, with a hinged snug-fitting lid. It will produce, vanish, or change a card or billet. This it does by means of an intermediate tray, hinged along with the lid. The tray fits tightly over the inside of the lid and loosely into the box proper (Fig. 190). At the start of the trick the duplicate card or message is in the bottom of the box and the tray is over it. The original is dropped into the box (actually into the tray), and the box is snapped shut. The lid thereupon picks up the tray, working the exchange. The box can safely be left for the audience to play with because, even when you know how, it is at least half a minute's work to pry the tray off the lid.

FIG. 190

The ancient wooden card box with a loose flap in the top will not go very far these days; it is one of the cheap substitutes for sleight of hand that I denounced in an earlier chapter. On the other hand the manufacturer's pride, the extra-thin metal card box, is altogether too good. The workmanship is beautiful, but the box won't hold anything except a card; it is pure "magic apparatus." You can keep a few cigarettes in the regular metal card box, and that's all the explaining you need to do. If you want to do the "card in cigarette" trick, the misdirection could not be more perfect.

The *card frame* is very popular with magicians, who are forever inventing improved models. Privately I suspect that audiences are impressed by it only in proportion to the showmanship of the performer, and that a good man could make his trick just as good without any frame.

At all events, the apparatus is a glazed picture frame just about big enough to display a card in. It is shown empty at the start of the trick, then laid down or held under the cover of a handkerchief, and eventually a card, chosen or otherwise, appears in the frame.

My *Cyclopedia of Magic* describes four entirely different card frames, and there are others.

The version that works with the least stalling is the "sand frame." At the start of the trick it seems to be backed with gray paper, in front of which the card appears. The front glass is actually double, and between the two sheets is a layer of gray sand. One end of the frame is hollow. Hold the frame hollow end upward and the sand between the sheets of glass actually duplicates the paper backing. Turn the hollow end downward and the sand trickles into it, exposing the card that was there all the time.

When the reproduction of a chosen card in the sand frame is to constitute the whole trick, magicians quite often have the card torn up, and ask the chooser to keep one piece. Of course they switch pieces, giving him a corner previously torn from the card in the frame.

Pulls I have already discussed. For objects not quite so long drawn out as a large silk, you can use a sleeve pull anchored directly to an elbow strap, without resorting to double action.

Cigarette pulls (usually but not necessarily of elastic) receive the burning butt in a metal tube, which holds them either by a constriction at the inner end or by a piece of flat spring pressing inward.

Billiard-ball pulls, naturally, must go under the coat instead of up the sleeve. They catch the ball with either a rubber sucker, a four-pronged spring clip, or a cloth bag with two flat pieces of spring steel in the mouth, which can be bowed open to receive the ball.

Percy Abbott's "Squash," the vanishing glass of whiskey, is one of the cleverest pulls—a rubber ball just big enough to be jammed hard into the mouth of a shot glass.

There are various other pulls, but their use is on the decline. I think you can contrive for yourself any that you may need.

Hooks I have already mentioned in describing the Roterberg vanisher (chapter 15, section 1). Coins and manipulator's dummy watches are also often provided with hooks.

In addition, you can put a hook on a bunch of cards or any other thin article by going to a stationery store and buying a few of the tiny black spring clips with one arm ending in a sharp hook that used to be called "Excelsior clips." You often see them used to hang announcements on cloth bulletin boards or over strings in show windows. The vanish and recovery of five cards together becomes a very simple matter with an Excelsior clip. Hook it to your trouser leg on the down swing, and they're gone.

Conjurers have a passion for wrapping things in handkerchiefs, which true wizards certainly would not do. In the handkerchief coin fold you have already seen one reason why magicians like handkerchiefs. Another reason is the variety of *handkerchiefs prepared as vanishers*. Any small object, such as a coin, billet, or folded dollar bill, can have a duplicate or reasonable facsimile sewed into a corner of a handkerchief. In putting the object under the handkerchief, you tuck under the faked corner of the handkerchief, palm the original, and ask someone to hold the object in the handkerchief for safekeeping. When you are ready for the vanish, of course a shake of the handkerchief does the work.

There are also various collapsible hollow shapes of wire or cardboard that can be hidden within a double handkerchief to simulate the presence of a glass of water, a wooden die, or a birdcage after the genuine article has been abstracted. The profession used to have a veritable craze for vanishing glasses of water from under handkerchiefs. As the craze has subsided, I shall leave you to find descriptions in the same books I would have turned to.

Tumblers can themselves be tinkered to render them more useful. Perhaps the best way is one that you might think would destroy the glass altogether—cut out the bottom. But you can easily see some of the tricks this makes possible. Set the bottomless glass on your palm, drop in a billiard ball or an egg, cover the glass with a handkerchief, and away goes the ball.

The old favorite "Kling Klang" (an egg in the glass changes places with a silk in the performer's hands) can be done with no other props than the silk, the egg, the bottomless glass, and a handkerchief to serve as cover. (It can, in fact, be done even without the bottomless glass by swiftly reversing an ordinary cylindrical glass under cover of the bandanna used to hide it, and so stealing the egg, which is switched with the rolled-up silk by palming.)

At page 600 of *Greater Magic* is an ingenious "visible penetration" trick with a bottomless glass.

The *mirror glass* will likewise produce, change, or vanish things. It has a double-faced reflecting partition down the center, either two mirrors cemented back to back or a piece of polished steel trench mirror. If not looked at too closely, the mirror glass seems empty when there is nothing in the front half. You can put a handkerchief or a handful of candy in the back half, and by giving the glass a half-turn either produce the object or exchange it for something put in the front half. Whatever you use should seem to fill the glass completely up to its own level. If it doesn't, it will be reflected in the mirror with fatal results. For instance a billiard ball would look like two, whereas a cupful of rice would simply look like a cupful of rice.

The principle of the mirror glass has been applied to cylinders, bottles, and other round glass containers.

The mirror glass and especially the bottomless glass have a wider usefulness for the sort of shows described in the chapter on platform magic than for close-up work.

17. *Standard Stuff*

MOST of the tricks in this chapter are more or less closely allied with platform magic. Though they *can* be done in the living room, I find myself almost necessarily telling you to go to the right or left of the stage, to do so and so on your way back from the audience. Naturally enough, the great majority of effects big enough to show to a large crowd are better for a crowd than close up.

In other words, the standard stuff is intended to make part of a set program. Set programs are discussed under platform magic.

At all events, here are some raw materials for your act.

1. *Cut and Restored Rope.* This trick has a dozen variants and fifty methods. It is another of the ones that magicians too often like better than audiences do.

Nevertheless it is a good, natural, real magic effect so long as you keep it simple and don't add improvements.

What you want to do is cut a piece of rope in two and make it whole again. It is customary to do this twice; even that is perhaps more than I should think necessary.

The normal rope for the effect is clothesline. Of methods you have basically three. One (the original) is some move that gets a spectator to cut the end off the rope, under the impression that he is cutting the middle. The modern form of this is called the Turban Trick, and is done with a piece of cheesecloth possibly a foot wide and ten feet long.

Toss an end to somebody, and have him pull. Next, clip one end of the turban in the crotch of your left thumb, with about six inches of the short end sticking up. Get the same grip on the other end with your right hand. That leaves the middle trailing on the floor.

Grab about eight inches of the middle between your two hands, holding it taut between *second* and *third* finger of each hand. The ends of the turban are still sticking up in the crotches of your thumbs.

With the turban in this position, make a downstage promenade from left to right. Over toward the right you ask someone to take the scissors and cut the turban in half between your hands.

Meanwhile, however, you have made a switch. When you swing to the right you drop both hands by bending your wrists, and at the same time close your fingers to make fists. Just then your left second and third fingers drop the piece of the middle they hold, and instead scoop in the right-hand piece that is dangling from the crotch of your right thumb.

With both hands now closed, all that shows is the short ends sticking up from your hands like a rabbit's ears, and a piece of turban (actually, of course, the right end) held out in the middle, ready to be cut.

After the cut, both ends of the actual turban are in your left hand. Your right hand holds a six-inch scrap of cheesecloth against the center of the turban. Drop everything from your left hand, and tie the scrap around the middle to form a "square knot."

This you get rid of by snipping off one bit after another with the scissors until nothing is left, and the turban is restored.

The second method is nearly as old, and consists of introducing a short extra piece of rope. You may double your long rope, apparently pull the center loop up through your fist, and actually pull up the short piece for someone to cut.

The short piece is also used to make a sliding fake knot. Simply tie the short piece around the rope. Leave the fake knot near one end and keep it out of sight; a good way is to hang the rope over a chair back. In handling the rope and tugging at it, keep one hand over the fake knot. Then tie the ends of the rope together and slide the fake knot up hard against the real one. This gives you a rope ring, which you yank at, and in the process slide the fake knot down to the far end of the loop. Bring your hands together for a moment, thus folding your big loop into two half loops. Yank at these, then let the fake knot fall from (say) your left hand, keeping the real knot in your left fist. With a pair of scissors, cut the rope twice, once on each side of your left hand. This eliminates the real knot, which you unload in your left pocket along with the scissors as you take the rope in your right hand. You can slide the fake knot off the rope in any way you choose; a conventional method is to wind the rope around your left fingers as if you were saving a piece of twine, and slide the knot off as you go.

Your third recourse is the first novelty in three centuries of Cut String tricks. You can prepare the ends of the rope so that they will stick together again. The cut-rope gimmick now usual is a metal cap to fit over the end of the rope. The caps are made in pairs, one with a short length of screw projecting, the other with a hollow thread to receive it. A single quick twist of the rope will fasten or detach the gimmicks.

The standard routine calls for two pairs of gimmicks, one pair fastened to the ends of a five-foot rope, the other pair on a scrap eight inches long. You now screw the short piece between the ends of the long piece, forming an endless loop around six feet long. In addition you need another short piece, which you tie in an overhand knot around the center of the long piece.

At the start of the trick you undo this knot, leaving the ends sticking up above your fingers in such a way that the rope is apparently held double, with the center trailing and the two ends sticking up. Then retie the overhand knot, drop it on the floor, and get a hand over each pair of gimmicks at the other end of the loop.

You have someone cut the rope between your hands—in other words he cuts the short gimmicked rope. These cut ends you hold up side by side, just as you did the alleged "ends" at the start of the trick. Trim these ends down with the scissors almost to the gimmicks; then unscrew the short remaining stubs, and unload them in your pocket along with the scissors.

You are now able to hold the two cut ends far apart. Bring them together, screw in the gimmick, and show that the rope has been rejoined into a circle. Your fake knot, of course, is still doing its duty at the center of the rope.

Finally, put one hand over the joined gimmicks, cut the rope on both sides of the hand, unload the gimmicked section along with the scissors, and finish by winding off the fake knot as you did in the original fake-knot version.

2. *The Egg Bag.* Here we have another prime example of presentation outweighing method. Mechanically the egg bag could hardly be simpler, and in fact the current version is cruder in working than the type used a century ago. But the old performers relied for their humor wholly on the intrinsic comedy of eggs and on the cumulative effect of repeated production.

The modern wizard has built the egg bag into a classic sucker routine. Such great professionals as Horace Goldin and Arnold de Biere have built their reputations quite as much on the comedy of the egg bag as on their new, huge, and expensive illusions.

Goldin said the whole secret of success lay in the way one handled the volunteer assistant, and Goldin is too great an authority to quarrel with.

I have described in Lesson 8 of *Learn Magic* two detailed routines with the egg bag. You can look there or in Hugard's *Modern Magic Manual* for the trimmings. The skeleton is here, to be clothed as you like.

The egg bag is made of cloth, often red or black flannel. It is rectangular, perhaps eight inches across and twelve deep. The trick about it is that one side folds inward at the mouth, and is doubled back on itself to within two or three inches of the bottom of the bag. In other words, it has a secret inside pocket, closed at the mouth of the bag and open toward the bottom. The whole art of deceiving with the egg bag consists in hiding this pocket. The art of entertaining with the egg bag is a more difficult matter, but not beyond the reach of any reasonably lively performer.

The egg itself could be an ordinary fresh one except for the attendant hazards. You can buy dummy eggs from magic dealers; de Biere used a blown egg. A hard-boiled one should be safe enough.

At the start of the trick the egg is in the secret pocket, and the bag is bottom side up, either crumpled on the table or stuffed into your coat pocket. When you first show the bag, hold it by one corner, with the pocket side toward you. The bag can be handled quite freely (more so if the egg is not too heavy—an argument against hard boiling). If you take the bag with your fingers inside the edge, covering the hidden egg, you can beat the bag against your knee or twist it up. When you turn it inside out, of course the pocket must stay toward you. With a little care, you can even stamp on the bag.

Finally you turn the bag right side out and hold it mouth upward, catching the egg through the cloth at the top of the pocket while you are getting a spectator to volunteer. When he comes up, he is told to feel in the bag, and see if he can find anything. After one or two futile searches, you release the egg, and so the volunteer finds it.

The sucker routine consists of apparently palming the egg and sneaking it out of the bag, and furtively stuffing it in your pocket. Actually, you poke the egg back into the secret pocket and simulate a clumsy palm of the egg.

When you show the bag empty, therefore, nobody is impressed, yet actually the egg is still there. They begin shouting for your pockets. You pull out all the wrong pockets, and finally, when the tumult is at its most deafening, the pocket where you supposedly hid the egg.

The egg then reappears in the bag, and is found by the volunteer.

You next say you are going to explain. You accompany each word with the appropriate action.

"I hold the egg like this" (pressing it to your palm with the second finger; *don't* actually palm it), "and then I put it in the bag, and then I sneak it out again" (simulating the presence of the egg, which you have once more tucked into the secret pocket), "and then I slip it into my pocket."

Here you stop suiting the action to the word. You simply explain, "And then I sneak it back into the bag the same way."

Have the volunteer hold your wrists. "Now we'll see if you can stop me from finishing the trick. If you think I'm trying to reach my pocket, stop me." Meanwhile you are holding the egg through the cloth at the mouth of the bag, where it fell after you slipped it into the secret pocket and turned the bag upside down.

The main part of the comedy lies in the ensuing tug-of-war between you and the volunteer. Finally you say, "Oh, all right, I can't do the trick. There isn't anything in the bag, is there?"

Whatever the volunteer says, make him reach in, and there is the wandering egg.

3. *The Passe-Passe Bottle and Glass.* This elderly trick still seems to knock them in the aisles. Just what is so funny about it I don't know, but with it a good performer can be sure of an extra crop of laughs.

You have a bottle, a glass, and two cardboard cylinders that just fit over the bottle. You put one cylinder over the bottle, the other over the glass, and then the bottle and glass change places at will under the cylinders.

The covers are the one part of the outfit that looks entirely like "magic apparatus"; but there is nothing wrong with them, and you can throw them around so casually that people will soon accept them at face value.

All the trickery is in the bottle. Actually there are two, both made of tin, and one fits over the other. The outer one is a mere hollow shell, with no bottom and no cork. The inner one has a bottom up near the neck, and is usually shown corked at the start of the trick. Each bottle has a hole cut in the side opposite the label.

In addition, you have a duplicate glass.

The routine is that you start with the two bottles nested; the top compartment of the inner bottle is full of beer, or whatever the bottle is supposed to contain, and the cork is in place. The nested bottles stand on the table with the duplicate glass inside (hence the raised bottom of the inner bottle).

You show off the two covers; you could hand them for examination except that this would emphasize your not handing out the bottle. My own suggestion would be to toss one cover up in each hand, flipping it over, and then to lay the two down on their sides so that the audience can see through them.

Next you uncork the bottle, pick it up—holding the duplicate glass in place by a finger tip stuck through the hole at the back—and pour out a drink. Drink it up, but don't put the cork back in. Set the bottle and glass down on the table, fairly well separated.

Now you explain that either cover will fit over either the glass or the bottle. Set one cover over the glass, then over the bottle, then lift it off the bottle and set it behind the glass. When you lift the cover off the bottle, lift it by the sides, squeezing gently, and the outer bottle comes off with the cover.

Then put the other cover first over the glass, then over the (remaining) bottle. Put the loaded cover over the glass, and you are set to make bottle and glass keep changing places as often as the audience remains amused. You can pick up the bottle inside the cover either by squeezing the outside or by poking your middle finger in at the top and stopping the mouth of the bottle. Whenever you like, you can pick up the visible bottle, and keep the glass inside it by pressure through the side hole.

At the end, you can pour yourself another drink, or (better yet) hand one out to the audience. You should plan your routine to leave the two bottles nested again.

4. Liquid Tricks. Apparatus designed to handle liquids generally works on the principle that water will not flow out of a single small hole in a closed container because air pressure keeps it in. If you open a second hole, the water flows out.

The oldest liquid trick has enjoyed a great revival in the past fifteen or twenty years: pouring many liquors from one vessel. In the seventeenth century this was known as the Inexhaustible Keg; by the nineteenth, a bottle with five interior compartments controlled by air holes to correspond to the finger tips had replaced the keg. The effect of inexhaustibility was produced by switching bottles as the supply ran low. Modern performers have used teakettles, pitchers, and cocktail shakers. The tremendous variety of drinks is accounted for by the presence on the table of a great many glasses, each with a few drops of a different flavoring essence in the bottom; the body of the drink is plain brandy or neutral spirits.

So much for history, past and current; the following standard liquid tricks are of more general use.

4a. The Lota. This is not an independent trick but a piece of apparatus that makes an excellent comedy obbligato (or "running gag") for almost any set program. You show a metal vessel halfway between a deep bowl and a vase. (I have seen some plastic ones that were practically indistinguishable from cuspidors; and, while the association may be disarming, I feel that the magical effect is substantially lessened.) It is full of water, which you pour out.

Periodically throughout the act you turn the lota upside down again, and each time it emits another gush of water.

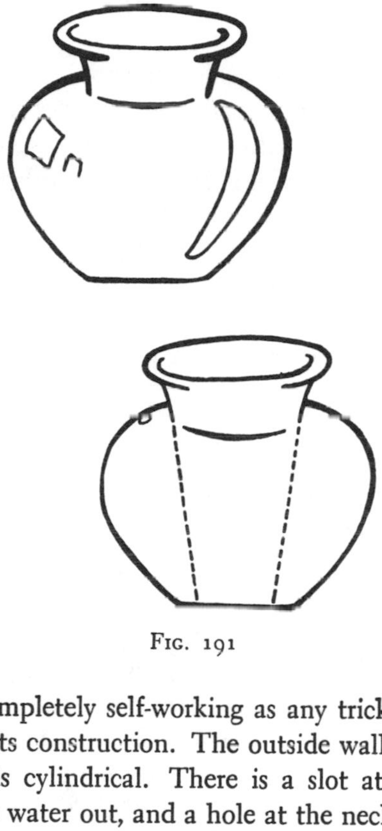

Fig. 191

The lota is as completely self-working as any trick in magic. Fig. 191 shows a diagram of its construction. The outside walls bulge very sharply, whereas the inside is cylindrical. There is a slot at the bottom of the inside wall to let the water out, and a hole at the neck of the outside wall to let air in. You prepare for the trick by standing the lota under a faucet and letting the water run until the lota is full. Lotas come in many shapes and sizes and differ greatly as to speed of flow.

When the lota is full, all you must do is put your thumb over the air hole before you pour out the first load. The moment you set the vessel down, water flows from the outer chamber into the center until it reaches its own level. At any time from then on you can pick up the lota, cover the air hole again, and pour out another load. Of course each load is smaller than the last—an unfortunate feature that makes it necessary to intersperse other effects, giving people time to forget the size of the previous load.

I sometimes use two small lotas, one filled with liquor and one with soda water; you can offer people drinks without making the small load so conspicuous.

The lota is a real East Indian trick, and its name is simply the common word for water vessel. The East Indian magicians load their lotas right in front of the audience by the simple expedient of dunking them in a bucket.

4b. The Rice Bowls. This is another trick that looks Oriental and is Oriental. There have been several methods devised to copy the East Indian effect. Though they satisfy the craze for having things examined, I don't think them nearly so neat as the original way.

The effect is that you show two bowls—brass in the East Indian version, white china in the imitations. One bowl you fill with rice. You clap the other bowl over it, and in a moment there is twice as much rice. It overflows on the table. You level it off with the upper bowl. In another moment the rice has turned to water, which you pour merrily back and forth from bowl to bowl.

One of the bowls is just a bowl. The other is a sort of lota, with the inside shallow instead of cylindrical. The outer air hole is at the middle of the bottom, and the inner water hole is near the rim of the bowl.

To work the trick, you fill the secret compartment of the faked bowl with water and plug the air hole with a bit of diachylon plaster. Then you put it mouth down on a tray, and the plain bowl mouth down on top of the faked one. You also need a bag of rice.

You pick up a bowl in each hand, toss them in the air, and possibly bang them mouth to mouth. Then set down the plain bowl mouth up, the loaded one mouth down. Fill the plain bowl about level full of rice. Sweep the loaded bowl across the top of the rice, and set it down over the plain bowl.

Now pick up the two bowls as a unit and wave them over your head. But in picking them up, put your thumbs forward and your fingers to the rear. After the proper amount of shaking, set the bowls down, this time with your thumbs to the rear. You have thus turned the bowls over.

The loaded bowl is less than half as big inside as the plain bowl. Consequently the rice towers in a great heap, spilling off in every direction.

Level this off with the plain bowl, privately trying to scoop away as much rice as possible. Pick up the two bowls, making your turnover again. When you set them down, scrape off the wax from the air hole. Of course the water starts running into the lower bowl, and a moment later you separate the bowls, pouring the water to and fro. The small remaining amount of rice is lost in the gush of water, which keeps increasing until the secret chamber of the loaded bowl is empty.

Various expedients (such as a raised false bottom in the bag of rice) have been devised to switch the loaded bowl for an ordinary one before or after the trick; but I seriously question whether they are worth while.

4c. The Funnel. Here is another evergreen old-timer—an empty funnel that pours out water on command. It is double, with an air hole (to be plugged with wax) at the top of the handle.

Of course the funnel is not an independent effect but is used for comedy in some set trick with liquids. Its most familiar job is to recover from a boy's elbow some water or soda pop that you have just given the victim to drink. You make him bend one elbow, under which you hold the funnel. You or another volunteer work the other arm up and down as a pump handle, and the liquid comes out through the funnel. I think a country audience would be much amused if the first pumping produced no results and the volunteer had to be primed with another drink.

4d. The Ching Ling Foo Water Can. This is the crudest piece of standard apparatus for liquids—a tin vessel shaped like Fig. 192. The dotted line represents an extra inner wall at one side of the can. The compartment thus formed is closed at the top and open at the bottom. Obviously, you can pour water from the can by turning the secret chamber uppermost; by turning it downward, you catch the liquid. The can may be turned upside down and spun on the end of your wand while loaded. Since the inside is painted dead black, a casual glimpse within will probably not tell the audience anything; but they shouldn't have the glimpse if you can help it.

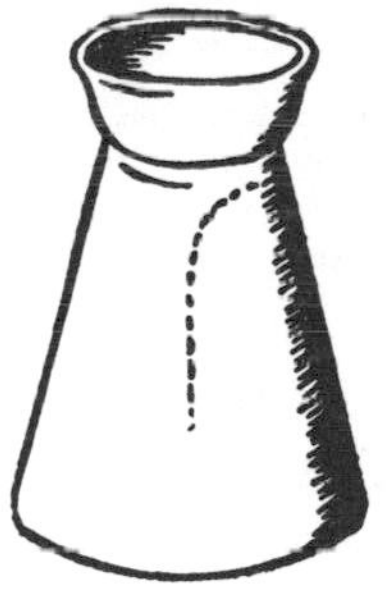

From *An Introduction to Magic* by Sherman Ripley (Sentinel Books)

FIG. 192

5. *Productions.* When the layman thinks of magic, four times out of five he thinks of the rabbit from a silk hat—a production. It seems to me as if productions had suffered a decline in favor among magicians during the past twenty years or so. The silk hat has disappeared altogether; and conceivably the good taste of professional magicians has been sufficient to make them shy away from the more obvious "production" contraptions.

Nevertheless, if only for background, you should know something about productions. They rest on a twin foundation: some method of hiding the objects to be produced, and a selection of articles that can be compressed or collapsed when hidden, and that fill a great deal of space when produced.

As for the objects produced, your dealer has paper ribbon, tightly wound into small "mouth coils" or large, flat "tambourine coils"; silks of all sizes, which pack small and fluff out marvelously; and such "spring goods" as collapsible cloth balls, carrots, sausages, even plucked chickens and unplucked skunks. You should be wary in buying spring goods: their collapsible nature is generally obvious, and all you can hope is that the low comedy of a string of sausages in someone's hat will outweigh their not very sausagy look. In the last couple of years some very lifelike rubber articles—fruit, vegetables, bottles, and what not—have been put on the market.

The method of hiding the load varies with each production trick.

5a. *Hat Productions.* These are most effective when done with a borrowed bowler, and so the trick is to hide loads in your clothes or behind furniture, and get them into the hat undetected.

Magicians who work in evening clothes sometimes still use "loading pockets"—pockets with vertical openings inside the breast of a tail coat. If you hold the hat to your chest while saying something to the man you borrowed it from, you can contrive to dump in a load.

The first big load is your only difficulty; after that, you can always find chances to pick up a new load while putting down the articles you have just produced. As a crude sample, you may hang a load on a brad behind a chair, and pick it up with the hat as you spread the silks from your first load over the chair back.

Any excuse to stoop will allow you to load from under your coattails or from behind a chair or table. You can get this excuse by loading in, say, a lemon from your palm, then carelessly turning the hat over and spilling out the lemon.

If you use a table servante (see platform magic), the correct way to load is to put the hat mouth down on the table, your fingers below the brim at the rear. Your middle fingers pick up the load as you lift the hat back and up.

Tambourine coils are often used for the finish of a hat production. You reel them out on the end of your wand with a quick circular motion. Jean Hugard remarks that every so often you must reverse the direction of your circles or you will get snarled up in the paper ribbon and bog down your production.

If you want to know the ultimate limits to which a hat production can be carried, read the description of Hartz's "A Devil of a Hat" in Professor Hoffmann's *Magical Titbits,* usually printed as a supplement to *Later Magic.*

5b. The Tambourine. Tambourine coils were first made for this trick, the description of which I borrow substantially from Lang Neil's *The Modern Conjurer.*

Effect: A small tambourine is improvised by pressing a sheet of paper between two metal rings, and trimming to shape. The performer taps with the wand on the center of the tambourine, making a hole in the paper, through which is drawn an apparently endless strip of colored paper. Finally from this bundle of paper are produced flowers, a rabbit, dove, doll, or candy, as the case may be.

Requisites and preparation: Two metal rings that fit exactly one over the other, so that when a piece of paper is placed between them and they are pressed together the paper is firmly gripped and stretched; a tambourine coil; a sheet of white paper; flowers, or whatever it is desired to produce from the paper at the finish; a pair of scissors.

The rings, paper, and scissors are laid on the table. The coil is slipped under the cloth of the table with its edge about an eighth to a quarter of an inch beyond the table edge, the cloth being previously turned under at the back so as to be flush with the table edge. Whatever is to be produced from the paper is on a servante behind a chair or the table.

Show the rings and paper, then lay one ring on the table, and over it the paper. Press the second ring from above over the first until the paper is tightly gripped, and show it casually to the audience from both sides.

Lay the rings and paper carelessly on the table over the hidden coil as you pick up the scissors in your right hand. Then your left hand takes up the untrimmed tambourine, carrying away the coil behind it inside. Trim off the paper around the tambourine.

Put down the scissors, take your wand, and make as if to play a tune on the tambourine. In a moment, however, you unfortunately break the paper. Reach through, and catch the center end of the tambourine coil, which you start reeling out.

Reel out the coil on your wand until you have a great mass of ribbon. Put down the ribbon long enough to lay aside the tambourine; this gives you a chance to get your last load from the servante, and you produce it from the midst of the ribbon.

5c. The Carpet of Bagdad. Servante loading is the secret of this effect too. You show a small oblong piece of carpet, the more Oriental looking the better—even a prayer rug, if you can find one small enough. You show both sides, then fold it in half, holding the ends together in one hand, with the fold hanging down. The production comes out of the fold.

The load rests on a servante, usually behind the table. To it is tied a piece of stout black thread not quite half as long as the carpet. The other end of the thread is fastened to the middle of one end of the carpet.

So long as you pick up the carpet by the other end, you can handle it quite freely, spinning it around to show both sides. You lay it down for a moment for some reason (such as tugging at your sleeves), then pick it up by the end where the thread is. This lifts the load up behind the middle of the carpet, and you simply swing the lower end back and up, to be caught by the upper hand.

If you wanted to continue loading, you might roll the carpet into a cylinder, rest the lower end on the back of the table, and boldly shove the stuff up from the servante.

5d. The Jap Box. This name covers two quite different production boxes. Nowadays one thinks first of the Jap Hank Box—mahogany, about 5 inches x 8 inches, 5½ inches deep, with no top and a removable bottom with a thumb-sized hole. Box and bottom are separated and shown empty. One side wall has a secret compartment covered by a flap hinged along the lower edge. This contains a load of silks. The hole in the bottom is for your middle finger to reach through and activate the flap.

Some models have compartments in both side walls, and two finger-holes in the bottom to match. The flaps may also have spring catches.

The original Japanese Inexhaustible Box, from the 1800s, still embodies a useful principle. You show it empty by tilting it forward and opening the top, then set it upright and start taking things out.

The box is rectangular, of any dimensions so long as the depth and width are equal. The trick is that the box has two bottoms, fastened at right angles to each other, and at that angle pivoted along one bottom edge of the box (Fig. 193). When the box stands upright, what you might call "the" bottom is flat on the table and doing its normal duty;

the other, or false, bottom is upright against one side of the box. When you tip the box over on the edge where the pivots are, the bottom stays flat on the table, and the false bottom, remaining upright, forms a bottom to the box in its new position.

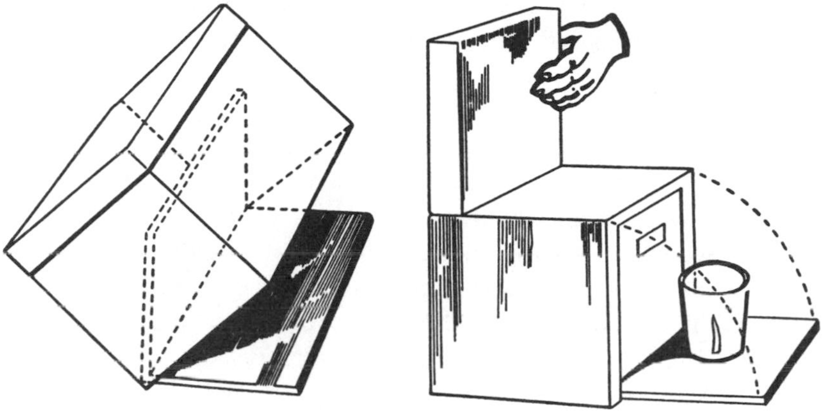

Fig. 193

You merely put your load in the box beforehand. Tip the box over and it looks empty; tip it back, and you can start producing.

When the box is tipped forward, naturally you can lift anything you please off the servante and put it on the bottom.

5e. *The Organ Pipes.* This ingenious production has the usual drawback that the apparatus is made solely to produce things from; still, the tubes are plain enough so that you can defy, even if you don't disarm, people's natural suspicion.

The organ pipes are a series of several (often six) metal tubes, all of them the same height, twelve or fifteen inches, but in diameter graduated downward from about six inches. They stand on a table, a low trestle, or the floor.

You show the biggest tube empty, drop the next one through it by way of emphasis, then show this one empty, drop the next through it, and so on. Then, with no further suspicious moves, you start hauling things out of the tubes.

The loads are hung inside all the tubes except the biggest by picture hooks (painted black, like the inside of the tubes) over the rear edge of the tube. When you drop the second largest tube through the largest, the edge of the latter catches the hook, and so retains the load, while the second tube is momentarily empty, and can be shown. You go through the same procedure with all the other tubes.

One reason for having as many as six tubes is that no load comes from the smallest tube, and you may prefer to lose this in the shuffle.

What you produce is a matter of your own choice. Originally the trick was called The Devil's Supper, and a complete table setting, with bird and bottle, was produced. You got the tablecloth from one of the tubes, and then produced from under the tablecloth two plates, which, since they were bigger around than the tubes, you loaded from under your coat.

6. *The Chinese Wands.* One of the old, old tricks used to be known as the Pillars of Solomon—two sticks with a string running through holes bored side by side in an end of each stick. The string was cut between the sticks yet continued to run back and forth nevertheless. Actually, the string ran down inside one stick, across at the bottom, and up the other stick, instead of crossing where it appeared to. The two "pillars" could not be separated at the bottom.

This was never a very good trick, even in its youth; but some clever Chinese devised what has become the only modern version, and so we have one of the inherently comic effects that will get a laugh from almost any audience.

You have two sticks—bamboo in the original version (which I think is still the best), red lacquered metal in most sets that you buy from dealers. Through the top of each stick runs a string with a button above and a tassel below. The two sticks are altogether separate—no sockets, threads, or other surreptitious connections. If you lift one button, naturally the tassel attached to it rises. The strings run perfectly freely through the holes drilled in the ends of the sticks.

The comedy begins when you pull one button, and incongruously both tassels rise.

Then you drop the button you hold, and its tassel falls again. A moment later, you pull the other button, and once more the wrong tassel rises. When you drop the button you have just pulled, its tassel falls full length.

For a time you hold the sticks together side by side. Then someone will probably demand that you separate them. You separate only the outer ends until the crowd grows altogether too noisy.

Finally, you put one stick under your arm, hold the other away from it at arm's length, and still the wrong tassel rises when you pull the button.

I have given you the whole presentation—everything but the working. The secret is a small cylindrical weight with a pulley at the top inside each stick. If you hold the stick horizontal, and draw the string taut, it will drop down until the button stops it; the pulley offers no hindrance. But if you tilt the stick, the weight slides down to the lower end, drawing the string with it. When you pull up on one button, and want the other tassel to rise, you merely slope the sticks upward. When you hold the sticks level, they behave normally.

As I say, the comedy of this trick is inherent. Attempts to strengthen it by "funny" patter are usually a mistake.

7. *The Linking Rings.* Here we have another real Chinese trick, introduced to the Occident in the early nineteenth century by the brilliant French performer who called himself Phillippe. The outstanding feature of Chinese magic is its misdirection; and the Linking Rings is misdirection at its best.

The plot of the trick is absolutely simple and magical: you link and unlink solid steel rings. Though you may make chains and figures, basically what you do is link and unlink the rings.

Misdirection comes into play in that the audience believes you are constantly linking rings that they have inspected and found solid; whereas really you don't perform the linking action more than half a dozen times throughout the trick. The rest is just association.

To succeed with the Linking Rings you must be deft, graceful, and not talk too much. You must also learn some one routine absolutely by heart.

I am giving only parts of a routine; you can plan a finished product to suit yourself.

The outfit consists usually of eight chromium-plated steel rings, eight inches in diameter and a quarter of an inch thick for close-up work, perhaps a foot in diameter and five-eighths of an inch thick for the platform. Only two of the rings are what the audience supposes them all to be—solid, separate circles. Two more are permanently linked, three are permanently formed into a chain, and one has a cut or opening a trifle wider than the thickness of the ring. Of course all the actual linking and unlinking you can do is with this "key" ring. The clever planning of your routine makes people suppose the linking is indiscriminate.

The one special move to be learned is the art of linking or unlinking the key ring from a solid ring. Hold one ring in each hand as in Fig. 194. Slide the key ring straight down and straight up, the solid ring straight up and straight down. When the solid ring goes past the break in the key, your right forefinger simply puts it through. Don't turn or "hook" either ring.

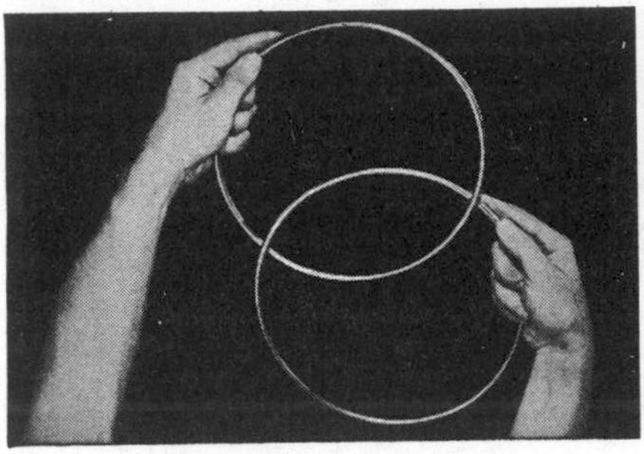

FIG. 194

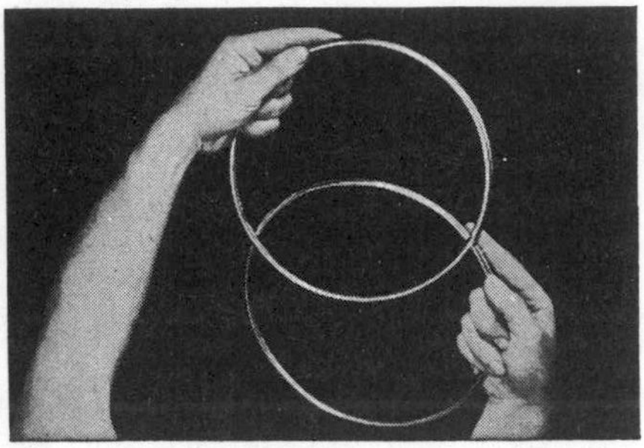

FIG. 195

Separating the rings is the exact reverse of the movement (Fig. 195).

A more spectacular way to join the rings is by "driving" the key ring through the solid one. Hold the solid ring upright in your left hand; hold the key ring crosswise and tap it on the solid ring. At about the third tap, you let the key ring pass into the solid one as in Fig. 196.

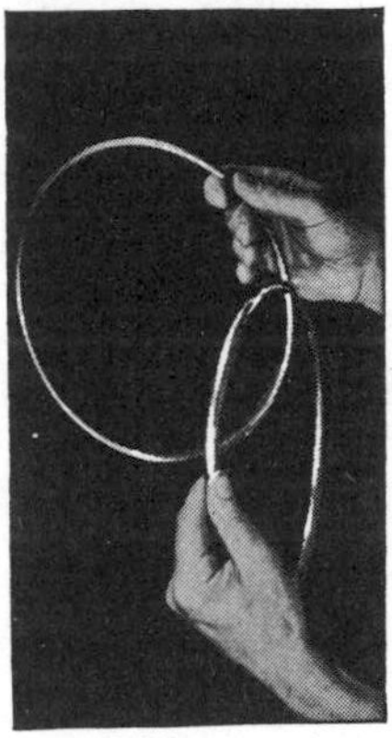

FIG. 196

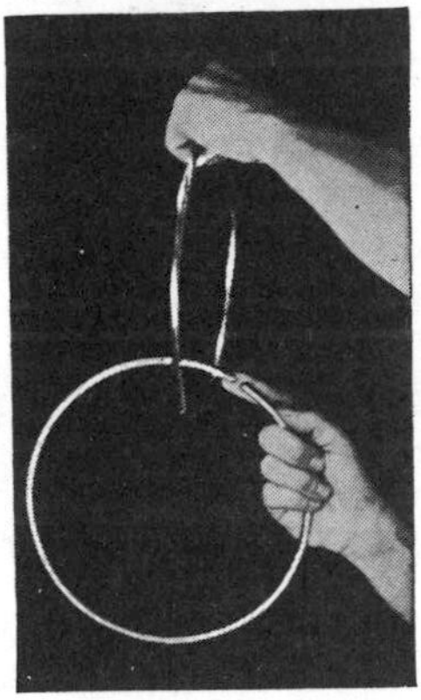

FIG. 197

To drive the rings apart, hold the solid one upright and knock the key ring against the bottom (Fig. 197).

Once you have learned these moves, the rest is routine.

Start with all the rings over your left arm—the three linked rings nearest the elbow, then the key ring, then the two linked rings, then the two separate ones.

You may count them by holding them in your left hand, holding your right hand not quite the diameter of the rings below, and dropping the rings one at a time, counting as you do so. In this way even the linked rings can be counted separately without betraying their connections.

Hand the two single rings to a spectator, and ask him to link them for you. Just as he is starting to try, pick up the two joined rings in your right hand, give them a shake, and let one fall. "Like this, I mean," you say. Allow him time to wrestle a little longer, then hand the two linked rings to someone else. "Well, maybe it's easier to take these apart."

Take the key ring in your right hand, and retrieve the separate rings from the spectator.

"See? Like this." Take a solid ring in your left hand, and link it with the key. "Just link them so, and then take them apart so." You unlink them again.

The really deceptive way to do the unlinking is to separate the rings as shown in Fig. 195, but keep the right ring pressed against the left one. Then walk up close to someone, and draw the rings slowly apart. The bright plating confuses the eye so that you can hardly tell when the rings are really linked, so this slow separation is perfectly baffling.

The various routines diverge somewhat at this point. Probably you will "link" the chain of three, link the key ring to that, and then the two joined rings to the key, making a swinging, clashing chain of six. Then you unlink the two from the key, and with the key and three are ready to start the figures.

With the key ring at the top, in your right hand, bring up the bottom ring of the chain, and link it into the key so that it rests parallel with the one already through the key ring. Don't hesitate, but clap the now dangling bottom (originally middle) ring up against the key. "One of the most difficult things you can do—linking two rings into two."

Fig. 198

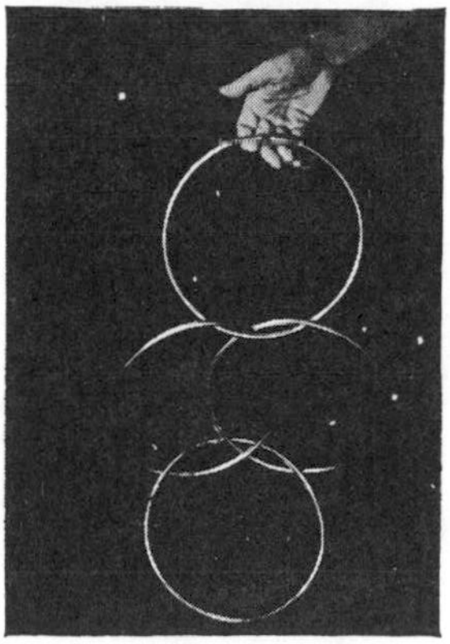

Fig. 199

Then let the solid ring beside the key fall again. "A chain of three." (Fig. 198.)

"A garden chair." Reach between the two middle rings, catch the top of the dangling ring, and pull it up and forward until the rings make the figure shown in Fig. 199.

"A globe." Catch the bottom of the lowest ring, pull it up (Fig. 200), and grab it in your right hand along with the key (Fig. 201). If you revolve your wrist, the figure looks even more like a globe.

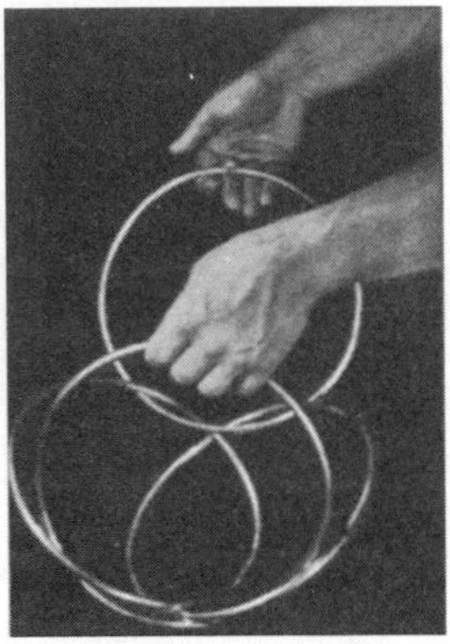

FIG. 200

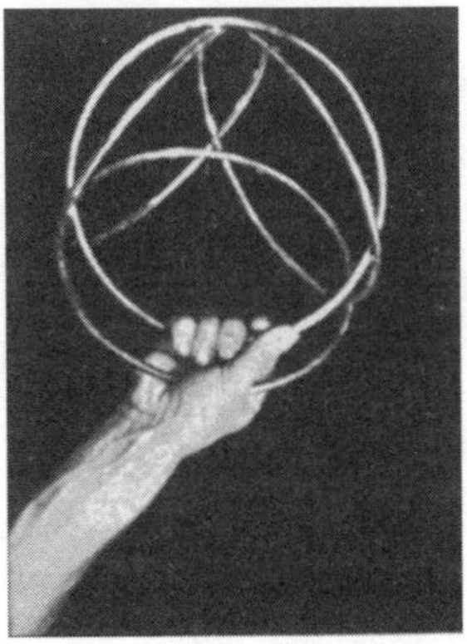

FIG. 201

"The lotus blossom opening." Relax your grip very, very gradually, and the four rings will part at the top (Fig. 202), opening into Fig. 203. Sometimes you have to help them at the start with your free hand.

The "falling link" is done with the four rings in a straight chain again.

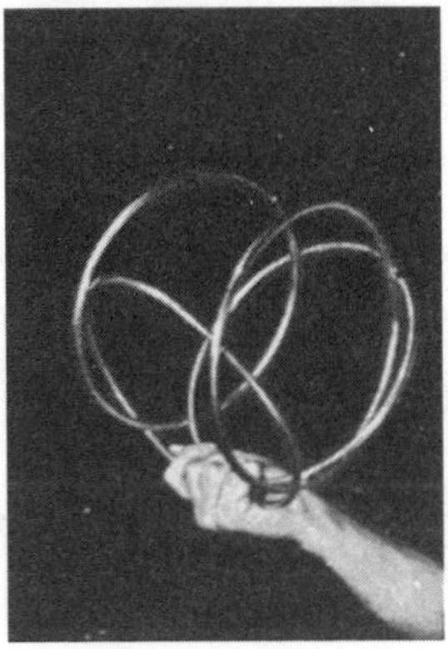

FIG. 202

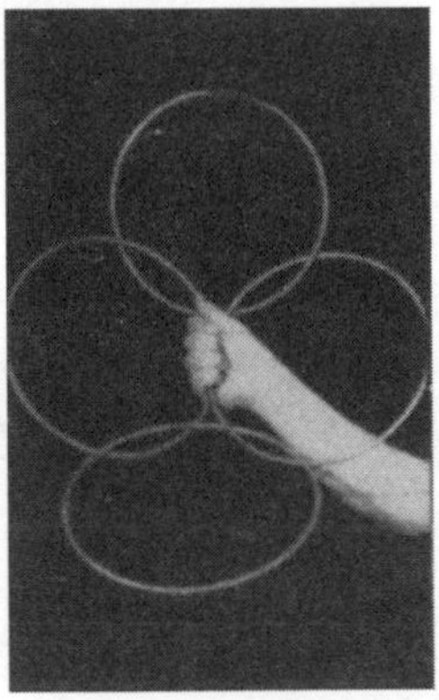

FIG. 203

Hold the chain by the key ring in your right hand. Give the chain a sharp twist to the left, so that all the rings swing as far around as they will go. Then take the bottom ring in your left hand, palm to the front and thumb to the right, so as to give one more twist. This folds the next to the bottom ring over on the bottom ring. Raise your left hand and lower your right (Fig. 204).

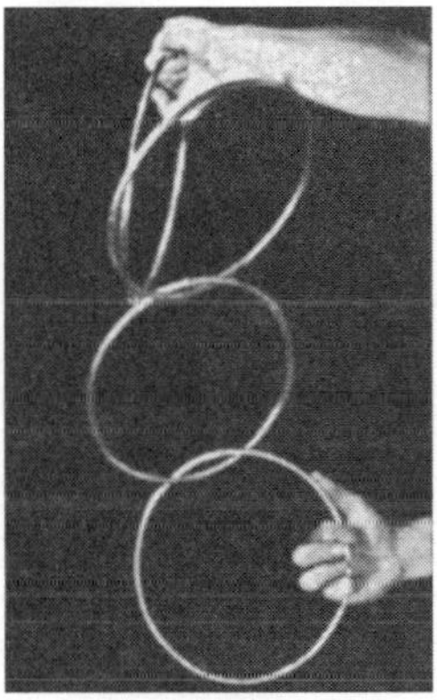

FIG. 204

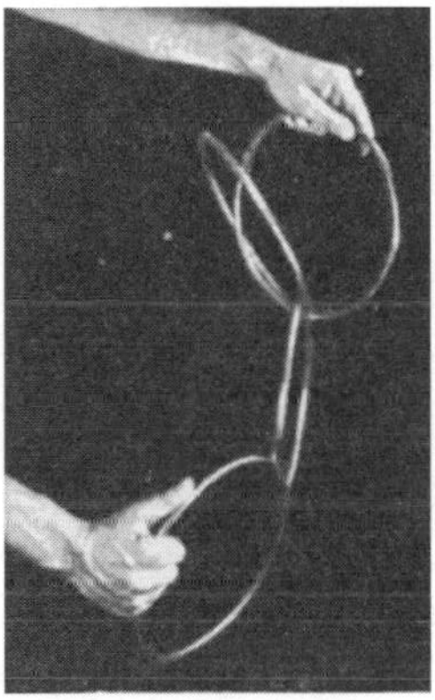

FIG. 205

If you loosen up on your grip of the chain, the ring folded over the left-hand one will flop down (Fig. 205), followed by the next one (Fig.

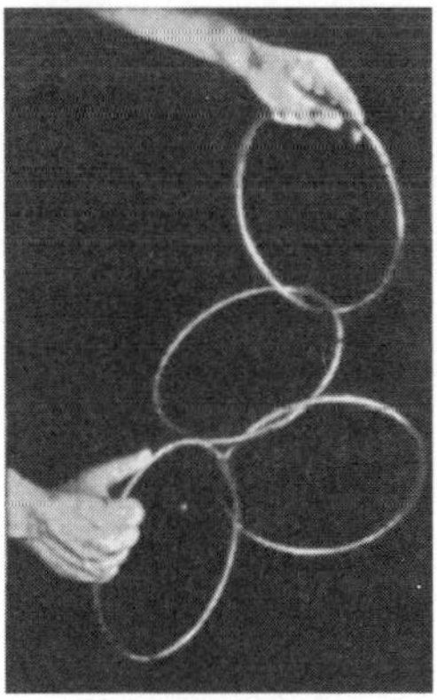

FIG. 206

206), and finally by the key ring, which you can instantly unhook, giving the effect that one link has traveled right down the chain and fallen off.

There are many different conclusions; simply bunching all the rings together and putting them aside after one of the spectacular figures is one perfectly sound way to advertise that the trick is done.

There is an extremely useful chapter on "The Chinese Rings" in *Gre·iter Magic,* besides which Dariel Fitzkee has practically exhausted the subject in his book, *Rings in Your Fingers.*

PART FOUR

18. Mental Magic

I MAKE no apology for basing this chapter on the work of Theo Annemann. If you want to specialize in mental tricks, the first thing you will have to do is relinquish several dollars for *Annemann's Practical Mental Effects.* Annemann was not the highest-paid "mentalist" of his time, but he did the widest and clearest thinking about mental tricks. He was constantly shearing away complications and fancy moves. He never forgot to ask himself, How would a real magician do it?

This is particularly necessary in mental effects because usually there is not much for the audience to look at; and without complications there is too often no trick.

Recent magical generations have also come to swear by *Corinda's Thirteen Steps to Mentalism,* a stout volume broken down into sections on nail writers, pencil, lip, sound, touch, and muscle reading, mnemonics, predictions, blindfolds, bullets, two-person telepathy, etc.

1. *Magician or Mind Reader?* Annemann recommends this as an opener for a mental act. You begin by saying that people often want to know the difference between a magician and a mind reader. Well, you say, a magician would have somebody draw a card, look at it, shuffle it back into the pack, and then the magician would find it.

And this is what a mind reader does. You bring out two packs of cards in their cases. Have a volunteer choose either pack and put it in his pocket. You take out the other deck. "The mind reader just fans the cards without looking at them, and lets some stranger remember any card he likes."

Your volunteer does so. Then you shuffle the pack and give it to the spectator. You remind him that he has not touched the cards; the selection remains locked in his mind. And now he himself is to take the pack and spell out the card he was thinking of. Naturally the correct card turns up on the last letter.

This, you point out, could have been done only by your reading the volunteer's mind, and then putting his card in the correct place.

But what would the volunteer say if you were to tell him that you knew before the performance what card he would think of?

The rudeness of his reply may vary, but the answer will not—nonsense!

All right, let him take the deck out of his pocket, remove it from the case, and spell out his card again.

Once more it turns up right.

Now does he believe you?

No matter what he says, you next pull a sealed envelope from your pocket. He tears it open, and inside is a slip saying, "You are going to think of the" (whatever the card is).

Since you have already learned the mental-selection Spelling Master (chapter 5, section *4b*), I need only tell you that both decks are set up with the same six cards ready to spell out. As for the prediction in the envelope, you have six different ones in different pockets, or arranged in order in one pocket.

2. *The Psychic Slate Test.* This is Annemann at his best—the method utterly simple, the presentation striking yet not pretentious. Most slate tests are rather flat, but here Annemann contrives to give people something to look at besides.

You announce that the image of a card can definitely be transmitted by thought waves alone. You have a pack of cards and two plain school slates. Spread the cards on the table face down, and let a spectator look at one.

Tell him that if it is a face card he is to put it back and take another, because pictures are altogether too hard to transmit; spot cards are all you have managed to receive so far.

Next give him a piece of chalk and send him to a far corner of the room. You take the other slate and some more chalk, and go to the opposite corner.

Have him draw on his slate the best picture he can of the card in his mind.

You stand there, concentrating intently to catch the thought waves. As he draws, so do you.

When both slates are turned over, the pictures are the same.

Instead of a mental marvel, this trick becomes a marvel of showmanship when you know that the spectator chooses his card from a set-up pack (chapter 13, section 3). After his card is removed, you pick up the part of the deck above it, then drop the remainder on top of that. A glance at the bottom card gives you a very clear mental image of the next one in the setup, which the spectator is so assiduously drawing on his slate.

3. *Extrasensory Perception.* This is a version of the last trick, but even better and even easier.

Instead of playing cards, you use thirty-two pieces of white drawing or bristol board five inches square. On each one a different simple design is drawn boldly in black India ink. You may use a circle, a crescent, a dollar sign, a star, a stylized flower, a flag, and so on—thirty-two different elementary drawings.

In addition, you have a school slate and a piece of chalk.

You show off the cards, spreading them casually in your hands, and explain that pictures are easier to visualize than letters or figures. You mix the cards up in a casual way, lay the stack face down on the slate, and then ask someone to pick off a bunch of the cards. He is to hold it against his chest for the time being, so that no one can see the drawing at the bottom of the bunch.

You go on to three or four other spectators, who also lift off bunches of cards. You put away the few remaining cards.

Now you ask one volunteer to look at the bottom card of his stack and concentrate on it hard. You too seem to concentrate; then you make a sketch on the slate. When you turn it over, it is the same as the drawing the man was concentrating on.

You do the same with the other volunteers.

I think Annemann's working here is the nearest human approach to perfection. After you make your drawings on the cards, mix them at random; then draw a series of tiny sketches in pencil on the middle of your slate, reproducing the order in which the cards happen to lie. You thus have a haphazard setup before your eyes, with nothing to memorize.

In mixing the cards, slide a few off the top of the stack into your right hand, then a few from the bottom of the pack on top of those in the right hand, then some from the top of the left stack underneath the right stack, then some from underneath the left stack on top of the right stack. This is known as the Charlier false shuffle, and the very clumsiness that renders it useless to the modern card worker is its best recommendation for this trick. It leaves the cards cut, but not disarranged.

The rest of the working will be obvious. After the last man has taken his cut of cards, you glance at the top card left behind. Your penciled setup shows you what design is on the bottom of the volunteer's stack.

After you have reproduced his drawing, which you do in such a way as to obscure the penciled list, you take back his stack of cards. A glance at the top card tips you off to the one at the face of the next man's stack; so you go through the line.

4. The Stolen-Center Ruse. This is one of the very best and cleanest ways to read a message written by a spectator. "Message" is perhaps not the word, since what the spectator writes must be confined to a small area; but anyway, here it is.

If you take any piece of paper about two by three inches, and fold it in quarters, naturally there is one corner where folds only, no single edges, meet. If you tear the folded paper in quarters, and keep the corner I have just mentioned, you will have a surprisingly large area from the middle of the slip intact.

The customary method is to draw a circle about an inch in diameter at the exact center of the slip. "To concentrate the impression" you ask a spectator to write only inside the circle.

You then tear up the folded slip, and burn it—all but the stolen center. This you open out behind the screen of a notebook or pad as you try to reproduce with a pencil what the victim has written.

Annemann, ingenious as always, turns this method into a first-rate publicity effect.

Publicity effects are not very necessary to an amateur who works only for his friends, but they are part of the professional's bread and butter. A good publicity trick is one that can be worked apparently impromptu on newspapermen—something to convince them that your powers are news. The ordinary conjuring trick merely puts you in a class with all the other wizards who pay for advertising space. Something like what follows will lift you out of that category.

Take any newspaper that comes to hand, and tear out of the reading matter (rather than the ads) a piece about two by three inches. Hand it to your victim, and tell him to ring with a pencil any word he likes. Then he is to fold the piece of newspaper in half, with the circled word inside, and in half again. All this time he is to keep concentrating on the word he has ringed.

The rest of the working is obvious enough. You tear up the paper, drop the bits (minus the stolen center) in an ash tray, and set fire to them. If you work seated at a table—the best way—you can unfold the center in your lap to read it.

5. *Question and Answer.* In chapter 16 I gave a billet switch with a thumb tip. This is the trick for which it was devised.

You have someone write on a slip of paper a question that he wants answered. He folds it up, and a second spectator puts his initials on it, and holds it in plain sight.

You write something on another slip of paper, crumple it up, and get a third spectator to hold it.

Now you unfold the slip held by spectator No. 2, and read the question aloud. Spectator No. 3 opens out his slip, and finds that you have written an answer to the question.

The slips are about two by three, previously folded as described for the billet switch—in half the long way, then in thirds crosswise. A blank slip thus folded is in the thumb tip where you can get it. The other slips, unfolded, are in your left coat pocket.

Bring out the slips from your pocket, hand one to the first volunteer, and put the other slips back in the pocket.

As he writes his question, you have plenty of chance to steal the thumb tip.

Have the man refold his slip and put it on your left palm.

You now make the billet switch and walk over with the substitute to spectator No. 2. He puts his initials on the outside and holds the slip over his head.

Turning away from him, you stick your left hand in your coat pocket, drop the thumb tip, and unfold the stolen slip flat in front of the others in your pocket.

Bring out the bundle of slips, swiftly memorize the question, and draw a blank slip from the bottom of the pile. Put the other slips away again.

With the blank slip you say you are going to do automatic writing. Write some sort of answer, the best you can, to the question you have just read.

Crumple up the slip instead of folding it; you want the two visible slips plainly distinguished. Have spectator No. 3 hold that.

Take the initialed substitute slip from spectator No. 2, open it, and pretend to read the question aloud. Actually you just repeat what you memorized from the slip now in your pocket.

Stuff the substitute slip also in your pocket and have spectator No. 2 read what he finds on the crumpled slip—a direct answer to the question.

6. *Stuart Robson's Newspaper Test.* The same switch with a thumb tip plays a part in a beautifully clean and direct "newspaper test"—you read a classified advertisement secretly chosen from the day's paper.

"In book tests and effects of this nature," remarks Annemann, right as usual, "I have always objected to the introduction of . . . foreign objects such as cards, dice, counters, numbered papers and what not that immediately gave the effect an air of preparedness and trickery."

Stuart Robson, the New York dealer whose hobby was thumb tips, did away with all the nonsense. He simply took a newspaper—it could be a borrowed one so long as he had two minutes alone with it beforehand—and tore out a page of classified ads, which a volunteer held.

Then he tore off the upper right corner of the entire newspaper, containing the page numbers. Someone chose a corner scrap, and the volunteer used the number on one side (his option) to indicate a column, the number on the other to indicate an advertisement in that column.

Robson gave the substance of the ad by "telepathy" from twenty feet off.

The two minutes' preparation is as follows: tear off the upper right corner of one sheet, making sure that the even page number is not higher than the number of advertising columns on a page. Say the numbers are five and six: on the ad you are going to tear out, read and remember the sixth ad in column five and the fifth ad in column six. Wad up the stolen corner and put it in your thumb tip.

In the routine, start by tearing out the ad page and giving it to a volunteer. Then, with one deft motion, tear off the upper right corners of the remaining pages, and drop them into a hat or bowl.

Ask another spectator to mix them up well, pick one out, and crumple it into a pellet without looking at it. Meanwhile you get the thumb tip on to your right thumb.

He gives you his pellet; you make the switch by means of the thumb tip in handing the pellet to the spectator who holds the page of ads. Walking away, you drop the tip and the original pellet into your left pocket.

All that remains is for you to watch the volunteer counting columns: you can tell from behind the page which column it is, and from that you know which ad to "read off."

As a matter of fact, any reasonably competent sleight-of-hand operator could make the pellet switch from hand to hand or by the De Manche change without the thumb tip. What matters is the admirable straightforwardness of the whole effect.

7. *Sid Lorraine's Forty Thousand Words.* I had my unenthusiastic say about book tests in chapter 2, and Ted Annemann had his in the previous section. Here is a version that meets all our objections, and also gives the volunteer something more interesting to do than counting pages and words. Lorraine's presentation is alone among book tests in exploiting the dictionary as a source of fascination instead of merely a lottery.

You hand somebody a pocket dictionary. Lorraine used one about three by six inches, bearing the cover title *Webster Dictionary—Forty Thousand Words,* which gave him his name for the trick. Literal pocket size is the only technical essential.

"When you ask a person to think of a word," you say, "he often finds it difficult on the spur of the moment to name a hard one. He may think of 'house' or 'rabbit,' but scarcely of anything like 'muscovado' or 'antidisestablishmentarianism.'

"That's why we'll use a dictionary. You can pick out a word as unusual as you like, and still there won't be any arguments over whether you dreamed it up yourself. Besides, you can read the definition. Naturally it's easier for me to get an impression of an idea than just of a collection of letters.

"All right, will you please hunt out a word that takes your fancy? And read over the definition? Thank you.

"And now if you'd write the word—not the definition, just the word—on one of these cards, and turn that face down on the table.

"If you'll concentrate on the word, and perhaps back it up with a bit of the definition, let one try to get an impression of what it is.

"Mmm . . . Lll . . . Sss . . . I don't really seem to be getting it. Rrr . . . Uh . . . Nope.

"Here, would you slip the card into the dictionary for a moment? Keep it face down, of course. You can concentrate more actively, and so can I, if nobody actually sees it.

"All right, would you take the card back and put it in your pocket? We want it out of harm's way.

"Hmm. I'm beginning to get the feel of a word . . . Sss . . . Ses. . . . Do you mind if I use the dictionary too?

"Ah. *Sesquipedalian.* 'Of a word, cumbrous and pedantic.'

"Would you let our friends see your card now, to show them I hit the right word?"

For this miracle you need two identical pocket dictionaries and a handful of blank calling cards whose longer dimension is about one-third greater than the width of the dictionary—in the case of Lorraine's three-by-six volume, say four inches.

One of the dictionaries is gimmicked by cutting a horizontal window about one and five-eighths inch by one inch, around mid-height of the book, through all the pages from 10 or 12 on to the back, including the back cover. The front cover, title page, and a few more are normal (not that you want to show them, at least not "intentionally").

Put the faked dictionary in your right coat pocket. The straight book and the cards are on the table.

The patter outline above gives you the main sequence of events. The trick moves are as follows:

After the volunteer has written on his card and turned it face down, you retrieve the dictionary without saying anything, and stick it in your right coat pocket. It seems to be rather an awkward fit, so with the same motion you pull out the window book and put it front-side-up on the table.

You make as much of your unsuccessful mind-searching as you think the crowd will believe, then hold out the dictionary with the edge toward the volunteer, letting him insert the card crosswise. What he must do, though you'll hardly tell him so, is get his word in the window.

Take the book in one hand, then lay it flat on the table. In the process you must tilt it just enough to read the word through the opening. Lorraine advised turning the front edge upward and saying that the volunteer had given you an unconscious hint by sticking the card in the letter S, which narrowed your field since there were four thousand words or so starting with S. I'm a little doubtful about this, partly because you might seem to be stealing a peep by turning the projecting card upward. And you don't want to make the insertion of the card in the dictionary any more interesting than necessary; you'd like it forgotten.

I think you might do better to tilt the backbone up in laying the book with exaggerated fairness on the table. Try it for yourself and see what works best.

After the volunteer has taken his card back and pocketed it, you start getting your impression, then pick up the dictionary to verify this. Unless the printed word has been eliminated by the windows, you find it and read off the definition (keeping your right hand thick and heavy over the back book cover). If it's missing, you know the word at least.

When the volunteer's written card is being shown around, you can switch dictionaries again.

As I hinted to start with, Lorraine's book test is admirable because it makes your volunteer feel like a personality rather than like your errand boy. You can discuss words with him at the beginning, suggesting that he not pick one he'd be afraid to have anyone read out loud, or that you'd find *psychic* more flattering than *charlatan*, but anything he likes, anything at all. Lorraine himself closed the number with a gag about someone who had chosen the word *nothing*, which made it hard to read what was in his mind.

It will all depend on you and on the mood of your crowd. Anyhow, if I ever ventured on a book test it would be this one.

8. *One-Ahead Reading.* You have two or three people write questions on billets, or on blank cards that they seal in envelopes. Then you ask other people to write such things as their telephone numbers, birthdays, or mother's maiden names. The billets or envelopes are mixed, yet you read off the items and answer the questions before you open them.

As you learned in hand magic, chapter 7, section 16, you can read a whole series of folded or sealed messages if you can just manage to discover one of them. For this purpose it has long been customary to plant one question, either getting a friend to write it for you or having him acknowledge as his own a question that you write and load into the pile. For a platform show in a strange place, that is still the usual way.

But at a social gathering Annemann would use another of his marvelous short cuts. In the first place, he found that the writing of "items" instead of questions lent variety to the trick. And in the second place, he coolly asked one spectator to write a specific item (usually the telephone number) that Annemann had just contrived to find out.

Then he had only to keep track of that message, "read" it first, and actually open it last in the series.

9. *A Day of Your Life* shows what Annemann could do with familiar elements when he put his mind on it. "Most billet reading routines," he wrote, "depend upon the assistance of several spectators, and there is a need for 'reading' tricks wherein only one person is the subject throughout. I recall occasions [see above, 4, on publicity tricks] when it would have been to my advantage . . . to do a good, solid test for a single person. . . . It is very essential that a test of this sort be personalized so that the subject can truthfully swear that he was given information absolutely impossible for the performer . . . to know. Besides, when you are making someone think of his personal doings, he has to keep his mind on himself, which is to your advantage in working."

You and your subject sit down face to face beside (not across) a table. You say you want to get impressions of a few ordinary events in a day of his life—that day for an evening performance, otherwise the day before.

You give him a piece of paper, and ask him to write down one item of food he had for dinner the night before. He does so, folds the paper, and you put the billet under his right foot, handing him a fresh piece of paper. On this he is to write one dish he had for lunch.

That paper, folded, goes under his left foot. Next he writes on a third slip something he had for breakfast. After a moment's discussion he is asked to clench that in his left fist.

Finally you ask him to put down on a fourth slip the approximate time he got up this morning.

That billet you burn, and read the hour in the smoke.

Next you touch your subject's forehead, and announce his breakfast food. You divine the luncheon and dinner dishes in turn, and wind up, "And those are only some minor details of your day. It's probably just as well if I don't try to get impressions of the important phases of your business."

The trick is typical Annemann: all you need is a pad of paper about two and a quarter by three and a half inches, writing instruments, an ash-tray, and matches. Tear off five or six sheets and fold them once the long way, once and once again the opposite way. Open them all out again except for one, lay them back on the pad, and put the lot in your side coat pocket, loose slips toward the body. The folded dummy is also in the pocket.

And here is the sequence. Take out the pad and stack of slips; remove the top one and give it to the subject for his "dinner" item. Put the packet back in your pocket, finger-palm the dummy, and pull out one fresh slip.

When the spectator has refolded his billet, take it in your right hand (containing the finger-palmed dummy), and with your left give him the new slip.

Suggest putting the "dinner" billet under his right foot, and do so—except that you switch it for the dummy. Already you are "one ahead."

Keeping the "dinner" billet finger-palmed, take another slip from your pocket. Take the billet from the subject in your right hand as before, handing him a fresh one with your left.

Make the switch and put the "dinner" billet (which you describe as the "luncheon" one) under the subject's left foot.

The procedure for the third round is the same except that when you take the "breakfast" billet you don't hand out a new slip. You finger switch as you ask where to put the billet; then say, "Why don't you just hold it in your left fist for safekeeping?" This, says Annemann, is important, because afterward he will always remember that he held his own paper, quite forgetting that you ever touched it.

With the "breakfast" billet palmed, reach in your pocket for the stack of papers and pad; open out the billet on top of the stack before you bring forth the lot. Read the breakfast item, then pull out two loose slips and lay them on top of it.

"Now one last test. Would you sketch here the hands of the clock for the time you got up this morning?" You draw a circle in the center of the top slip, which you pass to the subject.

Return the pad and stack to your pocket. Move the ashtray to the front of the table.

When the subject gives you his folded "clock" billet, take it at your fingertips and open out one fold, so that the paper is folded only once each way. Need I do more than whisper the words "stolen center"?

Set fire to the torn remnants. As they burn, bring out the pad, taking a quick look at the stolen clock face; pull off a blank slip, returning the rest to your pocket.

Gazing into the smoke, draw a duplicate of the clock hands.

Now you start pacing to and fro before the subject, with both hands in your side pockets. Refold and finger palm the "breakfast" slip. Pause, look piercingly at the subject, and name the breakfast food.

Take the paper from his left fist, open it, nod, refold the billet, switch it for the finger-palmed one, and toss that on the table. You now know the luncheon item, and have the appropriate slip finger-palmed.

Ask which foot the "luncheon" paper was under, as if you'd forgotten. The subject gives you what he thinks is the right one—actually the "dinner" slip.

You divine the "luncheon" dish, open the billet, note what was for "dinner," switch, and drop the actual "luncheon" slip on the table.

Finally, pick up the dummy billet from under the subject's right foot. "This is the most important meal of the day," you remark, switching billets and handing the real one to the subject.

"Hold the paper against your forehead and imagine what the food tasted like." You tell him what it was, and he is left with all the correct billets as souvenirs.

Surely this represents absolute perfection in one-ahead reading.

10. *More Alive Than Dead*. "Living-and-dead tests" are popular with mentalists, one supposes, because of the link with spiritualism. This usually means a certain solemnity in presentation, though there's nothing to

prevent your using real people and characters in novels, for instance, to lighten up the tone of the proceedings.

Annemann devised two corkers. For the first, you give your subject four paper slips, asking him to write on them three living names, and one of a person who has passed on. The volunteer folds each slip once each way, with the name inside.

You take the slips one after another, tear them up, and drop them into an ashtray. Each time, you hold a match to the pile of scraps. As the third slip is burning you say, "This is the dead name burning now!" and reveal what it is. The fourth, "live" slip remains on the table.

You will have guessed most of the routine already, but not all. You use four pieces of blank paper two by three inches. Mark one, preferably by nicking it with your thumbnail.

Give the subject a slip, asking him to write the name of a living person; another slip, another living name; another, another living person. The last slip you give him is the nicked one, on which he is to put a dead name. Have all the slips folded in quarters and dropped on the table, where you mix them around a bit.

Pick them up one at a time, tear each into quarters, and set fire to the scraps. The first two times you shake your head; "No, this is a living name."

Pick up the nicked billet third, tear it, steal the center, light the remaining scraps; drop your hands into your lap and read the "dead name." As the flames die down, reveal it. Leave the last "live" slip on the table for people to look at.

Dead or alive is a related effect on a somewhat larger scale, which Annemann recommends for press appearances with more than one "sitter."

You use five or six small blank cards and a "drug envelope," an oblong one opening at the end. Four people write names of living persons; one writes the name of somebody no longer living. The cards are collected by one of the spectators and mixed. You take the pile (writing side down, of course), mix it a little more, then seal the packet in the envelope. Holding this to your forehead, you slowly divine the dead name.

Then you take the cards out of the envelope and spread them around on the table, writing side down. Wave your hand over them and finally pick the card with the dead name, which you hand to the writer.

What you need is the envelope, a stack of blank cards about an inch shorter and correspondingly narrower, and a small pair of scissors. Across the face of the envelope, say half an inch from the flap end, cut a slit going nearly but not quite the full width. Mark one card on the upper left and lower right corners by pressing your thumbnail into it against your forefinger, and put this card on top of the rest. Stow the cards in the envelope until you're ready to show the effect.

And here's the routine. Take out the envelope (don't give anyone a flash of the slitted face), withdraw the cards, and drop the envelope face down on the table.

Ask someone to think of a dead person, and hand him the top (nicked) card to write on. Pass out the rest to other spectators for living names.

Ask someone to collect the cards, writing side down, and mix them on the table. You pick them up and mix them a little more. "Don't try to shuffle them like playing cards or do anything fancy," Annemann warns. "Just mix them carelessly with your two hands while they are held horizontal." In the process, get the nicked card to the bottom of the pile.

Pick up the envelope by the closed end with your left hand; with your right, insert the cards. Shove the bottom, nicked, card a little ahead so that you can guide it through the slit in the face of the envelope; then tilt the outer end of the stack down to prevent the other cards from following. Turn the envelope vertical, with the open flap facing the audience; moisten your right forefinger, rub it down the gummed side of the flap, and seal this by folding it over away from you.

This procedure brings you face to face with the dead name written on the nicked card. No matter if it should be upside down. In carrying the envelope to your forehead you can reverse the envelope as you ask the volunteer to concentrate on the name. This you reveal as impressively as you know how.

Hold the envelopes by the closed end in your left hand, flap side to the audience; with your thumb, draw the exposed card to the left until it is clear of the slit. Then pick up the scissors in your right hand and cut off the end of the envelope along the slit, which thus ceases to give anything away.

Stick your right first and second fingers inside the cut end of the envelope and draw out the cards; your thumb carries the card on the back along with them. Thus you take out all the cards in one motion; drop the envelope, mix the cards again face down, and spread them on the table. Wave your hand slowly over the cards and finally pick out the nicked one, which you turn face up and hand to the volunteer who wrote it.

11. *A Mentalist with Money.* Another class of effects uses paper money, either for the long serial numbers (what chiefly concerns mentalists) or for the thrill of seeing property wantonly destroyed with only the performer's assurance that it will be restored. The serial-number business is easy to overdo; Annemann gets around that here with his usual virtuosity.

This time you borrow everything; first a hat, then seven or eight dollar bills. Before you start collecting the money, ask one volunteer to write his name in pencil on the bill so that he can identify it later. When he has signed it, he is to fold it over and over into a small square. The other prospective lenders are to do the same. Collect the money in the hat, which you hand to a spectator on the other side of the room.

Ask the custodian with the hat to take out one bill while your back is turned, to hold it up, and say, "All right."

"Put it on the table and take another," you say. "No, that's not it either. Put it aside and try again."

About the third or fourth pick, you say, "That's it." You take the bill from him and hand it to the original lender, who finds his signature large as life.

"Wait. Look at the serial number. Don't read it off, just look at it. Now . . . mmmm . . . I get Q 8148825 B. Right?" Right.

The routine: While the man is signing his dollar, you collect a couple from the audience. Take the signed one in your right hand, and in apparently dropping it into the hat, slip it under your left fingers against the sweat band. Then gather the rest of the money.

Hand the hat, minus marked bill, to a spectator across the room. Walk back to the other side of the room and turn your back.

While the custodian is picking bills out of the hat, unfold the marked one in your left hand and memorize the serial number. "You'll find when you try this," says Annemann, "that you have more time than you think. Also you may think it hard to remember the number, but if you'll try this . . . before saying you can't, you'll be surprised." Refold the bill and keep it in your left hand.

When you stop the man with the hat, go over to him and take the bill from him in your right hand. Going toward the lender, pass "the" bill to your left hand, actually palming the one and bringing out the other, signed bill. When he opens it, it's the McCoy. Meanwhile you retrieve the hat and drop in the palmed bill.

Ask him to concentrate on the serial number; "read" it; take your bow, and ask the other lenders to raise their hands so that you can pass back the loot.

Annemann remarks that a somewhat worn bill is easiest to handle.

12. *The Lyons Bill Switch* is not a trick but a neat and ingenious sleight for money, billets, and other paper folded down to roughly an inch and a half square. Its uses are endless.

What apparently happens is that you receive the folded bill in your right hand; crease it more firmly with your left; show both hands and the bill innocent; and take the bill away with your left hand. Ordinarily you won't need to make much play with showing empty hands—the assurance that you can is enough for your peace of mind, and hence for the audience too.

The method of folding is important. It's the same we've been using in this chapter: fold the bill in half lengthwise, then in half crosswise, finally in half crosswise again. This produces a sort of little tent—one and a half by one and a quarter inch with a dollar bill.

Finger-palm your dummy in the left hand, with the last fold (the ridge-pole of the tent) toward your wrist. You'll find the folded paper is exactly the right size.

Instruct your spectator to fold the bill in this way. Take it from him in your right hand, with the last fold outward and the tent held shut between the tips of your thumb and middle fingers.

Bring your hands together, let the palmed bill open out just enough to stuff the right-hand tent into the left-hand tent, and run your left thumb and fingers up and down the last fold to crease it.

This gives you the whole bundle at your right finger tips with no way to tell from any angle that there is more than one bill, and both hands are otherwise empty.

Raise your right thumb so that the outer (dummy) bill opens somewhat; put the thumb on the inner (borrowed) bill, which you draw back into finger-palm position as the left hand carries away the dummy.

Working with dollar bills, you will need two dummies ready, one folded green side out, the other black side out, inventor L. Vosburgh Lyons warns us, because you don't know which way the spectator may fold his bill.

13. *Dr. Daley's Slates.* Annemann's slate tests, described earlier in this chapter, were not the conventional ones used for a century and more by spirit mediums. Neither are Dr. Jacob Daley's, to follow in a moment; but you might as well know what the old methods were.

The easiest depends on a "flap," a sheet of silicate that fits neatly inside the wooden frame of a school slate and looks exactly like the slate itself. Usually you have two slates, one with a message written on it beforehand and covered with the flap. The inside of the flap may also bear writing. You put the unprepared slate over the flap side of the prepared slate; when you turn the two over, the flap drops into the unprepared slate, showing the message.

Al Baker, possibly the most ingenious inventor of small effects and the most truly gifted comedy performer America has had, devised a folding-flap slate in which the flap is loose for only half the length of the slate. Hinged at the center, it is normally locked in place by the frame, which can, however, be slid endwise enough to release the flap. You write something on the slate, then fold back the flap. When you swing it down during the performance, the message appears, and the slate will defy examination.

Dr. Daley, an ingenious amateur, used four silicate flaps, four by five, instead of the customary school slates. He brought them forward in a stack, wiped both sides of each flap with a cloth, and spread them in a row on the table. A spectator indicated any two, and two were put aside. The chosen two were picked up, laid together, and handed to a volunteer to hold. When the flaps were slid apart, nothing appeared. A second attempt also gave no results. But on the third try one flap was completely covered with a message in chalk.

The working: The four flaps are stacked, with the message on the upper side of the third flap from the top. Dot the top flap so that you can always tell the top of the stack.

When you pick up the flaps in your left hand, take a little-finger break between the third and bottom slates. Wipe the face of the top flap with a cloth, then flip the piece over with your right finger and thumb at the lower right corner, as you would a playing card on the deck.

Wipe the side now exposed, and slide the flap off and drop it on the table. Wipe the face of the second slate.

When you go to turn this over, you actually turn the second and third flaps together, the equivalent of a two-card turnover. Wipe the exposed surface and put that flap (with the message on the under side) on the table.

Clean the two remaining flaps in the same way as the others, and put them in their turn on the table. This gives you a row of four flaps; the message is on the under side of the second flap in line.

Ask your spectator to touch any two slates. You either remove or leave his choices, depending on whether they don't or do include the second (message) flap.

Lay the message slate on the other one, and give the two to the volunteer. After an expectant wait, slide the top flap off with your right hand. Nothing.

Put the top slate under the other. (This brings the message to the bottom.) Another wait. Open the two slates bookwise. Still nothing.

Again you put the top flap underneath. This time, however, you turn the two over before giving them back to the volunteer. On your final try the message stares him in the face.

If you look on p. 173 of *Practical Mental Effects* you will find a combination of this trick with the torn center that is hard to beat.

14. *The Mystery of the Blackboard.* Expanding from slates to a large blackboard, Annemann devised an effect that depends, more than almost any I ever heard of, on sheer stage presence; and his planning provides you with the stage presence automatically.

On the platform, stage, or at the front of the room is a blackboard facing the audience, with chalk and an eraser. You announce that you are going to make a difficult experiment in telepathy, for which you need three subjects. They come forward and stand by the blackboard.

You take out a handkerchief and explain that you are about to be blindfolded and led to a far corner of the stage. Each member of your "committee" will then write on the blackboard—one, a three-digit number; the next, a word of at least seven letters; the third, any geometrical diagram that occurs to him. "This covers all the ways of expressing oneself in writing—with figures, letters, and lines."

You are next blindfolded and led off. The committee are set to their task: the word, the figures, the drawing. When they are done, you ask the audience to remember what your volunteers are thinking of. "Never tell them to remember what is on the blackboard," Annemann warns.

Now ask them to erase the blackboard, to lead you to it and give you a piece of chalk.

After a few prefatory marks, you write the number (not too neatly, but very well for someone who is blindfolded), the word, and finally a rather sprawling version of the drawing.

The only actual preparation is to take a large-sized man's handkerchief, roll it inward from opposite corners to the middle, fold it, and put it in your pocket. When it is unfolded and used as a blindfold, you can see straight ahead through the single thickness of fabric at the center. The great secret of the effect, though, is that you *actually keep your eyes tight shut* except for the one crucial moment about to be described. When you really can't see, you act like a blindfolded person; a silent script with a vengeance.

Stand in the corner with your back turned, directing the proceedings up to the point where you ask people to remember what the volunteers are thinking of.

Then you say, "Now, gentlemen, please erase the blackboard thoroughly so as not to leave any trace of what you put there." Here you wave your hand toward the blackboard, swing half around, and open your eyes just long enough to scan the board before it is erased.

Quickly turn back, and shut your eyes. The rest of the effect is performed by the truly-blindfolded you.

Annemann suggests writing the figure and the word, then taking off the blindfold and saying you would like the committee at a distance for the picture test. They go back to their seats, and you make the drawing, which the volunteer verifies (the audience knows anyway). The advantage is that it leaves you alone on the stage to enjoy your triumph.

15. *Taps*. Dr. L. Vosburgh Lyons, the inventor of the Lyons billet switch (12, above), created this little masterpiece. As I mentioned on an earlier page, I once bought a finger tip just for the one trick.

You undertake to produce spirit rapping through the medium of a steel ball isolated between two soup plates. (There is nothing wrong with any of the props.) Drop the ball into a plate three or four times to show off the sound.

Then put the ball back in the plate, invert the other over it, and hold the plates together at your finger tips. Though you keep them steady, with no motion at all, the ball raps several times.

Ask someone to hold the plates while you let another spectator choose a card. Take the plates back, and tell the spectator to concentrate on the number of spots on the card. He is to hold the card in his left hand, and with his right fist to imagine himself knocking on a door once for each spot.

The steel ball follows each imaginary knock with an audible rap.

You could also let him name the suits, rapping for the right one.

The secret, as you already know, is a finger tip, which you wear on either your left or your right third finger. You make the raps on the bottom of the lower plate. Watch your angles, says Dr. Lyons, and don't bare your forearms, because the muscles ripple revealingly.

The card is forced.

PART FIVE · INTIMATE MAGIC

19. *Close-Up Performance*

THE FURTHER the full evening show and the variety turn fade into history, the more likely magicians are to find themselves working under the noses of a small audience.

"Close-up magic is more popular than any other with the amateur, as often it is the only type he gets a chance to perform," Lewis Ganson wrote when I asked him what might most usefully be added to this book.

Actually, of course, a good half (perhaps two-thirds) of the tricks already described can be shown at close quarters: nearly all card tricks; most coin work (the Eureka pass perhaps better than the Miser's Dream); sponge balls; cups and balls, within limits; some cigarette effects; all the material in chapter 14, Varied Head Magic; silk knots; the tricks done with the small gimmicks and fakes in chapter 16 (except for the faked tumblers); the turban trick; the egg bag; the Chinese wands; a good many of the mental tests. The dollar-bill tricks sketched in the appendix are fine.

By this point in your study you'll have no shortage of potential repertoire. Martin Gardner's *Encyclopedia of Impromptu Magic* also lives up to its name.

Probably the best current source is Lewis Ganson's two splendid volumes on *The Art of Close-up Magic*. I was flattered that he opened Volume I with a quotation from these pages: "The surprising thing, really, is that in the electronic age conjuring should have changed so little. The decline of the waistcoat has affected magic more than the invention of communications satellites."

And then he turned around and on p. 25 gave an electronic device of his own that may have enlivened close-up performance quite as much as any single trick since the sponge balls or perhaps long before: it gives the wizard music at his elbow on command.

"Ganson's Personal Orchestra" is a battery-operated, transistorized miniature tape recorder (he uses a Philips 7¾ by 4½ by 2¼ inches) set in a leather attaché case fourteen by nine by four, which also serves as the magician's box of tricks—he carries all his small props in it. The tape cassettes will record thirty minutes on each side.

The performer, says Ganson, sits behind a table and places the case on it, to his right, with the lid opening away from him. All the signs point to a common-or-garden-variety close-up act, one if anything rather tamer than usual.

The performer opens the case and quietly switches on the recorder. Pause. Fanfare of trumpets. Voice: "Introducing . . . Lewis GANSON!"

"Now we act a little over-pleased with ourselves," Ganson explains, which justifies the voice in saying, 'Stop swanking, and get on with it!'

"Performer: 'Sorry.' Recorder: 'Well, they're waiting.' Performer: 'Well, how about some music to get us all in the mood?' "

The recorder thereupon blares out "The Stars and Stripes Forever" until the performer protests. Recorder: "Sorry, try this." The performer then goes into a silent routine, keeping time with the softer music.

"After this, we do not use the recorder again until the end of the act. . . . We perform a selection of close-up routines to patter, then we go to the case again for our Giant Fans and switch on the recorder. Giant Fans are performed to music, finishing with the complete circle of cards which is carried down below table level to the case, and recorder switched off as the cards are ditched. . . .

"Resist the temptation to over-use the recorder. We have found that the novelty is sustained with a short sequence at the beginning as described—it really gets attention and makes them sit up—then a musical finale at the end."

There are now some excellent noncopyright musical recordings, as well as various "effect" records of barking, infants crying, and so on, from which you can splice together whatever you want on your tape.

In thinking about close-up work you may find it useful to subdivide what someone has christened "intimate magic" into three or four forever overlapping groups: the impromptu; the dinner table (almost always at least seemingly impromptu (a special case is treated in chapter 22, section 4, Night-Club Shows); the table show with the performer seated behind, the audience in front, on which Ganson concentrates as the trend of the present day; and "vest-pocket," "micro"-magic with small apparatus.

Impromptus, again, break down technically into things you can really do on the spur of the moment and effects where your first problem is to make someone ask you to show a trick you have secretly prepared for. ("I brought my harp to the party, but nobody asked me to play.")

In either case, deciding *when and whether* to perform intimate magic is an art in itself, just as important as *what* to perform. You have one strategic advantage: you can choose your own public, with regard to both size and gullibility. Henning Nelms carries this further by the process he calls "casting the audience." "Just as you must select a role for yourself that fits your personality, you must select a role that fits the makeup of your audience." As broad categories he lists *onlookers; witnesses; participants; prospects* (to whom the performer pretends to sell something); *pupils;* and *victims of mass hypnosis.*

Whatever the audience, furthermore, you can pick the moment when they are most likely to enjoy your stuff. And you can stop when they have had enough—probably the main consideration.

Still more significant, Nelms points out, is the fact that you can learn to sparkle in a social gathering even without magic. You may arouse interest *before* you talk tricks. "If you have enough interesting material to contribute, you and your friends can discuss a subject like freak shows or extrasensory perception for ten or fifteen minutes merely as conversation and find it pleasant and stimulating. . . . Conjuring [may add] an exciting climax. Nevertheless . . . the conversation can be thoroughly entertaining without the conjuring."

Remember the performer Al Baker used to tell about, who billed himself as "Magician, Ventriloquist, and Entertainer." After the show the program chairman said, "Well, the first two parts were fine. Now how about the entertainment?"

Nelms again: "A young performer often has trouble in arousing interest for an 'impromptu.' If he says, 'Would you like to see a trick?' His friends either say, 'No' or look bored. But if he does not offer to perform, he cannot get started at all. . . .

"The process of establishing the appropriate atmosphere for an 'impromptu' illusion can almost be reduced to a formula. Arouse interest in some topic connected with the illusion." (When Nelms says "illusion" he means a dramatically compelling effect, not a large-scale one.) "Encourage spectators to increase their interest by contributing to the conversation.

Try to start an argument between the spectators. Bring the discussion around to the specific power that you plan to exhibit. If possible, lead someone to challenge you. *Although conviction is weakened when you challenge the spectators to see through a trick, it is strengthened when one of them challenges you to display your powers.*"

Another wise warning he gives is that even impromptus with genuinely innocent props shouldn't be quite impromptu—"You may be compelled to let interest sag for several minutes while you assemble the necessary glass, thread, and pencil." When you read Nelms's book you will see the pains he takes in preparing without letting on.

The opposite extreme is Lewis Ganson, who has a section on containers—the literal packaging of your tricks. Unless you are working entirely out of your suit pockets, he suggests you have a separate pouch or case for each trick, or else store everything in fitted compartments of a special attaché case. "Briefcases, trinket boxes, bags can all be adapted to hold props, the main considerations being convenience of storage, ease of transportation and pleasing appearance."

Another concern of Ganson's is the working surface: "It is desirable to carry some form of covering which can be spread out to work on. . . . We have found that a piece of red felt, 20 inches long by 12 wide, with a border of yellow ribbon, is pleasing to the eye, ideal to work on, and has the additional advantage of focusing all attention on one spot. . . . The covering can be rolled or folded to fit into the container." Elsewhere he calls this mat a "close-up pad."

For a set show, Ganson's system is hard to beat. Sneaking up on people cold, however, you must seduce them with apparent impromptus.

Dinner-table tricks accordingly have not only a couple of obvious technical limitations but a tone-setting peculiarity often overlooked.

Technically you are anchored to one spot; the angles are restrictive, though the table top may also serve you as a screen at times (Ganson puts "lapping" as a standard move on a level with sleeving and vesting); your closest spectators are very close, probably at your elbow, while people farther away at a banquet table may not realize you're performing at all. (Which is practically certain to raise choruses of "Do it again, we didn't see it!" So be prepared. Ganson sometimes does the same ten-minute act at six tables of a dinner party in succession.)

Your tone-setting limitation is that people have gathered expressly to eat and talk among themselves, rather than to watch you. Ordinary conversation being what it is, you can easily claim your share of attention; but a spectacular, interruptive trick will tend to break up the dinner and transform the occasion. This may work (say when you're the guest of honor, or after the dishes have been cleared); if it does, the process is usually self-terminating: you get up from the table and perform for a larger and remoter audience.

You might also put it that dinner tricks are bait for a challenge to do more. Seen in that light, they needn't even always be tricks at all. Puzzles and catches have a place here—usually to be followed up, since you are a magician, by stronger stuff.

Often someone else will start the puzzles. You may then confront the decision whether it's tactful to trump your host's parlor trick: a typical instance where social instinct must take precedence over your professional pride.

One way to steer a middle course is with unpretending little feats on the borderline between joke and trick. These are a prime example of what I said in chapter 2: as a working conjurer, you can carry them off with an air, but if you start your career with them, they won't necessarily make a magician of you.

1. *Matches.* The Linking Matches (chapter 14, section 11) is hard to beat. Then light one match and run the flame along the fingers of your left hand: no damage.

Blow down your left sleeve: the match in your right hand abruptly goes out.

1a. The Fireproof Hand is not a trick but merely a fact: so long as you keep the flame moving, you barely feel the heat at all. (The same thing will work with a napkin twisted ropewise and drawn through a candle flame. If you try it with a handkerchief, beware of perfume or cologne.)

1b. The Extinguisher effect, needless to say, depends 98 per cent on your acting and timing, 2 per cent on the trick, which is as follows: Hold the match near the unlit end between first and second fingers, short end toward the inside of the hand. Snap the short end with your thumbnail, and the jerk puts out the match. Try it a few times until you get the snapping movement down to the essential minimum.

1c. The Balanced Match is sheer clowning, and sometimes useful for that very reason: toss half a matchstick in the air, and catch it upright on the end of your thumb.

Quietly break the match in two beforehand and stick one half under your left thumbnail, hiding it by bending the thumb. Toss up the other half, catch it in your left hand, stick up the thumb. Marvelous.

1d. The Leaping Flame appears when you blow out a candle, then hold a burning match five or six inches above it. The candle relights.

The agent in the trick is a gray column of gas that continues for a time to rise from the hot wax; if this column touches flame, it takes fire and relights the wick.

With paper book matches you can do the same thing more comically: a burning match in each hand, blow one out, hold the other *above* it to relight; then reverse the roles of the two matches. (Wooden matches won't work for want of wax.)

1e. The X-Ray Cross uses a burnt match as a marking pencil. You draw a heavy black line on your left palm, then another line, crosswise to the first, on the back of the hand.

Close your fist, rub off the outside mark (openly with your right fingers or secretly against your coat when you hold the fist behind you), open the hand: the outside line has reappeared inside, crossing the original mark on the palm.

The secret is in the exact way you draw the line on your palm. The line, as I said, should be heavy and black. About three-quarters of an inch long, it runs diagonally from a point near the base of the little finger, inward and downward toward the center of the palm; it must lie in equal parts athwart the line or wrinkle that slants across the hand from between first and second fingers.

You make your second mark, on the back of the hand, in such a way that the two lines would form a cross if your hand were transparent.

From here on the trick works itself: simply close your fist, folding the fingers down tight but not curling them in. This prints a mirror image of the mark on your palm—two connected V's that form a cross astride the wrinkle.

The X-Ray Cross is a natural lead-in for the Potsherd Trick (chapter 14, section 13). Just remember that the Potsherd Trick may sometimes be *too* good for the dinner table—what can you do for an encore when they say, "Oh, I didn't see that"? The best bet is probably the X-Ray Cross first; if that earns you the spotlight, you go on to your crusher.

2. *Coin in Roll.* All a magician of your experience really needs for this is the title: it was a publicity trick with which eighteenth-century wizards used to make reputations, buying a series of cakes from some street vendor, breaking them open one after another, and finding a gold piece in each, until the superstitious vendor refused to sell any more.

Routine: Borrow a coin and vanish it, leaving it finger-palmed. Pick up a roll in the other hand, then take it in both hands, thumbs on top, fingers underneath. Press down at the center with your thumbs and up at the ends with your fingers, breaking the bottom of the roll across; feed in the finger-palmed coin, then press up with your fingers, breaking the top of the roll and revealing the coin.

3. *The Torn Cigarette* is a beautifully quick and simple effect by Ken de Courcy: borrow a cigarette, tear it into three pieces, drop them into your left hand, and pull out the cigarette in one piece again.

Finger-palm a cigarette of a popular brand in your right hand. Notice who around you is smoking these, and ask him to lend you one. Take it and neatly break it into three pieces, dropping them one at a time on the table.

Spread out your left palm for a moment, then with your right hand drop one piece on the palm and close your left fingers. Repeat with the second piece, opening your left hand a moment beforehand, then closing it promptly.

The move with the third piece looks the same, but actually you drop the finger-palmed whole cigarette in as well. Turn your left fist knuckles up.

Make a pass or two around your left hand, so that the right can be seen empty. Then put your left thumb tip against the end of the cigarette, and push. The cigarette glides slowly out of your fist through the curled little finger.

When it is almost out, extend your right hand, palm up, under your left fist, and take the cigarette between right thumb and forefinger. At this moment you quietly dump the torn pieces from the left fist into the right palm. Close your right hand, carrying the cigarette away and handing it to the lender.

Look back at your left fist, and open it. Empty, what did you expect?

4. *Tumblers.* For *4a, Balanced Liquid Diet,* you carefully clear the tablecloth in front of you, then take a glass about a third full (of water, for safety's sake), and balance it at an angle of sixty degrees or so. Anyone else who tries it will get a bath.

Secret: A matchstick tied to a thread. Slide the match under the cloth beforehand, with the thread leading out to you. The stick will prop up the tumbler quite steady once you've learned the proper amount of water and the corresponding angle of balance to use. If you repeat, shift the match around with the thread, and finally withdraw it to leave no traces.

4b. A follow-up is Douglas Francis' *Glass Levitation,* which I borrow from Lewis Ganson's Volume II. His version uses a glass, a table knife, and a handkerchief; if I were doing the effect I should look for means to get along somehow without the handkerchief. Anyway, you show around the props, then thrust the handkerchief into the glass, and finally the knife. The knife sticks to the glass so firmly that you can lift the whole thing by the handle and swing it pendulum-fashion. In the end, of course, everything is clean.

The gimmick is a double-faced rubber sucker—two suckers back to back. Francis recommends a touch of Vaseline on the surface to make working easier. Using the handkerchief, you will want a routine that ends with the sucker between your right thumb and the cloth; you then pop the kerchief into the glass, where you press the sucker against the inside about an inch from the top. There it sticks.

Francis himself uses a glass with an opaque pattern painted on it—a figure, or perhaps a college coat of arms—and this cover was what gave me the idea that one might possibly dispense with the handkerchief (say by sticking the finger-palmed sucker to the knife first, as one accepted the latter from a spectator, and casually "showing both sides" with the up-and-down variant of the double turnover used for the Jumping Peg trick (see Appendix): point the knife at the ceiling to exhibit one side of the blade, then swoop it downward, turning it over in the process). Naturally this is idle theory unless you can be sure of a decorated glass.

However you work, the next step is simply to thrust the knife into the glass and press it to the inside, where the free sucker takes hold. Between knife and painted design the gimmick is safely hidden. (Or grasp the glass for a moment in the other hand.) You can swing the glass by the knife handle, or invert it without spilling the knife.

Afterward a slight twist releases the knife, leaving you with the sucker in the glass to get rid of. The Vaseline makes dislodging it easier; finger-palm the gimmick as you put down the glass.

4c. Coin Through Glass is an invention of the Canadian coin manipulator Ross Bertram. It is quicker, easier, and more magical-looking than the Coins to Glass (chapter 7, section 19) on which I squandered my boyhood. The only drawback is that passing more than one coin would be rash.

You take a tumbler (not too large in diameter, for choice, and cylindrical is better than tapering) in your left hand with the palm covering the mouth. With your right hand you tap a half dollar on the bottom of the glass. A throwing motion, and the coin is jingling inside.

Hold the glass by clamping the rim between your left thumb and little finger. This leaves the other three fingers free. Hold the glass out in front of you horizontally—with the bottom to the right. Tap the coin, held between right thumb and middle finger, on the bottom.

For once in your life the throwing motion is real: extend your right hand a little farther than your left, and throw the coin sharply to the left. Instead of hitting the bottom as you pretend, it passes along the outside of the glass, and you extend your free left three fingers to catch it. Swing your left hand in a short arc, getting the coin inside the glass; then take the glass, still horizontal, between your palms. Shake the glass.

4d. The Vanishing Tumbler is *the* dinner-table trick par excellence: you can hardly do it under any other circumstances. You put a coin on the table, and invert a tumbler over it. You propose to extract the coin (the reverse of the previous trick, if you like) without touching it. (This may lead parlor-trick-loving spectators to expect the old puzzle in which one scratches the tablecloth to fetch a cent out from under a glass jacked up on two nickels.) You cover the glass with newspaper, then (on pretext of safety) with your napkin as well.

Suddenly, wham! You bang your fist on the package. The glass is gone, to reappear under the table. The coin is still there—no longer under the glass, as you point out to any strict logicians.

Method: You mold the newspaper over the glass so that it holds the shape. In covering this with the napkin, you move the package toward you to the edge of the table; call attention again to the coin, and at that moment let the glass slip into your lap. Set the package (which continues to simulate the glass) over the coin. The rest is acting. You will probably want to let the glass slide down the trough between your shins on the floor.

Here again I should make some experiments to see if I couldn't eliminate the newspaper, perhaps with a heavy, crisply ironed brocade napkin that would hold its shape alone. You could shift the package toward you in making sure the coin was still there.

4e. The Ghost Echo is another table-only trick. You talk about acoustics, cat-whisker tuning, and that sort of thing. To illustrate, you pick up your fork in your left hand, pinch the tines with your right, and move your right hand (carefully maintaining some mysterious gap between thumb and second finger) across the table to poise over your glass, empty or half filled. In that resonator the dead note from your "tuning" fork comes to life.

Secret: The fork goes on vibrating inaudibly. When you touch the butt to the table top, the glass resounds with a thin, unearthly tone.

4f. A related effect, equally simple in method, has a lot more possibilities, as you can see by following the way Henning Nelms evolves it in *Magic and Showmanship* from a humble card divination called the Singing Glass to a detective story titled the *Mongolian Marble* and finally to almost real witchcraft with the understated tag, the *Peculiar Pellet.* This is a trick than can, but need not, be shown at table.

The essential mechanical element is a way to evoke a musical note at will from a tumbler hanging by a thread tied to a pencil. Make a loop—

it can be a running noose—around the glass about two-thirds of the way up. Tie the other end of the thread, snugly but not too tight, around the butt of the pencil.

As you dangle the tumbler over, say, a row of cards, you can call forth the note by simply giving a twist to the pencil, which sets the thread and thus the glass to vibrating.

The simplest application is to have a card drawn from a set-up deck (so that you instantly know what it is), shown to the audience, and shuffled back in. Have the pack spread face up on the table, and tell the spectators that if they concentrate on the chosen card, they will begin to imagine they hear the glass singing when the card is reached.

(Nelms uses this to exemplify casting the audience as "victims of mass hypnosis." He also points out that unless the card is shown around rather than peeped at, you can't ask the spectators to concentrate on it.)

You will probably agree that the misdirection here is good; but it still attaches some unwanted interest to the glass. In Nelms's final version, the Peculiar Pellet (which I shan't detail here because it would be a crime for you to miss the way it's built up in *Magic and Showmanship*), the tumbler has barely a walk-on part. A mysterious-looking small object painted in strange colors is introduced as a device used by Mongolian witch doctors. (Toying with this before you start, you can make someone ask you what it is.) The object originates the sound, and you put it in the glass so as not to damp the vibrations.

Nelms then goes into a blindfold (see chapter 18, section 14) divination routine in which the pellet sings once when suspended over a man's hand, twice over a woman's; finally it detects an "assassin" as determined by who among the participants draws the lowest card. (You force the two of clubs on someone, or note who draws it from among a handful of cards presented.)

This is a classic example of the difference between a device, a trick, and an effect.

5. *Stringing 'Em Along.* Among fairground and sidewalk gambling swindles, the Shell Game (see Appendix) and the Three-Card Trick (chapter 4, section 7) have long been a regular part of magicians' repertoires. A third class is beginning to get some attention again after a forty-year interval: string puzzles, "catch-or-not?" challenges.

The operator lays out a piece or an endless loop of string in some tricky pattern on the table, then defies a spectator to put his finger down in a position that will catch the loop when the string is pulled away.

Instead of the traditional soft string, Lewis Ganson suggests four feet of thin ball chain. Ordinarily you fasten the ends together to make an endless loop; for the first effect below you don't.

5a. *The Spiral* has the peculiarity that even a spectator who knows the trick can't win unless you let him. Fold the chain in two, but not in equal halves; one end should be a couple of inches longer than the other. Putting the loop in the middle, you lay the double chain down in a spiral, taking care that the longer end (A) is the inner of the two.

Tell a spectator to study the figure as long as he likes, then to put his finger in the loop that will catch the string when you draw it away by both ends, held together.

The true center loop is the one around which you coil the spiral. The spectator will probably manage to put his finger in it.

If he does, pick up end A, which goes about halfway farther around the circle than end B, and carry it another half turn around the spiral, bringing A outside B. Seize A and B together, and pull. The string comes away clear.

If the spectator picks the other loop, simply grab A and B together as they lie, with no preliminary turn for A.

5b. *The Snare* is done with a closed loop. Hold the loop open between the fingers of your two hands, knuckles underneath. When you lay it down, you thus have a rough oblong maybe eighteen inches long and four deep.

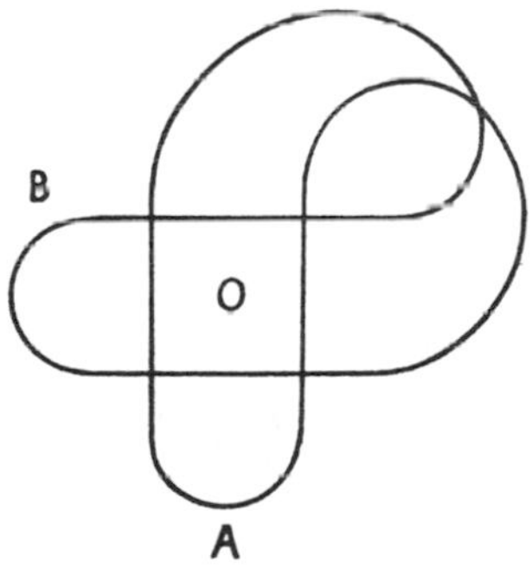

FIG. 207

Hold on to the right-hand end (A), and carry it in a semicircular motion away from and back toward you, so that the two halves of the loop cross to form a rough figure 4. The center of this pattern is a square (O). Here the spectator is to plant his finger. You can catch the finger or not, as you please.

This is the trick: if you keep your right hand palm upward in laying out the pattern, you give the card a twist before the square O is formed, and when you pull A the spectator's finger will catch in the loop. But if you turn your right hand palm downward as you lay A across B, there will be no twist; when you pull A, the spectator's finger comes free.

5c. The Triple Circle Routine by Jack Salvin and Fred Lowe is given in admirable detail in Ganson's Volume I. I will simply describe the lay-out and the device, with a hint of the misdirection.

Hold the loop up in your right hand, then lower it to the table top (which, incidentally, should not be highly polished) until about half of it lies there. With your right hand give a slight counterclockwise twist to the farther half of the chain, forming a small loop on the outside of the main loop. Make a second and a third small loop in the same way at intervals of about two inches. Carry the rest of the chain toward you so that a piece of it hangs over the edge of the table. Then lift this back away from you to form a big circle surrounding the small loops.

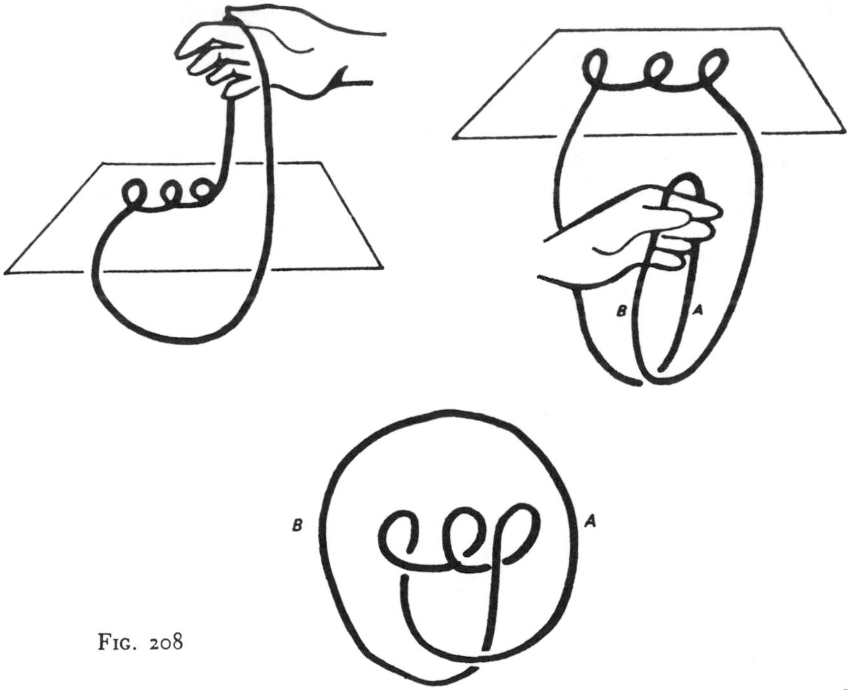

FIG. 208

The game is for the volunteer to guess which one of the three small loops will catch his finger; and this is the beauty of Lowe's misdirection, because, as in the Snare, either any loop will catch, or none.

If you flip the dangling end of the loop over to the right—that is, the left strand crossing over the right strand—before laying out the final surrounding circle, then any little loop will catch when the chain is pulled away.

If you cross the chain the other way, no loop catches.

Fred Lowe's routine starts by laying out the pattern to catch, and saying, "Only one of these circles will trap the finger when the chain is pulled. It is this one." Demonstrate. You lay it out again to catch, but say you can vary at will the circle that will trap. Demonstrate with another circle.

Call for a volunteer, lay out the chain not to catch, and let him try his luck. None. To "shorten the odds" you make only two small loops, and finally just one, but it's no use. For a finish, you put your own finger in the single loop, and it catches.

5d. The Jumping Rubber Band, though hardly more than by-play, is neat and puzzling. Put an ordinary elastic around the first and second fingers of your left hand. Show the hand open, front and back. With your right hand, snap the elastic, first against the inside of your left fingers, then against the back. On the third pull, from inside, close your left fingers, so that all four go inside the rubber band. From outside, the band still encircles only the first two fingers.

Flip your fist open and shut: in a flash the elastic jumps to your third and little fingers. Snap the band again. If you like, you can make it return to its starting position.

5e. Wild West. A combination of old material to give a fresh effect, devised by Norman Hunter. You come on in Last Chance Saloon fashion with a pair of dice and ten or fifteen feet of light rope—a lariat, if that's the presentation you're using. The bigger the dice, the better.

Someone rolls the dice several times, and finally (while your back is turned) sets one die on top of the other so that three faces are hidden. (You knew, of course, that the singular of *dice* is *die;* but too many magicians are still heard talking about *a dice.*)

Meanwhile you have been flinging out and coiling your rope. "This truly is a trick rope. It can tell how many spots on those dice are hidden. Stand back!"

Again you fling it out, holding on to the near end; this time the rope is full of overhand knots. Ask a new volunteer to count them. The first assistant adds up the hidden spots on the dice, and sure enough, they tally with the knots.

To learn the number of spots, you simply steal a glimpse at the top face of the top die (one reason for preferring big dice). Subtract that number from fourteen, and you're in. As you probably know, the opposite faces of any honest die always total seven: 6–1, 5–2, 4–3. The hidden faces of the bottom die come to seven, the hidden face of the top one is seven less what's showing.

Now for the knots. They are much easier to make than to explain, but I'll do my best. How you coil the rope is the whole secret.

LARIAT TRICK

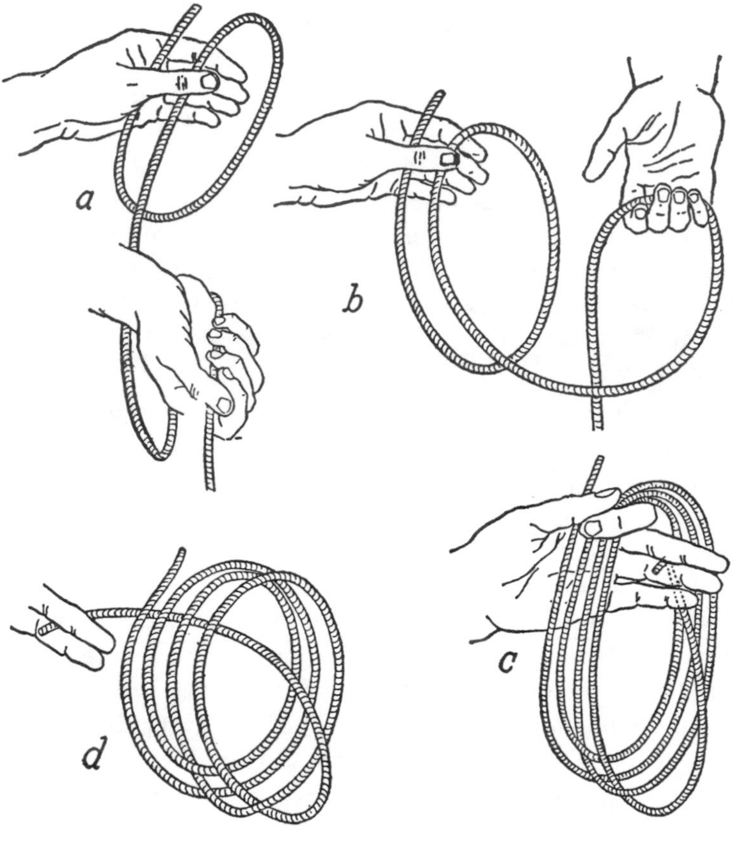

Fig. 209
(a) Starting to coil the lariat; (b) making a phony loop;
(c) the lariat coiled and ready; (d) making the knots.

Hold the end of the rope in your left fist, thumb up, with the short end sticking up, the long end hanging straight down to the floor.

Bring a piece of the long end around forward with your right hand, up over your left knuckles, then down through your left fist. This makes one plain loop, perhaps a foot long. The long end of the rope passes to the *right* of the short end as it comes down through your fist.

That's the natural way to start coiling a rope, and I describe it in such detail because from here on you start cheating. This first, normal loop is needed, but you don't count it toward the knots.

To make the rest of the loops, stick out your right hand palm up, then dip your thumb so that the palm turns to the right.

Grasp the long end of the rope *from the left, with your right palm.*

Now bring your right hand up and over the left knuckles, swinging the *right thumb to the left* before you lay the rope into your fist. This carries the long end of rope to the left, *behind* the first part of the loop. An ordinary coil is a simple spiral, but these fake loops are turned backward and interlocked.

Make eight fake loops. You know beforehand that there must be at least eight hidden spots on the dice. This is probably the moment to steal your glimpse at the stack—"All piled up so that nobody can see how many spots are hidden?"

Make as many more fake loops as you need. That leaves an end of rope still hanging down. Bring it up and catch it between your left middle fingers. If it's very long, make a few honest coils first.

To produce the knots, simply fling out the rope, holding on to the *far* end, the one caught between your left second and third fingers. The toss pulls the outer end through the reverse loops, tying a corresponding number of knots. (The first and any other honest loops don't make knots.)

If you could actually do a little rope-spinning first, it might be a big addition to your effect.

6. *Knocking the Spots Off.* This dice trick is at least two hundred years old, more likely three hundred, but when the Japanese conjurer Ten Ichi showed it with Oriental style and guile, it seemed brand new. I suspect you'd better not combine it with Wild West, because it would tend to raise suspicions of the dice and divert attention from the rope.

Let someone roll a pair of dice and count the spots showing.

Pick the dice up very slowly side by side, touching, between your right forefinger and thumb; turn your hand over to expose the spots on the lower faces. Have your spectator count those spots.

Put the dice back on the table right way up. Tell the volunteer to tap them gently, once, with his finger tip. Then he is to pick them up and count the spots. He finds his tap has added one.

You go through the procedure again, this time telling him to blow on the dice. Seven spots have vanished.

The only trick move is in turning over the dice when you pick them up; by raising your thumb and lowering your forefinger you give the cubes a quarter turn. Thus the audience sees the back, not the true bottom, of the pair.

Since you know from the top faces what spots are really underneath (subtract from fourteen), you can tell how many more or fewer spots the back faces show; in other words you know whether to have the spectator tap for addition or blow for subtraction.

Sometimes by bad luck the true and false totals will be the same, and then all you can do is clumsily drop the dice and start over.

7. *Coin Boxes* are perhaps the typical specimens of "vest-pocket" "micro"-magic: small pieces of neat workmanship, faked unobtrusively or not at all, they permit effects that even a good coin worker could not do by pure sleight of hand. At the same time they call for a good coin worker to get the best out of them.

7a. The German Box is a cylindrical brass cup just big enough to hold a stack of six coins (normally half dollars). There is a recess at the bottom with 1oom for a single coin, which is usually stuck in position with a dab of wax. As a result, the full box looks the same whether it is right side up or upside down. If you flip it over in your left hand, you can take it away with your right, leaving the stack of coins behind.

Lewis Ganson gives a routine developed by his father, Jack Ganson, that would be hard to beat. I borrow his description, compressing it somewhat because by now you will need only the sign posts.

The performer opens a little cloth or chamois bag and pours out six (English) pennies and a brass box. Giving three pennies to a spectator and keeping three himself, the performer tells the spectator to put one penny in the box; the performer then places one of his pennies in the box. This is repeated until all six pennies fill the box. A handkerchief is handed to the spectator with the request that he cover the performer's left hand, which is closed and back upward. The box full of pennies is stood on the handkerchief and the four corners lifted to form a bag. The spectator is asked to hold his cupped hands under the performer's hand. The performer lifts and lowers the handkerchief three times to strike the back of the left hand through the cloth. The third time, the pennies fall into the spectator's cupped hands, having penetrated kerchief and performer's hand.

You need seven pennies, two of them conspicuously alike. One of these is stuck into the recess on the bottom of the box. The handkerchief is in your breast pocket.

When you tip up the pouch, box and coins fall on the table. The box, being weighted by the coin in the recess, almost invariably lands right way up. (Occasionally, says Ganson, it lands on edge; keep your left hand ready to knock it over.)

Push three pennies toward the spectator, and pull three toward yourself, making sure you get the one that matches the coin in the recess. When the spectator and you alternately fill the box, keep the matching coin until last, and remark casually, "King George V," or whatever it is. Don't make a point of it; it's just a side remark.

Lift the box with the left hand and place it at the base of the right fingers. With the left hand again, pull the handkerchief from the breast pocket and hold it out to the spectator. At the same time (if not actually under cover of the kerchief) close your right fingers slightly, flipping over the box.

Transfer the box to the base of the left fingers, holding the stack in place with the right second finger tip. Make a fist of your right hand, back up, and ask the spectator to drape the handkerchief over it. Change your mind: "No, let's use the other hand."

Pick up the box by the sides between right finger and thumb, curling the left fingers upward, then closing and reversing your left fist with the stack of coins inside. Have the left hand covered with the kerchief, then set the box on it over the back of the hand.

Ask the spectator to pick up the corners of the handkerchief; by way of illustration lift the corner nearest to you with the right hand. Take the other three corners from the spectator with your right, quite concealing the box.

Say, "Ready—steady—go!" dipping the handkerchief each time. The unseen result is that the box, weighted by the coin, rights itself, and is seen empty when the pennies have passed and you drop the corners of the handkerchief. (To make sure of this, says Ganson, don't start out with the box dead center in the kerchief.)

7b. The Okito Box has no gimmick at all: it is like the German box without the recess, but with a loose-fitting lid. The story goes that Okito (Theo Bamberg), toying with a cardboard pill box, found it looked the same whether the lid was on the top or the bottom.

Lewis Ganson, in *Close-Up*, Volume II, gives a number of excellent coin tricks by Horace Bennett. Here is one called *Tea for Okito.*

The box is shown to contain five or six coins, and the lid is put on. The box is covered with an inverted teacup; another inverted teacup is put about a foot to the left of the first.

Then the magician claims he will cause the box of coins to pass from the right-hand to the left-hand teacup. After a mystic pass, he announces he has succeeded—but does not lift the cups to prove it. Instead, he says the really hard part is to pass the box back to the cup on the right. Another mystic pass, and the cups are lifted to show the box under the right cup, nothing under the left.

"But an even more difficult feat is to make the box pass from the left cup to the right." Here the magician takes the box from under the right cup and puts it under the left one.

Once again the magic gesture; but when the left-hand cup is lifted, the box is still there.

"See," cries the conjurer, "I told you this was the hard way. All I could make pass from left to right was the coins." He lifts the right-hand cup to reveal the stack of coins. The box is opened and shown empty.

All you need is the box, the coins, and the teacups. Perform on a cloth surface or close-up pad, says Bennett.

Bring out the Okito box, remove the lid with your right hand, hold the lid roughly in finger-palm position, dump the coins on the table, and set down the box. Replace the coins in the box with your left hand.

After dropping the last coin into the box, reach out with your left hand for the right-hand teacup. At the same time replace the lid on the box with your right hand, but fake it: turn the hand palm down, holding the lid finger-palmed or clipped between forefinger and little finger. As the hand moves back, the thumb presses on the rear edge of the box, causing it to turn over under cover of the fingers; then the fingers deposit the lid on the bottom of the inverted box. Additional cover comes from your left arm, reaching for the right-hand teacup.

Once this move is completed, take the cup from your left hand with your right, show it empty, and put it over the box. With your left hand show the left cup empty, and set it down a foot to the left of the other.

Now you go through your farcical feat, at the conclusion of which the audience won't be too attentive as you tilt the right-hand cup forward to lift the box, then replace the cup, hiding the stack of coins left behind on the table. "Just watch your angles and keep your attention on the spectator," is Bennett's warning.

Put the Okito box under the left-hand cup and go through the business of passing the box back to the right. Lift the left cup to reveal the box still there. The spectator naturally thinks you have failed, or are putting him on again.

But after a brief pause, explain that you have failed only partially; lift the right-hand cup slightly and move it off to the right, spreading the coins across the table.

Finally, pick up the box in your left hand with thumb and forefinger holding the lid by its sides, second finger pressing the box itself sidewise, third and little fingers slightly closed. Free the box so that it drops on the ring and little fingers. It rests for an instant at an angle, which the fingers increase until the box turns over and drops, right side up, into your right palm or on the table. Show the inside of the lid as an afterthought.

One advantage of the Okito over the German box is that you can do routines with a single coin, or with too few to fill the box.

7c. *The Boston Box*, named after its inventor, George Boston, is simply a German box with a lid; or an Okito box with a bottom recess, if you like.

Lewis Ganson (*Close-Up*, Volume I) gives an elaborately worked out routine by Fred Lowe called *Boston Three-Step*. To cripple it by abstracting would be a shame, so I refer you to Ganson. But you can practice evolving routines if I tell you the effect and a couple of hints on method.

Effect: Six (English) pennies (or half dollars) are placed in a small round metal box. A sixpence (or copper cent) is placed on top of the pennies.

First the sixpence passes through the pennies, the box, and the performer's hand. Next the sixpence passes through the lid to reappear on top of the pennies. Finally all the pennies and the sixpence escape from the box and penetrate the performer's hand.

To load, you have one penny waxed in the recess, with a sixpence glued on top. In the box are a sixpence, six pennies, and a third sixpence on top. The first special move takes the pennies and top sixpence out of the box, leaving the second sixpence behind. The next steals the top sixpence in putting on the lid, leaving the coin in the left hand for the "penetration." The third apparently slides the sixpence off the top of the box into the left hand, but actually brings it to right finger palm. The rest is turnovers of the box.

See what you can figure out before you refer to the authorities.

PART SIX · CHILDREN'S SHOWS

20. *Performing for Children*

AS we've noted earlier, children can be a difficult audience for a novice wizard. They care nothing about a performer's skill as such, and take noisy pleasure in some quite simple effects. Children seldom remember a magician's name, even if they loved the show; perhaps an effect or two will stay with them.

On the other hand, those whose vocation or avocation involves them with children can easily learn enough magic to help them with their work. Dr. Abraham Hurwitz, professor of physical education and recreation at Yeshiva University, was Peter Pan the Magic Man in playground shows; his daughter Shari Lewis developed TV programs for parents and children, with magic and ventriloquism thrown in as needed. Father and daughter have also written a book, *Magic for Non-Magicians.*

John Mulholland began his working life as a schoolteacher.

A valued correspondent and adviser, Dan Barstow of Hartford, Conn., teaches in a bilingual public school and leads a second, interwoven life as Merlyn's Apprentice. Conjuring can be used as a reward, he writes. "That's how I got started in magic. I offered to perform a trick if they behaved well. They did, and I soon ran out of tricks. It works (most of the time)."

In a rural retreat a German wizard named Hardy holds special magic seminars for schoolteachers.

Norman Hunter (see the Lariat Trick, page 317 above) is a prolific British writer of popular children's fiction (his hero is called Professor Branestawm) and a former big-time advertising copywriter. His *Puffin Book of Magic* is published by Penguin.

What Frances Ireland Marshall once called the "Heartbreak Circuit"—children's institutions and hospitals—offers the most direct personal contribution anyone could make to charity, more involving for all concerned than any amount of money, besides giving you a chance to take your first step in the art. This grows more and more important as the number of "places to be lousy in" for amateurs dwindles. (Mrs. Marshall will be on in a minute for an encore.)

At the other end of the emotional scale, many a conjurer's first paying engagement will be a juvenile birthday party. He gets the job as a young neighbor, and as such can gracefully accept a modest fee. This may offer a convenient launching pad for a magic career. Once started, you can spread out to nearby towns where your neighborhood rates are less binding. There are still ways to avoid being typecast forever as the Kiddies' Friend if your ultimate ambition runs more toward the *-inis* (Houd-, Card-, Mal-, or Slyd-).

Assuming that you want to try entertaining children, let me offer you the accumulated wisdom of some master practitioners. The great treasury is Frances Ireland Marshall's *Kid Stuff*, currently numbering six volumes; the first came out in 1954, the fattest (544 pages) in 1975. All are published by Magic, Inc. in Chicago, the company that Mrs. Marshall built up with her first husband, L. L. Ireland, and renamed after his death when her second husband, Jay Marshall, came into the business. Mrs. Marshall combines the lore of a magic dealer, writer, editor, and a dedicated children's performer, and her Chicago Magigals are among the few clubs of female wizards.

Other useful sources are a double-header in one volume published by Louis Tannen, *Doing Magic for Youngsters* by Bert Easley and the (British) *Art of Conjuring to Children* by Eric P. Wilson; Bruce Posgate's *Kid-show Showmanship* (Colon, Mich., Abbott); and two books from Goodliffe (Alcester, Warwickshire, England), Fred Barton's *The Land of Make Believe* and Ron Bishop's "*Laughter All the Way*."

David Ginn's *Professional Magic for Children* (published by the author at Norcross, Ga. 30093) is just what the title claims: practical and theoretical advice from a young man who makes his living by working school, shopping-center, convention, and party shows for youngsters. Ginn's experiences in developing his effects provide a first-rate workshop for budding troupers.

Now let's talk about your audience. *To begin with, "children" is a convenient but misleading term for your public.*

Frances Marshall says your first question when asked to perform for a private party should not be "When do you want me?" but instead, "How old are the children?" Sorting youngsters out into age groups is a vital and not entirely easy part of your job. What a five-year-old can understand and enjoy may need an apology or at least a conspiratorial wink for the eights; whereas a Bang Gun (a large pistol that is expected to give a loud report, but instead unrolls a silk bearing the word "BANG") is not funny unless you can read.

An advantage of birthday parties as well as school classes is the guests tend to cluster in one age group. School assembly shows have to be programmed adroitly to entertain the various ages successively without automatically boring the others. Company and organization parties are "the best pay, but the worst to play, because they are big, unorganized, and given in big, bare places," Mrs. Marshall warns.

She and David Ginn agree that you should flatly reject all requests to perform for children under five. Ginn is willing to work a birthday party where the majority of the children are five years old *and in kindergarten;* not in nursery or day-care centers, where discipline may be less formal.

The Swiss psychologist Jean Piaget and others have long studied the developmental stages of thought and behavior in growing children. Even chronological ages aren't the whole story, Dan Barstow points out. "For example, before children have developed the concept of *object permanence,* they cannot appreciate the magic of a ball disappearing from under a cup. And when their analytic thinking and independence are driving forces, they can be too busy trying to figure it out. But ages are not rigid. As the need for personal identity and expression develops (around 10–16 years), youngsters are most apt to be obnoxious skeptics.

"Another aspect of development is *energy level.* Kids reach a peak of energy level somewhere between 6 and 10 years. Then they develop more self-control. The energy level is not bad, because it also relates to attention—they pay more intense attention too. Take advantage of it."

Apropos of object permanence, Mrs. Marshall gives the general rule that juvenile audiences expect a vanished object to reappear; total disappearance gives them a sense of incompleteness.

Next caution: My much-quoted remark about the insignificant effect electronics has had on magic does not hold at all for magic *audiences.*

When this book first came out, television was a bit of a luxury. A school principal wrote, "Children up to the age of eight accept magic as a reality; after that, they regard it as a game." That distinction might make sense today if we set the boundary at age four; even a few years ago Mrs.

Marshall could say, "With new ideas in education aimed at the infant, we find tots of four and five picking out their college." At the upper end she had reported in 1959 that grade-school graduation "seems to make them adult overnight, because after that, as teens, their actions, amusements, lives, are those of grownups." By 1968 it was, "Childhood, per se, ends around 12 years of age." From then on conjuring is certainly a contest, not a joint undertaking. And an interest in learning magic oneself tends to sprout at ten or twelve: accepting wonders is an art you have to relearn then along with your sleights, as Picasso said, painters painfully relearned to draw like children—an act of faith under the old adage: *Believing what you know ain't so.*

Television, we always hear, has erased national boundaries and reduced the world to a global village. Magic on television in Europe has indeed brought forth a lot of silent acts (often more skillful than entertaining) and some gaudy illusion numbers that lose little by telecasting from a Paris theater to other countries, but this internationality is deceptive. Though conjurers complacently say everyone everywhere loves magic, the truth is mercifully otherwise. Mediocrity alone is international; entertaining ability tends to halt, with the dialogue, at the language barrier. A really great silent act is the only exception, and even those are not aimed at youngsters.

It is comforting, then, to find certain constants for magic acts nevertheless—prerequisites, of course, rather than guarantees of success.

Shows for children in particular depend on the spectators' getting a piece of the action. They must not only, like all conjuring audiences, recreate the show in their heads, they must get a feeling that it is mostly their show.

Just one common quality embraces every juvenile age group (and adults as well): the magic of make-believe. When Nelson Downs came on stage, did he quack, "It's great to be here tonight with all you wonderful folks"? No. He said, "Imagine me a miser, dreaming of money." That was the show. Make-believe is your overriding function as a children's performer: the only thing you have to sell. It's a game, not a contest. Your toys and costumes have more visible life of their own than the ones at home; your dolls may answer back audibly if you're even a fair ventriloquist. That's why you get engagements—that and because you're good company for children.

Being good company for your juniors is a talent some people are born with—they hardly know how they do it. Others acquire it. Here are a few principles they have worked out by their own efforts and the help of child psychologists.

First and easiest: Cast yourself as an uncle or aunt—familiar, well loved, more indulgent than a parent because less often around the house, but not to be treated like furniture.

A number of professional kid-show specialists actually call themselves "Uncle Bruce" or "Uncle Max," and their first order of business at a show is to say, "Good evening, boys and girls. My name is Uncle Bruce. When I say 'Good evening, boys and girls,' I want you all to answer and say, 'Good evening, Uncle Bruce.' Shall we try it?" When the first attempt comes across a little half-hearted, the performer invites them to "blow the roof off." "Now that we've been properly introduced," and he goes into his song and dance.

"Though this method may date from Adam," explained Uncle Bruce Posgate, "it is still effective. The children shout back at you, at your request, and they let off some of the steam of their over-excitement. It is like a safety valve. It has a further important effect. It often quiets the noisy adults, chattering away at the back of the hall!"

Casting yourself as an uncle doesn't interfere with your casting the uncle, in turn, as Santa Claus or some other entertaining figure: "My uncle, the magician," is double make-believe right there; Dan Barstow completes a triple play with "Merlyn's Apprentice."

If you enjoy poking into the whys and wherefores of performing, you should make acquaintance with the books of Prof. Erving Goffman. A small one issued by Penguin, *Encounters*, deals brilliantly with "Fun in Games," and "Role Distance," two subjects very appropriate to our present theme. And my friend Dr. Edward de Bono's *The Dog Exercising Machine* casts a bright light on children's practical imagination.

Second principle, too easy to forget if you're fresh from adversary conjuring against your contemporaries: *the children, particularly the ones who help you, are your guests.* You owe them the consideration an uncle would show to his young relatives, plus a bit more, because they *aren't* relatives. And still a bit more, since you have every advantage of stature, age, experience, and authority over them. In a show, the hospitable relationship governs your whole treatment of the audience, from seating through the recruitment and handling of assistants to clearing the house. The way you treat your guests tends to be reflected in the way they treat you, in their behavior as an audience.

At small parties the children are probably seated on the floor, and as the performer you must expect them to creep up on you as the going gets lively. You can't just order them back as you might at school or church; this is a party, remember? Instead you may put down chalk lines or white ropes, explaining that you want everyone to see, and so can't call on anyone inside the line to help you when the time comes.

Another dodge, if you set up your show in a living room before the audience comes in, is to spot the table about four feet in front of where you actually intend to work and to post yourself in front of that. Once your audience is seated, move the table back and go into your opening.

Choosing and using assistants is more than half of any kid show. Every child in the audience except two or three wants to get into the act; those two or three are terrified lest they have to. In sheer self-defense you must never say you want "a boy" or "a girl" or "a volunteer" to help you—you'll be mobbed. Instead, play the role of a sergeant at boot camp and announce, "I want three volunteers: you, and you, and you."

For that purpose, says Bruce Posgate, "When you first walk on stage, smiling, and during the first part of your show, you have plenty of time to look over the first few rows of the audience and pre-select your assistants . . . mentally select a child of the right age and sex, according to the type of trick. Choose a bright-looking youngster; avoid the dull or too-shy type. Then when you are ready, make it a personal invitation, such as 'the little boy in the red sweater' or 'the little girl in the pink dress,' etc. Your specific choice . . . avoids the rush of unwanted volunteers."

Frances Marshall says, "Keep your ears open beforehand to pick up some of their names, and summon them personally. They love it."

Another tip from Posgate: "If you have very small children on the stage to help you, squat down on your haunches when you talk to them. Don't forget that to them, you are a very large person, perhaps a little bit frightening. . . . By putting yourself on a physical level with them, you'll minimize your terrifying height."

Every effect in your act except the first and last can, and most should, depend on assistants. "Depend" is the key word: the best part of your make-believe lies in presenting the magic as done by them, while you merely manage the properties. You get the audience cheering for them, not for you. (N.B. You'd better believe this, literally: the faintest hint of condescension will ruin you. Don't demand approval when there's obviously nothing to approve.) *An aside on applause:* Children do not naturally clap their hands in concert; they have to be actively cued to applaud. Children show their pleasure in other, sometimes noisier ways. Your role of uncle puts you too close to be treated like a paid entertainer.

As an entertainer, however, you have long learned to take at least part of your pay in applause; without it you feel something is missing. At a children's party there is a further consideration. If the adults in the next room hear clapping, they assume the kids love you; and who are you to contradict potential future employers? So wind up a few of your best effects by loudly leading the applause for the assistants (or for a hand puppet, or an animal you have just produced). "In 30 minutes you ought to get applause about three times," says the sage Frances Marshall. "What do you want to do, wear out your spine taking bows?"

David Ginn has devoted a whole book to the problem, *Comedy Warm-Ups for Children's Shows.* "With some children's groups I would often be 10 minutes into the show before I would get any applause, regardless of the miracles I was performing. The children watching that pantomime opening were so amazed and/or unaccustomed to seeing a live magic show that they sat there in total silence. No applause, no laughs, nothing.

"But Harold Taylor solved the problem by suggesting that I go out in front of the curtain and warm up the audience before I actually started the show. 'Get the children clapping their hands and shouting and laughing and stamping their feet and so on,' he told me. 'Just be your own Master of Ceremonies before you start the show.'

"Now I come out, warm the kids up, *then* open the curtains and begin my show. . . . Remember, every time kids raise their hands, shout out things you've asked for, clap their hands for you and so on, they are participating. . . . In warming them up, you are allowing them to feel a part of the show because they are helping you."

The ultimate in audience involvement is *costumes for the assistants.* Dr. Peter Kersten of East Berlin uses them as a regular thing—magic cape, funny hat, huge spectacles. "Dressing up is still great fun," he says, "and it adds a spot of color to the act."

Fred Barton offers a chapter of seven costume playlets based on a stolen pearl necklace (costume: policeman's helmet); Sir Galahad and the Black Knight (cloaks, helmets, swords, shields, tunics, conical hat; steed with cutout head and hanging curtain flanks, suspended around rider's waist by shoulder straps); The Crown Jewel (Sir Walter Raleigh's cape and plumed hat; Good Queen Bess's cloak and crown; sword); Way Out West (chief's headdress, headband with feather, Davy Crockett coonskin cap; tomahawks, comedy rifle, peace pipes); Totem Pole (headdresses, tomahawks, Totem Pole illusion); Sherwood Sorcery (Robin Hood hats and jerkins, cape, feathered hat, helmet and sword); Jimmy and the

Magic Telescope (a pirate drama using a ship modified from Sir Galahad's horse). Barton warns that here a professional assistant is needed to handle the wardrobe.

Your position as host also governs a matter much argued by magicians: *sucker gags.* These are worthless for very small children who haven't learned what a guileful world this is: they're experiencing magic, not dissecting it. They've never heard of false bottoms, wires, or mirrors. Hardened juveniles who realize there must be a trick to it can take in a sucker gag, all right; if they become magic enthusiasts they will soon delight in trapping their contemporaries. But that's a fair fight. You as uncle-host owe more consideration because you start with all the advantages.

Here's the rule: sucker gags are all right, so long as you play the sucker yourself. The "adult-in-trouble syndrome," David Ginn calls it, is sure-fire for the young. The Breakaway Fan should disintegrate on *you,* not the assistant; if a missing silk or cutout figure reappears unexpectedly on somebody's back, let it be yours. When you explain about switching torn newspapers, the restored scraps are *your* cue to be surprised. You can survive these self-inflicted setbacks; a nine-year-old helper shouldn't be asked to. David Ginn has an entire chapter on sucker tricks, but when you study them you find that he bases most on the adult in trouble, and he says one per show is enough.

You want to involve all your audience all the time, and since you can seldom get everyone on the stage, you do the next best thing: ask everybody to help in concert. Mr. Bink of the Magic Zoo (Air Force Col. George D. Oetting) tells how in *Kid Stuff* V: "At the beginning of the show, teach them your magic word—'Hocus Pocus' or some other words, and tell them you really need their help to make each effect work. Then you can add bits of participation like having them give a magical whistle, wiggling their fingers together or any other device to get them to help to make each effect work. It doesn't need to be much, but it does keep everyone actively involved throughout the show. It's amazing how this simple technique will reduce the noise and possible unrest in the audience. It allows the kids to make some noise and let off steam, but in a way that relates to the magic taking place."

Bert Easley suggests suiting your magic word to each occasion—the name of the birthday child, of the club, firm, or school sponsoring the show, of a product or institution. Good fun and rather like a joke commercial.

Ask questions that call for obvious answers—"It's blue, isn't it?"—and get a good loud reply.

Now we come to the matter of *discipline,* of *staying in charge of the show.*

First rule: Never lose your temper. Never seriously scold a child (or adult) during a performance. Sarcasm is unforgivable. *Never argue.* Even avuncular teasing must be obvious and self-deprecating; children take your words as well as your make-believe seriously.

Merlyn's Apprentice, speaking for experienced teacher Dan Barstow, says, "It's important to be flexible. Some situations demand tighter control, some can be more open. *Whatever it has to be, act as if that was the way you wanted it to be.*"

Hecklers who shout that it's up your sleeve are a very small problem: ignore them the first time, the second time say something like "We can talk about that afterward; some of us haven't seen it yet." Or, with Bruce Posgate, in a stage whisper: "Shh! Don't tell anyone!" Barstow adds, "In small groups, parents often help out at this point."

Persistent interrupters can be invited on the stage, not for a set-to but for a sense of conspiracy. Working sucker gags on them is sometimes advised by performers who are, I trust, a good deal more simple-minded than you. I advise against it.

Arnold Furst, a very old stager, writes, "Once I begin the performance I pay no attention to individual remarks from one or more members of the audience. I sometimes speak to an individual boy or girl as a matter of discipline to maintain order, but I never respond when they ask me to repeat my remarks or to obey any of their requests. As soon as they discover that the performance continues and that their interruptions are ignored, the older boys and girls will automatically demand silence from the little tots since they realize their loss is irretrievable when they miss part of the program."

The *noise level* is a dilemma inherent in children's shows: if it's too low, you're a flop; if too high, the show is drowned out.

To begin with, of course you can't shout children into silence. That's the worst form of scolding, even if it worked. Some rough-and-ready performers blow whistles or shoot off pistols—a likely way to frighten really small tots, and no great testimony to the magician's self-confidence.

You can stop and hold up your hand. In an earlier edition of this book, Doris Robbins said, "Sometimes even a thoroughly happy juvenile audience begins to get out of hand. This must be stopped for the children's own sake, and the magician must momentarily drop his identification with the young audience. A very brief display of calm, cheerful, but firm authority will suffice. 'That's enough; give someone else a chance to see,' said crisply and with conviction, calms almost any tumult without hurt feelings." Or again, "The noisier the children, the more softly the performer speaks; or he may fall completely silent."

Eric Wilson carried it further: "Suddenly stop talking but keep moving your mouth as though you are still speaking . . . the decent kiddies in the audience, thinking that they cannot hear you owing to the noise of the others, will soon start shushing and you will get quiet. Then, when the silence comes and they find that you are just opening and shutting your mouth without actually saying anything, they realize how you have caught them, and once again you get a laugh and their respect."

When you get beyond the scale of birthday parties, you can profit by the advice of young trouper David Ginn: "One of the most important things you should learn in working children's shows is to use a microphone. A proper sound system can be a life-saver, or a voice-saver. If there is a sound system available, use it. And if you plan on working a lot of shows, a sound system makes a good investment.

"Why? It's simple. You want every person in the audience to hear every word you say. If they can't hear you, they turn you off. And if that happens, they are not entertained and they end up by not liking you, the performer, because they couldn't hear you.

"Not only does a microphone amplify your voice so you can be heard, but it also gives you the power to control an audience of children. Even though you may provoke the kids with a 'turn-it-around' sucker trick or an 'oh no, not again' running gag, as long as you have that microphone you can top them with your voice, getting above them in volume, and thus you can bring them back into the order you desire so the performance may continue.

"Make the microphone your friend. Don't be afraid of it. Use one every chance possible so that using a mike becomes natural to you.

"*One tip:* Keep the microphone about six to eight inches away from your mouth when you speak into it. Don't eat the mike as some singers do.

"As far as microphone types go, my preference is the removable microphone on a metal pole stand. . . . I personally do not care for lavalier mikes (attached to the performer's shirt or lapel) because the cords tend to get in my way and because those mikes pick up everything the magician says, which isn't good if you want to whisper something to a volunteer without letting the audience hear it."

As to *closing the act*, Bruce Posgate gives useful advice: Don't have any helpers on the scene for the last trick, because you want to be up there taking your bow, not escorting them to their seats. A production number, with distribution of loot, is a good finale, but unless you're safe on a stage don't toss things up for grabs. Announce that the candies or novelties will be given away after the show. Pass the tray, bowl, hat, or whatever to the hostess, asking her to make the distribution in the next room. You can do the same with a live animal you have produced: let someone hold it to be petted while you clear away. What you want is simply a moment's respite while you pack your props away from prying eyes if there's no curtain.

At parties, ask the hostess beforehand what comes after you. It it's a meal or a game in another room, offer to announce it at the close of the show, thus getting yourself off the hook.

Time is your next concern.

For private parties, you run over half an hour at your peril. Frances Marshall points out that magic acts are easier to sell precisely because such competitors as jugglers, marionettes, or animal numbers are quite brief, and party-givers want more for their money.

Accordingly, "They will try to hire you for at least an hour. No matter what the price, don't do it. In schools, where the children are regimented by instructors, assembly magicians will present hour shows. You have no such help. I can practically guarantee, no matter who you are, or how good you think you are, that somewhere between 30 and 45 minutes those little angels are going to start to change into little imps."

Mrs. Marshall suggests thirty minutes as the length of your show. You should explain to the party-giver that you know from long experience that the very best period of time for a children's show is a half-hour, and for that time you will keep the children happy and delighted. Suggest allowing 45 minutes for the arriving and gift opening, another 45 for the ice cream and cake, with you, the magician, sandwiched in between, as the perfect party.

More of a science is the question of time per effect. Says Merlyn's Apprentice: "Attention span changes. Young children need more brief and simple tricks; older children prefer longer, more involved stories."

Doris Robbins: Not more than one minute without something going on; preparations must be short and simple, or else must have an element of comedy. No trick consuming more than five minutes altogether should be used for audiences that include the youngest age group. "Of course every audience anywhere must be judged by its lowest common denominator—the youngest, the slowest, the farthest away from the stage."

David Ginn passes on the wise counsel of a magical friend: *Don't take so long between your tricks. It slows down the pace of your show.* "Since then my show has been *blam-blam-blam,* a fast-moving series of magic, comedy and audience participation."

Harold Sterling, an old pro: "Routines have to be tight and brought to a good climax while the audience is still interested and eager to see what is going to happen. What happens now in school shows has to be modeled after what the kids are used to seeing on television."

Back to Square One: *How should you dress?*

There's no agreement on this; here are some possibilities, with pros and cons.

One school, British and understated, says for parties you should be a guest—casual clothing in the afternoon, dinner jacket at night; dazzlingly fresh linen always a must.

No, say others, everyday dress does nothing for you except put you in a class with working parents; costume is what you should have.

The next step is a blazer or bright-colored jacket with dark trousers.

Beyond that, what costume?

The likeliest is that of a magician. If Occidental, perhaps a tail-coat with high wing color, heavy watch-chain, carnation, waxed and curled moustache (prop is better than real), and white gloves for entrance—a slapstick Alexander Herrmann.

If Oriental, there's a wide choice. Looking back, I don't think my own as shown on page ??? of the foreword was too well conceived, barring the bright-colored authentic Oriental silk; you can do better. (Later I got a real North African outfit made in Tunis.)

Merlyn's Apprentice (Dan Barstow) works in an astrologer's long-sleeved robe bearing cabalistic signs, with a tall conical hat (which even has room for a bird's nest, he reports). The sleeves fall back, leaving his forearms free and clear for hand magic.

A Pied Piper costume would have its advantages, including a toot on the pipe for the magic word. But it does, at least in theory, call for rats.

An American Indian medicine man is appropriate, although perhaps not easy to reconcile with an uncle role. And not much jollity.

A significant point too often forgotten: if you're dressed as an exotic figure, you should know something about your model. John Mulholland never forgave Dr. Harlan Tarbell's uninformed efforts at a Chinese act, because they cut the ground from under John's scrupulously authentic Oriental numbers without giving Tarbell any corresponding advantage.

What counts in the end is authenticity of spirit—in Japanese garb, say, ceremonial politeness and restraint.

This leaves stock TV figures, notably the cowboy. There are successful cowboy magic acts, but outside of the circus what do you do about your horse? (One performer showed a movie of his Thunder.) What of rope spinning? Your character limits your choice of effects; your roles compete.

As to clowns there are opposing schools of thought: the circus clown is the kids' delight, and if asked what she wants at a party, the birthday child may well say "A clown." The atmosphere is one of jollity. *Kid Stuff I* and *III* are informative on the subject. The other side says small children may easily be frightened by a figure in strange garb and startling white makeup, and that clownship, essentially pantomime, doesn't go well with storytelling patter.

Frances Marshall observes that youngsters often ask for clowns simply because they've never heard of any other solo acts. She also warns, "Only the great, legendary clowns have the privilege of sadness. The Pagliacci mood is not for the amateur." Practically, she advises no makeup beyond a round spot of dry rouge on each cheek; and a coverall costume.

Finally we have the arbitrary fancy costume—leisure jacket with bright, coin-dotted lapels and patch pockets, Superman-style jump suit. Before you embark on one of these, consider that modern sports uniforms, for instance, are designed chiefly to distinguish the teams on television: they are deliberately created as a glaring least-common denominator. So long as the game is good, little else matters. You may say the same of your own show; still, you don't want your clothes outshining your apparatus.

Piet Forton, an experienced Swiss kid-show performer, warns, "The properties should be designed in harmony with the costume, or at least provide a good contrast (e.g., black tails or dinner jacket with bright-colored objects). Often apparatus and clothing vie with each other in color and vividness. Avoid this, so that the child may concentrate on one thing without being completely bewildered."

It's better to aim at a middle level of taste and hope to elevate the stragglers without offending the fastidious (who may include some of your employers).

So much for costume; now for the act.

We saw in Chapter 15 that the *apparatus for kid shows* follows rules of its own: it has to be showy, with a lot of primary (not pastel) color, and indeed it had better not look too realistic except at the points where it's actually faked. (Silk-dyeing, however, where the kerchiefs are the display, is better with a neutral manila folder than with a painted tube.) Always use the biggest silks you can handle, Ginn advises. In general, your apparatus stakes your claim to the world of make-believe.

Some employers, such as school principals, may judge your act partly by the amount of apparatus you display. (And if you display something, use it; just letting it adorn the stage is seen as false pretense.) You will soon find yourself as a professional, on the other hand, judging tricks by the extent to which the props pack flat.

When performing on the same level with a young audience you run the constant risk that some urchin will break away to explore the scene. So long as you are safe on an assembly-hall stage, the danger is small. Frances Marshall said in her first volume, "I strongly urge those who wish to be happy and confident while working at children's parties to eliminate entirely such tricks as milk pitchers, passe passe bottles, square circles, and other production cabinets, all tricks which cannot be looked into, tipped over, put away quickly, or grabbed suddenly. Try to use nothing that will be exposed by a child's quick glance or sudden yank."

This is one among a series of don'ts Some others:

Vest-pocket, micro-magic is not effective for a child audience. (You may, however, take along one or two good pieces and a pack of cards on a date. If you get to talking with the grown-ups before or after your appearance, you can let them see what a wizard you might be at an adult function.)

No manipulation. (Exception: Miser's Dream, either with assistants or passing among the audience. Ordinarily coins are too small to show up except at very close quarters. Merlyn's Apprentice advises that ages 3 to 8 respond well to cups and balls.)

No card tricks. (For possible exceptions see chapter 4, above.)

Important: No effects that would bring harm to a child imitating them at home—no penetrations, guillotines, no fire, nothing burned and restored, no mutilation of neckties, no needle trick; don't "swallow" billiard balls for the youngest. No rope ties or escapes; even liquids demand second thoughts. This is one place where you must go well beyond the limits of common sense: not only are small children literal-minded (for all their imaginings), but parents may prefer to blame you (along with television) rather than themselves for their offspring's foolhardiness. Remember the little boy who blithely jumped off the roof in his new Superman suit.

David Ginn thinks otherwise; he always uses one trick with "the element of danger," and he describes five in a special section of his book. Admitting that it works for him, I still believe newcomers to kid shows will be wise to sidestep the problem.

Strategic rule: Never leave the stage (or your piece of living room) unless you must. "You have gone to great lengths to build up audience interest and attention," says Bruce Posgate. "Leave your stage empty for fifteen seconds and you have lost your grip on your audience. Children do not concentrate too long on any one thing. Up to the moment, you have succeeded in getting them to concentrate on *you*. Why destroy this hard-earned advantage? Once you let them go, it is twice as hard to get them back.

"If you want something examined, get a member of the audience up on the stage to do the examining. If you take your apparatus down into the audience for examination, only a small proportion of that audience can see you: the others will stand up or come crowding around you while those at the back will lose interest altogether, because they can't see what's going on."

He allows one exception for a platform show: guiding volunteers up the steps. "You will not be absent long enough to lose contact with your audience, because they are all interested to see who is going on upstage. Guide your assistants on to the stage, because in their excitement at being selected, they may fall *on* to the platform: avoid the risks of bruised knees and weeping assistants." For the same reason he favors escorting helpers back to their seats. David Ginn has his regular assistant do this.

Music is becoming more and more of a must; and luckily also easier and easier to provide. We have already met with Lewis Ganson's Personal Orchestra (chapter 19). Chapter 22, section 3, below, gives expert advice on the music itself. Fred Barton has a whole chapter on sound in *The Land of Make Believe*. He tells how to produce your own sound effects. One suggestion: "It will amaze you to see what can be achieved by recording at one speed and playing back at another. If you have a three-speed recorder make all your sound effects at the middle speed and play them back at each of the three speeds in turn. Each step-up in tape replay speed, i.e. from 1⅞ inches per second to 3¾ or from 3¾ to 7½ i.p.s., will raise the pitch of the recorded sound by one octave. . . . Try this: First record your voice, speaking very slowly and enunciating as clearly as possible at 3¾ i.p.s. Rewind the tape and play it back at 7½ i.p.s. If you do it carefully your words should be completely understandable, but you will sound like one of the wee people. In the same way, futuristic or 'space-ship' sounds can be built up."

Live animals, yes or no, is a real dilemma that grows acute as you evolve from a friendly neighborhood celebrity into a semi-pro. The rabbit is, as you don't need to be told, virtually synonymous with conjuring. So long as your pretensions remain modest, you can make do with rabbit cutouts, stuffed figures, or the version called Kicker that wiggles, kicks, and collapses to a third of its fifteen-inch size. But the day will come when you must give thought to real four-footed or winged friends. Most substitutes are feeble makeshifts.

Under city living conditions you may be able to strike a deal with a pet shop—either to rent the animals or to board your own.

You can't go very far unless you like animals and get along with them. Make pets of them if they'll let you. Water, air (in load containers as well as hutches), and exercise are the great essentials, along with proper diet.

Cultivate your veterinarian (perhaps not so far as a friend of mine whose dachshund has had a heart bypass operation; but cultivate him).

Never lift rabbits by the ears; it injures them painfully. Pick them up by the scruff of the neck, and quickly support the body with the other hand.

Some big-time performers have given rabbits away at the end of the show. Howard Thurston met this problem by wrapping the bunny in paper to be taken home, often dismaying the young recipient's parents; the package on opening proved to contain a box of candy instead. Mrs. Marshall passes on another system: explain that the rabbit in the show, being experienced, cannot be given away, but here is a card entitling the bearer to one rabbit, with parents' permission. The card is that of a local breeder, who will hand out a bunny on demand and charge it to the performer. The cards that aren't turned in cost nothing yet spread good will.

Instead of livestock you can have *hand puppets*. (This may be one exception where the substitute comes across as more real than the live rabbit.)

Topper Martyn, a prominent Swedish magician, remarks of his rabbit puppet routine, "Among small children, right in the middle of a routine, a child might ask, 'Is it a real rabbit?' You answer: 'No, he is a make-believe, but he is nice, isn't he?' You will find that you can continue as if nothing had happened, because kids can live in two worlds at once—reality and make-believe. You must not let them think you are trying to deceive them that you have a live rabbit. They know it is not alive, and their reaction will be: 'It's not real—it's a fake!' But they will accept make-believing together with you and enjoy it."

Ron Bishop says, "A glove puppet comes to life if, when you speak to it, it appears to react to your spoken word—talk to any inanimate object and you immediately endow it with a presence.

"Allow a ball or handkerchief or any prop to react to you of its own accord and at once it appears to have a built-in thought process—the magic wand that jumps up in the hand, the box lid that opens or closes on its own. . . . The simple secret of 'living' props—props with the 'thought process'—is what a child can understand; you are meeting him on his own ground. Every child has a private world of toys or dolls with which he or she converses . . . the children themselves show you how to entertain them if you watch and see what keeps them occupied and makes them happy."

He has a chapter on glove puppets in *Laughter All the Way*, concluding with a knotted-handkerchief puppet that I heartily recommend to your attention. "There is a great deal of impromptu entertainment to be got from an ordinary handkerchief."

William Larsen's *Puppetrix* is a book entirely devoted to the subject.

In *Kid Stuff* V, veteran Harold Sterling gives seven rules for ventriloquism, which of course hold good for hand puppets as well as dummies. To summarize:

1. Cultivate a tone of voice for the puppet that is distinct from your natural voice. It can be pitched either higher or lower than your natural voice. To test this, have someone in another room listen to both voices; if he says they are too much alike, try another tone for the puppet.

2. To create the illusion of two voices: if you are naturally a fast talker, talk slowly for the puppet; and vice versa. You can make the puppet stutter and stammer.

3. Synchronize the mouth movement of the puppet to the words you utter for it. Practice speaking very slowly as you open and close the puppet's mouth for each syllable; then gradually speed up.

4. All movements of the puppet must be natural (nothing a real person or animal could not do).

5. When talking for the puppet, avoid moving your mouth; hold it just slightly open and practice talking without lip movement. Slight movements, in words with *m, v, p,* etc., don't matter too much, because all eyes are on the puppet.

6. If you are talking to the audience, look at the audience. If you

talk to the puppet, look toward the puppet. If the puppet talks to the audience, it looks toward the audience. If the puppet talks to you, it turns *slightly* toward you. When you speak to the puppet, it turns slightly toward you as though listening. When puppet talks to you, turn slightly toward it.

7. "The real secret of ventriloquism: If you, yourself, in your own mind cannot convince yourself the puppet is alive and real, then it will be just a mechanical puppet. If you can present your act, keeping always in mind that your puppet is a human being, it will become endowed with human movements and emotions which in turn are transmitted to the audience. So help me, this is the secret, and an invaluable one that can lift you from mediocrity to perfection."

Giveaways: We've already noted the precaution of saving major distributions for the close. But Frances Marshall says: "Accent all the give-away tricks, even though you are presenting them with nothing but bits of cut rope. Children love getting something. Such standbys as the corn stalk or Christmas tree, the Afghan Bands, the paper hat, etc., in which the finished item is given to a child are still your wisest selections. . . . What they saw on TV was just a picture. Never lose sight of the fact that you are a flesh and blood magician, making tangible objects that they can touch and handle. You can't get that on TV!"

The one major exception to the ban on cards is your own advertising cards, which you can scale out (with a boomerang variation or two, cf. page 88 above) or distribute on some other pretext. Mrs. Marshall reproduces in *Kid Stuff I* a drawing of a rabbit that swallows a carrot if you move the card from arm's length to the tip of your nose; she suggests handing it out as an ice-breaker to introduce yourself. Other optical illusions like the ball that travels around in the wheel when you move the card in plane circles would do about as well.

And now we're down to particulars: *What tricks?*

Frances Ireland Marshall, wearing her dealer hat: "In selecting tricks, look at them as we have described. . . . Do they use children, are they for stage or parlor use, what kind of story can I use, is it really a theme for a child?"

Don't forget the hazards of apparatus that may be exposed by a quick glance or grab from the audience. Caution with liquids. (Lota safer than Ching Ling Foo can. Parenthetically, the original version of the Wine and Water trick was done with potassium cyanide, which Professor Hoffmann earnestly warned the performer against drinking.)

For hospital shows, says Mrs. Marshall, "In making your selection of tricks at home, take those suited to almost-surrounded conditions. Take nothing that requires floor space, nothing that can spill, or tip, or give any kind of trouble in case it is bumped or shoved. Do not figure on any trick where you give out anything to eat or drink. . . . I can almost guarantee that before you leave, the nurse will tell you that there are two or three kids down the hall, too sick to come to the show, but who have heard about it and want to see the magician." For these she counsels one or two simple tricks, perhaps winding up by sneaking a real or magic coin under the pillow, and telling the child to count to 10 and see what he finds.

Special apparatus for particular effects is described in all the books I have listed and many more. If you are a home handyman, you can keep busy for months just building your own.

Among the standard effects you have met in this book, some of the best for juvenile audiences are: Chinese Wands; Cups and Balls (with discretion: see above); Egg Bag; Funnel (don't "bore a hole" in the assistant's elbow with a trick ice pick); Goldfish Bowls (see Appendix); Inexhaustible Bottle (sometimes); Kling Klang; Knot that Unties Itself; Linking Rings; Lota; Miser's Dream; Productions (practically mandatory as a source of giveaways); Ring on Stick; Rope tricks; Sponge Balls; Torn and Restored Paper; Turban Trick.

A final hint on programming for novice children's wizards: in general, novelty of effect is not required, because *all* tricks were invented years before any of your audience were born. But if you work often in one neighborhood, you'll want to replace an item or two early in the act with others, lest "repeaters" in the crowd be moved to announce they've seen it all before. David Ginn has standard Birthday Party No. 1 and No. 2 shows, alike in structure but using different tricks. This takes care both of two dates in one neighborhood and of successive birthdays for one child.

Take the advice in chapter 21: type each program (counting any change whatever as a separate program) on a page of a loose-leaf notebook. In addition, jot down the place and date of each performance using that program. Then you won't need to worry about wearing out your welcome in the community.

Finally, here are a handful of *old standbys* that tend to be overlooked just because they have been so familiar to generations of performers. They will still fool adults, properly done; but more important, they offer absorbing make-believe for your ever-renewed audience of youngsters. In alphabetical order:

1. *The Afghan Bands.* This effect is not like real magic; it *is* real magic, drawn from the science of topology, "the study of those properties of geometric forms that remain invariant under certain transformations such as bending or stretching." The mathematician August Möbius (1790–1868) invented something that sounds as impossible as a description in a dealer's catalog: "a *one-sided surface* that can be formed from a rectangular strip by rotating one end 180° and attaching it to the other end."

The impossibility becomes reality when you cut or rip a Möbius band lengthwise down the middle: what comes out is two rings linked. Rotate one end 360° before attaching, and the result of tearing is one long ring, which you can rip as often as you please, and it still comes out one longer and longer ring.

The Möbius band remained largely a scientific puzzle until my late friend James C. Wobensmith, a Philadelphia patent attorney, put it in the form that two generations of conjurers have known as the Afghan Bands.

You start with a ring or endless band of cloth (usually dyed red) about four inches wide and three feet long. You tear it lengthwise, producing two rings. Tear one ring again, and the two narrow rings you get are linked; the other tears into one big ring twice as long as the original.

To make the band, take your strip of cloth, and fold it in half crosswise so that the ends lie together. With scissors, cut both ends together straight down the middle for about nine inches. Eventually you must glue the two ends together so that they overlap about two inches. But before you glue the left-hand half-ends together, turn one around so that the inside comes to the outside of the loop; then glue it. Before you glue the right-hand half-ends, give one a complete turn, so that the inside is twisted around to face in again. Glue that.

After the glue has dried, snip short center slits in the two halves. (See illustration.) Common practice is to make the bands up in batches and dye them.

This is your chance to make real magicians out of two kids: get them up on the stage, show your one band, rip it down the middle by starting at the center slit, and hand one resulting band to each helper. The trick works for them, though it didn't for you.

(By the way, a turn and a half before pasting will make a band tear into one long ring with a knot in it. But enough is enough.)

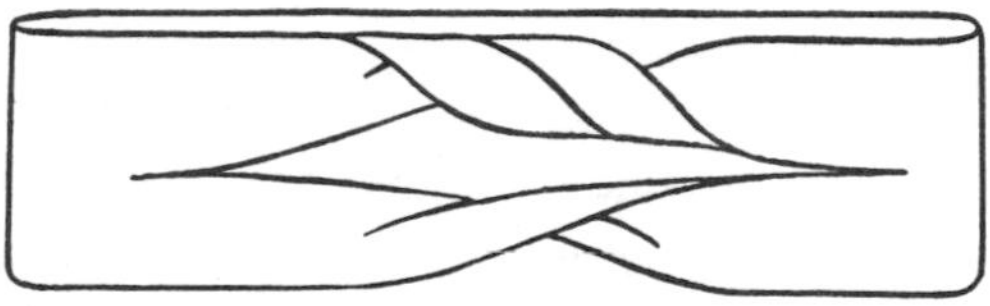

From *Learn Magic* by Henry Hay (Dover Publications)

2. *The Breakaway Fan.* Not a trick but a comedy accessory, the fan has served for a century or more to get mild laughs at the expense of volunteers. Remember, as an experienced children's entertainer you will probably prefer to turn the laugh on yourself.

The fan is strung in such a way that when opened from left to right "it assumes the customary appearance of a respectable fan; when opened from right to left, however, it comes apart" (Professor Hoffmann).

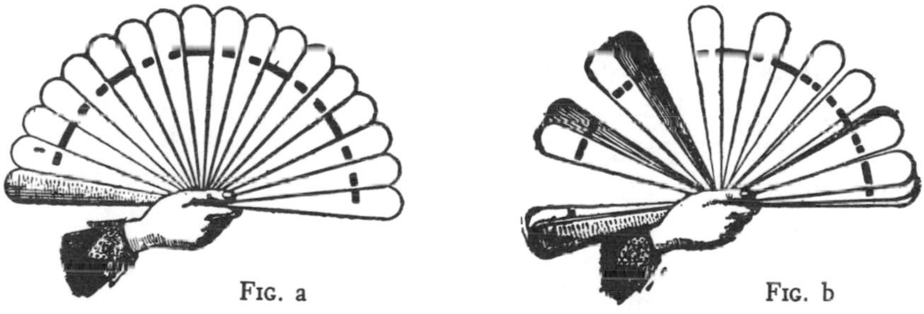

FIG. a FIG. b

From *Cyclopedia of Magic* (Dover Publications)

My own first exposure, at the age of eleven or so, was on the stage with, I think, Howard Thurston. He handed me the fan; having boned up on Prof. Hoffmann, I opened it backward. Thurston could only retrieve it, open it the other way, and say, "Oh, you've broken it." (This won't happen to you if you work the gag on yourself to begin with.)

3. *The Cake Baked in a Hat.* If I may quote from my younger self, "Al Baker's best trick for my money is the cake baked in a hat—one more proof that the secret doesn't matter. If my great-grandfather ever saw a magician, he probably saw a cake baked in a hat; and if I live to have great-grandchildren, I shan't forget the farce that Al Baker makes out of the trick.

"He borrows a hat; in looking for his cake recipe he makes a false start with one that turns out to be for home brew; as he breaks raw eggs into some perfect stranger's hat, he tosses away the shells, remarking, 'Just throw them in the sink—you know, the place where you scrape the toast.' He hunts for a red-headed girl over whose hair he can warm his felt saucepan; finally, when the gooey mess in the victim's fedora proves instead to be a fluffy sponge cake, he passes out pieces as magicians always do, but first he helps himself with relish, like you or me."

That was written after a superb performance before a crowd of magicians—a completely different trick, really, from what Frances Marshall reported: "He used to have ten or twelve youngsters trailing him about the stage as he did his famous Cake Baking Trick . . . he was smart enough to know that for the kid show you must use the type of trick that is not dependent on a fixed audience."

Along with the borrowed hat, the mixings (don't include salt; it's hell on pans), and the cake you need a plate (to serve the cake on) and the venerable prop called a Cake Pan. This consists of two nested round pans, an inner one, tin or aluminum, 4 inches deep and tapering from 5 inches at the big end to 4½ at the small, and an outer one 5½ inches deep. The inner pan is open at each end, and divided in two by a horizontal partition about two-thirds of the way down. This inner pan is never seen.

In its larger end you put the cake.

Soon after borrowing the hat you load the small tin into it, big end down. Professor Hoffmann used a servante (see next chapter); you may also dump the tin in from the outer pan while fooling around with pan and hat.

Either way this leaves an open receptacle mouth upward but unseen in the hat. Now begins the mixing. You have your choice of putting the ingredients into the outer pan and pouring them into the hat, finally lowering the pan clear in and thus picking up the inner tin; or absent-mindedly putting the flour, milk, etc. directly into the hat. This makes more fun, but the resolution of the dilemma raises a problem of bad example: it is conventional next to splash in some lighter fluid and set the "batter" on fire, then clap the pan into the hat to put out the flame.

This of course picks up the inner lining and leaves the cake in the hat.

Tactical considerations: This is not a birthday-party trick, because you can't provide a proper birthday cake. At big unbirthday parties you may have to pass a loaves-and-fishes miracle of your own, with more cakes waiting in the wings. Consider the predicament of my mother, presiding over a long-ago birthday at a boys' summer camp: one oval cake to be divided (on pain of insurrection) into seventeen exactly equal pieces.

4. *Nest of Boxes.* This name also covers a number of stage illusions, but here I use it for the clincher to the ancient Ball of Wool effect. It is one of the few coin tricks that show up well for young audiences. The plot couldn't be simpler: a borrowed and marked half-dollar disappears, and is found inside a nest of locked nickel-plated boxes, which in turn are wrapped in a big ball of wool. The key to the boxes is on the inner end of the wool.

For kid shows the only problem is dressing up and delaying the vanish, while the advantage is that you can involve at least three assistants: one the lender or custodian of the coin, two to unwind the ball of wool and rewind it into a skein.

J. B. Bobo suggests elaborating the vanish with a glass "dissolving" disk and glass of water: your assistant, holding the "coin" under a handkerchief, at whispered instructions from you drops the disk into the glass, then drinks the water when your back is turned. You retrieve the water with an Inexhaustible Funnel, but the coin remains missing.

The necessary equipment consists of the nest of two or three nickel-plated boxes (carried by dealers); a flat tin tube wide enough for a half-dollar to slide through, with flaring lips on one end to facilitate both the insertion of the coin and the withdrawal of the tube from the wool; 25 to 30 yards of very heavy, bright-colored wool; six or eight stoutish rubber bands.

From *Cyclopedia of Magic* (Dover Publications)

The boxes lock when snapped shut. To load, insert the flat end of the tin slide in the partly opened nested boxes; wind two sets of rubber bands tightly around the boxes from back to front, one set on each side of the slide, and a third set crosswise. When the slide is withdrawn, the bands will snap and lock the lids. Tie the key to the end of the wool, and wind the wool around the boxes, forming a big ball with the flanged mouth of the slide sticking out.

Put the ball, slide-mouth upward, in a container or behind something on your table.

You won't need much further mechanical explanation. At the start, borrow a half-dollar, have it marked, and hand it to a young caretaker —perhaps most plausibly to hold under a handkerchief. What you must do is switch the coin (whether for a substitute or for a glass disk) before you fetch the ball of wool. At that point you drop the marked coin down the slide, withdraw this just enough to clear the nest of boxes (which of course snap shut with the coin inside), and hold back the slide in lifting the ball into view.

Your trick is now done, and the show can begin, with as large a cast as you care to muster for skeining the wool, unwrapping and unlocking the nest of boxes, and returning the coin in triumph.

5. *Sun and Moon.* One last old-timer with ample employment opportunities for the audience. You show a red handkerchief, recruit an assistant (No. 1), to hold it, and ask to borrow a similar handkerchief, but white. The lender of this one becomes Assistant No. 2 and brings it onstage.

You say the handkerchiefs should be marked so that we will know them again, and for this purpose you cut a piece out of the center of each. (Tradition calls for an assistant to do so, but he is made to look a bit foolish; and remember our avoidance of bad examples.)

Give the cut center pieces and your wand to a third assistant, with instructions to tap his fist three times so that the pieces will go; meanwhile you fold the handkerchiefs together. When he fails, hand the handkerchiefs to the left-hand assistant, and then help out his colleague, who succeeds by tapping *your* fist with the wand.

The handkerchiefs are restored, but wrong: red center in white handkerchief, white center in red. In your embarrassment you offer the lender of the white handkerchief (Assistant No. 2) both monstrosities, wrapped in newspaper, as a sort of amends. The package, torn open, contains both handkerchiefs properly restored.

You need, obviously, two red handkerchiefs, one white, and the "sun and moon" pair. Fold the white one small and put it in a right pocket; "sun and moon" folded together small go into a handy left pocket. A newspaper is prepared by pasting together the top edges of its first two sheets, the right-hand edges down to the middle, and a strip right across the middle. In the compartment thus formed you put one of the red handkerchiefs, folded four times. Scissors and wand complete the outfit.

The classic working taught by C. Lang Neil relied heavily on vesting. A simplified version is this: for safety's sake bring along an extra white handkerchief, in case you have reason to think everyone uses Kleenex. You can give it to a child beforehand, asking him to offer it if you call on him. You will use him as an assistant at some point anyhow.

Start by choosing the red handkerchief, folding it up, and entrusting it to Assistant No. 1. Assuming that a proper handkerchief is forthcoming, its lender becomes Assistant No. 2. (Otherwise take your young confederate.)

Your first problem is to switch the borrowed handkerchief for the white duplicate. Take the lender's property, refolding it if he has shaken it out, in your left hand, guiding him into position with your right. Pass the handkerchief from your left to your right hand behind his back, which gives ample cover for stealing the duplicate from a righthand pocket and pocketing the original on the left. (If you are using your own planted handkerchief you just skip this switch.)

Now have both handkerchiefs shaken out again and shown, held up by the upper corners. "Mark" them with the scissors by cutting out the centers. Recruit Assistant No. 3 (your confederate with the spare handkerchief if that has not been needed), put the cut pieces in his left fist, and tell him to tap the fist three times with the wand.

Meanwhile collect and fold the two cut handkerchiefs. Create a diversion by talking with Assistant No. 3, steal the "sun and moon" bundle in your left hand, and clap the cut bundle on top—a version of the familiar dodge with torn paper. Turn the bundle over.

Since the cut pieces don't seem to be vanishing as they should, you hand the bundle to Assistant No. 1, casually stealing and pocketing the damaged hankies. Take over the cutout centers, palming them in your right hand as they seem to go into your left fist, and have Assistant No. 3 get in another lick with the wand. Gone at last.

But what of the handkerchiefs? Assistant No. 1 opens them out, and horrors! Give the white one to Assistant No. 2 for symmetry. Then fold both together. Pick up the newspaper, wave it casually, and tear off the front two pages, loaded with the duplicate red handkerchief. Wrap the folded bundle in the paper, and hand it to Assistant No. 1.

Magic words from the audience in chorus. Take back the newspaper package and break it open, bursting the paper with a sharp bend but not undoing it. This reveals the duplicate red handkerchief.

Pull it out, crumple up and toss away the paper (which still contains the "sun and moon" handkerchiefs).

Your concluding maneuver is to retrieve the original white handkerchief from the pocket where you left it at the start, and smuggle it under the red one, to be unfolded and shaken down with it.

Present both to Assistant No. 1, and heave a sigh of relief.

PART SEVEN

21. *Platform Magic*

A SENSIBLE amateur magician starts his career by doing just a few tricks for his friends, *when they ask him*. Naturally he will have family or intimates on whom he can try his stuff until he knows it will work. But I have already spoken of the pest who insists on doing card tricks; and the pest who insists on doing any trick that nobody wants to watch is close behind him.

You will find, though, that the showing of good tricks on request soon makes you a marked man. Before long, people will ask if you ever give shows for school functions, for children's parties, for charity.

The next thing you know, you will be in the ranks of semiprofessionals, doing set performances for pay.

This chapter is a roundup of things you should know in addition to your actual tricks. Programming and stage management need to be learned almost as much as showmanship, of which, indeed, they are a part.

The basic requirement of professional magic (as distinguished from showing a few tricks to friends) is that you must always know exactly what you are going to do next. Programming and stage management alike are nothing but system. You decide on your best tricks, on the best order to show them in, and you arrange everything so that you can follow this order without fumbling or confusion.

We may as well start small. Say you are to have ten minutes at an adult party. That means your program will probably be just two or three routines—sequences of small tricks that you have learned as a unit. You may show card flourishes, working into one chosen-card trick; then a sponge-ball routine; and then a coin routine. The simple fact that you have a routine means there will be no awkward *inner* transitions. The card flourishes will flow smoothly into the choosing of a card—for instance by your producing a one-handed fan and immediately having someone draw a card from it.

Unbroken transitions *between routines* are a matter of taste. In a short act you can transform a card into a sponge ball, and later a sponge ball into a coin. Or you may simply lay down the cards and take your bow, then produce the sponge ball. In long programs, the definite break between routines is desirable; the audience should have a chance to relax their attention.

As soon as you have learned any routine, and showed it enough to get the habit, you should time it in minutes and seconds. Time it more than once, and take an average. You will then know how much of any given program your routine or your trick will fill up.

Keep some record of each trick. I suggest three-by-five index cards. At the top write the name of the trick—not the dealer's name, but your own identification. Abbreviate if you like; the file is for your eye alone. At the upper right-hand corner put the time the trick fills.

What you put on the rest of the card I shall discuss a little later.

You now have the raw material for a program. When you know how long the act is to be, you can pick out the tricks to fill the time.

A good program, however, does much more than fill time. Like individual tricks, it needs a beginning, a middle, an end.

The opening trick is vitally important. It establishes your footing with the audience. You must jump right in and give them an eyeful. Prove yourself a man of magic, not a lecturer.

In other words, you must win your audience quickly, with *magic*. The opening trick must not necessarily be soon over, but it must be quick starting. Don't borrow anything; don't pass among the audience. If you can do it silently, so much the better. Most mental tricks and chosen-card tricks are poor openers. Flourishes, manipulations, bare-hand productions, and sudden vanishes are natural openers.

For the love of Heaven, don't make a brief introductory address saying you will endeavor to entertain people at this time with a few feats of legerdemain. The introduction by the m.c. or chairman will be quite ordeal enough. I repeat, there must be magic happening from the moment you come out.

This isn't to say that you must rush on breathlessly, waving the flag. The billiard-ball manipulator must still give people time to realize that one red ball is the hero of the piece; the man who catches a silk in the air must let his hands be seen empty. The common rules of presentation still hold for the opening.

The middle of the program is the easy part. You have a wide choice of tricks, but still you follow the laws of common sense and dramatic climax.

First you weed out tricks that look too much alike—Cut Turban and Rope Trick, Cards Up Sleeve and Coins Up Sleeve. Next you put aside for some other program effects that are worked by the same method—two or three black-thread tricks. Save up a spectacular one for the end.

For special occasions you want special kinds of tricks. The following chapter gives particular requirements for various kinds of show, and the Appendix is full of other popular effects.

When you whittle down the possibilities to a manageable number, you start arranging them. Naturally they should get better and better as the show goes on.

On the other hand, change of pace is a welcome rest in any show that lasts more than a few minutes. After a silk routine, a mental effect may be good. Though the tricks must get better and better, they need not get faster and faster or bigger and bigger.

Use your head about tricks that demand volunteers. At a dinner table or private party, every trick may legitimately be worked *on* someone. The person who has chosen the card or marked the lump of sugar will remember you forever. Audience assistance is the life of any children's show.

On the platform, however, the recruiting of each volunteer takes precious time. The people who don't volunteer like the trick rather less well than they would if it had not been done specially for someone else. They are quick to suspect stooges. A platform show where even a competent and lively performer keeps dragging reluctant victims from the audience is likely to be a painful failure as entertainment. You can't afford to make devoted slaves of a few at the cost of boredom for the many.

Passing things for examination, borrowing property from the audience, and having the cards shuffled are other time wasters that should be largely avoided in a platform show. I have already said what I think of apparatus that invites examination, though of course special tricks (for example, escapes) and special audiences make exceptions. Also, some very good tricks are pointless unless the articles are borrowed. All I contend is that one trick like this is enough in a program.

The length of the program may be established for you, or you may have leeway. John Mulholland gives as his rule, "The larger the audience, the shorter the show." Twenty minutes is the most you should offer to do for a platform show if you are consulted. The stage of your career is still some time off when you can tackle an hour's entertainment in a hired auditorium. Children's party shows should not exceed half an hour.

Remember that no night-club act ever runs more than fifteen minutes, and most take seven or eight.

In short, always leave everybody wanting more.

Your next consideration in arranging the program is technical: will the loads and preparation allow you to do the tricks in the order you propose? Obviously you can't steal two billiard balls, a hand dye tube, and three thimbles all in succession from your right trouser pocket; you can't do Squash and a cigarette vanish by adjacent pulls under your coat.

The remaining space on your index cards comes handy now. In it I would put all the preparations and requirements for the trick. "Silk dyeing, paper. 4 min. 30 sec. Dye tube loaded with green, blue, red silks, in fold of manila folder on table. Three white silks from Symp. Silks."

I have already said that the closing effect should be spectacular. A production trick that leaves the stage loaded with tambourine coils and silks is an excellent finish. For a show of hand magic, many good openers are also good finales, if you bear down on them a little. I need hardly say more: your closing effect is the big bang that sends them away popeyed.

Once you have chosen and arranged a particular program, type it out, just the main headings on a small slip of paper. Unless you show this program constantly, you will find it helpful to put the typed list on your table where you can steal a glance at it.

One good suggestion from Jasper Maskelyne, of the English conjuring family, is a loose-leaf notebook with all your programs in it. Even if you change only one trick, make a new page for the new program. The time, loading, and other requisites (dinner plate, newspaper, two chairs) should be on the same page. Then you can pick out a suitable program at a moment's notice for any occasion and prepare for the show almost as quickly.

Don't leave out a program just because it is a six-minute impromptu. Your routines are programmed too. They deserve to be recorded.

In addition to your reference program on the table, you want a careful, detailed loading list. This, like the page in your program book, includes not only gimmicks, loads, and preparations, but the unprepared articles you will need. This list is sometimes called a "cue sheet."

Take those articles along. Anything that can possibly go wrong in a magic show will go wrong sooner or later. Having to leave out a favorite trick because you can't find the properties is a poor beginning.

I don't mean to be silly about this. You can certainly find two chairs, *probably* water to fill your lota with. Yet the number of times when you can't get some ordinary article is surprising.

Your program is planned, timed, recorded, loaded for.

Now rehearse it. Go through the whole act from start to finish. Again. And again. Time the whole thing; entrances and exits may chew up the time for a complete trick. You have to memorize not only the sequence of tricks, but the location of everything.

Stage management is knowing where things are when you want them. If you have to root under silks to find your forcing deck, your stage management is faulty.

Good stage management requires you to consult your loading list three times: when you pack at home; when you load just before the show; and afterward, to make sure you have left nothing behind. The loading list may well be pasted into the top of your suitcase.

What I have said so far applies to any set magic program, whether platform or close up. We now come to the distinguishing features of platform shows. You can give a platform show without these features, but you can't give a close-up one with them.

They are *wand, clothes, prepared furniture.*

The *wand* is, as I remarked in another book, the badge of the professed magician. A wand means that you ask to be taken seriously as an entertainer. Of course you may not offer serious entertainment; but even your comedy is to be seriously *regarded.* Displaying a wand is an admission that the show is planned and prepared. If the act doesn't entertain people, they may legitimately complain.

Once you are prepared to meet your audience on those terms (which you should be, many times over, after studying these pages), the wand can be a big convenience. When you have to palm something a little too big for you, pick up the wand. When you want to shed something that you have palmed, lay down your wand. A touch of the wand wakes the audience up for the climax. When you do use volunteers, you can make a lot of fun by letting them wield the wand.

Furthermore, past generations of wizards have invented innumerable trick wands—silk producing, silk vanishing, coin producing, exploding, collapsing—a wild profusion. The appearing wand (drawn from the sleeve through the slitted bottom of a small change purse) is a good opening trick.

Most of the mechanical wands strike me as labored contraptions; yet if one fits smoothly into your routine, why not use it?

Many professionals do without a wand. It would look silly in Cardini's act; I believe Downs once used a coin wand, but later he disdained it. Suit yourself; you know what you're undertaking.

Clothes are less and less of a factor nowadays even in stage shows. Most performers manage with the ordinary pockets in the clothes appropriate to the hour when they are performing. No trick in this book demands anything more. Yet, if only as history, you should know how your predecessors a few decades ago used to tog themselves out.

The older magicians always wore tailcoats. Inside the breast of the coat on each side was a vertical "loading pocket." Inside the tails at the height of the knuckles were two pockets called *profondes*, much used for steals and disposals. The vest had an elastic around the bottom, to hold anything that was poked under it. The practice of "vesting" has died harder than any other recourse to magicians' clothes. At the back of the thighs were small pockets in the trousers called *pochettes*. These were used mostly to make steals from.

Chapter 1 of Professor Hoffmann's *Later Magic* describes the conjurer's dress when it was at its height. Possibly one reason that clothes are so seldom faked nowadays lies in the decline of made-to-measure tailoring. As we have seen, children's shows invite fancy dress. Television and stage performers too now tend to parody traditional society and cartoon costumes.

Faked furniture comes under two main headings—servantes and black art wells.

A *servante* is a hidden receptacle, usually a shelf or open bag. Servantes have been devised for the unlikeliest places, including the opening of a dress vest; but the standard kinds go behind tables and chairs. The bag servante, with a cloth body over a wire or strap-metal frame, has nearly displaced all others. Different kinds are shown in Figs. 210 through 215. All, however, are tending to go out of use in these close-up days.

Chair servantes can be hooked over the back of any borrowed chair

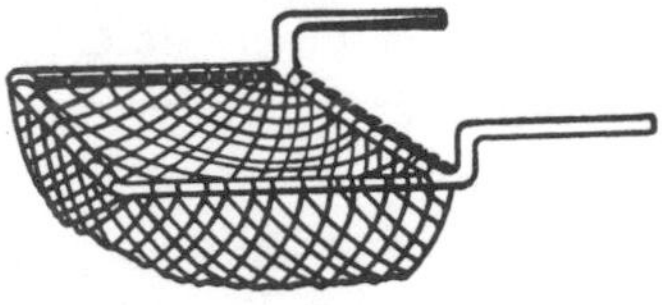

FIG. 210

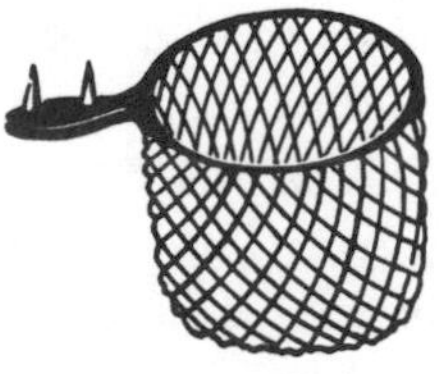

FIG. 211

FIG. 212

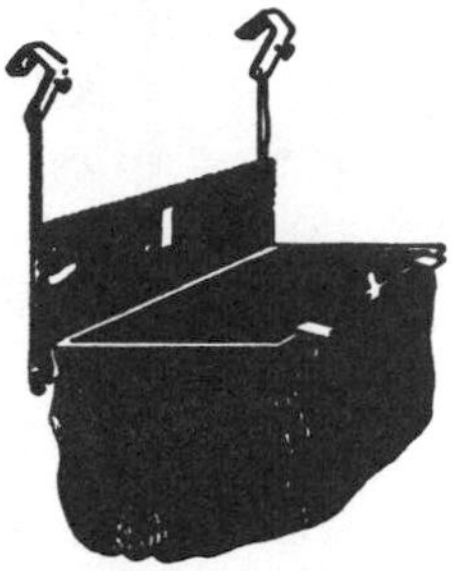

FIG. 214

FIG. 213

FIG. 215

and hidden by a shawl over the front. I believe it is better to use a table servante only on your own center table, not on borrowed tables.

Most magicians nowadays carry center tables that would have been side tables in an earlier day—a small top on a single column with short tripod legs. In fact a good one can be made out of a music stand. Get one the top of which can be set to any angle, and you will find it easy to attach a plywood or fiberboard top. Over this you put some kind of black velvet cover with a fringe. The cover hangs down far enough to hide a servante if you use one. The fringe may be either narrow or else tacked to the edge of the table top, hanging down the full depth of the cover (Fig. 216).

This illustration shows a top prepared with ***black art wells***. Black art wells have succeeded the table traps of a century ago. They are invisible, cloth-lined pockets in the top of the table. Dead black against dead black does not show—hence the invisibility. The table top has black felt or black velvet glued to it; the surface is broken up into convenient areas by a design in yellow ribbon. Some of these areas (three in the illustration) are cut out, and underneath is a velvet or felt pocket.

You can buy black art table tops from dealers, or you can find directions for making one in Downs's *Art of Magic.*

A black art table has many uses. Such gimmicks as the dye tube can be dropped down a well; so can any object up to a large tumbler, if appropriately screened with the hands or a handkerchief. The bottomless glass (chapter 16), was first invented to go with the black art table. You put a thing in the bottomless glass, and set it down on the table. When the thing is to vanish, you just shift the glass over a well.

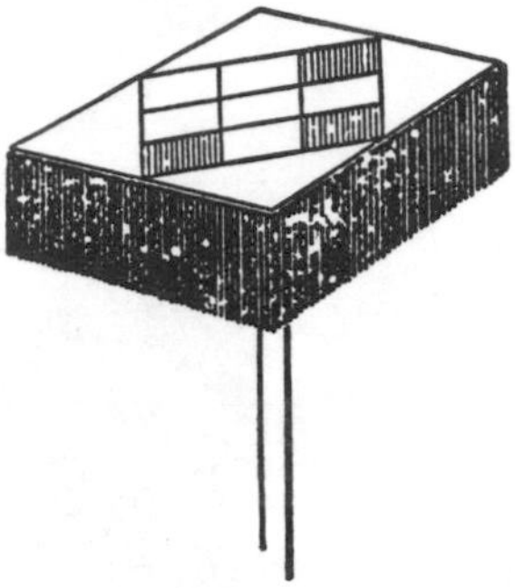

FIG. 216

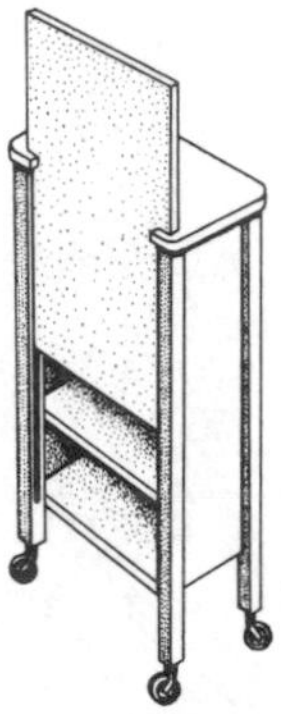

FIG. 216a

The one limitation of wells as against servantes is that you can only drop things into them, not load from them. For production tricks you will probably need servantes. Cups and Balls is much easier with a servante; but then Cups and Balls is not a platform trick.

A more recent development is the "night-club" table or trolley, an upright cabinet three feet high including the feet (which often have casters for rolling onstage), with a top about one foot by two. Shelves to hold equipment, and for ditching and loading, are accessible from the back. (Servantes and wells would be too risky for night clubs.)

Most knock down flat for transportation; one form serves as a container for the whole act, to be stowed in the back of the car. *The Table Book*, edited by Frances Marshall, gives working drawings for several.

All mechanical devices are trifles compared to the priceless asset of a good stage presence.

Stage presence is made up of so many elements that I dare not tell you how to get it; yet certain points are obvious. Absolute serenity, calm knowledge of what you are doing, is one great factor. Doubt and fumbling immediately spread to the audience, totally destroying your stage presence. Good stage management takes care of that part of you.

Good posture and deft motions also help. (Remember what I said in chapter 2 about turning your back on the audience.)

Voice plays a great part in stage presence. Two or three lessons from a good teacher in voice control are as sound an investment as you can make. (Often you can trade a show for lessons—something to remember whenever you need professional help.)

Not being a voice expert myself, I can't teach you in print how to speak from your diaphragm, how to stop talking through your nose, how to make your voice carry. A strong regional or foreign accent is likely to be a handicap if you travel far from home, unless you can use it as a comic asset. Some speech teachers specialize in eliminating accents; you can help yourself by becoming aware of your own pronunciation, recording yourself on tape, and comparing it with what you hear over the air. (Many people find the first time they hear themselves on tape an unsettling experience.)

Speak just loud enough so that the back row can hear you; you will find you can judge this quite easily. The bigger the audience, the slower you must talk and the slower you must move. A chain is as strong as its weakest link; a crowd is as quick as its slowest member.

One paradox goes with big audiences. You must do everything plainly and simply enough for the *slowest* member, yet you must talk smoothly enough for the *most cultivated* member. The educated speech that might be downright affected in some private gatherings is essential before a crowd. If you doubt your ability to talk up to your audience, get help. You can always find at least a high school English teacher to correct you.

A bright, friendly, unforced smile is a great prize for a magician. Remember, *unforced*. If you can't make it look natural, play it dead pan.

With assurance, carriage, neatness, voice, and a good smile, your stage presence can't be so bad.

Then you can put your mind on the tricks.

COACHING YOURSELF WITH VIDEOTAPE

By the Amazing Randi

Now that videotape recorders are being used in many homes, it is interesting and valuable for the amateur to collect performances by the pros, both for reference and pleasure and for instructional purposes. Collecting is becoming common among magicians around the world, and some video enthusiasts have hundreds of tapes, some made by themselves from television performances, some swapped with other collectors, and a few prepared in small home studios with the use of a television camera or obtained at live performances at theaters. A good videotape collection of magic and magicians is something that you couldn't have dreamed of owning just a few years ago. Take advantage of the available technology, and join the hundreds of magic fans who can conjure up a favorite magician by the touch of a button!

First we will consider the aspect of collecting performances for reference and for pleasure. The product the magician offers is something that he or she makes a living by selling, and one may not merely steal that product at will. The collector must know, from the start, that it is illegal to record any performance for purposes of a public showing for which an admission fee is charged. Furthermore, it may be illegal to record a performance for other purposes as well. I would advise you to look into the legalities as they apply to you since this situation varies from country to country, and according to program content. Remember to obtain the permission of the performer before using a television camera to capture a live show on videotape or film. Also, in many theaters it is against house rules to allow such filming. The offender may have the film or videotape confiscated.

Collecting can be done directly from television broadcasts or in person, if one is equipped with a simple camera. A black-and-white camera is quite inexpensive. A color camera requires more care than a black-and-white one and needs somewhat more light for proper operation. Ordinary theater lights are usually sufficient. A zoom lens is very useful since it will give you greater versatility in capturing a sharp picture over a range of distances than a standard lens would allow.

As for recording equipment, we find at present two main systems offered for the amateur market. They are the Video Home System (referred to as VHS) and the Betamax. Each system is manufactured by several companies. When choosing the individual model consider one having "freeze-frame" capability. Freeze-frame, the ability to stop a tape at a particular point and then advance it one frame at a time and return to its normal speed, is valuable for studying the action.

Consider carefully the circumstances under which you'll do most of your recording and choose the system that best fits your needs. You need not have one of the extended time systems either—in fact, the resolution tends to be so poor when using a 2-hour reel to get 6-hour playing time (since the tape is played out at one-third the speed) the tape is not as useful to collectors.

There is also a semi-professional system known as "U-Matic" which uses ¾-inch tape cassettes (very large compared to the other two systems mentioned above and also much more expensive). However, the resolution is of broadcast quality, that is to say, excellent. It is the system I use for making originals, and I dub copies onto VHS cassettes.

Making copies is not difficult. If the original is of good quality, the copy should be good. A copy made from another copy which is not an original, however, may exhibit serious stability problems (often the picture will roll and lack clarity). Try to make copies from the best original tapes available and never from extended time tapes. Keep both machines clean and properly tuned, and copying should be a cinch.

If you are going to play copies of tapes stick with a transistorized television receiver. For technical reasons that I'm sure I will never solve, copies made by us amateurs will sometimes exhibit a strange splitting image. This seems to happen usually when the copied tape is shown on a tube-type receiver, and not on a solid state television receiver.

Admittedly a television monitor, videotape recorder, and camera assembly can be expensive for a beginner. I suggest that you get together with a couple of friends interested in magic and pool your resources. The best way is to have one person assemble the equipment in that person's home, then arrange to let it out to others on a rental basis. A very modest per diem charge will eventually pay off the investment, or at least make it less of a burden. Since tapes can be used many times, their cost is of least importance. There will be very few deathless performances that will result from rehearsals. Most sessions will be erased immediately.

Since improvements are being made in the video market so quickly, used machines are often available. Consult the classified ads for bargains. Always test out a machine, examining the quality of a picture that you have just recorded for detail, stability, and color clarity. Sometimes, when a VTR is not working well all that may be needed to bring it back to perfect working order is a cleaning of the video recording heads. Cleaning the heads is a job for a professional or for one experienced in the work; amateur meddling can destroy the machine.

When you are taping, always record the date, time, station, performer, and other pertinent data. You may want to list the tricks being done as well. Make a catalog of performers and tricks, so you can refer to it and pick out any item easily. Videotapes have index marks that allow you to number the exact spot where something occurs. Note the counter number in your catalog to keep track of any event, since hunting through a 2-hour reel can be very frustrating indeed.

Videotape serves the amateur and professional alike for purposes of rehearsal in a way that a mirror cannot provide, and friends are not able to. For rehearsal and learning purposes, a camera is essential. A firm tripod is needed to hold the camera, and a fully adjustable mount so that it may be pointed at any angle. Be careful not to point the camera, even for a second, at any bright light or the sun. Some cameras will be permanently "burned" by such treatment. A black-and-white camera will usually have better depth of field than a color one. That means that the focus will not be so critical, since most practice (I hope) will be done in private when there is no one to adjust the focus during the performers' change of position.

Except for initial set-up of the equipment, I suggest that you not look at a monitor in which you can see your actions. Turn the monitor away from the line of sight while working, and play as if to a real audience. That way you will have a hope of approximating an actual performance.

Light the scene from as many angles as possible to provide flat illumination without heavy shadows. Most amateur set-ups will not accommodate shadow detail properly, and you can forgo glamor for harsh reality, during practice sessions.

The television screen is a harsh critic indeed. You may be in for a surprise. When you view your first few attempts, you'll probably want to jump off the roof. You may think your efforts are dreadful, and it's back to selling Tupperware. Remember, practice makes perfect and hopefully

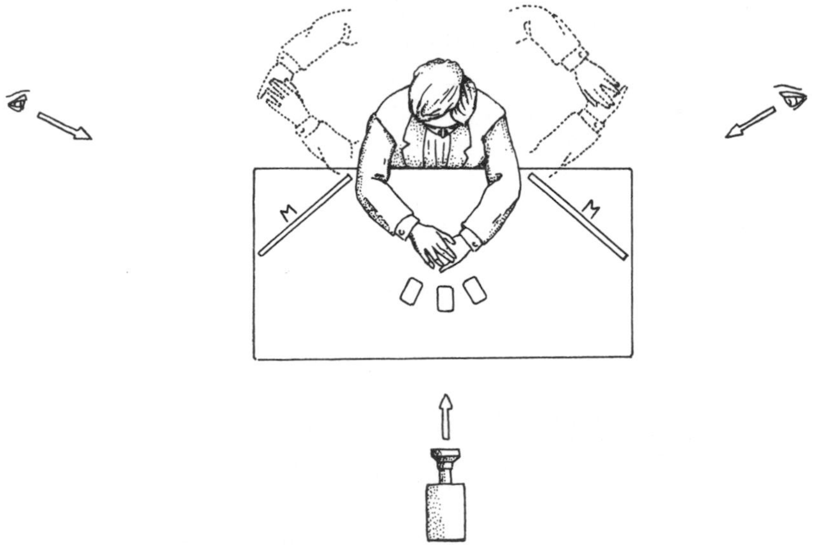

Fig. a

videotape will help you improve your performance. After a while, you will discover two things: you do some things badly, and you do some things very well. When I first began taping my performances, I discovered that I used several little movements and gestures that were instinctive—totally unplanned and unconscious. They add to the performance, and the only danger is becoming too aware of them and losing the spontaneity. Practice your technique and study the tapes of your practice sessions.

Practicing close-up is not easy with videotape. You get only one angle of view, as if working only one-to-one. That's fine, if that's the kind of work you want to do. Just arrange the camera where the eyes of the spectator will be, and you have an excellent tool working for you. But if you expect a few people at different angles to be watching you, you have to improvise some technical aids. See the diagram below:

This set-up, and variations, will allow you to see on screen what at least three spectators see. You may want to put an inclined mirror overhead also, though this requires special holders. Your picture should show about what you see here:

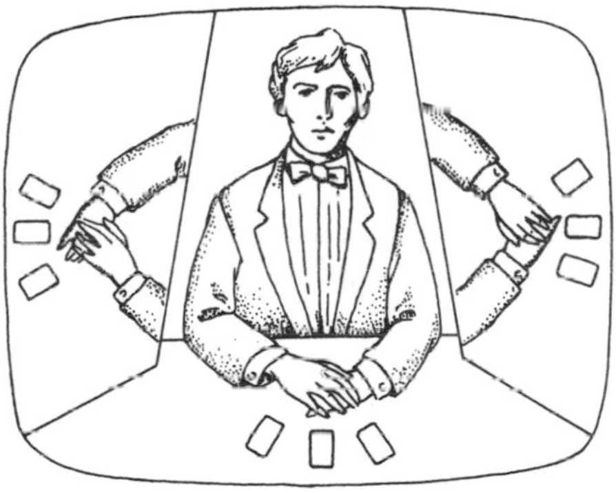

FIG. b

One thing your practice tapes may not show is misdirection, since most misdirection is accomplished by establishing eye contact with the spectator. If your face is not in the frame of the television shot, such contact will not be evident. Working for television is much different from working for a live audience, and this difference will show immediately on videotape. All this method can show you is the actual physical moves, not the overall picture. Keep this in mind.

When you record yourself doing a live performance in front of a real audience, arrange the microphone so that it also picks up the general audience reaction. You will discover that any dissatisfaction with the action on stage shows up as a rustling and murmuring sound. Take careful note of where this happens. It is something that might normally escape your attention.

Working with a closed-circuit television set-up will serve to instruct you in how to work for real television. Many performers who establish excellent stage routines are done in by television. For example, I have on tape a performance from a major television show in which a Las Vegas card-worker—well known to all magi—did some close-up one-on-one work for the show host, who was flabbergasted, as expected. The performer failed to instruct the director, who used the wrong camera angles, revealing almost everything to the viewing audience. It was a disaster.

As a performer you help not only yourself, but the show also when you go to the trouble of detailing shots for the director. Often the director is glad to have the information. Working with a small videotape arrangement in your own home will help make you a better television performer, by paying close attention to what you see on the screen, and by not allowing yourself to be fooled.

Videotape is a powerful device in learning magic, whether used to collect performances by others, or to provide a practice record and objective viewpoint. Its potential for instruction for actual television work is beyond evaluation. To fail to make use of this new technology is to lose a great opportunity. Wisely and frequently used, I consider it the greatest technical advantage magicians have ever had. I wish you luck with it.

22. *How to Stage a Magic Show—Some Professional Advice*

EVERY magician must know how to do tricks. But a successful performance depends on a variety of skills other than the tricks themselves. For that reason, I have chosen to end this book with a discussion of such general themes as comedy, pantomime, and publicity. Master the six subjects presented here—together with your knowledge of magic—and you'll not want for professional finish.

1. COMEDY

This subject is hard to write about, but it is something that the magician must certainly think about. Al Baker, probably America's most truly gifted comic magician, used to tell about a man who billed himself as "Magician, Ventriloquist, and Entertainer." When he had finished his act, the chairman of the entertainment committee said, "Well, the first two parts were fine. Now how about the entertainment?"

It is not strictly necessary to have any humor at all in a fairly short magic act; but the whole tendency of modern public entertainment is very strongly toward comedy.

Besides, the simple pleasure of an audience enjoying a good trick often expresses itself in laughter. Mind-reading and spirit effects follow different rules, but straightforward conjuring usually has something intrinsically comic about it.

There are three chief kinds of innate comedy in tricks: irrelevance or illogicality, petty misfortune, and repetition.

The Chinese Wands are comically illogical; people laugh automatically because when you pull up one string, it is the *other* tassel that rises.

The Sun and Moon Trick is inherently funny because people enjoy the small misfortune of the assistant and the owner of the handkerchief (but they would stop laughing if the damage were not repaired, and they would not *start* laughing unless they thought it was going to be).

They laugh harder and harder at the repeating three-sponge-balls-and-pocket routine, because the simple repetition of a small effect grows progressively funnier.

All three of these tricks are humorous in themselves; two of them can be very successfully done in dumbshow. (See below under "Pantomime.") One basic point about good comedy magic is that it must not depend *solely* on patter for the fun. Ready-made comic patter is almost never comic except (occasionally) in the mouth of its originator.

This is not to say that patter, as well as tricks, cannot be inherently funny. Remember Henning Nelms: "The conversation can be thoroughly entertaining without the conjuring." Al Baker was a star radio and TV gag-writer as well as a magician. Yet even he reached his zenith with tricks.

Max Eastman's "Ten Commandments of the Comic Arts" follow with a magician's interpretation of what each one means.

1. *Be interesting*. In other words, give your gags a buildup. Don't spring them until you have said enough to interest the audience in that particular subject. Don't jump people's attention around *at the start.*

2. *Be unimpassioned.* This does not mean you can't be absorbed in drama of your story; it means that you must not involve the feelings and beliefs of your audience too deeply. No jokes about religion, no tricks with dead animals.

3. *Be effortless.* Any sign of toil, says Eastman, destroys the playful spirit that all comedy demands in the listener. "Effortlessness" requires years of effort to escape from involved patter, the labored introduction, the "On my way here this evening . . . ."

4. *Remember the difference between cracking practical jokes and conveying ludicrous impressions.* By "practical jokes" Eastman means the humor that starts off in one direction and then dodges, or deliberately disappoints you. His kind of practical joke must begin plausibly and collapse suddenly. In a manner of speaking, sucker gags are practical jokes; so, again, are the Chinese Wands; whereas the Miser's Dream conveys a cumulative ludicrous impression, with no plausibility and no sudden collapse.

5. *Be plausible.* "By plausibility," says Eastman himself, "I mean successfully leading a person on." This is the very essence of all conjuring, and no more need be said about it. The Miser's Dream is not plausible in plot; but the motions of catching coins and tossing them into the hat must be so.

6. *Be sudden.* This is a general statement of the magical rule that you must never tell the audience what you are about to do. In jokes, don't telegraph the punch.

7. *Be neat.* An extension of Rule 3: the point must be right at hand,

with no explaining needed. Eight out of ten mathematical tricks are not neat, and the spectator is too weary by the time of the climax to feel any surprise.

8. *Be right with your timing.* In its way, the most important rule of all, and the hardest to teach. You must not rush either your trick or your joke so that people don't take it in; once they have taken it in, you must not dawdle and bore them. And, when your effect is over, you must give them time to appreciate it, yet not drag on into a stage wait.

9. *Give good measure of serious satisfaction.* This is meant to denounce the "anything-for-a-gag" attitude. There should be a little sense somewhere underlying even the most utter nonsense. The Miser's Dream is total nonsense, but love of money is not; to do the same trick with thimbles, catching far more than you could put on your fingers, would be stupidly senseless.

10. *Redeem all serious disappointments.* In its crudest application to magic, this means you must do something nice at the end for a volunteer whom you have made ridiculous. When Howard Thurston used to wrap up a live rabbit for a little girl to take home, he was skirting a double disappointment: the child's parents did not want to take care of any rabbits in a small apartment; yet when the rabbit vanished, that was a disappointment for the little girl. And when the package turned into a box of candy, both disappointments were redeemed.

2. PANTOMIME (by dance and pantomime director Louise Gifford)

As it concerns the magician, pantomime is the art of acting, apart from the spoken word. It includes the performer's carriage or posture, gestures, and expression. It is utterly impossible to do magic without pantomime; sleight of hand *is* pantomime of a difficult order. Unfortunately, it is all too easy to do magic without good pantomime.

Sleight of hand depends on skilled, well-coordinated muscle control of the arms and hands. For dramatic pantomime this muscle control includes the whole body—legs, feet, trunk, head, as well as arms and hands. This coordinated, designed body or muscle control in pantomime is called *body mechanics.*

Besides body mechanics the magician and actor use what are called *stage mechanics and transitions*. The simplest of the three—body mechanics, stage mechanics, transitions—is stage mechanics.

Stage mechanics concerns going from front to back or across the platform or acting space. The new names for old friends are "upstage," "downstage," and "oblique." "Upstage" (u.s.) means away from the audience, up to the back. "Downstage" (d.s.) means down near the footlights or audience. In pantomime or stage directions *d.s.l.* means downstage left—left from the *performer*; *d.s.r.*, downstage right—right from the performer. And so on.

A second and extremely important part of stage mechanics is the use of the *oblique*. When showing his empty palm the magician holds the palm at an angle visible to the audience sitting at the extreme left, full center, and extreme right. He is careful that neither shoulder hides arm or hand. He opens the upstage palm, points to the open palm with the downstage hand, keeping body facing front, shoulders on a line with the straight line of the platform opening. Often he moves s.r. to s.l., carefully keeping both shoulders visible to the entire audience. This is using or moving on the oblique.

To practice moving on the oblique, walk across the stage to s.l. naturally. Keep this easy natural walk going to s.r., turning the shoulders and head to the left as though talking to a person at extreme s.l. This will make a twist in the upper body. After practising in this extreme, modify the twist in the body just enough so that both shoulders stay visible to all the audience.

To acquire good body mechanics the use of observation and memory is important. In pantomime training, many exercises are given to sharpen observation of how people walk, sit, react, in everyday life. Everyone is aware that feelings and body attitudes are closely connected. Body attitudes are made through feelings, and are shown through, and only through, muscle contractions, muscle extensions, or muscle release. Our vocabulary to describe the physical coordinations called posture, carriage, or bearing consists of words for feelings. Posture is accepted as a symbol or indicator of an emotional condition. The words "dejected," "elated," "despairing," "hopeful," "joyous," "sadly" bring to memory various and contrasting pictures of posture. Take weariness or dejection as an exercise. Carefully observe the muscle pulls or posture of a dejected or very weary person. Such a person is easy to find on any street. Also we may remember the pulls of a very weary, unsuccessful walking jaunt. Observe carefully, remembering that the whole body—trunk, legs, and feet—is included as well as the already skilled arms and hands of the magician. Practice this pattern of physical coordination with the entire body as carefully as a palming pattern or coordination for magic.

Good posture is accepted as an indication of well-being, of confidence, of success. It may be described as standing our full height, giving our lungs full breathing space, standing "tall," pushing the sky up from the soles of our feet through the crown of our head. Practice walking in this pattern of elation.

Besides walks resulting from states of feeling, there is what is known as a balanced walk. This walk too is colored by feelings; that is, a balanced walk may be dejected or elated, but under the sway of any feeling the walk will still be graceful, or balanced. Grace and economy of movement are synonymous.

In walking, economy of motion is grace. Tension has no part in economy. Tension is a tightening, a holding back; economy is a wise, easy, full distribution of energy *where* energy is needed for action.

To get a balanced walk try an exaggerated *un*balanced or *un*economical walk in this way. Stand with the feet wide apart as though walking two lines. To progress forward keeping this wide base the body is lurched first to one side, then to the other. Walk with this wide lurch several times around the room, then begin narrowing the base, bringing the feet nearer each other; the lurching becomes less. Continue this until the feet barely miss brushing as they pass forward. The lurching is gone, the walk is *almost in one tread*. This *almost in one tread* gives grace and style to the body. To walk completely in one tread, like a tightrope walker, becomes artificial and looks affected for any use other than a tightrope walker. Try this walk—from wide to narrow base—before a mirror, and judge the effect for yourself.

With this balanced walk, practice the dejection and elation feeling patterns. Observe other muscle patterns, and practice them carefully and separately. For certain comic effects practice with the wide, lurching, uneconomical base.

Choice of a type character is one good way to start a story. Possibly two of the best types to begin with are a slightly intoxicated silk-hatted socialite suffering from hallucinations, and an irresponsible tramp carrying a torn and useless umbrella.

Suppose the tramp is unhappy, wants to play a game of cards but has no cards. The memory of wanting something is familiar to all, wanting money but having no money, wanting cards but having no cards, just "wanting." Then suddenly from out of the blue our want is satisfied; we are happy, gay. Two different muscle coordinations are here, familiar to the memory and experience of every audience. It is easy to "remember" seeing a character walking dejectedly, almost slinking, past a cafeteria door, stopping, searching through his pockets, even turning a worn wallet upside down and shaking it, sighing, then walking on in an unhappy, or "wanting," condition. This is an incident in pantomime.

Watching further this character with lowered head, slumped shoulders, dragging feet, we see him stop, examine a bright object. Suddenly his whole physical coordination changes. Quickly he moves to pick up the quarter—movement, pleasure, head and shoulders higher; now with confidence he walks into the cafeteria. The complete happening is a story in dramatic pantomime.

Between the two feelings shown by changes in muscle coordination is a place or *the* place where the change, or *transition,* from one to the other is made. The drama is in the transition.

This transition must be slowed down many times slower than the change, or transition, in a real happening. This is done so that the eye of the observer watching from a distance may have enough time to see physically and realize mentally what is happening. A transition for a dramatic story lets the audience see that something is about to happen, see how and what makes the happening, and see the conclusion, or result from this happening. The attention of the audience is kept on every obvious detail during the transition.

At the transition let the audience see something is going to happen, let the audience see this happening, then let them see the result of the happening. The magician may need to practice the dramatic transition by stopping suddenly, staring at a vacant spot, letting the audience see that nothing is present, reaching for this nothing and finding a dollar in his hand, seeing this himself, letting the audience see this, *then* adjusting to the new situation, now a happy one. Putting the three parts together with an interesting stage line of movement will result in a convincing pantomime of a wanting character finding money and becoming a happy character.

To re-create the muscle pattern does not mean that the artist gets his personal feelings into a state. The artist uses his mechanics—good body mechanics, the skill to choose a posture design—then coordinates his muscles into this design. Observation, memory, and practice make it easy for an actor to convey hope, joy, sadness, etc., one after the other.

When the whole body is coördinated for or in a chosen design, the gesture continues in the pattern. Here again the body is free of tension, so the gesture will be easy and broad. Gestures onstage must be broader than in a room, for the simple reason that they must be seen from a distance. When you beckon to a person at a distance you broaden, make larger, more open movements. The raised platform gives the performer distance from the audience. He must enlarge his gestures to reach the eye of the last seat in the most distant section of the house.

The audience follows the eye. The audience wants to see what the character is seeing. If the actor sees something, but his gaze becomes listless or moves on, the audience knows the object is of no value. The eye will reflect the body coordination.

The mouth is used only in the extreme of emotion, the dropped jaw of final terror, etc. Such extremes are best left alone by the beginner. The easy, relaxed face is best.

In really re-creating the posture patterns of muscle coordinations resulting from feeling, a *re-creation* rather than an imitation of the feeling is conveyed to the observer. This is the difference between the amateur and the artist. The amateur imitates, or tries to *pretend;* the artist *re-creates the pattern.*

3. MUSIC. The following suggestions come from singer and musical authority Henry Blanchard and high-fidelity expert Boyd C. Roche.

The importance of musical accompaniment is too little appreciated by any but a few professional conjurers. A silent act loses two thirds of its effect, and is twice as hard to do, without music; nearly all magic is better for good accompaniment.

Here the tape recorder is real magic for magicians. Compare the Ganson's Personal Orchestra device in chapter 19 and Fred Barton's hints in chapter 20. You can easily edit a tape to suit your needs. Remember, though, that most countries have vigilant organizations devoted to collecting royalties on every note of their members' work broadcast or performed in public. It doesn't pay to tangle with them over current or "evergreen" popular songs when you can use hundreds of classic and traditional tunes.

Music for the opening effect should always be bright and gay. Unless this quickens the pulses of the audience, the show is dead before it begins. Toreador Song from *Carmen*, Grand March from *Aïda, Tannhäuser* march, Strauss waltzes—that sort of thing.

For *manipulations* of coins, thimbles, etc. the music should have the lulling effect (in the hypnotic sense) produced only by the most utter familiarity. Some suitable tunes are *The Blue Danube*, the *Emperor Waltz*, and any of the Strauss waltzes; *Beautiful Ohio; The Merry Widow Waltz; Anitra's Dance*, by Grieg; *The Sorcerer's Apprentice*, by Dukas; Mendelssohn's *Spring Song and Spinning Song; Non Più Andrai*, the aria from Mozart's *Marriage of Figaro.*

Suspense will have to be created by music tailor-made (or in the case of a tape, spliced) from parts of pieces like Rachmaninoff's *Prelude in C*

Sharp Minor, the opening of Beethoven's *Fifth Symphony*, and the overture to *Carmen*, which is a very rich source.

Suspense followed by a sudden climax has to be created in the same way. The overture to *William Tell* has a great variety of material—storm, calm, dawn, and so on, which can be cut and repeated at will. The slow movement from Beethoven's *Sixth Symphony*, and, once more, *Carmen*, are an inexhaustible mine.

Productions, the reeling out of stuff by the yard, require music by the yard also: Chaminade's *Scarf Dance*; Chopin's *Minute Waltz*; Schumann's *Happy Farmer*; The First Movement of Mozart's *G Minor Symphony*; *Flight of the Bumblebee*, by Rimsky-Korsakoff.

Time-fillers, for use when a production of candy is being distributed, cards are being scaled into the balcony, or the magician is passing among the audience, should be tunes that can be whistled on one hearing; popular songs like *Home on the Range, Ol' Man River, Alexander's Ragtime Band*; patriotic tunes like *Yankee Doodle*; Strauss waltzes; Sousa marches; and the songs of Stephen Collins Foster, like *Oh Susannah* and *Camptown Races*.

Oriental music is recognized largely from the tom-toms and flutes. Among actual tunes, *Orientale*, by César Cui, a piece of the same name by Amani, and *Song from the East*, by Cyril Scott, are appropriate.

For children's shows, nursery tunes are very useful: *I had a Little Nut Tree; London Bridge; The Farmer in the Dell; Row, Row, Row Your Boat; Mulberry Bush; Baa, Baa, Black Sheep; Mary Had a Little Lamb; Little Jack Horner; Humpty-Dumpty; Sur le Pont d'Avignon; Au Claire de la Lune; Little Boy Blue; Rock-a-bye Baby; Pop Goes the Weasel; Hickory Dickory Dock; The Bear Went over the Mountain; The King of France.*

Manipulative routines, once the separate sleights have been learned, are best rehearsed to music. If secret moves are made in time with the music, they are much more likely to be detected than if they are slipped in, as they should be, *off the beat*.

4. NIGHT-CLUB SHOWS

After the decline of vaudeville, night clubs became almost the only place where magicians could find steady employment with a short act.

Night-club shows are of two kinds: floor acts, which are a modified form of vaudeville; and table acts, in which the performer goes from one party to the next, doing table tricks, and getting his pay directly from the patrons.

The requirements of all night-club work depend on the fact that none of the audience is in a mood to make any effort, and at least part of the audience will be somewhat drunk.

Therefore night-club magic must be fast in tempo, and it must require no concentration from the audience. In these respects Cardini's is the ideal night-club floor act. The floor act should not call for audience participation in any way more elaborate than the choice of a drink or the cutting of a rope; the choice of cards, for instance, should be confined to table acts.

Only Cardini's great skill enables him to do his particular work despite the third essential requirement imposed by the average night-club layout: the act must be angle-proof. This is true of both floor and table acts. Back-palming and servantes are practically ruled out; loads must be made with great care and discretion.

The tendency of magicians working a floor act is to forget that they are hired essentially as liquor salesmen; they are the entertainment that brings people into the place, but once the customers are inside, the magician must whiz through his act and get out of the way before he slows the flow of orders to the bar.

The night-club *table* magician has two special problems: an opening effect that will catch people's attention and make him welcome at the tables; and a finale that will forcibly suggest financial contributions from the party. Jean Hugard's *Close-up Magic for the Night-Club Magician* (now out of print) offers suggestions for both problems. The magician can kill two birds with one stone by producing several real coins from the clothes of patrons at the first table. The money is dropped carelessly on the table, and this helps people realize that they are expected to add to the pile. Production of a wand is another good opener. For a finale, Hugard strongly advises a trick with borrowed bills; some performers contrive to make it seem that the only gracious thing the patron can do is leave the bill with the magician.

Among effects suitable for night-club work are: Afghan Bands; Ball of Wool; Bird Cage; Breakaway Fan; Cake Baked in a Hat; Card in Cigarette; Cards Up the Sleeve (needs great care with angles); Chinese Wands; Cigarette manipulation; Cups and Balls (table only); Dollar-Bill tricks; Egg Bag; Funnel; Inexhaustible Bottle; Jumping Peg; Linking Rings (floor only); Lota; Miser's Dream; Needle Trick; Nest of Boxes; Organ Pipes (floor only); Rice Bowls; Ring on Stick; rope tricks; silk tricks (when angle-proof); Sponge Balls (table only); Sympathetic Coins; Sympathetic Silks; thimble tricks (floor only); Thumb Tie; Torn and Restored Paper; Turban Trick.

5. BUSINESS METHODS

While there are bound to be as many ways of doing business as of doing magic, a few general rules deserve remembering by the amateur who would like to develop an income from his hobby.

Free shows are legitimate and desirable if given for your own close friends or for organizations of which you are an active member. So are charity shows, provided you know that everyone else is also donating his services. Otherwise, remember that fund-raising is a big business that spends a lot of money to raise money.

Beyond this point, free shows merely destroy business that some professional may be depending on; furthermore, since people get such a show for nothing, they naturally decide that must be what it's worth.

How much to charge is always a puzzle for the new magician. In the first place, remember that your time is worth something, and that any show takes more time than you spend on the stage, or even traveling to and from the date. Naturally you would rather perform than not, or you wouldn't be a magician; but in business terms this is irrelevant. Even a schoolboy can be earning money some other way if he is not performing.

Partly, the price should often depend on what the employer can afford—less for a private party than for a club, less for small groups than for large ones.

Once you have decided on a price, never reduce it. It is far better to give a show free than to become known as a person who can be beaten down. Furthermore, if you are competing with another magician or some comparable act for a particular job, don't try to get it by underbidding, and don't even meet lower bids. The only thing you have to sell is the quality of your entertainment; purchasers who can't afford you today will be all the more anxious the next time.

You are required to keep a record of your magic income for tax purposes—something not even beginners can safely neglect. And it is a very good idea to keep books on what you spend, as well as what you take in through magic. You can offset the expenses against the income on your tax return, and besides you will be less inclined to think conjuring can be sold cheap if you realize what you have spent on it.

Sources of business must be found by each magician for himself. Schools, churches, and clubs are among the commonest employers of magicians. Making friends with the program director at a local TV station never does any harm. In large cities, business houses and conventions are another field.

One of the safest rules of selling is to concentrate on present customers rather than search indiscriminately for new prospects. Even a club that has just had you at its annual show can recommend you elsewhere—obviously the best form of advertising.

From this it follows that once you get a foothold in a particular field—fraternal organizations, children's parties, sales conventions, you name it—you should exploit that to the fullest before you go further afield. Your reputation spreads more quickly that way. Equally important, you have a known class of new prospects whose addresses you can get from directories or from satisfied clients.

So long as you are arranging your own booking, your mailing list is your most valuable single business asset. Keep it up to date; add names from news items (Mrs. William Snodgrass named Program Chairman of the Women's Club); make changes promptly; be sure that all names are spelled correctly.

Most American towns of any size have one or more lettershops. Find out the most expensive one, and go do a couple of quick tricks for the owner. He (or very likely she) can give you invaluable advice about selling yourself by mail. The bigger lettershops have someone on hand who specializes in writing sales letters, and someone else who knows about printing circulars and letterheads. If you have any friends in advertising, particularly in direct mail, put them to work. If not, there is an excellent pamphlet called *How to Think About Letters,* by Howard Dana Shaw, published by *Direct Marketing* magazine at 224 Seventh St., Garden City, N. Y. 11534. Also good is the same publisher's *How to Think About Direct Mail,* by Henry Hoke.

Newspaper and magazine advertising is usually too expensive to pay a magician; but small classified ads, or "professional cards," may be worthwhile in large towns if you know they reach the people you are looking for. A small ad on the society page, for instance, might bring you jobs at children's parties. Your name in the classified phone book can also be a good investment. Hint: list yourself as an entertainer, not a magician.

A booking agent will take many of these worries off your shoulders, but you must win a certain success on your own before any agent will handle your act. Here, too, only a good agent is good enough. Sign up with one you have confidence in, and leave him alone. He can make money only by doing his best for you; let it go at that.

One last rule, social as well as business: never knock another magician's act. In fact, if a dissatisfied employer complains in your presence, try to say something nice about the magician. A bad performer may give magic a black eye that you personally will suffer from.

6. PUBLICITY

In purpose, publicity is one form of advertising for the magician. In effect, it is better than any other form of advertising. In method, most magicians gravely misunderstand it, and so fail to get it when they could.

Publicity depends directly on newspaper, magazine, and TV reporters and on editors. Every magician, even the most resolutely amateur, should cultivate the friendship of journalists; that much is obvious. But friendship is not enough, and that is where most publicity-seekers (in the legitimate sense) fall down. A newspaperman's living depends on his printing what his own particular readers want to read—what will interest, impress, or move them. It would be quite futile for him, even through friendship, to print something his audience did not care about. There would be no publicity, because his readers would merely skip it, becoming nonreaders.

The conjurer's problem, therefore, is to convince journalists, whether friends or strangers, that something about him is especially interesting to the reading public. Actually the tricks themselves are usually interesting if well described by an impartial observer, but editors tend to feel that such descriptions belong in the advertising pages. It is up to the magician to prove that they deserve better.

Often the crucial thing is to get a reporter to your show. For a local event like a charity carnival, the papers will probably send someone. Just remember it's the event and not the attraction that has brought him. Otherwise, try to get an introduction to someone on the paper or, failing that, phone and ask the editor for five minutes of his time.

Keep your word. *Be ready to leave in five minutes.* If you have mastered the art of dealing with newsmen, he will probably keep you there for an hour. But put it on him. Make a real effort to leave as soon as you have exchanged civilities and shown one trick. You are trying to promote yourself not only as a magician but as a pleasant person to know. Overselling loses far more sales than underselling, no matter what your merchandise. And editors have more resistance to high-pressure methods than almost any class of men you can name.

Your chief resource in getting press attention is a small stock of impressive, ever-ready tricks. They need not be genuinely impromptu, but should seem so. They should be better and bigger than the average vest-pocket trick.

Mind-reading effects that can be shown quickly are very good (see Annemann's *Practical Mental Effects* for several beauties). So are quick, striking coin manipulations, dollar-bill tricks, Sympathetic Coins, a very, very few card tricks—anything that can be worked close up without fear of detection and has no flavor of apparatus, preparation, or laboriousness. Tricks involving liquor are made to order for some publicity, but not for all.

One inviolable rule in dealing with the press: don't lie, don't exaggerate. Only the truth is good enough to print. If a newspaper takes your word for a falsehood once, it will be the last time. And if you boast without foundation, the advertising pages are the only place for you.

John Booth's *Forging Ahead in Magic* is devoted to business and publicity methods.

There. So much for the nonmagical side of magic. If I hear of someone's studying this *Amateur Magician's Handbook* and then climbing out of the amateur class by getting paid for a show, I shall be satisfied.

APPENDIX

Further Tricks and Illusions

Glossary

ACQUITMENT. A sleight for showing the hands empty although something (especially a billiard ball) is palmed. Acquitments are very seldom convincing.

ANIMALS, LIVE. See chapter 20.

APPARATUS. Faked paraphernalia for tricks, as distinguished from ordinary articles used by the magician. See Part III.

BIRD CAGE, VANISHING. Invented by De Kolta, used with great success by Blackstone, Mulholland, and many others.

The cage is rectangular, six inches high and wide, eight inches long, made of wire on a frame of metal rods. It contains a bird, originally a live one, nowadays almost always a dummy. The performer comes forward holding the cage by the ends between his flat palms. He may ask a volunteer to put his palms on the top and bottom.

With no covering, the performer makes a tossing motion; the cage vanishes instantly.

The cage commonly used will collapse of its own weight, the bottom-right-rear corner and top-left-front corner pulling apart to draw the cage into a shuttle-shaped bundle. A pull is attached to the bottom-right-rear corner; when the magician actuates the pull by stretching his arms, the cage is drawn up his sleeve and between his shoulder blades, inside his waistcoat.

BLACK ART. The principle, used in some tricks and many stage illusions, that dead black against dead black is invisible owing to the absence of shadow.

BLINDFOLDS. Some tricks are more effective when the performer is blindfolded. By frowning and then raising your eyebrows while any ordinary blindfold is applied, you can get a clear view down your nose. If you roll a fairly thin handkerchief inward from two opposite corners, leaving an inch or so between the rolls, you can see through the single thickness of handkerchief. There are also various trick blindfolds on the market.

BODY WORK. Vesting, or the use of pockets, in operating a trick. Best avoided where possible.

BULLET CATCHING. A famous stage trick, mishaps in which have killed several performers. Volunteers from the audience fire rifles at the magician, who catches the marked bullets on a plate or in his teeth. Modern methods require the substitution of a blank dummy for the cartridge containing the marked bullet, which is extracted behind the scenes and secretly passed to the performer.

CARDS, MARKING OF. See MARKING.

CHANGE. An undetected substitution, often called a switch. Distinguished from a color change, which is meant to be seen.

CHANGING BAG. A velvet bag mounted on a ring with a long handle. Any small object put in the bag can be switched by a half-turn of the handle, which swings an inner half lining from one side of the bag to the other (Figs. 217 and 218). The bag bears some resemblance to a church collection bag, saving it from complete fakiness.

CHOPPER EFFECTS. A class of small illusions and pocket tricks using a sort of wooden pillory with one or more holes, through which a sharp steel blade slides, guillotine-fashion, from top to bottom. The blade is first proved sharp and solid by slicing a carrot. Then the blade and the top of the pillory are removed so that someone can put his head, wrist, or, in the pocket version, finger through the hole. The top is replaced, then the blade is forced down, apparently cutting the victim in two.

The pillory is unprepared; the blade, mounted in a wooden frame, is actually two thin blades lying together. The front one is only half the depth of its frame, and slides freely up and down in it. The rear blade, full width and fixed, has a large piece scooped out of the middle where the hole of the pillory is. A catch keeps the two blades together while the carrot is sliced; the performer undoes the catch when taking out the blade. Thus the front blade can slide upward in the frame when the assistant's neck stops it. The fixed blade does not

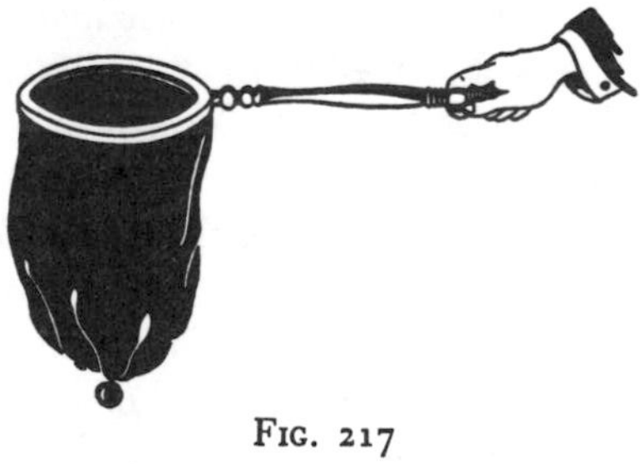

FIG. 217

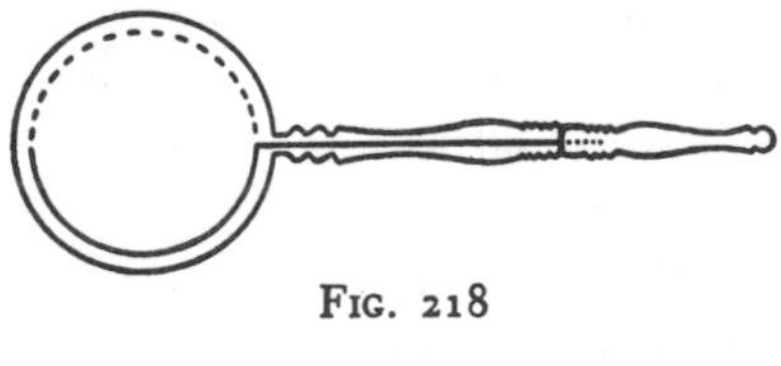

FIG. 218

touch the neck, being cut out there, but can be seen descending through holes on each side of the main pillory hole.

DANCING HANDKERCHIEF. Originally a parlor trick, done with a horizontal black thread, this became the showpiece of Harry Blackstone's repertory.

DEALERS. The larger cities have dealers in magical equipment and supplies, whom you will find in the classified phone book. Some are essentially practical-joke shops, not much use for a serious student. Some, such as Louis Tannen of New York, Magic, Inc. in Chicago, and Kanter in Philadelphia, are meeting places for the fraternity and storehouses of information. They are also the major publishers of professional books and magazines.

Tannen's catalogue of tricks, illusions, and books costs $3.50, which is not surprising for a 699-page tome containing something like 1700 items.

Abbott's Magic Co. of Colon, Michigan 49040 claims to be the world's largest manufacturer. Its 500-page catalogue costs $4.

DIE BOX, SLIDING. An old favorite SUCKER trick involving a large wooden die and a box just twice its size, with four doors, one on the front and one on the top of each compartment. Apparently put inside, the die can be heard sliding from end to end of the box as the performer opens and shows one compartment at a time. Eventually both compartments are shown at once, and the die reappears in a hat. Along with the die, a tin shell painted to look like it, but lacking two adjacent sides, is used. The die with the shell over it is put in the hat by way of illustration; the die is left behind there, and the shell put into the box, where its missing sides render it a mere thin lining for one compartment. The "sliding" noise is produced by a metal slug in the bottom of the box, which can be released by pressing on a spring.

DIVINATIONS. A class of effects in which the performer discovers which one of several similar objects the audience has chosen, or in what order they have been arranged. A simple example is Find the Dime, p. 229.

In apparatus versions, small slabs may be arranged in a case. Embedded in them are tiny bar magnets in different positions, which can be detected with a small compass in a metal or plastic "x-ray tube." Alternatively a panel in the lid of the box will slide far enough to give a glimpse of the slabs. The Mummy Case takes any one of three miniature mummies, one of which is unprepared, one weighted at the head, one at the foot. The case rocks or tilts accordingly.

The Diving Dial is a sort of watch case with a single hand, which spectators set to any hour, then close the lid. The secret is a counterweight on the hand; a star engraved on the outside of the case serves as a reference point when the case is stood on edge. The case rolls until the the weight is downward.

Luminous paint applied to a flat surface enables the performer to tell, for instance, which of three different-sized coins the audience has laid on it briefly. Held in partial darkness, the surface shows a dark circle where the coin lay.

Methods using skill involve such ruses as slightly opening the lid of a 3″ x 5″ card-index box closed with a rubber band, for a glimpse inside.

DOLLAR BILL TRICKS. The two major effects are the Torn and Restored Bill and the Bill in Lemon. The former differs from Torn and Restored Paper in that nothing is actually torn; a noisy ripping motion and the dumbshow of putting one half of the bill on the other create a deceptive illusion. On repetition, a second bill is used so that the two "halves" can be shown in different hands.

The bill in the second effect is caused to vanish from under a kerchief which has a duplicate sewn in the corner. The original is loaded into the lemon either by cutting a slit with the thumbnail and enlarging it with the forefinger, or by means of a sharp metal gimmick. The lemon is then cut in half with a kitchen knife, revealing the rolled-up bill.

DOLL'S HOUSE ILLUSION. A two-story dollhouse is wheeled forward on a low table. The front opens, allowing the performer to remove the furniture and the second floor; the house is seen empty. The moment the front is closed, a live girl pushes up the hinged roof and steps out. Fig. 219 shows the principle on which it works.

DROPPERS. Mechanical devices, usually worn about the person, that secretly deliver a succession of coins or cigarettes ready for production; a special form of *holder*.

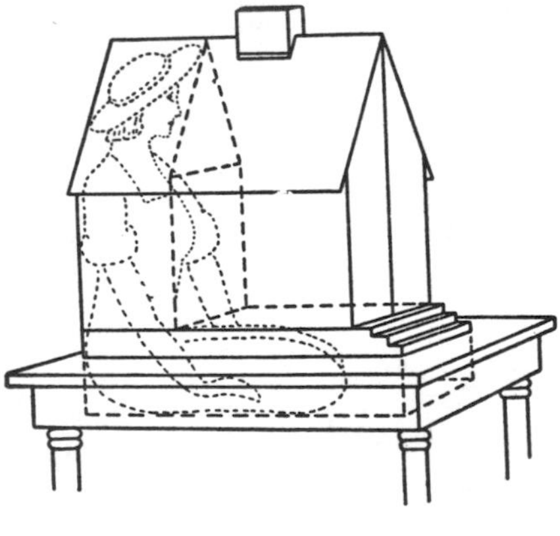

From *Greater Magic* by John Northern Hilliard (Carl W. Jones, Publisher)

FIG. 219

EAST INDIAN MAGIC. The big and spectacular miracles of the Indian magicians, such as the Rope Trick, in which the performer throws a rope in the air, chases his assistant up it, and disappears, are largely travelers' tales, founded on a thin basis of fact. John Mulholland has traced this one to a Chinese fairy tale, a cousin of our "Jack and the Beanstalk." The real virtuosity of the Indian conjurers lies in sleight of hand such as the Cups and Balls. A standard reference is Eddie

Josephs's *Magic and Mysteries of India.*

ELECTRIC PACK. Simulates the flourish of springing the cards, but requires no skill, since the deck is strung together with a double line of narrow white ribbon, allowing half an inch of play between each pair of cards. Now most often deliberately exposed as a gag.

ELECTRONIC EQUIPMENT. "Remote control" effects of course originally astonished because there was no such thing in real life. Now that such toys and appliances are commonplace, the tricks have lost most of their mystery.

The Belgian dealer Anverdi offers an electronic Rising Cards operated by a switch panel in your pocket. Conjurers' tables and inflatable robots wander about the stage on command. But have a care, dealer Victor Astor warns: they may answer to any chance passing frequency, e.g., a police car.

Shown as part of a drama, with no emphasis on the puzzle element, electronic gear offers a compact but expensive way to liven up the show.

There are books of puzzles and tricks with a pocket calculator.

ESCAPES. More and more an entirely separate branch of magic. Harry Houdini identified his name with it, and no other escape artist has ever come within miles of him. A selection of methods will be found in Downs, *The Art of Magic; Gilbert Knots and Splices;* Hatton and Plate, *Magicians' Tricks;* Burling Hull, *Thirty-Three Rope Ties and Chain Releases;* and Carrington, *The Boys' Book of Magic.* See page 19.

FIRING A GIRL FROM A CANNON INTO A NEST OF TRUNKS. A popular stage illusion. The cannon is a large wood and sheet-metal dummy, with a trap down through the carriage, allowing the girl to pass under the stage. Thence she quickly goes up through another stage trap; the two nested trunks have hinged double flaps in the bottom (Fig. 220),

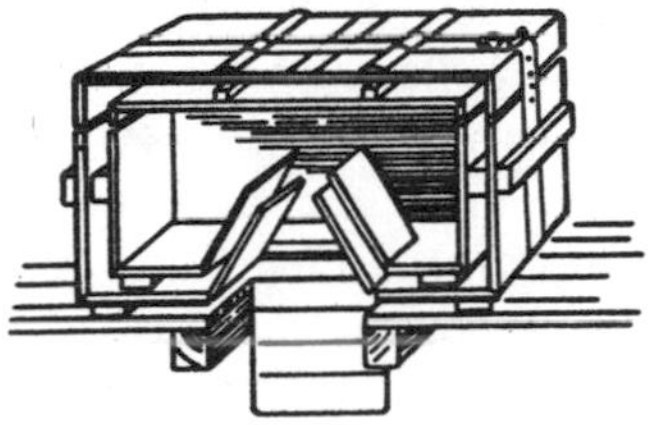

FIG. 220

which allow the girl to climb inside just before the trunks are swung up overhead with a rope and pulley. The cannon is not "fired" until after this has been done.

FLASH PAPER. Chemically impregnated tissue paper that burns with one swift flash when ignited. Used to "wrap up" articles that are to vanish. It is carried by all dealers.

GAMBLING METHODS. These may cause the conjurer some irritation because, although they are quite distinct from magic, people often feel disappointed that he is not proficient in them. Careful reading of Erdnase and *Scarne on Dice*, by John Scarne and Clayton Rawson, will at least enable you to talk a good game.

GOLDFISH BOWLS. A very old trick, of Chinese origin, which had a big revival when Ching Ling Foo puzzled western magicians with his version. The bowl is clear glass, full of water, with goldfish swimming in it (nowadays usually dummies cut out of carrots). It is produced from under a shawl draped over the magician's arm. The original method was to fasten a rubber cover over the mouth of the bowl, which was quite shallow, and was kept in a loading pocket or in a sort of cloth sling under the performer's coattails. Ching Ling Foo carried his slung between his knees, under his mandarin gown. A much deeper bowl can be produced by the use of a faked side table, the drape of which is just deep enough to hide the bowl, and is arranged to drop at a touch to the level of the actual table top. The performer pretends to catch a bowl under the shawl, realistically spilling some water with the help of a small sponge; he then sets the "bowl" down on the table, letting the drape fall to reveal the real thing.

GO SOUTH with an object. Secretly abstract or dispose of it.

HAND PUPPETS. See chapter 20.

HISTORY OF MAGIC. The subject is in rather a haphazard state; the best current source is Milbourne Christopher's *Illustrated History of Magic.*

HOLDERS. Devices suspended out of sight, often about the performer's person, to deliver into his hand any small load, such as a ball, silk, or stack of coins. Many varieties can be bought from dealers.

HOULETTE. A more or less ornamental container of metal, glass, wood, or plastic to hold the pack for the Rising Cards.

JUMPING PEG. The typical effect among a series of small tricks depending on a double-turnover move. The jumping peg is pushed into one of three holes bored through a small wooden paddle or pencil. It is put in the middle hole, and the paddle is shown from both sides. The peg instantly jumps to one of the end holes.

The secret of the paddle is that only two, adjacent, holes go clear through. Toward the handle end on one side and toward the outer end on the other is a hole burned part way through. From one side of the paddle the peg seems to be in the middle hole; from the other side, in an end hole.

A non-turnover move will serve for large paddles or for apparently showing both sides of the bare forearm, after which a design appears on the inside. Hold the hand (with or without the paddle) upright from the elbow, back of hand outward. Then point the arm straight down as if to exhibit the inside, but instead simply keep the back of the hand to the front.

The double-turnover move hides this fact. The two sides of the paddle are successively shown by a forward-and-back swing of the wrist. In addition, the paddle can be spun an extra half-turn by rolling it between forefinger and thumb. By a combination of both movements, the same side of the paddle will be shown over and over, although the audience seems to see alternate sides.

KELLAR TIE. The quickest rope release. Done with a two-foot length of clothesline or sash cord, which should be soaked in water to soften it. The rope is hung at the center over your right wrist, and tied on the inside of the wrist in a square knot. The left wrist is laid upon the right wrist, behind your back, and apparently made fast in exactly the same way, with a square knot over the exposed inside, or pulse, of the wrist. Actually, as the right hand goes behind your back, the fingers catch the upper piece of rope near the knot, and pick up a loop of slack, which they press against the heel of the hand for the brief moment before the left wrist is laid on top to cover the loop. If the hands are now clamped firmly together, the volunteer can pull hard in tying the second knot without dislodging the slack. Yet the hands can be instantly separated and brought together, the rope seemingly as tight as ever.

LEVITATIONS. Tricks and illusions in which something or someone floats in space without visible means of support. The inanimate objects that have been made to float include large balls, electric light bulbs, glasses of milk, and matches. All but the last are done by some arrangement of black thread. The various forms of Floating Lady were the most sensational illusions in use until the arrival of Sawing a Woman in Two. The most finished version was named Asrah. A girl was brought in, hypnotized, put on a couch, and covered with a sheet. The couch was faked, allowing a light wire form to take her place under the sheet, and she sank down into the couch. The arrangement of steel gooseneck and wires that supported the dummy in the air can be seen from Fig. 221. The gooseneck allowed a hoop to be passed over the floating form from head to foot, then back behind the form, then turned forward and passed from head to foot again, when it came clear at the feet. Eventually the sheet was shaken out, and the wire form either dropped on the half-darkened stage or collapsed.

LOAD. To introduce something secretly, before or during a trick; thing loaded.

MAGNETIC TRICKS. "The use of magnets has become increasingly popular

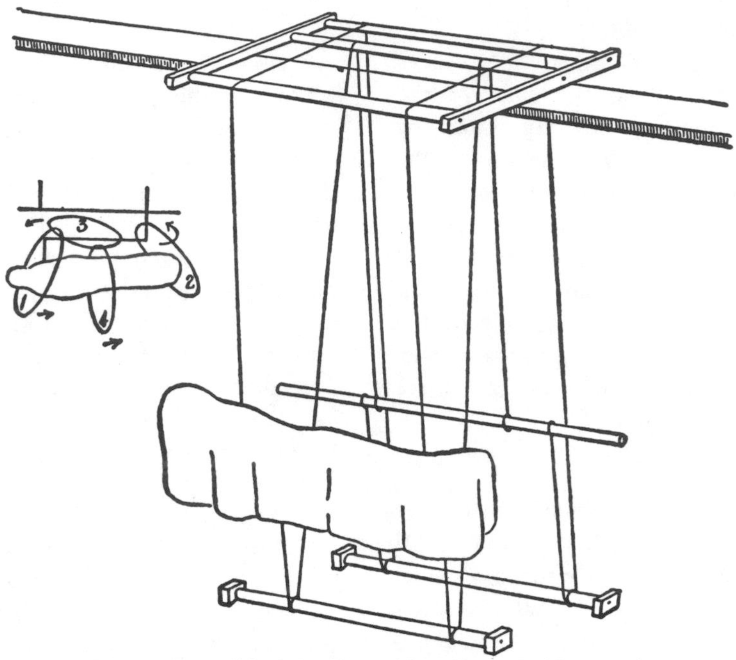

From *Learn Magic* by Henry Hay (Dover Publications)

FIG. 221

with magicians in recent years; so much so that the principle has been overworked to the point of giving the game away." Lewis Ganson wrote some years ago.

A strong circular magnet from a loudspeaker, fixed under the magician's working surface, will magnetize paperclips and the like held above it.

The commonest applications are in coin work. Coins are available either with a steel core, responding to a magnet, or magnetic, to stick to steel.

Dutch coins are magnetic, British not. Ganson suggests using a wand enclosing a strong magnet to sort out the Dutch currency from a fistful of change by passing the wand through.

MagnetiCoins and *Magnetrix* are two books on the subject by Frederick L. and Arthur Kraft.

MAKE-UP. Hardly necessary to the beginning amateur. In platform magic it will probably be needed. *Stage Make-Up*, by Richard Corson, gives complete instructions for every kind of face and hand make-up.

MARKING. The various methods that allow an operator to distinguish cards by their backs. Complete marked decks are known as "readers"; crude ones good enough for stage use can be bought from dealers. Gamblers and careful magicians mark their own according to some system that gives a choice of twelve distinguishable points for values (one remaining unmarked) on each card, and three for suits.

Individual cards (such as chosen ones) are marked during a trick by the pressure of a fingernail near a corner, or by "daub"—a marking ink to match the back color, usually carried in a pad or small cup. The performer gets a tiny smear of daub on a finger tip and so transfers it to the card.

MIRROR PRINCIPLE. In illusions, a method of masking by the use of two mirrors joined at right angles, each mirror making an angle of forty-five degrees with the footlights. If the sides and back of the stage or cabinet are identically covered, the eye of the spectator in front mistakes the reflection of the side wall for the back wall. Many stage effects have been, and still are, worked on this principle.

MUSIC. Greatly neglected by amateur magicians, musical accompaniment is almost a necessity for silent acts, and a valuable addition to many others. See chapters 20 and 22 for expert advice.

NEEDLE TRICK. A very old effect made newly famous by Harry Houdini, in which the performer apparently swallows a package of needles and several yards of thread, drinks a glass of water, then pulls the thread out of his mouth with the needles strung on it. The secret, of course, is a switch. The threaded needles may be hidden in the mouth beforehand and substituted there, or the change may take place before the needles are put in the mouth at all.

ORGANIZATIONS. Magicians are clannish and fond of one another's society. Groups of conjurers are often short-lived, but two are long-established, with local affiliates all over the country. The Society of American Magicians is the older; its branches are called Assemblies. The International Brotherhood of Magicians has branches called Rings, and publishes the monthly *Linking Ring* magazine.

PANTOMIME. Vitally important to the manipulator, and indeed to every magician, yet difficult to teach in print. See chapter, 22:2 above, Maurice, *Showmanship, and Presentation*; and particularly Nelms, *Magic and Showmanship*.

PLANT. A stooge or confederate in the audience. Most conjurers think this unethical and inexcusable at any time; a few eminent professionals make good use of plants for comedy, or occasionally to render a trick smoother, rather than merely possible. The amateur had better stay away from plants for his own convenience as well as self-respect.

ROUTINE. A set series of moves or small effects, learned as a unit, and constituting either a trick or a whole miniature program. No trick is ready to show until it has been thoroughly routined. Among the effects most completely dependent on routine are the Ambitious Card,

Cups and Balls, Egg Bag, Linking Rings, Sponge Balls, and Three-Card Trick.

RUNNING GAG. A comedy trick that owes its humor to cumulative effect, and is repeated at intervals throughout the act. The lota is the best example of a running gag, but there are others, any of which will liven up a program if intelligently used.

SALTING. Secretly hiding such things as duplicate cards and coins in a room where you are going to work "impromptu."

SAWING A WOMAN IN TWO. The most famous illusion of modern times. A girl is put in a long box, usually with her head, hands, and

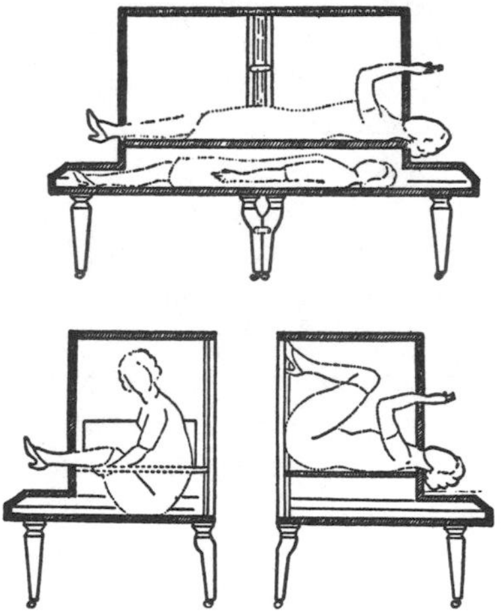

From *Learn Magic* by Henry Hay (Dover Publications)

FIG. 222

feet sticking out, and the box is sawed in two through the middle When the halves are slid back, the girl comes to life. The British P. T. Selbit and the Americans Horace Goldin and the Great Leon all developed methods independently. One version is explained by Fig. 222.

SHELL COINS. Used in pairs, they consist of a thin normal coin reduced in diameter, over which fits another coin, one side of which has been bored out to accommodate the smaller piece. Some very puzzling tricks can be done with them; the commonest version is the Penny and Dime.

SHELL GAME. A carnival and outdoor gamblers' version of the Cups and Balls, known in England as "thimblerigging" because it was usually done there with thimbles. There are three empty half-walnut shells and a "pea." The game is for the spectator to pick the shell where the pea is at a given moment. The pea is actually a piece of rubber cut to size, which is the main secret of the trick. If the shell with the pea under it is pushed forward by the forefinger, the rubber pea imperceptibly crawls out from under the shell, to be nipped between thumb and second finger. The pea is then introduced under another shell by reversing the process, pressing it with the second fingertip against the rear edge of the shell, and drawing the shell backward.

SILENT ACT. One in which the performer does not speak, but relies on pantomime and music. Silent acts are very difficult to do well, and make heavy demands on the performer's manipulation, pantomime, and misdirection; hence they are good training, though not necessarily the best showmanship. Cardini's is the outstanding silent act of the present time. Some tricks should always be worked silently, others cannot. See pages 12-13.

SPIDER. A mechanical device to facilitate back-palming.

SPIRIT EFFECTS. These reproduce the "manifestations" of spirit mediums. The chief classifications are billet-reading, slate tests, and rapping. Adjuncts are blindfolds and releases.

The chief rapping effects are The Talking Skull and The Rapping Hand, both of which sit on a table or sheet of glass. The papier-mâché skull answers questions by moving its jaw, actuated either by a horizontal black thread or by a wire gimmick in the board it sits on. The wax hand is essentially the same; in the modern form it rests on a mahogany board that has a hidden steel pin to tip it.

SPRING FLOWERS. Paper flowers with a split piece of watch spring inside that opens the flower unless it is held flat. A hundred will fold small enough to be loaded into a paper cone; open, they fill a bushel basket. Invented by Buatier de Kolta, and still a very pretty trick. The flowers are not so patently fake and compressible as the feather flowers made for other productions.

STEAL. To abstract or get possession of an object secretly. The opposite of *load*.

SUCKER GAG; SUCKER EFFECT; SUCKER ROUTINE. Method of leading the audience to think they have caught the magician, and then fooling them twice as hard.

TALK. Of an object or piece of apparatus, to make a telltale noise. See also page 134.

TEARING A PACK OF CARDS. To tear a deck of 52 cards in half requires a strong wrist and a powerful grip. The lower end of the pack, carefully squared, is laid across the ridge of the left palm exactly at the roots of the four fingers, the left thumb resting naturally on the lower left side of the pack. The four fingers are closed tightly, pressing the pack firmly against the palm. The right hand grasps the upper portion of the pack in exactly the same way, only the position is reversed; the right thumb is opposite the left thumb. The cards are thus held as if in a vise.

Twist the hands in opposite directions, right hand to the right, left hand to the left. Exert all your strength, and either your fingers or the deck will give way. At first you will find it wise to use 30 or 35 cards, and work upward.

John Mulholland introduced a version of the Card at Any Number, tearing the pack and making the halves of the chosen card appear at different numbers in the torn packets.

TELEPHONE TRICK. One or several spectators choose cards and are invited to call up a telephone number the performer gives them. The person on the other end of the line promptly names the chosen cards. The simplest method is by forcing. Another is to signal the chosen card by a code name the spectator is invited to ask for—Arthur Allen tor ace ot spades, Billy Allen for deuce of spades, and so on. Or the performer calls up his wife. She picks up the phone and starts counting aloud. When she reaches the correct value, the performer says "Hello." She then names the suits aloud until he says "Wait," and turns the phone over to the spectator.

THUMB TIE. The performer's thumbs are crossed, forming an X, and tied tightly with a cord that bisects the X perpendicularly. The two sides of this cord are drawn together by another loop wound around at right angles and tied tight. Although the tie is tight enough to stop the circulation, the performer instantly separates and rejoins his thumbs, catching on one arm a large ring thrown at him, etc.

The secret is in the cords, which must be strong and stiff. Most performers wind their own out of strong tissue paper. The first cord is eighteen inches long, tapering to pointed ends from a central diameter of one quarter inch. The other is half as thick and fourteen inches long.

When the thumbs are offered for tying, they cross at the base, the large knuckles one over the other. The longer cord is laid over, brought down underneath, back up on the opposite sides, and tied hard on top of the upper thumb, usually the right. As the tie is being made, the left thumb is withdrawn until its smallest part is in the loop, but pulled downward to hide the slack. The right thumb is driven into the loop as far as possible. The second cord bisects the X of the thumbs horizontally. During this tie the left thumb is driven in, the right thumb withdrawn to bring its smallest diameter into the loop. Both ties must be tight. Finally, one end of the long cord is knotted hard to one end of the short cord.

If the performer now brings his fingertips together and lowers his thumbs into the palms, the left thumb will slip easily in and out of the tie.

TRUNK TRICK, SUBSTITUTION. A popular old stage effect with which Houdini began his climb to fame. The performer's female assistant is tied up in a large sack, locked into a trunk, and the trunk is roped. The performer draws the curtain of a canvas cabinet in front of the trunk and himself. In a matter of seconds the girl has taken his place outside, and the performer is in the sack inside the trunk. The bottom of the sack is merely basted with one strong thread. The moment the girl in the sack is lifted into the trunk, she pulls out the thread. The construction of the trunk varies, but always has some sort of loose panel that opens inward, allowing the girl to get out and the performer to get in despite the roping. Much of the time needed is consumed, so far as the audience is concerned, by the roping and unroping of the trunk.

TWENTIETH-CENTURY HANDKERCHIEF TRICK. Two silks are tied corner to corner, rolled up, and put into a glass. A third silk of a contrasting color is vanished, and reappears tied between the two in the glass. The original method was to have a pocket sewn in the corner of one silk. A duplicate of the vanishing silk was tied to the corner at this pocket and then worked into the pocket, leaving the opposite, free corner exposed. This was the corner actually tied to the second silk before the two were rolled up. A yank in unrolling the bundle after the third silk was vanished brought the duplicate out, tied between.

The effect can also be done by a simple switch of the rolled-up bundle, either by sleight of hand or with a mirror glass.

VANISHING PERFORMER. Various methods used for vanishing a person in illusions can be employed. Two special methods:

1. The performer steps up onto a stool, holds a large shawl in front of himself, then vanishes when the shawl falls to the stage at a pistol shot. The shawl is held up by a horizontal thread across the stage at the height for a man's hands above his head, while the performer escapes through a swinging spring door in the center panel of a three-fold screen that serves as a background. He then fires a pistol and breaks the thread, dumping the shawl.

2. The performer wears some distinctive costume, while five or six assistants all wear a conspicuously different uniform. The performer, hidden for a moment behind a curtain, fan, or other concealment, strips off his own costume (it may be made of paper), revealing an assistant's uniform. He mingles with the crowd and one additional assistant is never noticed.

VEST-POCKET MAGIC. Close-up apparatus work. The dealers carry a variety of beguiling vest-pocket tricks, whose chief drawback is that they are one-effect pieces. The sleight-of-hand worker is not thus limited.

YOU DO AS I DO. A popular card trick having many versions. All are done with two packs, usually one red-backed and one blue-backed. A spectator chooses and shuffles one pack, while the performer does likewise with the remaining pack. The volunteer is told to make each move in step with the performer. The underlying effect is that the performer and the spectator each choose a card, and the cards are ultimately found to be the same. In most versions the two participants do not look at the cards they have drawn but each insert them into the other man's pack. The original method, still as good as any, required the stealing beforehand of one card from the spectator's deck. It was put into the performer's pack near the top. The same card from the performer's pack was on top. The performer "chose" this card; the spectator put his card into the performer's pack near the middle. The performer said, "You should have left it sticking out," and ran through until he came to the stolen card. Thus the performer's and the spectator's card were found to match. Many methods, some of them too complicated to be effective, are given in Hilliard's *Greater Magic* and Hugard's *Encyclopedia of Card Tricks.*

Biography and Bibliography

BOOKS are given under the author's name. Magic publications often have a short life in print, and many of the titles listed must be hunted for on the shelves of dealers, second-hand booksellers, and libraries.

Louis Tannen's Magic Shop (1540 Broadway, New York, N.Y. 10036) publishes and deals in magic books. Mr. Tannen has taken over and is reissuing the publications of Max Holden.

Another standby over many decades has been Abbott's Magic Mfg. Co., Colon, Mich. 49040. And another is Jay and Frances Marshall's Magic, Inc. 5082 North Lincoln Ave., Chicago, Ill. 60625.

The leading American magic periodicals are *Genii, The Conjurer's Magazine,* edited by William Larsen, Jr. (P.O. Box 36068, Los Angeles 90036), and *The Linking Ring,* the organ of the International Brotherhood of Magicians (headquarters, 28 North Main St., Kenton, Ohio 43326). In addition, there is M-U-M, published by the Society of American Magicians (David R. Goodsell, M-U-M editor, 11605 Victoria Drive, Oklahoma City, Okla. 73120). Abbott puts out the monthly *Tops.*

The most active British publisher of books and magazines is the Supreme Magic Co. of 64 High Street, Bideford, Devon; it issues most of Lewis Ganson's modern classics.

Goodliffe (Arden Forest Industrial Estate, Alcester, Warwickshire) issues a weekly called *Abracadabra,* and the Magic Circle of London publishes *Magic Circular.*

Abbott, Percy (1886-1960). Prominent Australian-born American magical manufacturer, dealer, publisher, and author.

Anderson, John Henry (1814-1874). Born in Scotland, the first great advertiser among magicians. He called himself the Wizard of the North, and was a huge success in Britain, Europe, America, and Australia.

Andrews, Max. *Sixteen Card Index Gems.*

Annemann, Theo (1907-1942). Brilliant American performer, inventor, writer and editor of mental tricks.

Annemann's Practical Mental Effects (New York: Max Holden.

1944). The mind reader's bible.

202 Methods of Forcing (New York: Holden, 1933). A pamphlet that every magician should have. Mostly cards, but many other kinds as well.

Baker, Al (1874-1951). Began life as a cigar-maker and became America's most truly gifted comic magician and an inventor of fiendishly ingenious small effects. Dean of the Society of American Magicians, "one of the best loved personalities in magic—consummate artist, ventriloquist, humorist, writer," as an obituary said.

Louis Tannen has taken over all the Baker books:

Al Baker's Book, 1933.

Al Baker's Second Book, 1935.

Al Baker's Ways and Means, 1941.

Al Baker's Mental Magic, 1949.

Al Baker's Pet Secrets, 1951.

Blackstone, Harry (Harry Bouton, 1885-1965). Outstanding American illusionist, one of the last to do a full evening's show; also a brilliant card operator. See page 42.

Blackstone's Modern Card Tricks and Secrets of Magic, two volumes in one (New York: Garden City, 1941). A very useful book intended for the beginner, but not to be scorned by experts.

His son Harry (Blackstone Junior) has succeeded to his father's mantle as an illusionist.

Blitz, Signor Antonio (1810-1877). European magician and ventriloquist, born in England, died in Philadelphia. He said that at one time there were thirteen imitators of his name and billing in America.

Fifty Years in the Magic Circle is one of the liveliest of conjuring autobiographies, although—as so often in magicians' publicity—it is hard to tell how much is fact.

Bobo, J. B. (born 1910). American lyceum and school performer. His one great book has become a classic. *The New Modern Coin Magic* (Chicago: Magic Inc., 1966).

Booth, John. *Forging Ahead in Magic* (Philadelphia, Kanter). No tricks. "Preparation, presentation, publicity, and profit."

Bosco, Bartolommeo (1790-1863). The greatest Italian conjurer, famous for his skill with Cups and Balls.

Braue, Frederick. Card manipulator and writer. See Hugard.

Breslaw, Philip (172?-1783). German conjurer who moved to England at about the age of 35 and became prominent in the earliest, outdoor period of conjuring. A book of tricks bore his name, *Breslaw's Last Legacy*.

Buckley, Arthur H. Card manipulator.

Card Control (Chicago: the author, 1948).

Cardini (Richard V. Pitchford). British-born American magician, the king of modern card, billiard-ball, and cigarette manipulators. A master pantomimist, he contrives to put real comedy into a silent act.

Carter, Charles Joseph (1874-1936). American illusionist whose greatest successes were won in Oceania, the Far East, and Europe.

Ching Ling Foo (Chee Ling Qua, 1854-1918). Greatest Chinese magician of modern times to tour the Occident. After he came to the U.S. in 1898 a whole crop of imitation Chinese acts sprang up, some excellent (notably Chung Ling Soo, q.v.).

Christopher, Milbourne. American performer, writer, inventor, and collector.

50 Tricks with a Thumb Tip (New York: Tannen).

Panorama of Magic (New York, Dover, 1962).

The Illustrated History of Magic (New York: Crowell, 1973).

The last two titles together offer the most comprehensive available history of magicians and their tricks.

Chung Ling Soo (William Ellsworth Campbell Robinson, 1861-1918). American performer who won international fame as an Oriental after the success of Ching Ling Foo (q.v.) He assisted Alexander Herrmann and Harry Kellar (qq.v.), then launched his own Chinese act. He died doing the Bullet-Catching Trick.

Clark, Keith. *Celebrated Cigarettes* (Cincinnati, Ohio: Silk King Studios, 1943).

Comte, Louis Appollinaire Christien Emmanuel (1788-1859). Geneva-born, "The King's Conjurer" operated a theater of his own in Paris, where "Robert-Houdin (q.v.) undoubtedly first thought of becoming a professional magician himself," Milbourne Christopher says.

Corinda, *Corinda's Thirteen Steps to Mentalism* (Cedar Knolls, N.J.: Wehman Brothers, Inc.). Placed by its devotees on a level with Annemann (q.v.)

Corson, Richard. *Stage Make-Up*, 6th edition (Englewood Cliffs, N.J.: Prentice Hall, 1981).

Dante (Harry Jansen, 1882-1955). Danish-born American illusionist who headed a touring company for Thurston (q.v.), then took his own big act all over the world.

deKolta, Buatier (Joseph Buatier), (1847-1903). One of the cleverest inventors in magical history. The Vanishing Bird Cage and the Spring Flower Production are among his innovations. Born in France, he performed largely in England and America.

Devant, David (David Wighton, 1868-1941). Brilliant English performer, inventor, and writer, possibly the greatest his country has produced. He devised the silk-dyeing effect, popularized thimble tricks, and made many other contributions to the art.

Lessons in Conjuring (London: 1922). A most regrettably scarce book on all the old magical standbys. Get a copy if you possibly can.

Magic Made Easy (London: S. H. Bousfield & Co., 1903). Much useful information on the easy ways to do things—no sleight of hand.

Tricks for Everyone (London: A. C. Pearson, 1910).

Our Magic. See under Maskelyne.

Dodson, Goodlette. *Exhibition Card Fans* (Atlanta, Ga.: H. R. Hulse, 1935).

Doebler, Ludwig (or Louis) Leopold (1801-1864). He and J. N. Hofzinser were Austria's greatest magicians. Starting life as an engraver, he became a conjurer, touring the Continent and the British Isles with huge success. A street in Vienna still bears his name.

Downs, Thomas Nelson (1867-1938). American magician, the creator of modern coin manipulation, and also one of the great showmen and great card manipulators of all time. In addition to the coin sleights bearing his name, he invented the side steal and pioneered with the one-way deck.

The Art of Magic, with John Northern Hilliard (New York: Dover Publications, 1980). No sleight-of-hand magician can afford to be without this epoch-making book, though he may have to hunt for a copy.

Eastman, Max. *Enjoyment of Laughter* (New York: Simon & Schuster, 1936). Should be studied by every intelligent magician who cares why comedy is comical.

Erdnase, S. W. An anagram or jumble of the name of Edward S. (or possibly Milton) Andrews, of whom almost nothing is definitely known except his invaluable book.

The Expert at the Card Table (Wilmette, Ill.: Drake, 1905). The card man's bible. See pages 53-56.

Farelli, Victor. Scottish magician, known in America chiefly for his books.

Card Magic, two volumes (Middlesex, England: Bagshawe & Co., 1934). A very sensible, practical, clean-cut book, highly recommended to the card worker who has gone beyond the kindergarten stage.

Fawkes, Isaac (d. 1731). The best-remembered of the early British fair and outdoor performers. In his booth at Bartholomew Fair he showed sleights and was early in the wave of automata that played a big part in the next century's conjuring. He accumulated a large fortune for his day, and left the show to his son, Fawkes the Younger.

Fischer, Ottokar. Austrian magician, writer, and eminent magical historian and collector. He was responsible for the universal respect paid to the memory of the great Austrian card conjurer, Johann Nepomuk Hofzinser.

Illustrated Magic, translated by Barrows Mussey and Fulton Oursler (New York: Macmillan, 1931). The most lavishly illustrated popular magic book in English. It has been justly condemned for explaining rather than teaching tricks, but nonetheless contains much material useful to a practicing magician.

Fitzkee, Dariel. American magical writer. His books are expensive, but well worth the attention of any thinking conjurer.

Magic by Misdirection (Magic Limited, Oakland, California, 1945).

Rings In Your Fingers (Magic Limited, Oakland, California, 1946). See page 286.

Showmanship for Magicians (Magic Limited, Oakland, California, 1943). See page 18.

The Trick Brain (Magic Limited, Oakland, California, 1944).

Frikell, Wiljalba (1818-1903). German conjurer, one of the first to work in evening clothes instead of flowing robes. He cleaned up his stage so that it looked like a drawing room of the period, and relied on skill, not on bulky apparatus.

Ganson, Lewis (1913-1980). British performer, editor, and writer on magic. His books are not for absolute beginners; they teach, and illustrate with his own photographs, excellent tricks from both his repertoire and those of today's magic greats—particularly Dai Vernon.

The Art of Close-Up Magic, Vol. I (Bideford, Devon: Supreme Magic Co.).

The Art of Close-Up Magic, Vol. II (Bideford: Supreme).

Card Magic by Manipulation (Bideford: Supreme).

Expert Manipulation of Playing Cards (London: Davenport). A book that helped launch the fanning craze among amateurs.

Routined Manipulation, Parts I, II, and III (Bideford: Supreme).

Unconventional Magic (Bideford: Supreme).

And the Vernon series:

The Dai Vernon Book of Magic (Bideford: Supreme).

Dai Vernon's Cups and Balls (Bideford: Supreme).

Dai Vernon's Inner Secrets of Card Magic (Bideford: Supreme).

Dai Vernon's More Inner Secrets of Card Magic (Bideford: Supreme).

Dai Vernon's Further Inner Secrets of Card Magic (Bideford: Supreme).

Dai Vernon's Ultimate Secrets of Card Magic (Bideford: Supreme).

Dai Vernon's Tribute to Nate Leipzig (Bideford: Supreme).

The Magic of Malini (written from Dai Vernon's recollections, Bideford: Supreme).

Gardner, Martin. Prominent writer on science, mathematics, mathematical magic. More comprehensive is *Encyclopedia of Impromptu Magic* (Chicago: Magic, Inc., 1978).

Gaultier, Camille. *Magic Without Apparatus*, translated by Jean Hugard and edited by Paul Fleming (York, Pa.: Fleming Book Co., 1945). Enjoyed a great European reputation, for which reason I list it, though I do not think American readers will find the reputation particularly well deserved. It goes to the point of manipulation for manipulation's sake, including many moves not practically useful.

Geller, Uri. Israeli night-club performer who adapted a schoolboy spoon-bending trick and standard mental routines to TV, and was hailed by the press and some scientists as a "psychic superstar" of the 1970s until exposed as a conjurer by Randi (q.v.) and others.

My Story (New York: Praeger, 1975), written by John Fuller, is far less useful to conjurers than James Randi's *Magic of Uri Geller*.

Gibson, Walter B. American magician and outstanding writer. He acted as amanuensis for Blackstone and for Thurston's later books. The long list of titles under his own name also deserves respectful attention.

Professional Tricks for Amateur Magicians (New York: Dover).

The New Magician's Manual (New York: Dover).

Houdini's Fabulous Magic, with Morris N. Young (Philadelphia: Chilton, 1961).

Gilbert, Alfred C. The manufacturer of Mysto Magic sets, a former professional conjurer.

Gilbert Knots and Splices and Rope-tying Tricks (New Haven: A. C. Gilbert Co., 1920). Good material on escapes, not to be despised because of its intended juvenile audience.

Ginn, David (b. 1946). A professional performer for children in the southeastern U.S. Of his more than 20 books, two are standard:

Professional Magic for Children and *Comedy Warm-Ups for Children's Shows* (both published by the author at 5687 Williams Rd., Norcross, Ga. 30093).

Goldin, Horace (Hyman Goldstein, 1873-1939). Polish-born American magician and illusionist. He was a superb performer of small tricks like the egg bag and also a whirlwind stage magician who made famous the "Sawing a Woman in Two" illusion.

Hatton, Henry (P. H. Cannon) and Adrian Plate. *Magicians' Tricks: How They Are Done* (New York: Century, 1919). The first American general textbook, still full of useful material.

Hay, Henry (Barrows Mussey, b. 1910). Former American professional magician; later writer, editor, translator, foreign correspondent, and advertising consultant. Aside from the present volume, two of his magic books remain in print:

Learn Magic and (ed.) *Cyclopedia of Magic* (both New York: Dover).

Henning, Douglas (b. 1947). Canadian performer, the first to obtain a foundation grant for the study of magic. His "The Magic Show" was a great hit in New York, "Spellbound" ditto in Toronto, and he has done widely praised television specials.

Herrmann, Alexander (1843-1896). Member of an Austrian conjuring family, known all over America as Herrmann the Great. To the older generation his name is still synonymous with magic; he was truly a great performer. Not to be confused with his father Samuel, his almost equally great brother Carl (or Compars), or his less-accomplished nephew Leon. See page 36.

Hilliard, John Northern (1872-1935). American magical writer. He did the writing of Down's *The Art of Magic*. Jean Hugard completed the manuscript of Hilliard's masterpiece:

Greater Magic (Minneapolis: Carl Waring Jones, 1945). One of the best as well as largest books ever written about magic. The emphasis is overwhelmingly on card work, but there are many other valuable tricks as well. Now out of print, but worth a long search to find.

Hoffmann, Professor Louis (Angelo John Lewis, 1839-1920). English barrister and journalist, the greatest of all writers on magic. His major books have unquestionably launched more magicians than any other one cause in all the centuries of conjuring. Not a professional or even an outstanding performer, he was on intimate terms with all the magical greats of his day. His major works, *Modern Magic* (1874), *More Magic* (1890), and *Later Magic* (1911), have been reprinted by Dover Publications, New York, and are still a fine source of information.

Hofzinser, Johann Nepomuk (1806-1875). The most brilliant inventor among Austrian magicians, introduced the roller-curtain card frame, double-faced cards, the counterweighted clock dial, and many effects still in use by men clever enough to do them. A book of his card tricks by Ottokar Fischer was translated by S. H. Sharpe, and published in England as *J. N. Hofzinser's Card Conjuring*.

Holden, Max. *Programmes of Famous Magicians* (New York: Holden, 1937).

Hopkins, Charles H. *"Outs" Precautions and Challenges* (Philadelphia: Chas. H. Hopkins & Co., 1940). A pamphlet that every card conjurer should have for reference.

Houdini, Harry (legally adopted name of Ehrich Weiss, 1874-1926). Incomparably the greatest escape-artist of all time, and also a brilliant general conjurer. His talent for getting publicity was miraculous. He was an erratic but persevering student of magical history, and his chief literary monument is the volume below. The standard biography is Milbourne Christopher's *Houdini: The Untold Story* (New York: T. Y. Crowell, 1969).

The Unmasking of Robert-Houdin (New York: Publishers' Printing Co., 1908). Although launched and written in a fit of ill temper, this book contains more authentic material than any other one volume on conjuring history until the appearance of Christopher's *Panorama of Magic*.

Hugard, Jean (John Gerard Rodney Boyce, 1872-1959), American performer and writer, of Australian origin. Prolific contributor to magical literature. Only a fraction of his output is listed here.

Close-up Magic for the Night-Club Magician (New York: Louis Tannen). Exactly what it pretends to be, and a most useful pamphlet.

Coin Magic (New York: Louis Tannen). A sound small book, less inclusive than Bobo's *New Modern Coin Magic* and less original than Eddie Joseph's *Coin and Money Magic*.

Encyclopedia of Card Tricks (Editor, with John H. Crimmins, Jr.) (New York: Dover). A good source of head magic; weak on sleights.

Handkerchief Magic (New York: Dover). A general roundup of silk methods and effects, extremely valuable to anyone interested in that branch of conjuring.

Modern Magic Manual (London: Faber & Faber). For some years the standard American text, this is now available only from England.

Silken Sorcery (New York: Louis Tannen). A general roundup of silk methods and effects, extremely valuable to anyone interested in that branch of magic.

Thimble Magic (New York:

Louis Tannen). Another of the author's special-subject pamphlets, containing some material not found in *Modern Magic Manual*.

Expert Card Technique—Close-up Table Magic, with Frederick Braue (New York: Dover Publications). Conscientious, clearly written, and well-illustrated treatment of card sleights and difficult tricks, admittedly in the Erdnase tradition. You should find lots of things in it that you like.

Jordan, Charles T. (1888-1944). California inventor, dealer, and publisher, of whom his friend and associate T. Nelson Downs (q.v.) wrote, "He is a genius for card ideas. . . . He is not a performer or clever manipulator."

The great bulk of his work has been assembled and edited by Karl Fulves in *Charles T. Jordan: Selected Tricks* (Box 433, Teaneck, N.J. 07666: Karl Fulves, 1975). Card effects predominate, but there is splendid material on coins, silks, mental magic, and miscellaneous tricks.

Joseph, Eddie. *Coin and Money Magic* (Colon, Mich.: Abbott, 1942). Full of interesting suggestions for coin workers. See pages 129, 169.

Magic and Mysteries of India (Colon, Mich.: Abbott, c. 1940). Mr. Joseph has lived all his life in Calcutta. The first part of this pamphlet, dealing with nonconjuring wonder workers, leaves one rather confused; when the author gets around to conjuring, he is admirable. You will want to try some of the small tricks as well as read about the big ones.

Kalanag (Helmut Schreiber, 1893-1963). The leading German illusionist during and after World War II. He had previously spent 25 years as a film producer, which no doubt explained the high ratio of show business to pure magic in his act.

Kellar, Harry (Heinrich Keller, 1849-1922). The dominant American magician between the time of Herrmann the Great and Thurston, who succeeded to Kellar's show. He was wholly an illusionist and apparatus conjurer, but a great showman, and is still remembered for his kindly personality. See page 19.

Lafayette (Siegmund Neuburger, 1872-1911). German-born American illusionist whose stage-settings, music, and showmanship were legendary. He was mauled several times by lions in his act, and lost his life in a theater fire in Edinburgh while trying to save the animals.

Leipzig, Nate (Nathan Leipziger, 1873-1939). Swedish-born American, the greatest specialist in close-up hand magic. He was an international success with his card, coin, and thimble act in vaudeville, but really came into his own at private gatherings. See under Ganson.

LePaul, Paul (Paul Braden, 1900-1958). An outstanding American card manipulator known for his fanning, back-palming, and regular card tricks. Howard Thurston, Nate Leipzig, and Hofzinser (qq.v.) were his idols. His one book has become standard.

The Card Magic of LePaul (first

edition 1949; now New York: Tannen).

LeRoy, Jean Henri Servais (1865-1953). Anglo-Belgian illusionist, brilliant inventor and performer, traveled the world with the act of LeRoy, Talma, and Bosco. Talma, his wife, did a coin number that Nelson Downs (q.v.) called the best of his imitators. Bosco was originally a German comic, Imro Fox. LeRoy's greatest invention was Asrah (see Appendix, Levitations).

Malini, Max (Max Katz Breit, 1873-1942). Polish-born American close-up performer of legendary nerve and ingenuity. See under Canson.

Mardo, Señor Ed. *Routined Magic* (New York: Holden, 1945). A pamphlet worth while well beyond its small size.

Marshall, Frances Ireland. Leading American dealer, publisher, writer, and children's performer. With her first husband, L. L. Ireland, she built up the company she now runs under the name of Magic, Inc. with her second husband, Jay Marshall. The most important of her many books:

Kid Stuff, Vols. I (1954) II (1959); III (1963), IV (1968), V (1975). (Vol. VI is a reprint of an earlier book by Arnold Furst.)

How to Sell by Magic.

(ed.) *The Table Book* (1961). (All are published by Magic, Inc., 5082 North Lincoln Ave., Chicago, Ill. 60625.)

Maskelyne, Nevil (1863-1924). In the second generation of the British conjuring dynasty that kept magic theaters running in London for more than fifty thousand performances. David Devant was the performing partner in Maskelyne & Devant, and also coauthor of one of the best books in magical literature.

Our Magic, second edition, (York, Pa.: Fleming Book Co., 1946). See page 17. The first and greatest book to treat magic as a dramatic art rather than a collection of ruses. Hardly recommended to the young beginner; essential to the working performer.

Maskelyne on the Performance of Magic (New York: Dover) is Part I, the theoretical section, of the above.

Maurice, Edward. English vaudeville magician.

Showmanship and Presentation (Birmingham, England: Goodliffe, 1946). A pamphlet packed very tight with important information on stagecraft (not tricks). It would be easier to absorb if it were not quite so concentrated. Hardly a wasted line.

Merlin, Jack. An obscure yet legendary American card manipulator, whose methods are treated in the book that goes under his name.

"*. . . And a Pack of Cards*" (New York: Holden, 1940). A standard reference on difficult card sleights of the Erdnase school.

Mora, Silent (Louis McCord). A witty Boston Irishman and memorable manipulator with a brilliant Chinese act.

Mulholland, John (1899-1970). American magician, magical historian, writer, editor and lecturer. See page ix in the front, and *passim* throughout this volume. A small selection of his books:

The Art of Illusion (New York: Scribner's, 1944). Entirely head magic—an excellent collection of tricks and much sound advice on presentation.

John Mulholland Book of Magic (New York: Scribner's).

Quicker Than the Eye (Indianapolis: Bobbs-Merrill, 1932). No tricks, but interesting sketches of magic and magicians.

Neil, C. Lang. *The Modern Conjurer and Drawing-Room Entertainer* (New York: D. Kemp, 1937). In its way this admirable book, with its hundreds of photographic illustrations, has never been surpassed. The magician who will pare down the patter can still make a success with every trick exactly as Lang Neil teaches it—more than can be said even of *Modern Magic*.

Nelms, Henning. An American of dazzlingly diverse talents—among others, artist, stage director, lawyer, and magician.

Magic and Showmanship (New York: Dover Publications) is the first book since Maskelyne & Devant (q.v.) to teach the why rather than just the how of our art. His message: "Tricks don't make magic."

Nicola, The Great (William Mozart Nicol, 1880-1946), American magician and illusionist, described at his death as the highest-salaried magician America had produced. One of the very few magicians who would never use a trick he had not acquired by purchase or gift.

Okito (Theo Bamberg). A member of the oldest surviving magical family, which began in Holland in the late eighteenth century. Okito's son David Bamberg (Fu Manchu) is an outstanding favorite in North and South America.

Quality Magic (London: Goldston, 1921). The small sleights are very good indeed; the big effects not so good for modern tastes.

Philippe (Jacques Andre Noel Talon, 1802-1878). A French confectioner who began his magic career in Aberdeen. He first introduced to the West the Linking Rings, Goldfish Bowls, and other feats he had learned from a Chinese troupe in Dublin. His performance and his automata strongly influenced Robert-Houdin (q.v.).

Pinetti, Giuseppe (1750-1800), the most important magician of the late eighteenth century. Born in Tuscany, he performed all over Europe. He finally settled in Russia, where he died having spent a large magic-based fortune on ballooning experiments.

Randi, The Amazing (James Randall Zwinge, b. 1928). Canadian performer and author. Stage, cabaret, and TV appearances worldwide. Escape artist (28 jails), only man to hang over Niagara falls in a strait jacket (for a TV documentary on magic). *Guinness Book of Records* listed his Frozen-in-Ice record (43 minutes), now pushed to 53½ minutes. Strident foe of "paranormal phenomena," especially the Israeli "mystic" Uri Geller.

The Magic of Uri Geller (New York: Ballantine, 1975).

Flim-Flam! (New York: Lippincott & Crowell, 1980).

Houdini, His Life and Art (New York: Grosset & Dunlap, 1978). Written with Bert Randolph Sugar.

Raymond, the Great (Maurice Francois Saunders, 1877–1948). American illusionist, of the globe-trotting generation of Carter, Goldin, Lafayette, and Leroy (q.v.).

Rice, Harold R. *Rice's Encyclopedia of Silk Magic*, Vols. 1, 2, 3 (Cincinnati, Ohio: Silk King Studios). Probably the last word on the subject.

Robert-Houdin, Jean Eugène (1805-1871). Outstanding French magician and magical writer, often called the father of modern conjuring. Probably he was neither so great as French magicians pretend, nor such a sham as Houdini makes out in *The Unmasking of Robert-Houdin*. His autobiography (republished by Dover Publications, New York), though very likely ghostwritten, is excellent reading. Among his technical books, one—unfortunately the scarcest—is still valuable.

Secrets of Conjuring and Magic, translated by Prof. Hoffmann (London: Routledge, 1878).

Sachs, Edwin T. (d. 1910). British journalist and amateur magician, now remembered solely for his one great effort.

Sleight of Hand, reissued edition (York, Pa.: Fleming Book Co., 1946). Usually mentioned in the same breath with *Modern Magic*. You can take your choice; Sachs lays perhaps more stress on presentation; Hoffmann impresses one as having the wider and sounder foundation. The later reissue, newly illustrated and provided with a modern commentary by the learned Paul Fleming, is far better than earlier editions.

Selbit, P. T. (Percy Thomas Tibbles, d. 1938). English magician, inventor and builder of illusions. Originally a journalist, he took up magic

Selbit, P. T. (Percy Thomas Tibbles, 1879-1938). English magician, inventor and builder of illusions. Sawing a Woman in Two was the best known among his dozens of successful creations.

Stars of Magic (New York: Tannen). A photographically illustrated collection of 39 tricks by leading performers such as Dai Vernon and John Scarne.

Siegfried & Roy (Siegfried Fischbacher and Roy Horn). German illusionists who have been a fixture at Las Vegas for years with a big act using lions and tigers.

Tarbell, Dr. Harlan. American magician and magical writer, the deviser of the Color-Changing Silk, the modern form of rope trick, and various other effects.

The Tarbell Course in Magic, 6 volumes (New York: Louis Tannen, 1941-1948). An expensive and inclusive series of lessons teaching nearly every standard trick with considerable care.

Thurston, Howard (1869-1936). American card manipulator and illusionist. In the great days of backpalming he was the leading performer with cards; later he bought Harry Kellar's show, and succeeded Kellar in the heart of the American public. See also page 123.

Four Hundred Tricks You Can Do, two volumes in one (New York: Blue Ribbon, 1939). Somewhat more elementary than Blackstone's *Modern Card Tricks*, but not unlike it—natural enough since Walter Gibson put both books together.

Turner, William O. *How to Do Tricks with Cards* (New York: Collier Books, 1970; first published 1949). A sound and sprightly introduction to modern card tricks as a specialty.

Vernon, Dai W. Canadian-born American sleight-of-hand artist, famous for his card work, and perhaps equal in skill though not in public reputation to Nate Leipzig.

Most of his work has been written up by Lewis Ganson (q.v.).

Dai Vernon's Select Secrets (Brooklyn: author, 1941). This pamphlet just touches on sleight of hand, but gives a number of excellent tricks and sound advice throughout.

Symphony of the Rings (Bideford, Devon: Supreme Magic Co.). Vernon's version of the Linking Rings, with photographs.

Watson, Donald ("Monk"). *The Professional Touch* (Colon, Mich.: Abbott, 1945). Good advice on presentation, born of long experience, and a number of suggestions about tricks.

Wyman, John (1816-1881). One of the first American-born magicians with a full evening's show. He started as a ventriloquist, then branched out into magic. One of the first magicians to present spiritualism in his act.

Index